COLLECTED ESSAYS IN LAW

Crime, Compliance and Control

The Collected Essays in Law Series
General Editor: Tom D. Campbell

Law's Premises, Law's Promise:
Jurisprudence after Wittgenstein

Thomas Morawetz

ISBN: 0 7546 2013 1

The Jurisprudence of
Law's Form and Substance

Robert S. Summers

ISBN: 0 7546 2024 7

Regulation, Crime, Freedom

John Braithwaite

ISBN: 0 7546 2005 0

Legal Rules and Legal Reasoning

Larry Alexander

ISBN: 0 7546 2004 2

The Great Juristic Bazaar:
Jurists' Texts and Lawyers' Stories

William Twining

ISBN: 0 7546 2211 8

Dispute Processing and Conflict Resolution:
Theory, Practice and Policy

Carrie Menkel-Meadow

ISBN: 0 7546 2305 X

Objectivity in Ethics and Law

Michael Moore

ISBN: 0 7546 2329 7

Doreen McBarnet

Crime, Compliance and Control

ASHGATE
DARTMOUTH

Published by
Dartmouth Publishing Company Limited
Gower House
Croft Road
Aldershot
Hampshire GU11 3HR
England

Ashgate Publishing Company
Suite 420
101 Cherry Street
Burlington, VT 05401–4405
USA

Ashgate Website: http://www.ashgate.com

British Library Cataloguing in Publication Data
McBarnet, Doreen J.
Crime, compliance and control. – (Collected essays in Law)
1. Sociological jurisprudence 2. Criminal Justice, Administration of
3. Justice, Administration of 4. Commercial Law – Interpretation and construction 5. Compliance
I. Title
340.1'15

Library of Congress Catalog-in-Publication Data:
McBarnet, Doreen J.
Crime, Compliance and control / Doreen McBarnet.
p. cm. – (Collected Essays in Law)
Includes bibliographical references and index.
1. Criminal Justice, Administration of. 2. Crime–Sociological aspects. 3. Social control.
I. Title. II. Series
HV7419.M397 2004
345'.001–dc22 2003070903

ISBN: 0 7546 2349 1

Printed and bound in Great Britain by
Antony Rowe Ltd, Chippenham, Wiltshire.

Contents

PART SIX: LAW, POWER AND CONTROL

Acknowledgements

My thanks to Tom Campbell for inviting me to put this collection of essays together, to the publishers, detailed below, for permission to reproduce articles and chapters, and to the institutions and funding bodies who have supported the research on which this book is based.

Planning a retrospective work brings back lots of memories and provides as good an opportunity as any to thank those who have provided institutional support and personal encouragement over the years. So thanks to my friends and colleagues at Glasgow University, where I began my research, to colleagues, visitors, students and administrative staff over a long period of time at the Oxford Centre for Socio-Legal Studies, and to those with whom I have done joint research, notably Christopher Whelan and Graham Mansfield. The Centre has provided a wonderful research community within which to work. Under both Centre directors, Don Harris and Denis Galligan, I have enjoyed complete freedom to pursue new directions in research, working in areas which must sometimes have seemed esoteric or quirky, particularly for a sociologist, and which often involved long periods of groundwork to get to grips with highly technical areas of law and finance. I thank them both for their apparently unwavering confidence through each new project that something interesting would emerge! My time as a visitor at other institutions, and particularly my extended visits at Australian National University and Edinburgh University, have also been stimulating and much appreciated experiences.

There have been many sources of research funding over the years and thanks are due to the organisations which have made possible the research on which this volume is based: the Jacob Burns Foundation, the Anglo-German Foundation, the European Commission, the Nuffield Foundation, the French Commissariat du Plan, Wolfson College, the Centre for Tax System Integrity at the Australian National University, and especially the ESRC which has granted funding over the years for two major projects on tax avoidance, a linked studentship, and most recently a generous professorial fellowship. The research programme proposed for the fellowship has developed out of, and will hopefully develop further, the research and ideas which are reported in this volume as a record of my core work to date.

Grateful acknowledgement is made to the following editors, publishers and institutions for their kind permission to reprint the essays included in this volume: Blackwell Publishing, Oxford; Sociological Review, Keele; Palgrave Macmillan, Basingstoke; Hodder Arnold, London; Elsevier Ltd, Oxford, copyright © 1984 Elsevier; Taylor & Francis Ltd, London, <http://www.tandf.co.uk>; Kluwer Law

International, Dordrecht, copyright © 1992 Kluwer Law International; LexisNexis Butterworths Tolley, Oxford; John Wiley & Sons Ltd, Chichester, copyright © 1999 John Wiley & Sons Ltd; Oxford University Press, Oxford, copyright © 1997 Oxford University Press.

A particular thank you to Scarlet McBarnet for editorial and production work in the preparation of this book.

Series Editor's Preface

Collected Essays in Law makes available some of the most important work of scholars who have made a major contribution to the study of law. Each volume brings together a selection of writings by a leading authority on a particular subject. The series gives authors an opportunity to present and comment on what they regard as their most important work in a specific area. Within their chosen subject area, the collections aim to give a comprehensive coverage of the authors' research. Care is taken to include essays and articles which are less readily accessible and to give the reader a picture of the development of the authors' work and an indication of research in progress.

Doreen McBarnet is Professorial Fellow at the Centre for Socio-Legal Studies, Oxford University, Fellow of Wolfson College, Oxford and Adjunct Professor at the Australian National University. She also teaches at Oxford's Said Business School. Having graduated from Glasgow University with first class honours in history and sociology, she became a lecturer in sociology at Glasgow before moving to Oxford to focus on socio-legal studies.

Introduction

Researching crime, compliance and control

The title, 'Crime, compliance and control' sums up the broad areas my research has addressed over the years. This introduction tries to give some insight into how and why that research evolved. It reflects on how I came to define specific topics as research problems, and it shows how one project led to another, demonstrating connections between what might at first sight seem quite disparate areas of study. Connections run deeper too. Through all my work, indeed providing its driving force, runs an underlying concern with certain fundamental social issues. These might be summarised as: inequality, power, and the ideas — and ideals — of justice and the rule of law. These will crop up, both explicitly and implicitly, as recurrent themes throughout both book and introduction.

Taking law seriously in socio-legal research

'Crime', in the title, has analytical connotations, as we shall see, but it also refers to the criminal justice system, the focus of my first foray into research, for the PhD which then became the book '*Conviction*' (McBarnet 1981). My first teaching included the honours course on 'Deviance', which was, in the heady days of 1970s and 1980s sociology, one of the most exciting areas of the discipline, posing real challenges to classic theories and reconceptualising the 'old criminology' into the new (Taylor, Walton and Young 1975). The choice of sociological research in criminal justice flowed naturally from this context. Yet the themes which came to preoccupy me in that first work focused not on conventional criminological concerns, old or new, but on the nature of law and the ideology of the rule of law.

The change of focus emerged from the research. Sitting in court, observing cases in process, I was surprised to note incidents taking place or being reported, which, in my layman's conception of the civil rights of the suspect or defendant, were impossible: a defendant's past record being produced before a jury as evidence; a suspect's exercise of the right to silence being treated as evidence of guilt; the right to legal advice at the police station being denied, and so on. What was happening? Were police, magistrates, lawyers, judges simply breaching the law on a daily basis? So I asked a lawyer: what was the law on all of these issues? That was my first encounter with the legendary inability of a lawyer to give a straight answer. The response was, of course, to cite a range of cases, specific and often apparently contradictory. This I found both frustrating and intriguing.

And so the sociologist began to focus on the nature of law, shifting method so that while I was still observing and interviewing, I was also spending time in law libraries delving into case law and the small print of statutes and regulations, and all of those puzzles — the hidden rules structuring what happened in court, the clash between my image of civil rights and their operation, and the inability of a lawyer to give a straight answer — became data needing explanation, and led to a rethinking of the project.

At that time, the main thrust of sociological analysis of law was a focus on the gap between law in the books and law in action. *Conviction* suggested a gap *within* the law between its rhetoric and its substance. Chapter 1 discusses the state of research on criminal justice at this time and sets out a number of 'false dichotomies' which characterised it and which needed, in my view, to be addressed. It also provides a useful starting point for this book, in that it sets out the approach I have taken to research throughout my work. First, there is a grounded approach, with theory, concepts and the more subtle questions for research arising out of the research itself. Distrustful of the blinkers grand theory can impose, I have preferred to explore social action from the bottom up, to learn, to empathise, to capture detail and nuance, to listen to and be led by the data. Second, all that micro level detail is only the base for trying to shed light on more macro issues: bridging macro issues and micro methods has always been the goal, with the hope that this results in a richer and more subtle understanding of the big issues. Third, there is a commitment to addressing, as a socio-legal scholar, both 'socio-' and technical legal material as data.

The research on criminal justice began the commitment to taking law seriously in what nonetheless remained sociologically framed research, as Part II demonstrates. Chapters 2 to 5 each examine a specific aspect of the criminal justice system — pre-trial procedures in chapter 2, legal proof and advocacy in chapter 3, arrest in chapter 4, and the right to silence in chapter 5. They demonstrate through examples observed in courts, how the gap between the rhetoric of civil rights and the small print of the law plays out in practice.

Legal form, legal ideology, legal actors — and the shift to research on business

That was only one level of interest however. The research also prompted questions on how the ideology of civil rights was maintained, despite the gap, and what all this meant not only for criminal justice but for the ideology of the rule of law. These are the issues addressed in chapters 6 and 7. The concern to grapple with questions of legal form and legal ideology — and the way they could be *used* — has remained a driving force in my work despite an apparently major shift of focus in the next phase of research from criminal justice to business. Hence the inclusion in Part II of chapter 8, a first exploratory piece on 'law and capital', but one which is still addressing the themes of legal ideology, structure and action.

The shift of focus to business practice and the law meant ploughing a fairly lonely furrow. This was a time when sociology could too often be accused of 'holding its hands up but keeping its eyes down' — looking to the 'rich and powerful' for research funding but focusing on the poor or powerless in the definition of the 'social problems' that needed empirical research. At the level of theory, while there was a great deal of macro level analysis on the role of 'capital' in the abstract, there was little sociological research on how business and finance actually worked. I wanted to explore those workings at operational level, and in particular to explore the relationship between business, finance and the law. The motivation was both curiosity about unknown territory and a wish to study empirically the interplay between law and class, the impact of law on economic power, the impact of economic power on law, and the consequent impact of both on society more generally.

The focus, at one level at least, on regulation, compliance and legal work emerged from the research rather than from any *a priori* theoretical starting point. My original notion had been a historical study (my first degree being in history and sociology not sociology alone) to explore whether and how law facilitated business — a micro analysis to complement and enrich macro studies of the role of law in the development of capitalism. But exploratory work, and the lessons learned from *Conviction* on the malleability of law, began to suggest there might be interest in how business *made* law facilitative, not necessarily in the conventional sense, through political power, but through legal practice, through the lawyer's construction of legal concepts and devices to solve a specific client's specific legal problems (chapter 8). The focus was the interplay of business practice and legal practice at a private level, not necessarily involving either legislatures or courts, often operating unobserved, and certainly, from a socio-legal perspective, unanalysed.

What also emerged was that business clients' legal problems were often simply their legal obligations, as imposed by statute, regulation or case law, the lawyer's role was to find a way to circumvent those obligations, and the mechanism for accomplishing this was manipulation of the words of the law itself. Law, as indeed had been implied in the criminal justice research, was a 'double-edged sword' not just a mechanism for providing rights or exercising control, but a mechanism for undermining both. Again we were back to the structural issue of the nature of law. But my interest in the nature of law was never deterministic. It was the interplay between the, as it were, passive, but perhaps facilitative nature of law, *and* its active and conscious *use* that was of interest. The focus was on 'legal form *and* legal actors', on the clash between idealist notions of the rule of law, and a conception of law in practice as 'a raw material to be worked on' (chapter 8).

Law, class and labelling

In terms of substantive areas of research, I have ranged quite widely over time, covering, to date, criminal justice, insolvency, tax avoidance and evasion, accounting, corporate finance, the Single European Market, globalisation and the law, and professional practice. The reason was not necessarily any great interest in those particular substantive areas, nor a masochistic desire to put myself in the position where I was constantly having to invest in learning about new areas of technical law, literature and practice, a time-consuming business not well suited to pursuit of the holy grail of constant publication. The reason for doing it was to try to find the optimal area for researching any particular analytical issue. An issue having arisen from exploratory research, the question, each time, was what was the optimal area for researching it in full?

My first explorations in business and the law were in the area of insolvency, in both historical and contemporary contexts. However, as my interest developed in the uses of the form of law, and in notions of manipulation, circumvention and avoidance, I sought an area where I could explore how and whether such issues had been tackled overtly in law itself. Hence the focus on tax avoidance. Widening that focus to include the definition in law and practice of tax *evasion* allowed me to explore how the line was drawn between the two, and how positioning on the right side of it was accomplished. It served a more pragmatic function too, allowing me to apply to the ESRC's 'Crime and Criminal Justice' initiative, where I became, thanks to the open-mindedness of the selection committee, the only recipient of funding whose prime interest lay in practices that were *not* criminal.

Of course the point was to ask *why* they were not criminal — to ask how the line between the criminal and the non-criminal, compliance and non-compliance, was constructed, to problematise the definitions of both crime and compliance, to reverse the normal focus on the criminal and ask: how do the *law-abiding* abide by the law? And this is the focus of Part IV.

Chapters 9 and 10 explore how the line between evasion and avoidance — with their very similar consequences for society in terms of tax unpaid, but very different consequences for the actor in terms of acquiring or escaping a criminal label — can be actively managed. Chapter 9 shows how the technical substance and form of law can be used; chapter 10, how disclosure of facts can be manipulated through techniques of 'non-disclosing disclosure' and 'fraud insurance'. Both chapters have implications for 'labelling theory' in criminology and deviance. It also emerged that what is claimed to be legal avoidance is not always in fact so clearly distinct from outright evasion, that one may in fact slip into the other, without necessarily being detected (chapter 9). The implications go deeper too. What is ultimately raised here is the issue of equity in law, since the capacity to use the law and manage the label is not available to all. Rather we are faced with a situation where economic elites with the resources to buy legal creativity and manipulation may also be able to buy immunity from legal control.

The focus on the law-abiding rather than the criminal perhaps demonstrates another characteristic of my working 'method', and that is a persistent intellectual curiosity about what might be thought of as the other side of the coin. Hence the focus, as a sociologist, on taking law seriously as data, on scrutinising what was at the time only a taken-for-granted backdrop in criminological research (Part II). Hence the switch from focusing on the criminal to focusing on the law-abiding (Part IV), or on rethinking an initial study of insolvency to one that focused on the construction of (technical) solvency, via creative accounting techniques (McBarnet and Whelan 1999; chapter 15). Hence too the shift of focus from regulators, which had dominated regulation research, to a focus on the regulated, the topic of Part V.

From regulator to regulated: creative compliance

From the tax research emerged a rethinking of the issue of 'compliance' and a new focus on the regulated. Hitherto compliance had been analysed predominantly as a construct of law enforcement agencies, and the social and organisational practices they brought to bear on their application of law (Hawkins 1984), or perhaps implicitly in work like Becker's (1963), as a construct of how law defined crime, that is to say, defined what was crime and therefore implicitly what was not.

From the work on tax avoidance, however, emerged the idea of compliance as a construct not just of regulation or regulators, but of the creative action of the regulated themselves. From their perspective there were a number of ways in which to respond to unwelcome law (chapter 9). We might think of these as non-compliance, capitulative compliance, committed compliance and, the focus of my attention, creative compliance (chapter 17). By 'creative compliance' I mean using the law itself, often in novel, unanticipated ways, to construct legal forms for business deals, or other transactions, which can claim compliance with the letter of the law, while totally undermining its spirit.

An emphasis on legal creativity and creative compliance has implications for our understanding of law and its role in society in a range of ways, including the making of law, the effectiveness of law and the role of the legal profession and legal work.

Creative legal work has to be seen as significant for the *making* of law through the construction of legal practices, which may ultimately be endorsed by judges or legislators (who may indeed be ascribed credit for their invention), but which in fact originate 'in the pragmatic practices of legal entrepreneurs serving their clients' interests' (chapter 8). Chapter 13 demonstrates how legal creativity can operate in the context of global transactions in a world without global law, to fill legal gaps and smooth conflicts. However it also demonstrates that serving clients' interests and solving their legal problems is not necessarily all positive. As noted above, a client's legal problems may be someone else's legal rights or a government's legal policy. And creative legal work is characteristically about circumventing and therefore undermining both.

Chapter 11 uses examples from legal avoidance in tax and rent control to suggest that legal policy — or social policy implemented through law — can prove ineffective in practice not just because of political compromises or drafting failures weakening the substance of law, not just through failures of enforcement, but also through the active role of the regulated, using the technical substance of the law to circumvent the policy behind it. Set originally in the context of a special journal issue on law, democracy and social justice (Cotterrell and Bercusson 1988), it raises the question: can law effectively implement egalitarian policies? The need to scrutinise the role of lawyers and legal work in all of this is also underlined, along with the implications for the ideology of the rule of law, particularly in the way it can be utilised, not just by the underdogs of society to further their rights (Thompson 1975), but by the 'top dogs' to undermine those rights and to defend their right to do so.

The impact of creative compliance on policy is not confined to national contexts or social (in the narrow sense of the word) policy, but can apply to any area of policy and any regulatory context. Chapter 12 demonstrates this in the context of the Single European Market, and chapter 13, in the context of transnational commercial and financial transactions. The often hidden nature of creative compliance also means policies may look as though they are working effectively when at the level of practice they are not. So institutional structures, legislation and enforcement agencies may be put in place 'only to be destroyed by stealth through private legal work' (chapter 13).

Chapter 14 briefly analyses some of the recurrent techniques used, in any context, in scrutinising the words of the law to construct creative compliance devices. Chapter 15 demonstrates creative compliance at work in the context of company law via a case study of a takeover by a relatively small UK company, of a US company worth twice its value. On the face of it, the market and legal hurdles to this should have made it impossible, and indeed the pundits declared it 'Sheer magic!'. The analysis shows how that magic was legally accomplished, its long-term consequences, and its wider implications. The fundamental technique used, off-balance sheet financing through an orphan subsidiary, was similar to the techniques used later by Enron, as revealed after its massive collapse in 2001, though Enron's 'legal carpentry' (chapter 9) was not always perfect enough to keep it clear of outright fraud. But chapter 15 not only provides another example of creative compliance, it has already moved us on to Part VI and the next significant issue raised by creative compliance, the issue of legal control.

Law, power and control

Creative compliance inevitably raises the issue of legal control. In its nature, and by design, it can totally undermine legal control as it stands at any given moment. More fundamentally, it poses a challenge to the feasibility of *ever* establishing effective legal control over those with the financial and legal resources to circumvent it, with the implication that 'creative compliance and the powerful economic elites usually associated with it, may be beyond legal control' (chapter 16). It was primarily the wish to research whether creative compliance itself could be constrained by law, that motivated the move to another substantive area, financial reporting, and indeed to corporate finance more widely, with much of this research conducted with Chris Whelan.

My awareness of and interest in creative accounting (now, after Enron, common knowledge, but then, in the mid 1980s, a highly esoteric subject) arose partly in the course of the tax avoidance research. Interviews, particularly those with merchant bankers, suggested that tax avoidance was only a relatively small part of the story of routine business circumvention of law, and that practices in corporate finance and accounting, even more fundamental (in the sense of striking at the very heart of capitalist markets) and at the same time even less visible, needed scrutiny too. In addition, earlier work on insolvency had made me wonder about the concepts of 'solvency' and 'profit', and how they were constructed in practice, suggesting a need to research accounting. From research on the workings of corporate finance there also emerged a wider perspective. It became clear that creative compliance was not confined to the circumvention of state regulation but occurred in the context of *any* legal constraints, including private law mechanisms such as corporate constitutional rules and contractual controls (chapter 15).

Tax and accounting were particularly apposite areas for empirically researching whether creative compliance could be effectively constrained by law because these were areas where legal avoidance was beginning to be both officially defined as a problem and overtly targeted for control. What is more, attempts at control, in each case, took different forms, providing a range of control mechanisms to assess. In addition, given the doubts that can be raised over what exactly the 'spirit of the law' is, financial reporting regulation was a good area for research precisely because the mission of controlling creative accounting was so overtly declared. A visit to Australian National University provided the opportunity to research Australian anti-avoidance rules in tax to widen the picture further still.

These various studies identified a number of major obstacles to the successful legal control of creative compliance, certainly as those mechanisms of control are currently conceived. Chapter 16 explores both the issue of how to control creative compliance and the more general debate over rules and standards, or principles, in law. Though vague laws can also open the way to creative interpretation, creative compliance thrives particularly on detailed prescriptive rules. This chapter analyses the consequent attempt by the UK Accounting Standards Board in financial reporting, and the judiciary in tax, to introduce regulations or doctrines which focus on principle rather than rule, on substance rather than legal form, and on the spirit rather than the letter of the law. But it also analyses the multiple ways in which these principles gradually 'drift' back to rules — or, ever emphasising action over determinism, are *steered* back to rules — making it extremely difficult to sustain broad principles over time. It might also be noted that the same forces can be seen as a means whereby the regulated can 'resist discretion', suggesting limits to the conventional focus on regulatory discretion in studies of law enforcement (McBarnet 1997).

Chapter 17 takes as its starting point a critique of the 'compliance' model of control (Ayres and Braithwaite 1992). In particular it criticises the model's ultimate reliance in its 'enforcement pyramid' on 'big sticks' since 'big sticks', or sanctions, can only deal with *non*-compliance. In tackling *creative* compliance the issue becomes one not of enforcement but of enforceability: one has to first of all *contest* the claim made of creative compliance that it is 'perfectly legal', for this, as with all legal constructs, is only ever a claim, potentially vulnerable to legal challenge (McBarnet and Whelan 1999). New 'big powers' could be expected to make that challenge easier. In the areas researched, however, problems still arose, not just the problems of sustainability noted in chapter 16, but problems in application on the part of regulators, problems of political legitimacy, and problems of attitude on the part of the regulated. This last is crucial. Chapter 17 argues that fundamentally creative compliance is a product not just of law but of the attitude taken to it. If change is to be accomplished, it is not just the law but the attitude that needs to be tackled.

Next

It is therefore to the interplay between law and ethics — business and professional ethics and culture — as well as to recent developments in the wider social context, that a key part of my next research programme will turn. The aim is to probe the nature and basis of the current approach to law, and to explore whether there are any factors in play that might foster or force a new ethic.

As things stand, what the research reported in this book shows is that law is operating as a double-edged sword. It is not just an instrument for implementing social policy, social control, social rights, but an instrument, in the hands of those with the motivation, power and economic resources to wield it, for undermining them.

Ultimately much bigger issues than crime, compliance and control are being addressed. For when law becomes, for some, no more than a series of obstacles to be circumvented, it is the social fundamentals of democracy, equity, justice, and the rule of law, that are at stake.

References

Ayres, I and J Braithwaite (1992) *Responsive Regulation*, Oxford University Press

Becker, H (1963) *Outsiders*, Free Press of Glencoe

Cotterrell, R and B Bercusson (1988) 'Law, Democracy and Social Justice', *Journal of Law and Society* (special issue), **15**(1)

Hawkins, K (1984) *Environment and Enforcement*, Oxford: Clarendon
McBarnet, D (1981) *Conviction*, Macmillan
McBarnet, D (1997) 'Resisting Discretion', in *Administrative Discretion and Problems of Accountability, Proceedings of the 25th Colloquy on European Law*, Council of Europe Publishing, pp. 121–128
McBarnet, D and C Whelan (1999) *Creative Accounting and the Cross-eyed Javelin Thrower*, John Wiley
Taylor I, P Walton and J Young (1975) *The New Criminology*, Routledge and Kegan Paul
Thompson, E P (1975) *Whigs and Hunters*, Allen Lane

Part One

Opening Perspectives

[1] False Dichotomies in Criminal Justice Research

Sociological research into criminal justice has painted a detailed and fascinating picture of the day-to-day running of the law: the policeman on his beat seeing drunks home from carnivals or organising arrests around teabreaks; the lawyer negotiating and string-pulling in his chambers; the probation officer fitting people into stereotypes; the magistrate and advocate performing with language, gesture and ritual in court; the mystified defendant being processed willy-nilly on 'the conveyor belt of criminal justice', (Bottomley, 1973, p. 217).[1] Social administrators[2] have barraged us with statistics on how many people – or more accurately how few – are granted bail, legal aid, access to solicitors in police stations; how many choose to plead guilty, appear in magistrates' or crown courts, have a lawyer representing them; how many are convicted, sentenced in various ways or successfully appeal.[3]

These are two very different approaches, positivist and interactionist, theoretically at odds, yet neat corollaries to each other, one providing the skeleton of figures, the other the flesh of how people experience and construct criminal justice. And in one sense, this is a mass of valuable information and explanation. But in another it is severely limited. For both approaches have offered almost exclusively a picture of how the criminal justice system *operates*, showing how its alleged aims are reinterpreted or distorted in practice by the people who operate it. Neither has focused on the system itself, seen its aims as problematic rather than to be taken for granted, treated its rules as a significant factor in explaining its practices, or seen its assumptions and rhetoric, its concepts of necessity, fairness and civil liberty, as requiring analysis and explanation too. The net result is that research into how criminal law works overlooks the most obvious element, the law itself.

Social administrators tend to shy clear of the task of analysing the system they are studying as a matter of policy. They are by definition less concerned with theory than practical information, less interested in structural change than increasing efficiency or fairness 'within a system whose broad parameters we endorsed', to cite the example of Bottoms and McClean (1976, p. xvi). Sociologists might more readily be expected to have turned their attention to this issue. Yet instead, they too have concentrated on behaviour within the system rather than on the system, have focused less on legal than on general social behaviour, showing how the informal rules of social interaction operate in legal institutions just as in any other. Thus the people who operate the law are studied either as *any people* or as *any occupational group*.

So their legal doings, arrests, strategies in and out of court, judgments, are explained by the fact that they are just human beings subject to all the biases, whims, ups and downs, vanities and self-interests of the human lot (Bottomley, 1973, p. 143; Box, 1971, p. 175). So judgments are related to the quality of the judge's breakfast, the organisation of the court list to golf matches (Carlen, 1976). Sometimes it is more explicitly a matter of the human element in a specific type of society. In a male-dominated society, the treatment of rape victims in court is explained by male bias (Holstrom and Burgess, 1974); in a capitalist or white society, differentiation in arrest, conviction and sentencing between black and white, working-class and middle-class people is explained by race and class stereotypes (e.g. Box, 1971).

Likewise law-enforcers are seen as subject like anyone else to the pressures of their occupational group. So the emphasis on speed rather than fairness in court cases is related to bureaucratic pressures (Bottoms and McClean, 1976), the arrest rate to career interests (Cain, 1973), negotiations over the defendant's fate to reciprocal obligations or professional practices (Blumberg, 1967), the isolation and degradation of the defendant to work routines (Carlen, 1976).

These are general social pressures, informal rules that you could find in any social situation. But this emphasis underplays two factors. First, criminal justice is a legal system, with not just informal rules of acceptable social behaviour to organise it but a massive volume of formal rules on how it may be, should be or must be organised. Second, there are the elements of power and structure in both society and law. The legal system is a hierarchy, and the petty administrators are not the only people engaged in constructing the operation of the law. There is a top to the hierarchy too, the élite of judges and politicians who make those rules; their activities in relation to law enforcement have been almost totally ignored.[4]

The reasons for this seem to lie in an interlocking series of questionable dichotomies, once useful analytical devices but now, arguably, straitjackets on research – dichotomies between the substance and administration of law (sometimes put in terms of 'the law in the books' and the 'law in action'), between macro- and micro-sociological theories, between the 'new criminology' and 'the old', between abstract theorising and empiricism.

Although the sociology of law has a long tradition in the classics, its current resuscitation is largely an outgrowth of the study of deviance in the 1960s, an outgrowth that took two forms to produce a bifurcated sociology of law. The sociology of substantive law grew out of the issue: who defines deviance and why? It took the criminal law as defining deviance and examined the people and processes of law-making. It led quite logically into questions of social structure, class, power, ideology and interests at the top of the hierarchy, in short into the politics and structure of law. The other fork grew out of the issue of defining at a different level: who defines *deviants* and why? The focus was on the labelling of particular individuals and particular actions as opposed to the broad categories of definition with which substantive law deals, defining at the level of the individual rather than the level of 'society', dealing quite deliberately in the areas of criminal justice where visibility is low and the scope for discretion high. Logically enough, the police and other agents of face-to-face social control were the subject matter, and the focus was on that face-to-face control, on interpersonal interaction and decision-making. Law enforcement therefore became the precinct of micro-sociology, separated off from concern with the structure of law *per se*.

This parallelled the bifurcation of theoretical development, one half highly abstract, relying heavily on Marxism, viz. the new criminology (Taylor, Walton and Young, 1973), the other very concrete and ethnographic, relying heavily first on interactionism then on phenomenology, really very empirical with the theory more terminological than explanatory. The result was macro- *or* micro-sociology, why questions *or* how questions, and no link between the two. Research into law enforcement, as though from some endemic appropriateness, but in fact by the historical accident of its own roots and the development of sociological theory, has remained almost exclusively the preserve of micro-sociological description within the legal system.

Bridging the gap, by linking analysis of the individual in the criminal justice system with 'society', was in fact theoretically pre-empted for micro-sociology, since its 'social construction of reality' perspective ruled out analysing 'social structure' as reification. 'Social structure' only existed and could only be analysed in the process of being built up Pisarro-like from the dots of individual action. Rules and roles could therefore be realistically described only as they were acted out not as they were prescribed.

This approach found a ready niche in traditional criminal justice research since it echoed an older dichotomy of the law from the legal realists of the 1930s. They argued that law was not the 'law in the books' (what the law should be according to statutes and authorities), but the 'law in action' (how it was actually interpreted, operated, acted out). It was not the legal reasons laid down in formal law that counted, but the real reasons—back to the human element—behind judges' decisions.[5] It also fitted with the lawyers' interest either in demystifying the law by showing the gap between the rhetoric of civil rights and the reality of legal practice, or in demonstrating the tension—yet another dichotomy—between the ideals of 'due process' in the law and the practical necessity for 'crime control' (Packer, 1964). So the law in law enforcement got lost in the fascinating analysis of human action; formal rules got lost in the unending informal methods of avoiding or redefining them; the intentions behind the law got lost in the unintended consequences of its operation; explanation got lost in micro-sociological description and indignant demystification.

Meantime macro-sociological research has stuck with analysis of substantive law rather than enforcement, or failed to operate at the level of empirical research at all. Any hope that the new criminology might provide a structural analysis of law enforcement has come to little. For although it has provided 'an immanent critique' (Taylor, Walton and Young, 1973) and raised vital questions, these questions remain at the level of abstractions. Indeed, if theory in the micro-sociology of law has been criticised as more terminological than explanatory, the same could be said, for all its grandiose claims to be bringing social theory to criminology, of the new criminology. Only the terms are different. What the new criminology has done, though, is create yet another unproductive split in the analysis of law, a split between the old criminology and the new, blending into the resuscitation of a much older split between theory and empiricism.

Traditional criminology with its positivist approach has come in for hard criticism by the advocates of the new.[6] It has been characterised methodologically as empiricist, isolated from the concerns of sociological theory; ideologically as geared to the *status quo* via either correctionalism or liberal reformism. The social administrators for their part respond by embracing this description and explicitly dissociating themselves from the 'cynics and revolutionaries' of the new criminology (Bottoms and McClean, 1976, p. xvi). And so a classical, not to say clichéd, position is set up: two armed camps, theory versus empiricism, science versus policy, radicalism versus conservatism.

Much of the new criminology's criticism is quite accurate and its demands for change quite valid. Many books 'conceived in the older tradition', to draw on Bottoms and McClean again as the most recent and explicit work of this kind, sadly fail to do their own findings justice because they are just too cautious, too afraid of being seen as revolutionary, too empiricist, to give the necessary emphasis to the blatant indictment of the judicial system and structural explanation of the defendants' plight clearly there in their own data. But there are two problems in the particular way in which the new criminology's criticisms and demands have been presented.

First, there is a distinct danger that in their concern for total revision of what has gone before they are going to throw the baby out with the bathwater. For there is also a great deal in the old criminology that is of value. For a start there is a lot to be said for doing rather than talking. The old criminology concentrates on empirical research, and if it is sometimes ill-conceived and the resulting data affected by that ill-conception, it is equally often information that provides a useful, indeed *necessary*, basis for explanation. (So, for that matter, does the data provided by micro-sociological interactionism.) Bottoms and McClean's book is a veritable mine of valuable data on the processing of the defendant through the criminal justice system. In fact, although they do not themselves play up the theoretical implications, focusing conventionally on the petty administrators for their explanations, this includes vital pointers to how the legal structure itself actually shapes the way people operate and experience the law. There are the penalty clauses that emasculate real choices of plea, venue or appeal (Bottoms and McClean, 1976, pp. 103, 121, 181), limitations on legal aid (p. 165), failure to check out a guilty plea (p. 232), the unilateral power of the police in the absence of a solicitor at the police station (p. 188)–all the product of formal legal rules. The irony is that the old criminology is providing data on which the new could feed to answer very different questions.

The second problem is that demands and criticisms are not enough. But the danger is that the criticisms may pre-empt the fulfilment of the demands. So thorough has the new criminology been in its criticisms of existing empirical work – whatever is is wrong – that it is scarcely likely to encourage the lowly, lonely, fallible researcher to opt for the minefield of the real world when he could dabble instead in the ideologically safe territory of debating again what type of research might be acceptable to Marx, Gramsci, Lukacs, Taylor, Walton and Young, or Paul Q. Hirst. If the new criminology is taken too much as doctrine, it could quite plausibly produce not the stimulus to research it sets out to provide but a desert of non-problematic, non-explanatory tenets of faith never put to the test of empirical research. Research in the criminal justice field would then, ironically, be left quietly under the aegis of the old criminology, whose monopoly is exactly what the new criminology set out to destroy.

So the criminal justice field has been beset by a series of dichotomies which threaten to stultify rather than stimulate research. But they are questionable dichotomies and there are signs that these are not only being recognised as such but are being confronted and bridged. Indeed, given the dialectical development of knowledge with old analyses leading to new syntheses, that is exactly what one would expect.

That theoretical and empirical work need each other should hardly need repeating and it is a sad comment on the discipline that it does. However, there are signs of some movement towards a bridging of the two. Bottoms and McClean, for example, despite their own caution, argue for the accompaniment of 'fact-finding research' by 'explanatory research': 'for ultimately (as we have shown from our own study), administrative research raises important explanatory questions' (Bottoms and McClean, 1976, p. 242). They add a significant corollary: 'Unless we know more of the answers to some of those explanatory questions our effort at policy-making will be hindered by operating to change the system in ignorance of the true nature of the system' (p. 242). Theory is as necessary for policy aims as data is for explanation.

More important than such programmatic conclusions to research, however, is the fact that the starting-point and aim of some current research is precisely formulated to move beyond these dichotomies.

Thus ethnomethodologists argue that the tendency for micro-sociology to stop at description rather than theory, appreciation rather than explanation of the subject's views and experience, is not inevitable. Recent work tries to make the study of interaction in situations like the courtroom more rigorous than the metaphorical explanation they see as all that has been offered so far. Thus Drew tries to relate information management, and specifically the build-up to an incontrovertible accusation, to the structure rather than just the content of court 'conversation'. Atkinson takes the degradation and mystification of defendants by the dock, the strange procedures or the constant sitting and standing, not as conclusion but as starting point. Why is this so? His approach is to examine the situation and purposes of the court to separate out ritual degradation from the methods necessary to produce order in court. Time-saving for example is seen as a product of the fact that time is not unlimited, and the issues involved not academic but practical. The court is not a way of adjudicating ideally but just a solution for the practical purposes of settling matters somehow. Finding a gap between ideals and practice is hardly a revelation but exactly what one would expect. The question from the policy point of view – for Atkinson tries to bridge the theory–policy gap – is rather how far the gap is inevitably tied up in the practical problems of the court and how far those problems could be met by alternative means without unacceptable side-effects, for example doing away with the dock as degrading and as fulfilling no necessary practical function anyway.

Of course Garfinkel's work or a day in court make one suspect the purpose *is* degradation and there is a distinct whiff in this approach of the old errors of functionalism, taking the aims of the system as given, focusing on the functions of existing situations rather than their historical purposes, on logical inevitability rather than social determinants. However it illustrates one current attempt to confront the empiricism–theory, theory–policy, law in the books-law in action dichotomies by moving micro-sociology beyond description to explanation, beyond demystification to practical policy recommendations.

The need to move beyond demystification is one of the changes Taylor, Walton and Young call for in *Critical Criminology* (1975, p. 6). The irony is however that few social administrators or sociologists have really succeeded in demystifying because they have only demystified practice not the legal structure itself. That formal legal rules are organised around civil rights is taken for granted by both the champions and the critics of the *status quo*. Thus those lobbying for wider police powers argue that the rights for the defendant built into the legal structure prevent the police from getting criminals behind bars. Due process prevents crime control. And the critics, rather than confronting this assumption, accept it, by focusing on police practices, not legal rules (Cox, 1975). Indeed, sociologists have endorsed the system by suggesting that, if only police practices could be brought into line with the law, the defendant and the citizen would be in a fairer position (Skolnick, 1966).

If, however, we question the dichotomy between due process and crime control, the substance of law and its enforcement, we are drawn to a rather different conclusion. Actually examining the rules of due process in statutes and precedents indicates that they are not dichotomies at all. Judges and politicians may deal in the rhetoric of civil rights and due process, but the actual rules they create for law enforcement and the policies they adopt on sanctioning police malpractices are less about civil rights than about smoothing the path to conviction, less about due process than *post-hoc* acceptance of police activities as justifying themselves. Thus a good many of the practices in criminal justice described as informal perversions of the formal rules are in fact allowed, facilitated or upheld in the formal rules of statute and precedent. There are inklings of this in earlier work, new and old research never falling into the neat categories overviews like this might suggest – in Bottoms and McClean, for example, or Greenawalt, or Green, in Skolnick's reference to the institutions of public prosecutor and defender facilitating plea-bargaining, or Stinchcombe's tying together of class differentiation in arrests and legal definitions of privacy and liberty. But one can go through the whole process of criminal justice and find the same systematic and pervasive pattern.

Thus arrest on suspicion is exactly what the Vagrancy Act, 1874, Prevention of Crimes Act, 1871, and local acts like the Glasgow General Powers Act, 1960, are about. Using a holding charge to arrest and question on suspicion of a different offence, quite contrary to the rhetoric of the Judges' Rules, is upheld in legal texts (Renton and Brown, 1972, p. 32) and judicial decisions (e.g. Christie *v.* Leachinsky). Search without warrant is accepted at law (Bell *v.* Hogg: Hay *v.* HM Advocate; Chic Fashions *v.* Jones; Jeffrey *v.* Black), while evidence obtained illegally is still accepted in court: 'It matters not how you get it; if you steal it even it would be admissible' [an opinion of 1861 cited in Kuruma 1955]. Access to a solicitor is quite legitimately refused if the police feel it might cause 'unreasonable delay or hindrance . . . to the processes of investigation or the administration of justice' (HO Circular 31), regardless of whether the lack of a solicitor might affect justice from the perspective of the defendant and due process rather than the police and crime control. The management and suppression of information in court is not just a product of informal techniques but is affected at the pre-trial stages by formal rules facilitating the preparation of the prosecution's case and limiting the preparation of the defence's, at the trial itself by the rules of evidence, all geared far less to civil rights and more to conviction than the rhetoric of justice suggests. In short, the dichotomies organising criminal justice research are false. The operation of the law is not a subversion of the substance of the law but exactly what one would expect it to produce; the law in action is only too close a parallel to the law in the books; due process is for crime control (McBarnet, 1976, 1977).

For a full explanation of how law is enforced then, substantive law, legal structure, the State must be added to[7] moods and bureaucracies and face-to-face interaction. It's a long way from the Law Lords to the Saturday night affray, from the corridors of power to the Monday morning guilty plea, but a clear chain links the two. Social structure and individual action are merely two sides of the same coin; macro-sociology has as much to contribute to the explanation of specific arrests or convictions as micro-sociology.

But bringing law in as an explanatory factor in the operation of criminal justice is not enough. We must examine the assumptions and purposes underlying criminal justice itself in terms of its social, historical and political basis, in relation to class, power, interests and ideologies; in short, we must apply the questions and concepts hitherto reserved for the analysis of specific laws to the legal system *per se*. We must do so not at the level of tautological assumption – taking it as unproblematic that in bourgeois society law will take bourgeois forms – but empirically, asking what this means, if it is quite so simple (is ideology only empty rhetoric or does it have some causal impact too? Thompson, 1975), and analysing how it is achieved. Systems do not operate themselves; people construct them. Exactly 'who' is important. So is 'how?' If law is an ideological tool, how is it operated? Douglas Hay's work on the apparent inefficiency of eighteenth-century criminal law enforcement – its 'inefficiency' was the key to its ideological strength – provides a fine example of the value of empiricising such questions. One might also ask how ideology is maintained in the face of blatant negations of it. How, for example do judges maintain the ideology of civil rights while satisfying in the same judgement the 'necessity' of conviction? Or more broadly, how is mystification achieved? Burton and Carlen's work on official discourse makes a start on just this type of problem. The implication is that, if macro-sociology has to be brought in to explain the operation of the local court, so micro-sociology must be brought in to explain the system, not to analyse the local bobby but the élite of the State, not the petty administrators but the creators of the criminal justice system, not to turn in scorn from abstract questions of power but to examine real people constructing and maintaining domination.

Bridging false dichotomies thus opens up a whole new level of problems for criminal justice research, combining the questions of macro- with the methods of micro-sociology, the critical insights of the new criminology with the dogged empirical work of the old.

Notes

1. See for example Blumberg (1967); Bordua (1967); Cain (1971, 1973); Carlen (1976); Chambliss (1969); Cicourel (1968); Garfinkel (1956); Hetzler and Kanter (1974); Newman (1966); Sykes and Clark (1975).
2. This is a broad term which includes lawyers and sociologists with a positivist approach (see Taylor Walton and Young, 1973, for an explication of positivism) as well as those who would label themselves social administrators. An overview of this kind necessarily if unfortunately (especially given the argument!) operates on broad categories and crude summaries.
3. For example: Bottomley (1968, 1973); Bottoms and McClean (1976); Dell (1971); Hood (1962, 1972); Justice (1971); King (1971); Zander (1969, 1972a, 1972b).
4. Chambliss and Seidman have analysed the Supreme Court, but in the conventional model, that is mainly for the purpose of demystifying its value-neutrality and showing how human and organisational factors influence judicial decisions at this level too. Even élite studies in sociology have curiously neglected the study of judges.
5. See how Chambliss and Seidman used this dichotomy as an organising model.
6. And of course, on some shared, some different grounds, by interactionists. See for example Cohen (1971), Introduction.
7. Note 'added to'. Structural analysis is a corollary to and context for, not a replacement of, interactionist analysis.

References

Bell *v.* Hogg 1967 *J.C.*

Chic Fashions (West Wales) Ltd. *v.* Jones 1968 1 *All. E.R.*

Christie *v.* Leachinsky 1947 *A.C.*

Hay *v.* H.M. Advocate 1968 *S.L.T.*

Jeffrey *v.* Black 1977 *Q.B.D. T.L.R.* 15.7.77.

Kuruma *v.* R. 1955 *A.C.*

Atkinson, J. M. (1976) 'Order in court: some preliminary issues and analyses', presented at the Conference of the International Sociological Association Research Group on Sociology of Law.

Blumberg, A. S. (1967) *Criminal Justice* (Quadrangle).

Bordua, D. (ed.) (1967) *The Police* (John Wiley).

Bottomley A. K. (1968) 'The granting of bail: principles and practice', *Modern Law Review*, 31. (1973) *Decisions in the penal process* (Martin Robertson).

Bottoms, A. E. and McClean, J. D. (1976) *Defendants in the Criminal Process* (Routledge & Kegan Paul).

Box, S. (1971) *Deviance, Reality and Society* (Holt, Rinehart & Winston).

Burton, F. and Carlen, P. (1977) 'Official discourse,' presented at the British Sociological Association conference.

Cain, M. (1971) 'On the beat' *in* S. Cohen (ed.) *Images of Deviance* (Penguin); (1973) *Society and the Policeman's Role* (Routledge & Kegan Paul).

Carlen, P. (1976) *Magistrates' Justice* (Martin Robertson).

Chambliss, W. J. (1969) *Crime and the Legal Process* (McGraw Hill).

——and Seidman R. B. (1971) *Law, Order and Power*. (Addison-Wesley).

Cicourel A. (1968) *The Social Organisation of Juvenile Justice* (John Wiley).

Cohen, S. (1971) *Images of Deviance* (Penguin Books).

Cox, B. (1975) *Civil Liberties in Britain (Penguin).*

Dell, S. (1971) *Silent in Court*, Occasional Papers in Social Administration no. 42 (Bell).

Drew, P. (1978) 'Accusations: the occasioned use of religious geography in describing events', *Sociology* (January 1978).

Garfinkel, H. (1956) 'Conditions of successful degradation ceremonies', *American Journal of Sociology*, **61**.

Green, E. (1961) *Judicial Attitudes in Sentencing* (Macmillan).

Greenawalt, K. (1973) 'Perspectives on the right to silence' in R. Hood, (ed.) *Crime, Criminology and Public Policy* (Heinemann).

Hay, D. (1975) 'Property, authority and law' in Hay *et al. Albion's Fatal Tree* (Allen Lane).

Hetzler, A. N. and Kanter, C. H. (1974) 'Informality and the court' in Sylvester S. F. and Sagarin E. *Politics and Crime* (Praeger).

Holstrom L. L. and Burgess A. W. (1974) 'Rape: the victim goes on trial' in Drapkin and Viano *Victimology* Vol. III (D. C. Heath).

Home Office Circular no. 31 (1964).

Hood, R. G. (1962) *Sentencing in Magistrates' Courts* (Stevens); (1972) *Sentencing the Motoring Offender* (Heinemann).

Justice (1971) *The Unrepresented Defendant in Magistrates' Courts* (Stevens).

King, M. (1971) *Bail or Custody?* (Cobden Trust).

McBarnet, D. J. (1976) 'Pre-trial procedures and the construction of conviction' *in* P. Carlen Sociological Review Monograph on *The Sociology of Law* (Keele University) (1977); 'The police and the state: arrest, legality and the law', presented at the British Sociological Association Conference.

Newman, D. J. (1966) *Conviction* (Little, Brown).

Packer, H. (1964) 'Two models of the criminal process' *University of Pennsylvania Law Review*, 113. p. 1.

Renton, R. W. and Brown, H. H. (1972) *Criminal Procedure According to the Law of Scotland* 4th edn (Green).

Skolnick, J. (1966) *Justice without Trial* (Wiley); (1967) 'Law and conflict resolution', *Journal of Conflict Resolution*, XI.

Stinchcombe, A. (1963) 'Institutions of privacy in the determination of police administrative practice', *American Journal of Sociology*, 59. p. 150.

Sykes, R. E. and Clark, J. P. (1975) 'A theory of deference exchange in police-civilian encounters', *American Journal of Sociology*, 81. p. 584.

Taylor, I., Walton, P. and Young, J. (1973) *The New Criminology* (Routledge & Kegan Paul); (1975) *Critical Criminology* (Routledge & Kegan Paul).

Thompson, E. P. (1975) *Whigs and Hunters* (Allen Lane).

Zander, M. (1969) 'Unrepresented defendants in the criminal courts', *Criminal Law Review*; p. 632 (1972a) 'Legal Advice and Criminal appeals', p. 132 *Criminal Law Review*; (1972b) 'Access to a solicitor in the police station', *Criminal Law Review*, p. 342.

Part Two

Taking Law Seriously in Socio-Legal Research: Explaining Conviction

[2]
Pre-trial Procedures and the Construction of Conviction

I Criminal procedure and the construction of conviction

In the revived sociology of law the procedures of the legal structure have been curiously ignored. Research has concentrated on either the power structure behind legislation or the day to day dramas of the courtroom so beloved and belaboured by the ethnomethodologists. The result is that two distinct lines have developed in the sociology of law with different methodologies and problems – why the substance of law takes the shape it does and how the routine outcomes of the law are achieved. This is what makes the failure to analyse procedure so curious. For legal procedures – in criminal law, the rules of investigation, trial and sentence, the establishment of rights and duties (and the lack of them) – bridge this gap. On the one hand they are part of the substance of the law and thus the product of decisions at the top of the legal and political structure, and on the other hand, one of the influences on how the law is routinely enforced. Legal procedure thus provides a clear link between the ethnomethodological concern with the law in action and the structuralist concern with the law in the books and the power structure behind it. It opens the way to an explanation of courtroom practices that goes far beyond the courtroom walls.

The criminal court determines innocence or guilt. It is the central point in the penal process described by Bottomley as:

> 'a conveyor belt . . . characterised by a lack of any overall guiding purpose.' (1973: 219–220).

However problematic the purpose there is no doubt about its outcome. Theoretically the output of the penal process could be acquittal or conviction; statistically, the end product is unequivocably conviction. According to Scottish criminal statistics for 1974, 91% of cases resulted in conviction, in English crown courts 82% and in the magistrates' courts 94%.[1] Some samples show even higher rates – a 98·5% conviction rate for magistrates' courts in Sheffield. (Bottoms and McClean 1976).

Conviction depends in court on the plea or the verdict. If the accused[2] pleads guilty to the charge against him, conviction follows as a matter of routine. If he pleads not guilty, a contested trial follows, evidence is presented by both prosecution and defence, and the judge, in summary cases, the jury, under solemn jurisdiction, decides on conviction or acquittal. According to Bottoms and McClean, 72·5% of those contesting the case in magistrates' courts, 55% of those choosing jury trials, and 71% of those allocated to the higher courts were convicted on some or all counts (1976: 106, 109).

The crucial decision in these contested trials is the verdict, yet it has received so little attention in research that Bottomley omitted it in his review of *Decisions in the penal process* (1973). Curiously the sociology of judicial behaviour has concentrated on sentencing practices, noted the wide-ranging variations that exist, (Hood 1962, 1972) approached the court with a decision-making model in mind, and reduced the problems posed by the court to the decisions made by individual judges and the perceptions of community, selection of information and general 'human element' (Bottomley) involved in the process. But one would expect sentences to vary. The law explicitly requires that sentences be tailored to particular cases. The decision which resolves the trial and precedes any question of sentence is remarkable for its consistency rather than its variability, and that decision is the verdict – finding the accused not guilty or, 90% of the time, guilty.

The verdict is clearly central and it is also highly problematic. In our adversary system, a criminal trial is a joust between two competing versions of reality, which must result in a clearcut unambiguous decision. The choices available to the accused, the judge and the jury are presented in the form of cut and dried, mutually exclusive categories. An accused person may plead guilty or not guilty, the case for the prosecution is either proved or it is not, a verdict is either conviction or acquittal.[3] There is no place in strict legal categories for the ambiguities which dog real life. The judge or jury in reaching a decision is charged that it cannot convict unless convinced 'beyond reasonable doubt' that the prosecution case is an accurate representation of what happened in the disputed incident. Conviction thus depends on a legal concept of proof, not on common-sense or scientific criteria which might well conclude the truth to be unknowable, not just in a philosophical sense but because of the circumstances and methods involved.

The incident itself is likely to have contained elements of ambiguity or greyness, and the methods of proof used are far from favourable to a precise reconstruction. The offence may have occurred months before; proof depends on human beings with memories of the event subjectively perceived at the time and liable to moulding after it; evidence is partial rather than total – the witnesses available and co-operative rather than all those with relevant knowledge; each side has a vested interest in distorting even their perceptions of what occurred; and all of this is compounded by the perceptions of the judge or jury receiving the evidence presented. The verdict is therefore a compoundly subjective construction of reality after the event – yet it is also a clearcut decision that the offence and the offender have or have not been proved beyond reasonable doubt. It is unambiguously black or white.

This is the first problem that the verdict poses for sociologists. In the face of all the implicit ambiguities, how does the judge or jury *become convinced* of guilt or innocence? How is conviction, in that subjective sense, constructed?

But in most cases conviction in the legal sense – a finding of guilt – is constructed at the same time. In court, both sides are given an equal opportunity to present their versions of reality, the balance of how much proof is required favours the accused since any reasonable doubt should, in law, result in acquittal, yet the joust is one that the prosecution can expect to win. Why?

The decision-making approach is one way to try to come to terms with this. The human element, prejudices, preconceptions, mood, might as readily affect the verdict as the sentence. The legal realists of the 1930s, many famous jurists themselves, called for a perspective on judicial decisions based on psychology rather than legality. The problems of access to such subjective matter might explain why judicial decision-making as a field of study has taken a long time to get off the ground.

A more recent sociological approach is to study interaction in the court. The court is not just a legal institution, it is the daily work-place of the personnel who operate in it, and operate on their own experiences, friendships and enmities, and personal rather than judicial aims and interests. Techniques for routinising the work of the court are developed informally to keep cases simple and clearcut and to operationalise the preconceptions of the policemen, judges, lawyers and social workers in court in relation to the accused. So it is that in contested cases where reasonable doubts might arise, alliances of alleged adversaries, techniques of cross-examination, the use of language and gesture, common-sense understandings of credibility, degradation ceremónies, remedial routines, and the symbolic position of the accused all provide valuable insights into how the outcomes of the court are routinely achieved. (Garfinkel 1956; Young 1971; Hetzler and Canter 1974; Carlen 1974, 1975). Informal routines and interactions contribute to the processes of conviction, in both senses, by limiting the information and opinion voiced in court to selected issues with no ifs and buts to raise doubts, and replacing the formal presumption of innocence with an informal presumption of guilt.

But interactionist detail in court cannot provide a total explanation of the processes of conviction. In the first place, it understates the structural influences of the legal system's rules, checks and definitions on the construction of reality. In the second place it underplays how much the events and information observed in court have been shaped long before the stage of public trial is reached.

The legal system itself presupposes and indeed provides for pre-trial 'clarification of issues', in the doctrine of no surprise (of which more later) and in the build up to the trial. If the prosecutor is to prove the unknowable beyond reasonable doubt he must come to court with a version of the incident as cut and dried and logically complete as he can. Criminal procedure includes a filter between the police and the trial for the specific purpose of establishing that there is a prima facie case for prosecutions brought to trial. The procurator fiscal's discretion to drop or pursue police cases fulfils this function in Scotland. The magistrates' decision in commital proceedings does the same in indictments in England. The filter is not so efficient in practice that only watertight cases come to trial.[4] But the presupposition that there is a prima facie case for conviction is thus built in to the common-sense assumptions of the court before any evidence is heard. As Sir Robert Mark put it:

> 'The procedural safeguards for the suspect or accused in our system of criminal justice are such that committal for trial, involving the participation of lawyers and bench, is itself an indication of strong probability of guilt'. (Alderson 1973: 16).

The informal displacement of the presumption of innocence by the presumption of guilt is not then just the product of the symbolic position of the accused in court, but of the pre-trial procedures assumed, as Sir Robert Mark assumes, to exempt the innocent (and the guilty who cannot be proved guilty) from the process of public proof.

If procedures do safeguard the accused to this extent there is a simple explanation for the large proportion of convictions – normally only the indisputably guilty with no reasonable doubts to offer would come through the filters to trial. Certainly only 62% of people apprehended came to trial in Scotland in 1974. So pre-trial procedures become an important focal point in understanding how the courtroom joust between two versions of reality is so often resolved in favour of the prosecution.

But what are the procedures? *Do* they favour the accused? Do they filter out the innocent? The problem is an empirical one, for though sociologists have recognised the significance of pre-trial *events* for the outcomes of the penal process, they have ignored the role of the formalities of the legal structure.

This is not surprising, especially after one glance at the material involved – the statutes written in the longest and most qualified sentences in the language, the lifeless reports, the shelves and shelves of dusty law reports where the common law is as convoluted as a maze and often seems about as purposeful. The law like so many of our significant institutions does not invite study, and the substance of procedural law does not excite the same immediate interest as observing the fascinating informalities of human beings presenting images of self, manipulating language, mystifying with knowledge, string-pulling, conniving, and organising cases around the tea break.

What is more, sociologists have not just ignored on grounds of interest, but scorned on theoretical grounds, the study of formal rules and roles. They have emphasised the significance of what really happens as opposed to what should, an offshoot of the legal realism of the thirties. They have stressed that roles and rules are problematic in the more recent fashion of phenomenology. They have concentrated on showing how what formally *should* happen is distorted by the informal realities of interaction, Goffman style, or by Weberian unintended consequences which lead, for example, to the secondary interest of efficient administration taking primacy over what the organisation was set up to do.

This microsociological side of the coin is both valid and important, but it is not the only one. There is a tendency to present formal rules and actual behaviour as mutually exclusive, but reality is never quite so simple. Just because people do not act out their roles to the letter, may 'make' rather than 'take' them, it does not follow that they do not act them out at all. One does not need to fall into naive role theory where 'ought' and 'is' are assimilated to recognise that people are constrained in socially – and legally – defined situations. The judge observed summing up:

> 'I have no alternative but to find you guilty as charged.'

or another even more poignantly:

> 'With great regret I must find this case not proven.'

is not merely exhibiting Sartre's 'mauvais foi' but reminding us that if he is no mere norm-following homunculus, neither is he a free agent in the court.

The same could be said of the police. Sociology has emphasised the discretionary side of the policeman's job, and the problem has been defined in terms of how the police come to select particular individuals who tend to be male rather than female, working class rather than middle class, black rather than white. What is not discussed is the procedural powers and legal definitions which enable, indeed invite, the police to use their discretion in this way. It is not just personal prejudice, nor bureaucratic secondary interests, nor the definitions of role imposed by wives, communities and colleagues, that are involved in the policeman's action, (Piliavin and Briar 1964; Young 1971; Skolnick 1966; Cain 1973) but the powers, duties and sanctions of the formal legal system itself.

In short, if interactionist analysis of events inside the court cannot offer a total explanation of the processes of criminal justice, neither can interactionist detail on the beat or for that matter in the probation officer's room (Cicourel 1968), the lawyer's office (Blumberg 1967), or the clerk of court's chambers, where individual rights may be sacrificed to the efficiency of 'liberal bureaucracy' (Bottoms and McClean 1976). The actors in the decision-making model and the interactionist model of law enforcement are affected by procedures beyond their control. Schutz, the arch antagonist of reification nonetheless noted that people often experience the world as reified:

> 'I find myself in my everyday life within a world not of my own making . . . I experience these transcendencies . . . as being imposed on me.' (Schutz 1970: 245–6).

More attention to the structural influences of rules, checks and definitions is required, and the study of precedures is one way to do that.

There is a second reason for the study of procedure. The emphasis on unintended consequences leaves a nasty gap on the equally interesting issue of how the penal process *is intended* to work. If petty officials are constrained by procedures, procedures in turn are created by decisions at the powerful peak of judicial and political hierarchies. What are the purposes behind legal procedure?

The first step towards these wider issues is to find out exactly what the legal situation of the accused vis-a-vis the prosecution is. We all know the rhetoric, the rights provided for the accused, the safeguards Sir

Robert Mark and others refer to. The accused has the right to a fair trial and the onus of proof rests on the prosecution. In the contested case, the crown faces a problem of proof involving three processes:

1. incriminating the individual
2. assembling a case against him
3. surviving the public joust in court.

At each stage the prosecutor must prove his point according to standards of fairness of method, sufficiency and quality of evidence, and credibility of presentation. What is more, the accused has a right to silence, he is not a compellable witness and he is protected from self-incrimination so that the prosecutor has to be able to prove his case without the co-operation of the accused. At any stage the accused can choose to establish a defence case to counter that of the prosecution, with the less stringent requirement not of 'proof' but merely of raising a reasonable doubt, and he may use legal expertise to do that.

In principle the accused is in a strong position. It becomes a wonder that 90% are convicted every year. But only if we look at the general principles around which the legal system is *discussed.* If we look at the actual procedures set up for operationalising justice, we are presented with a very different picture of what the legal system is for. The legal system *is* the procedures not the rhetoric, and procedures do not so much provide safeguards for the accused as powers for the prosecution.

This is true at all three stages of proof, and each stage affects the next. Thus the powers available to the police to incriminate an individual affect the kind of case each side can assemble and their relative chances of establishing it in court. This paper examines just one part of pre-trial procedure taking up the process *after* the stage of incrimination (dealt with in a separate discussion of police powers) and focussing on what happens between the charge and the trial. Whether the prosecutor has to go on to the second stage of proof and a full-blown case depends on how the accused chooses to plead. If he pleads guilty, conviction follows without further investigation; if he pleads not guilty each side must collect evidence for the trial, and conviction depends on the judge or jury deciding that the prosecution has the better case. In principle each decision could go either way; in practice most pleas are guilty and most contested cases result in conviction.

The point of this paper is to show that the subjective decision to plead guilty is directly related to the legally defined situation in which it is taken; that the tendency to conviction is not arbitrary but built into the pattern of rights, limitations and powers established in pre-trial procedures to the benefit of the prosecution and disadvantage of the accused; that this is not just the product of unofficial interaction at the lower levels of law enforcement but is official policy defined by statutes and decisions taken at the top of the judicial and political hierarchies; that the construction of conviction is not just a complex informal achievement but is endemic in the legal system itself.

Analysis is based on two years' observation in criminal courts, informal interviews and documentary research. The central focus is the Scottish legal system but those familiar with English law will find the situation much more familiar than nationalistic Scottish lawyers would have them believe, and references are made throughout to some of the clear similarities or glaring discrepancies between the two countries in their systematic construction of conviction.

II The Plea

By right, anyone can plead not guilty and make the prosecution *prove* guilt, but in practice the vast majority do not take advantage of this procedural safeguard. Official statistics do not provide information on pleas, but sample studies show that 76% to 93% of defendants in magistrates' courts and 57% to 75% in higher courts incriminate themselves in the most direct way possible by pleading guilty (Dell 1971, Zander 1969; Bottoms and McClean 1976).

This proportion includes not only those who see themselves as factually guilty, or as factually innocent but technically guilty, (both of whom still have a right to force the prosecution to prove guilt) but also those who, according to Dell and Bottoms and McClean see themselves as totally innocent. Why do they plead guilty and thus convict themselves?

Sociologists have emphasised the role of 'plea-bargaining' between prosecution and defence in explaining this, though mainly with reference to America (Blumberg 1967; Skolnick 1967; Newman 1966). Evidence in Britain on solicitor's advice to plead guilty is scantier, contradictory and less statistically significant, though that is partly because not everyone in the samples has a solicitor. In the Sheffield study only 7% of the total sample of guilty pleaders, but as many as 34% of the 'possible innocent' gave 'lawyer's advice' as the reason for their plea (Bottoms and McClean 1976: 112, 121). Dell however does not mention lawyer's advice in her discussion of 'innocent' respondents' reasons for pleading guilty, (perhaps they were not represented), and on the contrary, concludes that legal representation *does* help those, who believe themselves innocent, to plead not guilty.

Bottoms and McClean suggest indeed that bargaining is not so developed in England as in America and is discouraged officially, and they quote Lord Parker's disapproval of the involvement of judges in bargaining to support this. But bargaining does occur, as McCabe and Purves (1972) show in their small sample of changed pleas.

Informal extra-legal interests in a bargain exist for all the participants in it. Solicitors have interests to take into account which may run contrary to their client's right to trial as these excerpts from interviews show. There may be financial interests in keeping up a fast throughput of cases:

> 'You need five cases a day to make it pay.'

Or just the possibility of more time:

> 'I had three trials today and it's down to one now. With luck I'll get that over quickly at two.'

Then there are informal alliances to establish, cement and honour:

> 'You get more leverage to get the right sheriff or get the court adjourned to fit a case in quickly if you're a regular there and known to bargain.'

And these alliances in turn facilitate bargaining. Asked why he had just interrupted another trial to slip in a client who'd changed his plea to guilty, one solicitor explained:

> 'I knew (Sheriff X) would send him away, so I put pressure on to get in while this guy (Sheriff Y) was on and before (X) came back from the funeral. I knew (Y) would just fine him. The trick is to get a guilty plea and in return you get the charge reduced to two-thirds and a lighter sentence.'

The police and the prosecutor too have practical, personal, careerist and administrative motives for bargaining over a case (Blumberg 1967; Newman 1966; Skolnick 1966). What these authors don't mention is that more than time and efficiency is involved. There may simply *not be a case* for the prosecution that would stand up to the rules of evidence, so conviction *depends* on a guilty plea.

Finally the accused has advantages to gain from pleading guilty to a reduced charge if he expects to be found guilty anyway or to avoid being kept in custody awaiting a full-scale trial. Sometimes indeed it is the accused who tries to negotiate with the police, as this reply to a charge shows:

> 'Could I get bail tonight? I have nothing to say against the charge'.

But if informal interests provide the motives for bargaining, the legal system itself provides the opportunity. Contrary to Carlen's perspective *in the court* – that bargaining is something to be hidden from the magistrate, 'a betrayal of the ideal of the professional construction of justice' (1975: 355) – and to Bottoms and McClean's conclusion from a discussion *of the system* that negotiating is not encouraged in England either by the legal structure or by formal policy, the Scottish situation suggests it is promoted by both.

The charge, the allocation of a case to solemn or summary jurisdiction (with higher or lower maximum sentences), and the acceptance of the plea are left, with the occasional statutory exception, to the prosecutor's discretion, and can be changed without explanation. The legal structure in Scotland, as in Skolnick's study of the public prosecutor's role in America (1967), allows for bargaining. It is also officially endorsed, for example, by the Thomson Committee, set up by the Scottish Home and Health Department and Crown Office to investigate criminal procedure:

> 'There is no statutory authority for plea adjustment but it is accepted as proper practice for either the accused's legal adviser or the prosecutor to approach the other and negotiate the acceptance of a partial plea. Normally such an approach comes from the defence but it is perfectly proper for the prosecutor to intimate to the defence that he would be willing to accept a plea of guilty to less than the full extent of any particular charge'. (1975: 97).

It was noted that judges are not and should not be involved, which may explain why Bottoms and McClean discussing official policy, in England, only in relation to the judge's role, found little evidence of structural encouragement for bargaining (though even this is put in doubt by a recent case – Cain TLR 20 February 1976). The only criticism by the Committee was that it was wasteful for plea bargaining to occur at the last minute after the case had been prepared and witnesses called, so it was proposed that:

> 'While the practice of plea adjustment should continue, it should wherever possible be effected well before the trial', (97)

and that procedures should be used or adapted for this purpose. The period of time between the charge and the plea diet should be extended from six to twenty days (too bad for those in custody untried) to 'facilitate early plea adjustment in solemn proceedings', (97) and there should be a preliminary meeting between the two sides, at which

> '*We recommend that there should be informal discussion* between prosecution and defence . . . on, for example, the following subjects . . . plea adjustment . . .' (116 – my italics).

As this quotation shows, informal liaisons do not occur despite the system but because of it. The relationship may indeed be best seen as dialectic, as comes out forcibly in criminal procedure reports. The structure of procedures makes possible a practice which, while not necessarily planned, is nonetheless condoned and legitimised by legal authorities and then deliberately promoted by procedural change. Informal actors and formal structures are not distortions of each other, they are interrelated, and explanations of penal processes that emphasise one or the other are not conflicting but interdependent.

This is as true of the accused's choices as it is of lawyer's negotiations, as becomes apparent if we leave aside the source of plea-bargaining and consider the situation in which it occurs. Negotiation implies a bilateral exchange, and this might not quite reflect the situation the accused is in, both as objectively defined *for* him by the legal system and subjectively defined *by* him. Dell's and Bottoms and McClean's 'possibly innocent' respondents mentioned police advice or pressure (15% and 9% respectively) and 'it's only my word against the police' or 'it's not worth challenging the police' (14% and 8%) as reasons for their guilty pleas. This takes us back a stage to the accused's situation vis-a-vis the police. First, procedures relating to police questioning make the suspcct far more vulnerable than the rhetoric of a right against self-incrimination would suggest, and it is not surprising that 11% in Bottoms and McClean's study said they pleaded guilty because they had confessed to the police. However incrimination can take a more ambiguous form than out and out confession. To take just one example – replies to charges – out of 93 studied only 7 were directly incriminating – 'I'm caught' – but 13 were indirectly incriminating by way of justification – 'I was bloody angry' – or capable of interpretation as incriminating – the fatal 'I'm sorry' – with another 7 discrediting or hostile to the police – 'Fucking gestapo!' Since these statements are all admissable evidence the accused has damaged his credibility from the beginning and may feel it pointless to plead not guilty. Second, the police station is a degrading as well as a frightening place. After being charged, the accused may, in law, be searched, involved in an identification parade or have his finger prints taken, all, according to several accused, creating an atmosphere of guilt.

Third, the power to define the situation is very much on one side. The accused is alone with the police. He is not entitled to see a solicitor until after the charge, which normally means immediately before the court hears his plea. So, in the crucial period of weighing up his position, the accused is exposed to only one version of how the law interprets the behaviour he has allegedly or actually committed, how the evidence looks against him, what chance he has of establishing his innocence and what the outcome is likely to be. (In Bottoms and McClean's study 27% said they pleaded guilty because the police had a good case). Sometimes the police may use their aura of superior procedural knowledge to alarm the accused into a guilty plea, as in this reported case, quashed on appeal:

> The accused was arrested on Christmas Eve. His lawyer was informed but was not able to come at once. The police suggested that the accused would be wise to get the business over with rather than spend Christmas in custody awaiting trial. In fact the offence was a petty one and it was highly unlikely that bail would have been refused. However the accused was misled into pleading guilty. (Law 1965 JC 32).

Sometimes it is not so much a matter of misleading as threatening. According to the account of one interviewed defendant, the policeman who charged him said 'You plead not guilty and I'll come down and swear your life away'.

But there need be no intended or malicious influence exerted. It is just that in an undefined situation the dominant interpretation of the police is likely to be rather different from that of the defence. Yet the legal system explicitly prevents anyone being present to provide a defence perspective that might encourage the accused to think he has a chance and should take up the option of a trial.

However a guilty plea can also be a calculatedly sensible move on the part of the accused. The opportunity of trial is not automatically available but has to be chosen. So as in all rights which have to be claimed, there is a low take-up rate for all sorts of legally extraneous reasons. A good many of the predominantly working class people who come through the courts tend to see the law and the police, because of cultural assumptions, or as in these cases from experience, as an alien institution in which one might as well plead guilty because:

> 'You don't have a chance anyway'.
> 'People like us can't go against the police'.
> 'A copper's word would go against you if he came and lifted a bloke off the street'.
> 'I was surprised to hear them actually lie in the court but they can say anything and get away with it'.
> 'People like us don't have rights'.

Given this assumption, taking up the right to a trial is hardly worth the practical problems it involves. The respondents in Dell's and Bottoms's studies of guilty pleas both mentioned reasons like – getting it over, avoiding delay, less fuss, to avoid remand, too trivial to fight. Trial procedure is slow. Bottoms and McClean provide the most up-to-date and detailed figures. In the magistrates' courts they studied, 88% of those who pleaded guilty were dealt with immediately, whereas only 8% of those who pleaded not guilty appeared in court within 34 days and the majority were delayed by 56 to 100+ days (1976: 45). This delay might involve not just anxiety but imprisonment – 30% of those who pleaded not guilty on indictment were held in custody (211), of whom just over half spent up to 13 days, and the rest up to 83 days in jail awaiting trial (51). The 110 day rule is the only check, and that only in Scotland, on how long a person can legally be held in prison untried, and even that legitimises a 4 month period of custody while technically innocent, rather at odds with the rhetoric of justice – 'nulla poene sine crima', no punishment unless a crime has been committed. Pleading not guilty entails two appearances in court on a summary charge, three on indictment. Any of these stages can be postponed at the last minute after hours of waiting, the trial itself can last for hours, days or weeks.

The practical problems emerge when one considers difficulties like arranging time off work while not wanting the employer to know about the charge, or quite simply the loss of earnings involved in court appearances or custody. There is no compensation for the accused who is consequently found not guilty. On the contrary there is provision in England, though it is rarely exercised, for the costs of prosecution to be awarded against a defendant who is found guilty after pleading not guilty and thus wasting the court's time. Legal aid is far from available of right and the accused may be afraid he could not afford legal advice and afraid to take on the experts in opposition without it.

In short the legal system offers the right of trial only if the accused chooses to take it up, but the choice facing someone whose family depends on his earnings and freedom is not necessarily based on guilt or innocence or even the merits of the case. He may be unable to face the delays, publicity and ordeal of the trial. Or he may simply be unable to afford the luxury of acquittal.

These practical reasons for pleading guilty are not just subjective perceptions existing in an ethnomethodological vacuum. They represent an accurate assessment of the legal procedures in which the accused is caught. One need not look to phenomenological processes or cultural assumptions to explain the decision, but to the legal system itself.

Likewise, the advice to plead guilty by lawyers and policemen may not just be explained by informal interests, but represent sound legal advice in the light of procedural constraints.

The plea is made on 'the first lawful day' after the police charge – usually the next morning. This is after the prosecution has established a prima facie case but before there is much if any chance for the accused or his solicitor to collect evidence. Unless there is a clear cut defence like alibi there can be no assurance that it will be possible, however innocent one may be, to pick holes in the prosecution case or produce evidence to counter it. The accused, the solicitor and the police are all aware that a not guilty plea may result in a conviction anyway, and they are aware that if this happens the legal system has built in punishments for the individual who contests the case. Another reason given by the guilty pleaders interviewed by Dell and Bottoms and McClean – that they might get harsher sentences if they were to plead not guilty – is quite accurate, though the legal manuals prefer to put it in reverse, that a guilty plea counts as a mitigating factor. There are other advantages in pleading guilty, e.g. there is provision in solemn procedure with a special form available, to ask for an 'accelerated diet' – quick disposal – if you plead guilty. The legal system offers clear incentives against taking up the right to a trial.

What is more, there are *structural obstacles* to altering a preliminary guilty plea to not guilty which do not exist in the reverse situation. 'The Crown is master of the instance' as Thomson puts it, so the prosecutor can accept the change to a guilty plea any time he chooses without explanation. But in the high court and summary courts a change of plea to *not* guilty is only allowed at the discretion of the court if an adequate case is made out by the accused,

> 'it being necessary for him to satisfy the court that his plea was tendered under substantial error or misconception or in circumstances which tended to prejudice his case'. (Renton and Brown: 95).

Doreen J. McBarnet

In solemn procedure in the sheriff court there is no statutory provision for withdrawing a guilty plea at all. It is legally impossible to change one's plea to not guilty. The Thomson Committee recommends that this should be made possible but only at the discretion of the court not as of right.

Finally the legal system encourages people to plead guilty by failing to provide a systematic check on the plea itself. A guilty plea is accepted in court without examination of the circumstances or the intent, though both may affect the legal applicability of the charge.

In all these ways then, the pressures to plead guilty lie not just in perceptions, negotiations, informal liaisons and bureaucratic interests, but also in the legal system itself. Indeed it is a truism that the system, in terms of staff and facilities could not function without a vast majority of guilty pleas. The courts just could not cope with the added workload. Criminal justice in principle places the onus of proof on the prosecution and provides the accused with the right to a trial and a presumption of innocence. But it operates in practice on the assumption that for the vast majority these rights must be merely empty rhetoric. As one prosecutor put it when asked about expanding legal aid, 'Good heavens we couldn't do that. They'd all want trials then.' The procedural devices built into the legal system ensure that the vast majority do not.

III Assembling a case

For those who plead guilty the court appearance now becomes a routine conviction, while contested cases enter the stage where the prosecution must and the defence may prepare a case for public presentation in court.

In law whether the outcome is conviction or acquittal depends on
(1) the legality of the charge
(2) the sufficiency, admissability and weight of the evidence
(3) the competency and credibility of the witnesses who present it.
Knowledge of the law, access to evidence, and availability of witnesses before the trial thus become key issues in which side's version of reality will stand up best in court.

On all three counts the accused is placed at a structural disadvantage by the simple fact that in criminal, unlike civil, law, he faces the whole weight of the state. However unequal the joust between two individuals in the civil court may be, it cannot match the inequality of State v. accused.

Almost all prosecutions in Britain are presented by the state, not by an individual. This is even more clear-cut in Scotland than in England, where the police, even if only in legal fiction, prosecute as private citizens. Under Scots Law, the police do not conduct their own prosecutions but hand their cases over to procurators fiscal, legally trained and experienced civil servants under the aegis of the Lord Advocate. Prosecution is thus conducted by a professional public prosecutor who works full-time in court, for whom the establishment of a case in law and fact is a matter of routine, to whom the judges and clerks are colleagues, whose evidence is collected by a team of professional detectives, the police. The facilities for constructing the prosecution case are a publicly funded part of the legal structure, but defence is left to the private citizen and private enterprise.

This produces inequality between one accused and another according to class, since the accused has to buy the case he can afford. Legal advice, representation in court, the search for witnesses, the taking of statements, all have a price attached. It is market forces, tempered at the margins by legal aid, that count in the preparation of a defence case, not the merits of the situation. But even with the best of lawyers and unlimited funds the accused could not stand in the same position as the crown. Defence agents do not have forensic laboratories and teams of experts at their disposal, or the legal powers of search and detention available to the police. At best, placing the onus of proof on the crown is not so much an advantage to the accused as a compensation for the unequal start in producing cases. At worst it is meaningless since the pre-trial situation is such that the crown is far more likely to produce a plausible case than the accused is to raise a reasonable doubt anyway. There could be no pretence that accused and crown start off on an equal footing unless a public system of defence was set up in parallel to the public system of prosecution.

This situation has a direct effect on the accused's command over the first element of a case, knowledge of the law, since this presupposes legal expertise which may not be available to him. The accused has the right to use the services of a lawyer but not to be provided with them. Scotland has a duty solicitor scheme, but duty stretches only to those in custody and stops at the point of plea – legal advice is available of right only to answer a charge, not to contest it. From that point in Scotland, and from the beginning in England, only means-tested legal aid is provided by the state, legal aid which has to be known about and applied for, via a procedure so complicated that you really need a lawyer to apply for legal aid.

Not surprisingly, 'Justice' (1971) found that 96% of unrepresented defendants in magistrates' courts in England and Wales in 1969 had not even applied. The effect is, to take the Sheffield study again as the most recent and most detailed (Bottoms and McClean 1976), though 99% of defendants on indictment were represented, mainly on legal aid, just 19% of those appearing only at magistrates' courts were represented at all. Since the vast majority of cases are dealt with in magistrates' courts, the defendant operating without legal advice is in fact the norm.

This is not just the product of magisterial discretion – as suggested by those who note that applications are decided on by magistrates and concentrate on the variations between them. Selective criteria are set down by the Home Office in a circular of 1972 (No. 237) which stated that legal aid should be provided according to the likelihood of the defendant being sentenced to imprisonment. This means that legal aid is more likely to be awarded in the higher courts where the scale of punishments is more severe. What this ignores though, is that previous convictions have a cumulative effect that increases the likelihood of imprisonment even on summary offences, so that it is important even by the criteria laid down for even first offenders on petty charges to be represented. However the selective criteria reflect a conscious decision that legal aid is not a priority in budgeting scarce resources – the Home Secretary in 1966 tightened still further the already stringent conditions recommended by the Widgery Committee on grounds of cost. The accused's position vis-a-vis the state is the product not just of magisterial but of political decisions.

Having a lawyer does not necessarily win a case, of course. Even in jury cases where almost all defendants are represented, 55%–71% are convicted. Clients frequently criticise their lawyers as having added little to the case or not done it justice (Zander 1972). But at least the accused has the *possibility* of access to legal expertise. Without this he has to prepare a case himself in ignorance of the law. He may fail to prepare lines of defence, challenging the prosecution on a point of law like relevance, (whether the behaviour in question is illegal), or on a point of procedure like the admissability of his reply to a charge if he was not cautioned. Without the authority of a lawyer he may not be able to approach witnesses and persuade them to give statements. Without the training of a lawyer he may not be able to spot, in pre-trial interviews, points that might discredit crown testimony or support his own. He may quite simply not know what the procedural requirements for establishing a defence are, as in this account:

> Three youths on trial for breach of the peace and assault were discussing their experience in the police station with the policeman on

> court duty and myself. They said they had tried to counter the charges against them by complaining against the bouncers who had, according to them, started the fight. They showed the duty officer their injuries but the policeman on the desk advised them it was unnecessary for him to take a note of the injuries sustained since 'your mates can corroborate it in court'.
> *Court policeman:* But you shouldn't have taken that – you don't talk to the monkey if you want information from the organ grinder.
> *Accused 1:* That's O.K. but you know the ropes, we don't. I told them my injuries would heal by the time of the trial but they said it didn't matter. I *have* got medical evidence. There it is. But I'm not allowed to use it because the doctor isn't here to swear to it himself.

Evidence relevant to a special defence of self-defence is channelled out through ignorance of procedures. Even if that accused had cited his doctor as a witness the evidence would not necessarily have been admissable – special defences have to be declared before the trial. Consider this case:

> Six youths were on trial together. One cross-examined a police witness on the time of the incident.
> *Policeman:* 10.15
> *Accused (to judge):* Sir, I wasn't there then. I'd left to go to another pub.
> *Judge:* That's an alibi defence. You didn't intimate that.
> The accused's own testimony, that he had been arrested after the event, was corroborated by a co-accused. The judge in his summing up rejected this evidence:
> *Judge:* An alibi defence was offered. This is inadmissable evidence since no notice was given before the trial.

Procedural requirements can operate less to safeguard than to mystify the accused, to channel out of court information relevant to his case, and thus to diminish the legal credibility of his account. This is exacerbated if knowledge of the law is available to only one of the adversaries in preparing a case for trial.

Of course, since the onus of proof is on the prosecution, the defence need not present a case based on law or fact at all, but simply pick holes in the prosecution case or say nothing at all. It may even be judged after the prosecutor has put his evidence that there is 'no case to answer'. But if the prosecutor does assemble a legally sufficient and logically plausible case – and he is unlikely to take it as far as trial if it does not appear to meet minimal standards – the accused really has to present a positive alternative if he is to enter the battle for credibility at all. Given this task, the defence is ironically enough in a weaker position than the prosecution in building up a case exactly because he is responding to a charge not instigating it. The framework of relevant issues (in both common-sense and legal terms) is set up by the charge and the defence has to be constructed within this framework. Historically this fact was actually used to channel out possible defences:

> 'An ingenious prosecutor could render any defence inadmissable by explicitly contradicting it in the indictment'. (Gordon 1968)

This particular technique is no longer possible, since the introduction of the shortened charge in 1887 but the crown's prerogative in creating a framework of relevance for information remains.

Given the accused's position as respondent, it is obviously essential that he should know exactly what the charge against him is, and this is a procedural requirement in line with the doctrine of 'no surprise'. Also in line with this, the Thomson Committee recommend that since the esoteric language of the charge may in fact mystify rather than inform the accused, this should be simplified. However, there is also a procedural power to alter the charge before the trial. So it is that defendants complain that they are charged with one offence at the police station, come prepared to dispute that, only to find the charge has changed form:

> 'This is ridiculous. We want to complain about this. We were charged with resisting arrest then when we get to the court it's breach of the peace.'

The problem was acknowledged but sustained by the Thomson Committee:

> 'An arrestee must be told why he is arrested. As however it is the procurator fiscal who prepares the indictment or complaint which contains the charge against the accused in court, it follows that the charge made by the police may be different from the charge eventually libelled against the accused in court . . . We do not see how this could be changed.' (1975: 24)

Nor does the doctrine of 'no surprise' stretch to the accused being informed of the *case* against him, though this can significantly affect his ability to prepare a case in response.

> *Accused:* 'I had no idea of what story the police had till I got to court. When I heard it I wanted to get up and beat them.'

Pre-trial procedures and the construction of conviction

In Scotland there are no committal proceedings where the basis of the prosecution's case is publically stated. Rather the procedure is that the fiscal gives the accused a list of his witnesses and vice versa. (Even this is compulsory only in solemn jurisdiction not in the summary cases which constitute the vast majority of proceedings). Only the names of the witnesses are provided, not the statements the fiscal has put together from his witnesses. Though each side can interview the other party's witnesses it does not follow that this will reveal the points that the adversary is using to build up his jigsaw of a case. A witness for one side will not necessarily be freely co-operative with the other; so that the questioner only gets answers to the questions asked and without knowing the crux of the other's case he may not ask the right questions. Even the interpretation of the answers given may vary so that the final gloss on the statement for the crown and the defence may be quite different. A defence lawyer is not entitled to see any statement attributed to the accused even though it may be read out in court as evidence against his client, and may, as we have seen in the example of replies to charges, be damaging to his case. In the first requirement for collecting evidence – knowing the relevant issues – the prosecution has the double advantage of not only defining the issues, but of being under no duty to disclose them till the trial.

In the actual collection of evidence the advantage also lies with the crown. The prosecutor is more likely to come across a breadth of potential evidence because of his superior facilities, inside knowledge, and simply because he *has* to establish a case which need only be answered. There is therefore an expectation grounded on notions of fairness that any information discovered that is favourable to the accused should be provided to the defence. Lawyers feel this simply does not happen:

> 'The police don't help. They give you a list of witnesses but of course you don't know what the witnesses said to them. They select and omit to tell you bits that might help your case'.

This is partly an informal process of normal selective perception. People see what they are looking for and policemen who have taken a case as far as charge are, as one policeman put it, 'all out for conviction'. They are looking for incriminating evidence and they do not necessarily know what the defence case is. If the prosecution only turns up black points, not grey or white ones, it is only what you would expect as the informal product of a formal system of adversary investigation. This might be enhanced by the fact that it is the policemen on the case who normally take statements from witnesses in summary cases, and occasionally (though the job is then officially the fiscal's) in solemn cases. The Thomson report recognised the problem involved, but also recognised that time and staff did not allow the fiscals to do all this work themselves and that, if

> 'it is found necessary for the police to continue to assist with this work, it is preferable that an officer familiar with the case should precognosce the witness.' (p. 110)

Given that, it would seem sensible to allow the accused access to the information culled by the prosecution in order to assess its value for himself. But this does not happen. When it was proposed to the Thomson Committee that witnesses' statements should be exchanged – not, as it happened, to help the accused know the case and spot useful information, but 'to save the time of witnesses, especially the police, and facilitate pleas of guilty' – this was rejected on the grounds that confidentiality would be breached and people would be less willing to help the police (1975: 91), while the present situation is explained in Renton and Brown, the official manual of Scots criminal lawyers, in the same vein:

> 'Confidentiality of crown precognitions is, in general, necessary for the prosecution of crime.' (1972: 54)

Even the passing on of information by the prosecution is not a right, nor a duty with sanctions, and the exchange of names stretches only to those selected as witnesses, not the whole pool of people interviewed as potential witnesses whose contribution was discarded as not helpful to the prosecution. Information is thus filtered into as unambiguous an account as possible, and points that raise doubts, useful to the accused but available only to the police might never come to light.

In two special cases, the prosecutor has access to information that the defence has not, simply by virtue of representing and using the power of the state. One is access to documentary evidence. The police have powers of search and removal available which the defence has not. If the accused requires documents for his case, e.g. account books in a case of embezzlement, either from a third party or from the prosecutor, he cannot compel the possessor to hand them over but must take out a civil case of diligence, with all the expense that entails, to appeal for the right to see and use them. Though Renton and Brown (1972: 80) say 'such applications have been repeatedly granted' they are far from being cut and dried. In Hasson v. HMAdv (1971 SLT: 199), Lord Cameron rejected the taken for granted view that a statement from the defence lawyer to say the documents were required for the case would be sufficient grounds for granting the application. Rather, some indication of their role in the proposed defence was required. Documentary evidence thus becomes available only at the expense of disclosing the defence case.

The second example is access to police records and thus to valuable character evidence on witnesses. There are complex rules on the admissability of evidence that discredits the character of the accused, and the defence is discouraged from questioning the character and therefore the credibility of crown witnesses by the rule that the crown is then entitled to retaliate. But it is always open to the defence to use this tack, and if the accused has no previous convictions it can be a valuable way of undermining the testimony of a witness for the prosecution to show that he has. It is after all a battle of credibility. The problem is that only the prosecution has official access to information on whether witnesses on either side have records. So a 'catch 22' operates whereby the accused has the right to take an initiative on information he is not allowed to have. In fact taking that initiative in ignorance can backfire. The defence solicitor may attack a crown witness in the belief that his client has a clean record, only to find that the accused had been hiding his past, the prosecution brings in his previous record as evidence and for the sake of undermining one aspect of the prosecution case, the defence agent has jeopardised the accused through revealing him as a legally discredited character.

So the doctrine of 'no surprise' seems to work more for the prosecution than for the defence. Nowhere is this more obvious than in the procedures regarding special defences. These are alibi, self-defence, insanity, incrimination of a specified other person, and, oddly, 'that the accused was asleep at the time when he committed the crime charged'. In these instances prior notice must be given to the prosecutor at the plea diet. If notice is given later he is entitled to an adjournment for further investigation into the claimed defence. In short the crown's positive case remains something to speculate upon from the bare list of witnesses. But when the defence offers a positive case the prosecutor is not left to put two and two together from interviews with defence witnesses, but is provided with a right to prior notice about the case he will have to counter. Information on both sides of the dispute is more readily available to the crown.

Information alone, however, is not enough. Evidence must be presented at the trial orally, on oath or affirmation by first-hand witnesses, so that part of the preparation of a case is inevitably the task of finding people who are competent and willing to put the relevant information to the court. When it comes to procedural powers over witnesses the same imbalance is revealed.

The prosecutor's role as agent of the state provides both the aura and the sanctions of official authority. Potential witnesses for the prosecution are approached either by a uniformed policeman, or by an equally official letter of citation from the court. Potential witnesses for the defence are approached by the accused himself, his solicitor or by the solicitor's assistants. The latter are often ex-policemen as it happens but lack the authority of uniforms just as the accused and the solicitor lack the compulsion of officialdom. Being a witness is an experience but it is no fun. As one woman put it:

> 'I was terrified up there. My legs were quaking.'

Time at work is lost and expenses are meagre – unless the witness has some positive urge to contribute there is no obvious rationality in volunteering for the job. If a potential witness for the crown refuses to attend for precognition or to give information 'within his knowledge' he is liable to a £25 fine or up to 20 days in prison in accord with the Summary Jurisdiction (Scotland) Act 1954 s. 33(4). No such sanctions are available to the accused. He can cite a hostile witness to attend court but cannot compel that he be interviewed beforehand, as the prosecution can. To cite him on force of law as a witness would therefore be to do so blindly and take the risk that he might give evidence against rather than for the accused. This is why the Thomson Committee recommend that the defence be given the right to seek a warrant to cite a witness for precognition (1975: 91). For the moment, the informal advantages of state authority behind the prosecution are bolstered by the one-sided nature of formal sanctions.

In the elements required for assembling a case, access to evidence, knowledge of the law, and availability of witnesses, the prosecution has the advantage. Information games in court and information selection by judges, should be set in the context of pre-trial procedures which operate as filters on the knowledge available at the trial.

There are indeed procedures to ensure that the filtered versions of reality are the ones that appear in court – for example the policy of accepting without enquiry minutes of admission, that is, the accepted facts as negotiated by the defence and prosecution before the trial. The ways in which agreement is reached are not the business of the court and the points are simply presented as undisputed. If tapes of pre-trial events are introduced they will be discussed before the trial and only any disputed sections actually brought in as evidence for the judge or jury to decide on. The proposed revival of a judicial examination (after which the crown may use statements unfavourable to the accused, but the accused is not *entitled* to have any statement he made *favourable* to himself read out in court) would provide another filter on how much conflict, doubt or ambiguity actually reaches the stage of trial. The Thomson Committee recommended that such filters and negotiations be encouraged by increasing the time lapse between indictment and first court appearance from six to twenty days and persuading solicitors to

> 'use the procedure more extensively. We therefore recommend that the initiative for reaching agreement on these matters should lie with the crown.' (1975: 133)

Routines for clarifying issues, for all their informal appearances, are grounded in formal policy and procedure.

More generally, the procedures for collecting witnesses' evidence enhances the channelling out of contradictory information. Precognitions are not statements by witnesses but the fiscal's edited version of what was said, neither signed nor usually seen by the witness, himself. Though the value of the information will depend on the witness saying what the prosecutor selects as relevant not just privately to the fiscal, but in court, and though much is made of the rhetoric that the witness is not bound by his precognition, that indeed he has a right to have it destroyed before he gives evidence at trial (Renton and Brown: 398), there are actually ways of encouraging him to present the information wanted and only that. This is partly achieved in court by techniques of examination and cross-examination, but there are also procedural powers that can be brought to bear if witnesses do not reproduce pre-trial accounts. A witness cannot be attacked in court for failure to fit with the precognition taken by the prosecutor, but his credibility can be put in doubt and the pre-trial version brought in as information for the court by putting his police statement to him in examination, as in these cases where information was drawn out of very hostile witnesses after a gang fight:

Prosecutor: Do you know McN's sister?
Witness: Yes.
Prosecutor: Did you see her there?
Witness: Never noticed her.
Prosecutor: You realise you're on oath?
Witness: Yes.
Prosecutor: And you're on the crown list of witnesses?
Witness: Yes.
Prosecutor: But you saw nothing at all?
Witness I never seen them.
Prosecutor: Have you ever said anything different?
Witness: No.
Prosecutor: I suggest you have. I suggest you told the police that you saw these three accused and the girl coming along just at that point.

or with another witness:

Witness: I didn't see anyone else.
Prosecutor: Did you give a statement to the police?
Witness: Yes.
Prosecutor: Did you give a description of someone?
Witness: I just saw somebody in a denim jacket.
Prosecutor: So you did see him?
Witness: I only saw arms in a denim jacket.
Prosecutor: And you saw that piece of wood?
Witness: It could've been.
Prosecutor: Were you able to tell the police what happened?
Witness: No.
Prosecutor: Sure?
Witness: Think so, sir.
Prosecutor: Did the police take a note of what you said?
Witness: Yes.
Prosecutor: But you didn't say anything.
Witness: All I saw was something coming down on his head and he fell back into the shop.
Prosecutor: Then why didn't you say so?

Since the defence by definition has no police statements but only precognitions to work from, only the prosecution can use this means of ensuring that the case prepared before the trial is the one brought into court.

The Thomson Committee while declining to make precognitions a legitimate subject for examination, nonetheless took note of the 'strong feeling' that:

> 'so many witnesses who have given precognitions which incriminate an accused depart from their precognitions at the trial that something has to be done to overcome the problem.' (1975: 166)

They recommend three changes. First, prosecutors should be allowed to recall witnesses after all the evidence is led to prove that statements made to the police contradict testimony brought out by the defence even if this removes from the accused his traditional right to the last word in the trial. Second, witnesses should be allowed to see their precognitions before the trial to sharpen their memories, even though these are not their own statements but the edited version prepared by prosecutor, defence lawyer or police. Third, they suggest sharpening up procedure by not only allowing examination related to precognitions on *oath*, but attaching criminal sanctions to any departure from the pretrial statement, to the tune of up to two years imprisonment, a fine or both. This sanction would be available only to the crown. The problem is defined as one 'where the crown case fails' (168) and to stretch it to the defence too would be to make it' unnecessarily wide in its application'. This is based on the dubious assumption that:

> 'almost all Crown witnesses who have incriminated an accused in a sworn statement before a sheriff (and it will be on this incriminatory evidence or at least partly on the basis of this incriminatory evidence that the Crown will have launched its prosecution) will have told the truth in the statement.' (169)

So one more one-sided power for the crown is proposed despite the minority view on the Committee that:

> 'It seems wrong that a witness . . . should be liable to punishment for making a material change from an earlier sworn statement if that change helps the defence, but not if it helps the prosecution.' (171)

The recommendation is, in fact, only a strengthening of a sanction already in existence – contempt of court by prevarication which is liable to punishment by a £25 fine or 20 days in prison but can be 'purged' by giving the evidence required.

There are then systematic attempts to keep the issues raised in court to those 'clarified' before the trial, and particularly to see that the prosecution's pre-trial case survives the public joust – and if the Thomson Report becomes law they will increase. Adversary investigation filters out ambiguities and leaves only black and white cases – the caricature versions of reality offered by prosecution and defence; courtroom powers and sanctions help prevent any deviation from these filtered versions, especially the crown case in court; the unequal powers available to the adversaries before the trial help ensure that the prosecution case is the stronger.

IV Implications

The introduction to this article raised several central issues in the sociology of law which a study of procedure might begin to illuminate. The substance of the article has been much narrower. It has focussed only on pre-trial aspects of the penal process and only on two specific points, the circumstances surrounding the plea and the construction of knowledge for presentation at the trial. But in this narrow area it has shown that Sir Robert Mark's views of pre-trial procedure are not sustained. Pre-trial procedures operate less as safeguards for the accused than as powers for the prosecution. It cannot be assumed that only the unambiguously guilty come to trial, nor that no reasonable doubts exist in the cases which result in conviction. Rather this discussion has shown some of the ways in which the ambiguities of real life and the doubts that could be raised in a defence case are chanelled out in the pressures to plead guilty and in the imbalance of power vis-a-vis the crown in preparing a defence case. The effects of the pre-trial situation permeate the rest of the judicial process. If the construction of conviction in both senses begins outside the court in the filtering of knowledge before the trial, Coutts's contrast between the adversary criminal trial as one that offers 'a sporting chance' to both sides and the continental inquisitorial system where

> 'the trial is not for the purpose of determining guilt or innocence, for the result is predetermined; the trial itself is simply a demonstration trial'. (Coutts 1966: 15)

may be less than accurate. The rhetoric of the legal system does not stand up to scrutiny.

More theoretically, this paper has clear implications for the explanation of law enforcement and its outcomes. Pat Carlen shows how situational rules and information games in informal courtroom interaction operate against the accused. This review of formal rules would supplement her conclusion that 'situationally there is no equality before the law' (1975: 378) by adding that *formally* there is no equality before the law either.

Pre-trial procedures and the construction of conviction

Even before courtroom techniques and structures play their part the prosecution and defence cases are likely to be unevenly weighted by the pre-trial impact of the legal system – not just the legal system in the *administrative* sense of bureaucratic pressures for speed or efficiency (efficiency just happening to mean conviction); or in the *informal* sense of professional negotiations that lead to bargain justice and a high rate of guilty pleas. The legal system is weighted against the accused and towards conviction much more formally, precisely and substantially in the pattern of rights and opportunities it affords the prosecution, and explicitly withholds from the accused, rights and opportunities established officially by common law and statute.

The gap between rhetoric and reality is not just one between formal equality and situational inequality, between the law in the books and the law in action, but a gap between the rhetoric of justice and the reality of criminal procedure: it is a gap *within* the law in the books, which has to be traced not to the petty administrators of the law but to the people with the power to make it – the judicial and political elite of the state. In this way criminal procedure provides a direct entrée into the politics of law.

Doreen J. McBarnet

FOOTNOTES

1. The official statistics are to be found in
Criminal Statistics, England and Wales 1974 Cmnd. 6168
Criminal Statistics, Scotland, 1974 Cmnd. 6081
These percentages are not provided in them but calculated from them as follows:

Scotland

Persons proceeded against:	241,146	Table 8
Charge proved with conviction:	220,546	
Convictions as percentage of proceedings 91%		
England: magistrates' courts		
(a) Total proceeded against at magistrates' courts	2,051,680	
(b) Committed for trial	64,798	
Those appearing only at magistrates' courts		Table 7
(a – b)	1,986,882	
Found guilty	1,886,859	
Convictions as percentage of those appearing only at magistrates' courts 94%		
Crown courts		
Total proceeded against	56,403	Table 8
Found guilty	46,790	
Percentage found guilty 82%		

2. In legal terminology the English 'defendant' is known in Scotland as the 'accused' in summary proceedings, and the 'panel' in solemn proceedings. For simplicity's sake I shall use the 'accused' to cover all three terms. 'Solemn' jurisdiction means trial by jury. Summary proceedings take place either in the sheriff or the district courts, with only one judge, not a bench as in England.

3. The only ambiguity is introduced by the two forms of acquittal in Scotland, not guilty and not proven, the latter meaning that the prosecution case did not achieve the required standard of proof, not that the accused is declared innocent.

4. Conversely the guilty who cannot be proved so may be filtered out.

Pre-trial procedures and the construction of conviction

REFERENCES CITED

Cases: Law v. H.M. Adv. 1965 JC 32
Hasson v. H.M. Adv. 1971 SLT 199
R. v. Cain TLR 20 February 1976

Alderson, J. C. and Stead, P. J. (1973), *The Police We Deserve*, Wolfe, London.

Blumberg, A. (1967), *Criminal Justice*, Quadrangle, Chicago.

Cain, M. (1973), *Society and the Policeman's Role*, Routledge and Kegan Paul, London.

Bottomley, A. K. (1973), *Decisions in the Penal Process*, Martin Robertson, London.

Bottoms, A. E., and McClean, J. D. (1976), *Defendants in the Criminal Process*, Routledge and Kegan Paul, London.

Carlen, P. (1974), 'Remedial Routines for the Maintenance of Control in Magistrates' Courts', *British Journal of Law and Society*, I; 2.

Carlen, P. (1975), 'Magistrates' Courts: A Game Theoretic Analysis', *Sociological Review*, 23; 2.

Cicourel, A. V. (1968), *The Social Organisation of Juvenile Justice*, Wiley, New York.

Coutts, J. A. (1966), *The Accused*, Stevens and Sons, London.

Dell, S. (1971), *Silent in Court*, Occasional Papers in Social Administration, 42, Bell, London.

Garfinkel, H. (1956), 'Conditions of Successful Degradation Ceremonies', *American Journal of Sociology*, 61.

Gordon, G. H. (1968), 'The Burden of Proof on the Accused', *Scots Law Times, News*, 29.

Hetzler & Canter (1974) in S. J. Sylvester & Sagarin, *Politics and Crime*, Praeger, U.S.A.

Hood, R. G. (1962), *Sentencing in Magistrates' Courts*, Stevens, London.

Hood, R. G. (1972), *Sentencing the Motoring Offender*, Heinemann, London.

Justice, (1971), *The Unrepresented Defendant in Magistrates' Courts*, Stevens, London.

Newman, D. J. (1966), *Conviction*, Little Brown, Boston.

Piliavin, I. and Briar, S. (1964), 'Police Encounters with Juveniles', *American Journal of Sociology*, 70.

Renton & Brown, (4th ed. 1972), *Criminal Procedure According to the Law of Scotland*, Green, Edinburgh.

Schutz, A. (1970), *On Phenomenology and Social Relations*, University of Chicago Press, Chicago.

Skolnick, J, (1966), *Justice Without Trial*, Wiley, New York.

Skolnick, J. (1967), 'Law and Conflict Resolution', *Journal of Conflict Resolution*, XI.

The Thomson Report (1975), Criminal Procedure in Scotland, HMSO Cmnd. 6218.

Young, J. (1971), *The Drugtakers*, Paladin, London.

Zander, M. (1969), 'Unrepresented Defendants in the Criminal Courts', Criminal Law Review, 632–645.

Zander, M. (1972), 'Legal Advice and Criminal Appeals', *Criminal Law Review*, 132–173.

[3]
Convincing the Court: The Structure of Legal Proof

The core of the liberal democratic concept of criminal justice is that a person is innocent *until proved guilty*. Justice does not rule out punishment; on the contrary it deals in 'just deserts'. What the ideology of justice is opposed to is *arbitrary* punishment. The important criterion in dealing out 'just deserts' is that the recipient should have been *proved* guilty. The whim of kings, the barbarism of joust, the mysticism of magic should be replaced by a rational method of proof. The trial is where that process of proof is not only carried out but put on public display—where justice has not only to be done, but be seen to be done. The plausibility of the trial as a process of *proving* the accused guilty is one criterion by which the ideology of justice stands or falls.

But the trial is not self-evidently a process of proof. 'What happened', the incident under investigation or in dispute cannot be conceived of as some absolute—'truth' or 'reality'—nor as a simple objective thing, a jigsaw puzzle that can be taken to pieces and reassembled through witnesses' testimony exactly as it happened. First, the limits are not so clearly defined, for how is reality bounded? Where of all the events going on continuously and simultaneously in several lives did 'the incident' start and stop? Second, the pieces do not fit so neatly together. Conceptions of reality vary. 'What happened' is, to a witness, what *struck* him as happening; how he made sense of what he saw. Different witnesses with different perceptive filters may be struck in different ways. Truth and reality are subjective and relative. Third, the pieces are dynamic: 'what happened' is, to a witness, not just how he made sense of it at the time but how he has made sense of it reconstructing it later; not just how well but *how* he remembers it. And of course there are lies: witnesses may have vested interests more powerful than the oath. The *idea* of proving what happened is a complicated philosophical problem.

Not that the law admits to this. Witnesses are simply enjoined to 'tell the truth, the whole truth and nothing but the truth', a fine piece of rhetoric, devastatingly naive and blasé, but also extremely powerful. In what must be the most familiar of all courtroom catchphrases it deftly sweeps all the philosophical problems neatly under the carpet of mystique. But analytically the problems remain. Indeed when one adds the fact that most trials take place months if not years after the incident in question, and that the court in an adversary system is presented with two conflicting versions of that incident, it becomes incredible that any jury or magistrate can ever feel that what happened has been proved beyond question. Yet in the vast majority of trials it seems they are. The philosophical problem of how one reproduces 'reality' thus becomes a sociological one: how is it that in such a situation of ambiguity, conflict, subjectivity, fading or moulded memories, the judges of the facts can so readily find themselves convinced beyond reasonable doubt?

In part the answer lies in the skills of advocacy, 'the technique of persuasion', as David Napley (1975) puts it, but these skills are themselves merely adaptations to a particular structure of proof. This chapter focuses on the legal *concept* of proof and the legal *form* of proof as they have developed in the common law countries since the seventeenth century.

THE CONCEPT OF PROOF

The legal system copes with the philosophical problems of proof by redefining it into more manageable proportions. What is involved is not a philosophical or scientific concept of proof but a much less demanding *legal* concept. As David Napley (1975) puts it in teaching the techniques of the advocate:

> Whilst therefore the doctor and the scientist are engaged in an inquisitional pursuit in which they are seeking the truth, the lawyer is engaged in an accusatorial pursuit to see whether a limited area of proof has been discharged. (p. 30)

The justification lies not in any idealism that 'the truth the whole truth and nothing but the truth' results, but in pragmatics. The courts are there not to indulge in the impossible absolutes of philosophy or science but to reach decisions—quickly:

> If we lived for a thousand years instead of about sixty or seventy, and every case was of sufficient importance, it might be possible, and perhaps proper . . . to raise every possible enquiry as to the truth of statements made. . . . In fact mankind finds it impossible. (Rolfe, in *A.-G.* v. *Hildicock*, 1847, cited in Cross, 1974, p. 21)

So the courts have drawn a line at what will do as proof. Prosecutors do not have to prove everything a jury might want to know, they only have to produce a *sufficiency* of evidence. Juries have to be convinced beyond reasonable doubt—but they cannot choose the issues that they have to be convinced about: sufficiency and credibility are distinguished in law. The law defines how much evidence constitutes 'sufficient' to prove a case and it is the judge's role to decide that this standard has been met. The jury's role is to decide whether they believe it. But the legal demands involved in 'sufficiency' are often rather lower than one might expect. Indeed from judges' summing-up addresses it seems clear they recognise they have to persuade juries—whose only knowledge of the law is after all the rhetoric—that *enough* evidence is not as much as they might think.

In Case 103 where the accused was charged with theft but the goods were still alongside the car they had been stolen from, the judge took pains to point out this was not mere attempt but legally constituted theft:

> But note this, ladies and gentlemen, [then he picked up and read from a legal text] it is sufficient to complete the crime of theft if the thing be removed for the shortest time and [loudly] *but a small distance* . . .

and he continued for two minutes with the details.

In Case 91 the judge addressed the jury:

> You might expect you would need an eye-witness for proof, but that is not necessary in cases of theft. There are facts and circumstances from which theft can be inferred without eye witnesses. Here the Crown can infer theft according to the doctrine of recent possession . . .

In Case 93, where one of the charges was breach of the peace, the judge (the same one as in Case 103) again read from a law book on the definition of the offence (having prefaced the law with the comment that this was a common but fundamental offence, 'because without the peace there is no order, and if there is no order there is certainly no civilisation as we have been brought up to know it'):

> Breach of the peace is behaviour which "might reasonably be expected to lead to lieges being upset". Note that "might be". There is no need to lead evidence that anyone *was* upset.

He continued on the question of evidence for the second charge of assault with an ornamental sword:

> It was perhaps revealing that the accused's idea of assault was an idea held by many—hitting a person. That is not the law. An assault in law [and out comes the book again] is an intentional attack on the person of another whether it injures him or not. To aim a blow at a victim is an assault though the blow never lands, to set a dog on someone, to make a gesture of violence are all assaults. Disabuse yourself of the idea that there's got to be blood, got to be bruises. To aim a blow, a fist, a boot [pause] a *sword*, [pause] is assault.

Likewise a Scottish jury will be told that there must be corroboration for proof of a case, but they are not left with that as a *minimum* requirement to work from; they are not left to decide whether the general idea that two supporting pieces of evidence constitutes proof is valid; they are told it is. Corroboration equals legal sufficiency. The only question for the jury is whether they believe those two items of evidence, whether they are convinced by the evidence, *not* whether they are convinced by the assumption that such evidence constitutes proof.

They do still have to be convinced of the credibility of the evidence, of course; convinced indeed beyond reasonable doubt. They need not *all* be convinced though. The majority verdict institutionalises ignoring the doubts of two jurors in the 10:2 majority verdict allowed in England, seven in the 8:7 straight majority allowed in Scotland. Nor indeed do all doubts the juror may have count *per se* as 'reasonable doubts'. English judges have now been advised it is safer not to try and define a reasonable doubt but Scottish juries are warned in the judges' summing up that they cannot fail to convict because of 'frivolous' doubts or because of the 'strained or fanciful acceptance of remote possibilities' (*Irving* v. *Ministry of Pensions*, 1945). In Case 91 the judge warned that 'beyond reasonable doubt' meant 'not a philosophical doubt but a reasonable doubt'. In Case 103 the jury was told that proof beyond reasonable doubt:

> does not mean proved to a mathematical nicety because if that was so no case would ever be proved. Nor either does it mean a capricious doubt. It means doubt based on substance, and reason on the evidence before you. [And the judge thumped the table in emphasis.] If *such a doubt as that* exists the accused is entitled to the benefit of it.

In Case 93, the same judge began by reeling off the same definition almost verbatim, with a little extemporising as he concluded:

> If that was so, no criminal charge would ever be proved and God help us all then. Some doubting Thomases will doubt everything, even the evidence of their own eyes. You cannot indulge in that. Doubt must be based on substance and reason on the evidence before you.

The concept of 'proof beyond reasonable doubt' is thus redefined from the awesome heights of abstraction into pragmatic minimal standards that can be all too readily attained. At the same time the problem of 'unbounded reality' is tackled by the notions of admissibility[1] and relevance.

Relevance, with the related concepts of 'material' issues or 'the facts of the case' sets limits on what may be introduced as evidence or indeed on what may be taken into account as evidence: 'Your experience of him is limited to what you heard in that box. . . . Try the case according to the evidence.' (Case 93.) It is also interlinked with the accusatorial style of a trial: indeed in general terms it is this that gives it its substance: ultimately what is relevant is the facts of the accusation. The prosecutor thus sets the general boundaries of relevance in his charge. This point is also implied in Archbold's (1979) dictat (reserved only for defence counsel) that:

> the defence should exercise a proper discretion not to prolong the

case unnecessarily. It is no part of his duty to embark on lengthy cross-examination on matters which are not really in issue. (s. 525)

And it is the judge's duty to stop such irrelevant evidence. So in Case 29, the boys accused of suspicious activities around cars, who claimed they were in fact being arrested for nothing in order to be questioned about a stolen television set, were interrupted:

Magistrate:	I'm sorry—I'm not prepared to listen to information about a television.
Accused:	But he said he didn't ask us about a TV set and he did.
Magistrate:	It's irrelevant to the charge.

Information relevant to the incident but irrelevant to the prosecution's framing of the charge is thus edited out. More generally, how the concept of relevance transcends the problems of truth may be best illustrated by this example:

Witness:	The truth is, going back—you want the truth, you'll get the truth . . .
Assessor:	[interrupting] Just a minute.
Magistrate:	We're only concerned with what happened on this occasion. (Case 97)

The concept of relevance thus allows artificial boundaries to be drawn around unbounded reality, and 'the whole truth' to be replaced by 'the facts of the case'.

Indeed it is not just the concept of relevancy that does this; it is also the basic form by which proof is accomplished—by adversary advocacy.

THE FORM OF PROOF

Adversary advocacy helps solve the philosophical problem of reproducing reality quite simply by not even attempting it. Instead the search for truth is replaced by a contest between caricatures. Advocacy is not by definition about 'truth' or 'reality' or a quest for them, but about arguing a case. The concept of a case is such a fundamental part of Western legal thought that we may take it for granted, but it is a method of proof with a history of only two or three centuries, and one which provides a neat example of the abstraction which theorists of law under capitalism, like Pashukanis (1978), see as an essential element of the legal form. Just as the concept of the legal subject abstracts him from his real social being, so the case abstracts from the complexity of experience, and in doing so it helps solve both the practical and the ideological problems of proof.

An incident and a case made out about the incident are not the same thing. Conceptions of reality are multifaceted and unbounded; cases are 'the facts' as abstracted from this broad amorphous raw material. The good advocate grasps at complex confused reality and constructs a simple clear-cut account of it. A case is thus very much an edited version. But it is not just edited into a minimal account—a microcosm of the incident—it is an account edited with vested interests in mind. Hence the lawyer's approach 'that, so far as possible, only that should be revealed which supports his case' (Napley, 1975, p. 29). Far from being 'the truth, the whole truth and nothing but the truth' a case is a biased construct, manipulating and editing the raw material of the witnesses' perceptions of an incident into not so much an exhaustively accurate version of what happened as one which is advantageous to one side. In relation to an incident, then, a case is partial in both senses—partisan and incomplete. The good advocate is not concerned with reproducing incidents but producing cases, not with truth but with persuasion. Lord Denning makes this quite clear:

> the duty of counsel to his client in a civil case—or in defending an accused person—is to make every honest endeavour to succeed. He must not, of course, knowingly mislead the court, either on the facts or on the law, but short of that, he may put such matters in evidence or omit such others as in his discretion he thinks will be most to the advantage of his client. So also, when it comes to his speech, he must put every fair argument which appears to him to help his client towards winning the case. The reason is because he is not the judge of the credibility of the witnesses or of the validity of the arguments. He is only the advocate employed by the client to speak for him, and present his case, and he must do it to the best of his ability, without making himself the judge of its correctness, but only of its honesty. Cicero makes the observation that it is the

duty of the judge to pursue the truth, but it is permitted to an advocate to urge what has only the semblance of it. (*Tombling* v. *Universal Bulb Co. Ltd*, 1951)

The Bar is an apprentice-based craft, and the lectures and manuals on the art of advocacy by its 'masters' illustrate the same role. Sir William Boulton's *Conduct and Etiquette at the Bar* indeed quotes Denning's view, above, to summarise the advocate's role (1975, p. 69). Sir Malcolm Hilbery's *Duty and Art in Advocacy* takes pride in the transformation advocacy can bring to what witnesses have to say:

> His may be bad material, his opponent's good. One side is wrong and each side has its counsel. But even bad material treated by a good craftsman will take form and with that may even be made attractive. (Hilbery, 1975 p. 29)

Lord Cross observes proudly to the Holdsworth Club:

> I have seldom felt more pleased with myself than when I persuaded three out of five law lords to come to a conclusion I was convinced was wrong. (Cross, 1973, p. 3)

Coddington, in *Advice on Advocacy in the Lower Courts*, takes the same line, somewhat less pithily:

> One must never tell a lie oneself. One must never tell the witness to lie. On must never put forward a defence which one has been told by one's witness is not true. One must never express one's personal opinion of the truth and justice of one's case or of the reliability of a witness, because one speaks as an advocate not as a private person. But on the other hand, one is entitled to accept what one does not personally believe, if a witness has said it on his own account. One is entitled to argue that the court should accept this, that or the other evidence, whether one does so or not in one's own heart. (Coddington, 1954, p. 2)

And like all good writers of manuals on advocacy he cites an apocryphal case—the case of the trilby hat—to show what he means:

> There is an old Northern Circuit story that a woman was found

strangled on Ilkley Moor, and beside her body was a trilby hat which a witness recognised as that of the accused though it had no special marks of identification. Defence counsel cross-examined: 'Is not this a perfectly ordinary type of hat? Are there not thousands of others like it? Is it not an ordinary size? Would it not fit thousands of heads?' To all these the witness had to answer 'Yes'. At the conclusion of the prosecution Counsel submitted to the judge that there was not sufficient identification for the case to go to the jury. The judge agreed and told the jury to acquit. The prisoner was discharged, and as he was leaving the dock he turned to the judge and said 'And now pray Lord, may I'av my at?' (*ibid.*, p. 2)

The Bar's fondness for supporting descriptions of advocacy with apocryphal stories is itself a nice demonstration of the advocate's concern with a good story rather than an accurate one, while the habit of using such apocryphal stories in lectures and handbooks on advocacy, even if primarily to keep students awake with a joke, nonetheless suggests a latent socialisation function into manipulation and persuasion rather than 'truth'.

Of course there are professional ethics involved, for example, not arguing for a client one knows to be guilty, but there are also ways of coping even with this (spelt out alongside the statement of the ethic) namely by never asking a client directly if he is guilty, avoiding the ethic by making sure one does *not* know, or if the client volunteers the information anyway, by refraining from arguing a positive case *for* him in court, while nonetheless arguing against the opposing case (Napley, 1975, p. 43).

It is worth noting in passing that there are no such rules on arguing prosecution cases, just one example of the suspicion of guilt attached to the accused by virtue of being accused. On the contrary the prosecution's role is elevated in the manuals (Napley, 1975, p. 74; Boulton, 1975, p. 74) to one of public service, not just in Scotland where he is literally a civil servant, but in England where he is usually a barrister who may act either for defence or prosecution. In his defence role he is a biased advocate, as a prosecutor, an impartial 'minister of justice'. This role would seem to exist largely in ideology. Archbold, in a manual more concerned in the main with procedural rules than broad rhetoric, notes this prescription but on the same page lists legal rules which suggest the expectation of rather a different role. For example, it is noted that the prosecutor has a duty to give to the defence the names of witnesses whom he does not intend to call but who do have material evidence to offer (Archbold, 1979, s. 433). The word 'material' is the key. It indicates that the prosecutor is assumed to present a case selected for conviction rather than one that sets out all of even what *he* sees as the *material* facts. Again, the prescription for how and to what end examination-in-chief should be conducted—'to adduce relevant and admissible evidence to *support the contention* of the party who calls the witness'—makes no exception for the prosecuting counsel (*ibid.*, s. 512).

At the level of practice there is no doubt that prosecutors do act out the normal advocate's role of arguing a one-sided case: the examples throughout this book are readily supported officially by the Fisher Report on the *Confait* case, in which three youths—two of whom were mentally subnormal—were convicted of murder on the basis of impossible confessions—impossible, because it was subsequently proved that Confait could not possibly have died as late as the confessions alleged. But ambiguities over the time of death were filtered out by the police and prosecution in constructing and presenting their case. Fisher (1977) notes of the prosecutor's courtroom examination of a pathologist on the crucial issue of the time of death:

> It might well be that, if Dr C. had been given sight of the other evidence and asked to reconsider his evidence in the light of it, and had been asked the relevant questions in a neutral way instead of being asked to suggest ways in which the period for the time of death could be extended after midnight, the course of the trial would have been different and an acquittal might have resulted. (Fisher, 1977, p. 223)

Or again:

> . . . far from trying to make the time of death more precise, those concerned with the investigation and prosecution . . . made every effort to keep it as vague as possible. The reason for this was that they were concerned to establish a case which rested wholly or mainly on confessions which could not be entirely true unless the time of death was outside the brackets given by [the experts]. (*Ibid.*, p. 20)

Indeed a closer look at the legal sources suggests it would be very hard to find a *legal* prescription for the prosecutor to behave as a 'minister of justice'. The *Puddick* case from which the phrase is quoted and the *Banks* case which cited it as law, were cases of rape and unlawful carnal knowledge. The prescription made in *Puddick* was very much in relation to the specific difficulties of knowing what happened in sexual cases, and explicitly related to them, not to the role of the prosecutor in general:

> Counsel for the prosecution *in such cases* are to regard themselves as ministers of justice, and not to struggle for a conviction . . . (1865, p. 499, my emphasis)

What is more, the *Banks* appeal which tried to establish this as law *even* in a sexual case, was dismissed (1916).

Nonetheless the notion of the prosecutor as a 'minister of justice' not only functions at the ideological level both in the rhetoric of the Bar as to their role, and in general to support the view of a system of justice bending over backwards to ensure the innocent are not convicted, but is also an idea that is put to good practical use by prosecutors in court to support the credibility of their cases as opposed to the biased nature of the defence's:

> Prosecutor: Ladies and gentlemen, my function is to elicit as much evidence as possible to put before you. My friend's is to defend his client's best interests. *I* act in the public interest. (Case 103)

The emphasis in advocacy on both sides on persuasion rather than 'facts' is reflected in and promoted by the structure of the profession, with its separation of solicitors and barristers—a separation which incidentally is emphasised in the pages and pages of Boulton's *Conduct and Etiquette at the Bar* (1975) devoted to the rules of barrister–solicitor relations, right down to the undesirability of a barrister being an honorary member of a local law society, or of purchasing tickets for a local law society dinner (though there would be 'no objection to accepting gratuitous invitations'). The roles of the two should be quite distinct. The barrister is not allowed to interview witnesses. His task is to take as given the facts assembled by the solicitor and to argue from them not about them: Boulton asserts: 'It is essential that he should be able to rely on the responsibility of a solicitor as to the state of the facts put before him' (p. 8). Hilbery (1975) notes that 'a Barrister is required by his professional code to make use of the material which is contained in his instruction, and nothing else' (p. 11) and he has an extreme story to demonstrate this with Mr Justice Swift, in his days as a counsel recognising an opposing witness in a case of fraud as an ex-solicitor once convicted of forgery and embezzlement, but concluding 'Well, I cannot make use of it. It seems a pity.'

This separation of processing from presentation encourages a narrow persuasive role with emphasis on skill in the use of words and manipulation of witnesses rather than in any concept of search for 'what really happened'. It also means the barrister has no direct experience of the negotiation that may have lain behind the 'facts' as he has them, the questioning behind statements for example. He may therefore argue for 'the facts of the case', without any subjective knowledge of how they have been processed, and avoid the ethical limitations on wilfully misleading the court. Working from a prepared case, with its ambiguities and ifs and buts filtered out, he may also argue the more convincingly. The public presentation of evidence may thus carry an aura of subjective conviction that is not just produced by the art of the advocate but by the structure of the profession. The conceptual distinction in advocacy between incident and case is hardened in the practical separation of its private preparation by one professional and its public presentation by another.

A further feature of the form of presenting proof is that it is interrogatory. Evidence is not presented directly by witnesses, but indirectly in response to questions by counsel. The rules prohibit leading questions but the very framing of a question, whether leading or not, and the context in which it occurs, set parameters on what can be an acceptable answer. The witness is a respondent, 'he is there to answer questions, that is all' (Cockburn, 1952, p. 10), and the person who asks the questions is structurally very much in a position of control (Atkinson and Drew, 1979) and quick to interrupt witnesses or warn them to confine themselves to the essential facts they are being asked about, or indeed merely to answer yes or no:

Prosecutor [to victim] Did you know him [the defendant] previously?

Witness: Yes we had a scuffle the night before.

Prosecutor	[sharply] Mr Sweeney, the question was very simple. Please answer yes or no. Don't volunteer anything. Understand? (Case 98)

The questions 'should be clear and unambiguous and as short as possible, each raising a single point' (Walker and Walker, 1975, p. 360) so particularising and abstracting the facts relevant for the case from the multiple possible facts of the incident. This style of presentation helps construct an idea of clear-cut proof, by filtering and controlling the information witnesses make available to the court, and so transforming what could emerge as an ambiguous welter of vying and uncertain perceptions into 'the facts of the case'.

Interrogation means not just filtering potential information but imposing order and meaning upon it by the sequence and context of questions asked—whatever meaning it may have had to the witness, control by questioning can impose the meaning of the questioner. The case thus takes on its own logic within the framework of the 'facts of the case', and any other issues mentioned, hinted at or unknown, lose any relevancy to the meaning of the case that they may have had to the meaning of the incident. What is more the order and logic of a controlled case is much more visible than that in the welter of social reality, and therefore, arguably the more persuasive in carrying its evidence along. Questions can be both selected and ordered to lead, as it were inexorably, to a given conclusion, to proof.

Hence the style of asking a series of questions to which the individual answers must be 'yes', then summing them up into the logical total to which they add up—*logical* viewed in the abstract, but with an implication which would not of itself either reflect the incident, or be accepted as accurate *in toto* by the witness. This occurs not just in apocryphal tales of trilby hats but routinely in court:

Prosecutor:	Weren't you making as much noise as the others?
Accused:	No I was trying to quieten them down.
Prosecutor:	You were saying 'Ssh' in a whisper?
Accused:	No I was saying 'be quiet or you'll get into trouble'.
Prosecutor:	And they were making a lot of noise.
Accused:	Yes.
Prosecutor:	So you had to raise your voice so they'd hear you.
Accused:	Well maybe a wee bit.

Prosecutor:	So you were shouting and bawling.
Accused:	No.
Prosecutor:	You just said you were! (Case 19)

The right of the advocate not just to question but to sum up—a right denied to the witnesses themselves—allows still further editing, abstraction, and imputation of meaning to be imposed on what witnesses say.

Interrogatory, adversary advocacy has another function. It not only organises proof; it also helps legitimise the outcome. Doing the best one can with a client's case means taking it to extremes, one side taking the grey areas of 'reality' and turning them into 'black', the other turning them to 'white'. This is why cross-examination is often no more than bringing ambiguity back into an extreme case. Being an artifice, adversary advocacy makes for thoroughly artificial ways of discrediting people. A witness's credibility is attacked by bringing into cross-examination *what he would have liked to say in examination*, given a chance to do so:

Prosecutor:	You didn't tell my friend [the defence agent] that.
Defendant:	He didn't ask me.
Prosecutor:	You're on trial—did you not think it was up to you to say that.
Defendant:	I've been told not to say other things. If he had asked me I'd have said it. (Case 103)

Indeed for a witness to suggest there *is* common ground, some truth in the adversary's version, rather than grossly distinct black and white cases, is also to invite imputations on his credibility:

Prosecutor:	[to defendant] So only those bits of evidence that go against you aren't true? (Case 26)

But more generally the presentation of cases as mutually exclusive extremes provides a potent legitimation for whichever version is accepted—the whiteness of one extreme is all the more readily displayed by the blackness of the other. Wiping out the grey area means very often that to believe one case is necessarily not to believe the other.

The method of proof by advocacy thus focuses on the case not the incident; on manipulation, persuasion, and caricature, not 'truth' and so sweeps the problems attendant on reproducing 'what happened' neatly under the carpet. Both in its concepts and its form the legal system copes with the problems of proof and truth by redefining them. And the problem of how the judges of the facts can so readily find themselves convinced beyond reasonable doubt that a case is proved, is explained, in part, by the legal meaning attached to their task and the method by which they are presented with the information on which they must decide.

But the question of conviction is not just how juries or magistrates are *convinced*; it is also how they are convinced of *guilt*, particularly since the rules of evidence, the concept of admissibility, and the legal structure in general are so routinely presented as biased in favour of the accused. It is one thing to say the concept of the case obviates the philosophical problems of proof and truth; it is another to show how the prosecutor manages to construct a case in the face of all sorts of general principles which set limits on the methods by which evidence against the accused can be acquired and indeed exclude all kinds of information unfavourable to him. In assembling and presenting a case for conviction the police and prosecutor must abide by the demands of legality: how then is it that, in the face of such obstacles, the prosecution case normally succeeds? That is the question addressed in the next five chapters.

NOTE

1 Analysed in succeeding chapters.

[4]
Arrest: The Legal Context of Policing

In the ideology of the liberal democratic state, the rule of the state over the individual is closely circumscribed by the notion of legality. Citizens should be subject to the rule of law not of men, to established law not individual whim or retrospective decision, with all citizens equal before the law and free from arbitrary arrest or imprisonment. An essential ingredient is that state officials, especially the police, operating the most explicitly oppressive of routine state powers, criminal law, should themselves be subject to laws that protect these civil rights. This imposes recognized limitations on the effectiveness of police work, but the rhetoric goes that it is better for ten guilty men to go free than for one innocent man to be wrongly convicted.

Hence the basic protection against arbitrary arrest in English, Scots and American law is the principle that a person may be arrested or searched only in relation to a specified offence: 'A citizen is entitled to know on what charge or on suspicion of what crime he is seized' (*Christie* v. *Leachinsky*, 1947 AC). In other words, policemen 'cannot compel any person against his will to come to or remain in any police station', to answer questions or be searched.

Hence too civil rights under arrest include the right of the accused to remain silent, indeed to be cautioned that 'you are not obliged to say anthing unless you wish to do so but what you do say may be put into writing and given in evidence', the right to be protected from induced confession by the principle of admitting only voluntary statements and the general right to legal advice: 'Every person at any stage of an investigation should be able to communicate and to consult privately with a solicitor.' These points are referred to in the English Judges' Rules (HO circular 1964 no. 31) but Scots common law and American constitutional rights involve similar maxims for controlling police behaviour. The warrant, the caution, legal aid, and the duty solicitor are all symbols of legality.

Sociologists of the police have tended to treat the notion of legality as

[2] This chapter is drawn from a larger project based on fieldwork in the period 1973-5 (observation of 110 cases in the district and sheriff courts of a Scottish city and informal interviews) and analysis of statute and case law. It is a modified version of a paper first given at the British Sociological Association Conference in March 1977 as 'The Police and the State: Arrest, Legality and the Law'.

unproblematic, not because they assume the police operate according to these principles, but rather because they assume the opposite, that they are largely irrelevant in practice. Thus Skolnick (1966, 22) notes that the purpose of his book is 'not to reveal that police violate rules and regulations. That much is assumed.' Rather, he seeks to show how the work conditions of the police produce pressures and preconceptions that lead to a presumption of guilt rather than innocence, to an emphasis on catching criminals, if necessary at the expense of the civil liberties embodied in legality. The same emphases permeate the literature on police behaviour vis-à-vis citizens. The dominant *issue* is the law in action – how the police do behave – rather than the law in books – how they should. The dominant *approach* is via the discretionary and discriminatory side of the policeman's role, how the police come to select for arrest particular individuals who tend to be male rather than female, working-class rather than middle-class, black rather than white. The dominant *explanation* is in terms of non-legal influences on the policeman – family, colleagues, bureaucratic demands, personal ambitions (Cain, 1973) – and in terms of informal interaction – police interpretations of behaviour, stereotyping, perceived lack of deference sparking off hostility on both sides (Skolnick, 1966; Piliavin and Briar, 1964; Kadish, 1962; Young, 1971; Sykes and Clark, 1975). Not surprisingly, then, with police studies dominated by interactionist rather than structuralist sociology, the key to police action is found in the informal, the situational and the subjective. If the police conduct arrests in a way that contradicts the spirit of legality, this is merely a by-product of informal interaction: the role of formal law and the potential constraints of legality are barely touched on.

Yet, ironically, the idea of legality is almost always taken for granted as embodied in a formal legal standard from which practices deviate. Cain (1971, 88) quotes the policeman's view that 'you can't play it to the book. You'd never get anywhere in a job like this.' Skolnick bases his work on a dichotomy of law versus order on the same assumption; Reiss and Bordua (1967, 31, 49) refer to the 'institutionalized distrust of the police' at the trial and talk of the suspect who 'demands all the safeguards of due process', assuming thereby that they exist. Indeed, so much is the law itself assumed to incorporate real rights that Skolnick argues fairness and efficiency would result if only practice could be brought into line with existing law. More generally, it is almost mandatory to refer to Packer's (1964) two ideal types for describing law enforcement, 'due process' (or legality) and 'crime control'. The point is made that in practice policemen veer towards the crime control approach to enforcement, which is empirically scrutinized for all the non-legal reasons involved. Due process, meantime, remains simply the other half of the dichotomy, the assumed legal standard, unproblematic and unexplored.

If sociologists have tended to take it for granted that the law on criminal procedure embodies legality, so too have those making policy proposals to widen police powers. Working with an unproblematic conception of due process means working on assumptions, and the dominant assumptions at the moment are framed by those with a vested interest in assuming the law not only *does* provide safeguards for the citizen vis-à-vis the police but provides so many safeguards that the police task is impossible; in short, that due process *prevents* crime control. Sir Robert Mark's views (1977) are the obvious example. These opinions in turn become the basis of proposals for policy changes in favour of wider police powers, such as the recommendation of the Thomson Report (1975, 12) to move away from arrest only on a specific charge to detention on suspicion: 'We recommend, therefore, a form of limited, or temporary arrest – arrest on suspicion.'

Indeed, interactionist research on the police has lent support to such arguments exactly because it presents the views of policemen on due process, rather than investigating it. Take, for example, Skolnick's dichotomy of law (legality) versus order (crime control) or his testament that policemen see procedural rules as making their jobs more difficult by requiring them to prove to legal standards the guilt of someone they 'know' to be a criminal, a point Mack (1976) makes too. West Coast sociologists and the police lobby may make strange bedfellows but they share the same blind spot. Indeed, even the National Council for Civil Liberties accepts that civil rights are lost by police *abuse* of the law without scrutinizing the law itself: 'All policemen are under the same pressure; *bend the rules* to deliver the goods in the form of convictions . . . It is the *abuse* of police powers in these circumstances – arrest, search and questioning – that has created the most intractible police/civil liberty problem in recent years' (Cox, 1975, 164, my emphases).

Champions, critics and students of police powers alike, then, base their arguments on *assumptions* about the law. Meantime, those one might expect to turn a critical eye on the law itself – new criminologists and radical sociologists of law – have concentrated on armchair theorizing and conspiratorial models of police and state, which are again largely unexplored assumptions.

So the issue remains an empirical one. Are legal procedures distorted by informal police interaction? Do legal procedures safeguard the principles of legality at the expense of crime control? A straightforward need for information then, is the first reason for subjecting due process to empirical scrutiny.

The second reason is more explanatory. Sociologists studying arrest have concentrated on asking why policemen want to make arrests; the rules seen as significant have been not the abstractions of law but those informal rules constructed *in situ* for practical purposes. But there is another question: why may policemen make arrests? That involves looking at the formal rules of the law itself and at what judges treat in court as acceptable, accountable or sanctionable exercises of police power.

Sociologists have focused so far on studying police behaviour on the beat, but we must also study it in its legal and judicial context. This perspective is significant in two ways.

First, there is the potential casual influence of the law on police behaviour. To say this is not to fall into naive role theory; it is not just to suggest that what people ought to do affects what they do, but rather that what they can get away with affects what they do. The elements of accountability and sanctions introduced by formal rules make them more than just abstractions. Courts, after all, are taken for granted as sanctions on the police, in 'the book' and the safeguards for defendants mentioned by the police and those who study them. It may even be that the police take heed of the formal rules of admissibility that they may have to face in court, not only *retrospectively* in the accounts of their behaviour that they give in reports and court testimony, but also *prospectively* in their behaviour and decisions. There is, for example, some indication that a change in the District of Columbia rules of admissible interrogation in 'Mallory', which the chief of police predicted would make the collection of evidence impossible and lead to a 'complete breakdown in law enforcement', led instead to a redefinition of the possible and a new set of methods involving more investigation and less interrogation (Sowle, 1962, 167).

In short, if abstract rules are redefined and used according to practical purposes, then practical purposes, the 'needs' of crime control, may also be redefined according to the demands of formal rules. Rules and practice interrelate. Sometimes, of course, the sanctions are empty. Most studies on the police have paid scant attention to the judicial sanction exactly because most police work is 'justice without trial', where the police settle or punish disorder themselves taking it no further and where most cases that do come to court are guilty pleas with no trial involved. But as argued elsewhere (McBarnet, 1976) justice without trial is not just a product of informal police activity: it is also a product of the legal system itself. Police decisions are taken in a legal context which is significant as one formal parameter to add to the informal ones on why particular decisions are made in the process of law enforcement.

But what the police may do is significant from a second point of view; and that is the main interest of this paper. Studies of the police so far (for example, Skolnick, 1966; Cain, 1973) have in fact been less about the law than about an occupational group who happen to operate the law and incidentally impinge on it – a significant issue but not the only one. Law enforcement analysed instead from the perspective of how it is meant to operate provides a more direct entrée into the nature of the law itself and the judicial and political elites of the state who make it. Here, methods scorned for studying the police become vital for studying the law. Observation in court and study of police records may not tell us much about the actuality of police behaviour but do tell us what kind of police behaviour is acceptable in law. Analysis of the 'law in the books' on police behaviour does not tell us what the police do but a good deal about what the police are legally allowed and legally expected to do. Law enforcement, in short, is not exclusively an area for interactionist study at the micro-level; it is also an issue in the politics of law at the macro-level.

This means a change of focus, shifting attention from the routine activities of petty officials of the state to the top of the judicial and political hierarchies where rules are made and sanctions operated, switching our question from the effectiveness or otherwise of rules and sanctions (assuming they were intended to be effective) to the intentions themselves. *Is* the law formulated to control the police? *Does* the law incorporate civil rights as in the ideology of legality it should?

Posing the question at this level indicated that 'due process' is a more complex concept than Packer's dichotomy might suggest. Compressed into the vague concept are two quite distinct aspects: first, the general principles around which the law is discussed, and second, the actual procedures by which legality is operationalized. In short, between police practices and the rhetoric of legality lies the state – judges and parliaments, the actuality of legality in common law and statute. If police behaviour deviates from the rhetoric of legality therefore, we cannot just assume it does so despite the law; we must also investigate how far the law itself incorporates its own rhetoric. *Is* deviation from the standards of legality merely a product of informalities and unintended consequences at the level of petty officials, or is it also institutionalized in the formal law of the state?

Shifting the question like this raises a whole array of potentially significant issues on the state, the law and dominant ideology, on contradictions within dominant ideology and the mechanics of its operation. The first step towards these wider theoretical issues, however, is the practical one of describing empirically the current procedures of legality governing arrest. The main focus will be on the law of Scotland where court observation was carried out. But English law is covered too and, despite the much referred to variations in the two systems, shows remarkably little real difference on the basic points argued in this chapter. Indeed, significant judicial decisions, taken though they are in relation to specific cases and according to two apparently independent bodies of law, are often strikingly parallel and contemporary – a point which is not only ironic in these days of devolution but perhaps relevant to any study of the relative autonomy of law.

The law of arrest

Lawful arrest

Arrest, that is, the detention of a person against his will, may be legally carried out only in relation to a specified offence. Otherwise, attendance at the police station is purely voluntary. This is the spirit of the Judge's Rules. Barry Cox (1975, 172) points out succinctly the gap between this ideology and practice: 'Detention for questioning is therefore in theory impossible; in practice "helping the police with their inquiries" is a daily event.' How is this possible? Partly because of the simple fact that if such arrest is impossible in theory it is nonetheless perfectly possible in law. Although they are much referred to as a symbol of legality, the Judges' Rules are not law, only principles for administrative guidance. Authoritative law on arrest is rather different.

For example, the voluntary nature of helping the police with their inquiries has been interpreted in law, to say the least, very widely. Consider the Scottish case of *Swankie* v. *Miln* in 1973 which defines the current situation. This was deemed not only not to be an illegal arrest but not to be an arrest at all. The judges accepted that the police had stopped the accused in his car, taken his keys away, waited with him and would have prevented him from leaving if he had tried to. However, they concluded that the accused had remained voluntarily and had not therefore been arrested. What their judgment would have been if he had tried to leave is unclear. But it is also an arrestable offence according to the 1964 Police Act to obstruct the police in the execution of their duty.[2] Since this has been interpreted (Parker L.J.) as 'the doing of any act which makes it more difficult for the police to carry out their duty' and might include simply refusing to answer questions and any sarcasm[3] in one's manner (*Rice* v. *Connolly*, 1966), it is difficult to see how someone can avoid being arrested if the police have a mind to it. Furthermore, refusing to co-operate is not a far cry from resistance, which is, of course, an arrestable offence, nor is resistance far from another offence, assault.

Indeed, in court, resisting arrest tends to be presented by prosecutors

[2] J.D. Devlin in 'Police Charges' (1968) asserts there is no such power but it is assumed and used in the courts, e.g. *Stunt* v. *Bolton* 1972 RTR 435 (Leigh, 1975, 72).

[3] In *Rice* v. *Connolly* the conviction was in fact quashed but the possibility kept open that failure to answer questions *plus* some other circumstances could be grounds for arrest.

as indicative of guilt and therefore a justification of the arrest on the first charge anyway. 'Only the guilty take advantage of civil rights' is the line taken. On the other hand, with the nice skill lawyers have of always holding the winning trick, failing to resist is also suspicious. Witness case 8, in which the prosecutor was suggesting that the accused must have been committing the offence or he would not have allowed himself to have been seized (uncharged) by two men (the police were in plain clothes) without resisting:

Prosecutor	You didn't do anything?
Accused	I couldn't.
Prosecutor	You didn't say 'What are you doing?'
Accused	No, it was all too quick.
Prosecutor	And no explanation was given at all?
Accused	No.
Prosecutor	When did you gather they were policemen?
Accused	I asked them – they said they were taking me to the station.
Prosecutor	But why assume they were policemen? There *are* railway stations.

In his summing up the prosecutor considered it doubly suspicious that the accused's companion had not fought off the two policemen if his friend was being innocently seized:

Prosecutor	According to his story, his companion made no protest while the accused was dragged out by two unknown men. This is quite incredible. He is clearly guilty of this charge.

The companion in question might, however, have been relieved that he had not intervened if he had heard the accused's mother's account of her night in jail charged with breach of the peace when she went to protest, or if he had witnessed case 13:

Policeman	One youth ran towards us saying 'What are you taking him in for? It's a fucking liberty. He's done fuck all!'

He was cautioned and charged with breach of the peace and fined £10. In any case, the prosecutor's argument was only about the credibility of the accused not the legality of the arrest. Indeed, in cases of resistance or assault, even if the arrest was unfounded and illegal it is still, in English law, 'open to the jury to convict of common assault' (Halsbury, 634) and the charge sticks even if the resister did not know the person seizing him was a policeman. In short, the law itself does not encourage standing on one's right to freedom from arbitrary arrest.

Given this, the warrant system provides a potential method for safeguarding the citizen against *arbitrary* arrest since it involves a specific charge and acceptance by a neutral judge that there are grounds for suspecting the accused. However, in *R* v. *Kulynycz*, 1971, it was agreed that arresting without a warrant while pretending to have one was not fatal to the case, and the Criminal Law Act of 1967 allows a member of the public or a policeman to arrest without warrant 'anyone who is, or whom he reasonably suspects to be in the act of committing an arrestable offence'. A policeman may also arrest someone whom he reasonably suspects is about to commit an arrestable offence.[4] So in most serious cases a suspect can be arrested without warrant. The same is true of the all-embracing breach of the peace, while specific acts often have specific powers of arrest without warrant attached, for example, in drug offences, immigration offences and motoring offences. Under Scots law, the police may arrest without warrant for all common law crimes (most crimes being based on common law) and for statutory offences, categories which can cover most incidents.

In any case, the control function of the warrant seems rendered redundant by the view expressed in the authoritative manual on procedure (Renton and Brown, 1972, 28) that 'such petitions, being presented by responsible officials, are assumed to be well founded.' This is rather at odds with Lord Hewart's rhetoric (Ludlow, 1938) on the rule of law over officials: 'One of our most priceless possessions is the liberty of the subject. If once we show any signs of giving way to the abominable doctrine that because things are done by officials, some immunity must be extended to them, what is to become of our country?

However, the view that officials can be trusted was upheld by the Thomson Committee (1975, 20) in the face of requests for change and it was on this basis that they found it 'satisfactory' for judges to 'rubber stamp' rather than investigate requests for warrants. Lafave and Remington's American study (1975) of the warrant system points to informal judicial laxness as the source of its ineffectiveness but, from these views expounded by a legal authority and a committee set up by the government and crown office and chaired by a high court judge, it would seem in the Scottish case to be formally endorsed common law and policy.

With or without the symbolic warrant, however, an arrest is accountable and there must be grounds for it, although of course it is accountable only if challenged and, as Renton and Brown (1972, 28) point out in discussing arrest without warrant, 'it is not often challenged'. Given the methods available for challenging an arrest (in the course of a criminal trial, by a civil action or by a complaint to the police) and given that most cases do not come to trail, (Criminal Statistics), that most defendants are unrepresented and unversed in law, (Dell, 1971; Bottoms and McClean, 1976), that civil cases are costly and legal aid limited, and that police complaints are rarely effective (Box and Russell, 1975) this is hardly surprising. If challenged, however, an arrest is accountable on two aspects – first, on whether there is enough evidence to charge the suspect under a specific law with a specific offence, since an arrest must be accompanied

4 An 'arrestable offence' is a serious one for which the accused may be imprisoned for five years.

by a charge, (*Chalmers* v. *HM Adv.*, 1954); and second on whether it is necessary to arrest, that is, to keep him in custody after the charge rather than releasing him on bail until he comes to court.[5]

The legality of custody is defined in terms of reasonableness or the interests of justice (Renton and Brown, 1972, 30), neither of which sets the parameters very clearly, allowing wide scope for subjective discretion. Indeed, common law merely offers a post hoc check on the 'reasonableness' of the policeman's *belief* that arrest was justified. The law also accepts the belief that people ought to be taken into custody if they have a past record (*Carlin* v. *Malloch*, 1896) or are jobless or homeless. Lord Deas in *Peggie* v. *Clark* (Renton and Brown, 1972, 29) made it clear that the arrest of a member of 'the criminal classes' or of someone with no means of honest livelihood or fixed abode is easier to justify than that of someone who, 'even although expressly charged with a crime by an aggrieved party, be a well known householder – a person of respectability – what, in our judiciary practice, we call a "law-abiding party" '. This statement by a judge in 1868 remains the criterion today. What is more, the requirement in Scots, though not in English, law, of a cash deposit for bail rather than just a promise that the money will be paid if the accused fails to turn up in court, leads to the detention of the same type of people – the jobless and homeless – regardless of the trivial nature of their offence. Even the Ludlow case (1938), noted above, which found for the complainant in his action against the police for abuse of their powers of arrest and search and is full of civil rights rhetoric, nonetheless draws its indignation from the *status* of the citizen so affronted: 'Is it easy to imagine a more gross indignity offered to a perfectly innocent and respectable professional gentleman?'

Note the parallels in law with the practical grounds for arrests used informally by Skolnick's policemen, that the homeless or jobless were most likely to abscond, with King's account (1971) of police objections to bail (the two most frequently mentioned were that the accused had previous convictions or no fixed abode) and with Cain's account (1971) of the arrest of vagrants. In two police stations she found that twenty per cent and twenty-seven per cent respectively of those arrested for marginal offences were of no fixed abode. She links this to their vulnerability as 'a small exposed and powerless section of the population' who are therefore particularly at risk to the policeman's interests in making arrests, especially during 'the long cold haul between supper break and dawn' (Cain, 1971, 74, 75). But it is not just informal motivations and assessments that are involved, subverting equality before the law. Given the law's attitude to the homeless and jobless we could nto expect equality anyway. Pragmatics and

5 'There are many cases where arrest is competent but not justifiable in the particular circumstances, since the interests of justice can be sufficiently served by methods not involving arrest' (Thomson, 1975, 11).

rationalizations at the informal level – with the consequence, intended or otherwise, of class and racial bias – are also endorsed in formal law.

As for having sufficient evidence on a specific offence, there is also plenty of scope for legally circumventing that principle. The specific offence may itself be rather unspecific – breach of the peace (whose peace?), loitering with intent or being on premises for unlawful purposes (how does one determine purpose or intent?), possessing goods for which one cannot satisfactorily account (how many people carry receipts and what is satisfactory?), carrying implements that could be used for housebreaking (where does one draw the line?) or as weapons. Even an empty milk bottle has been defined as a dangerous weapon (Armstrong and Wilson, 1973). If the police operate at this level with wide discretion (Bottomley, 1973), it is not just because they surreptitiously take it into their own hands but because they are formally allocated discretion on what constitutes an offence via vague substantive laws and wide procedural powers.

So, in vague cases like breach of the peace, the offence exists because the police say they observed someone loitering, drunk, 'bawling, shouting, cursing and swearing', to quote the daily menu for the district courts, or more unusually but nonetheless an observed case, 'jumping on and off the pavement in a disorderly fasion' (case 30). These offences may be, in Maureen Cain's term, marginal. They are, as described, amazingly trivial. Recognizing the marginality of such offences, but recognizing too their numerical significance (seventy-six per cent of the arrests she observed) Cain (1971, 74) probes the non-legal reasons for police making such arrests. But what is also important is the formal structure which makes such arrests, whatever their motivation, legal.

Likewise, one must refer to more than informal stereotyping to explain the arrest of two young boys, a 'known thief' and his companion, who, according to the police evidence, were 'touching cars', according to the boys, 'just pointing at Volvos and things, expensive cars'. Whatever the informal motivation of the police, the legality of their action is indisputable and the stereotyping more than informal. The General Powers Act of 1960[6] lays down the law that known or reputed thieves in suspicious circumstances are subject to arrest. A known thief is someone with a previous conviction for dishonesty: previous convictions become therefore not just informal leads for narrowing down suspects on committed crimes but legal grounds for arresting them. A reputed thief is someone who keeps bad company and has no known means of honest livelihood: stereotyping

[6] This example is a local act specific to the Scottish city in question and thus the relevant context for this particular case, but other acts operate on similar stereotypes and fulfil similar functions in other parts of Scotland and England e.g. the Vagrancy Act 1824, or the Prevention of Crimes Act 1871.

and assuming the worst are thus written into the law. Suspicious circumstances are left to the police to define. Thus police evidence in this case (9) is expressed purely as subjective interpretation:

> 'they were touching them *as though to* open them'
> 'he *seemed to say* to Craig to stand back'
> 'they *appeared to be* watching and waiting' (my emphases).

Note that it is not just police practice but the formal law here which deviates from the ideals of legality, replacing arrest for a specified offence with arrest on suspicion or for prevention; replacing established law with arbitrary definitions; replacing the doctrine of trying each case on its merits with the relevance of previous convictions. Personal and bureaucratic motivations may explain why the police want to make arrests; the law itself explains why they may.

What is more, judicial sanctions on police arrests at this level are meaningless. Vague laws and wide powers effectively sidestep standards of legality and proof by equating the subjective police decision with substantive law and requisite evidence. The police are given the statutory powers to define the limits of the behaviour that constitutes public order. It is not necessary to prove intent in cases like these, by, for example, reference to 'any particular act or acts tending to show the purpose or intent; he may be convicted if, from the circumstances of the case and from his known character, the court is of the opinion that he was intending to commit a felony' (Vagrancy Act 1824, s. 12).

Nor is there any need to prove effect, for example in a breach of the peace, that anyone was offended or even affected. A breach has occurred 'where something is done in breach of public order or decorum which *might reasonably be expected* to lead to the lieges being alarmed or upset' (*Raffaeli* v. *Heatly,* 1949, SC). So the refusal of members of the public to say they were offended in witnessing the incident, a point regularly made in police reports, is rendered irrelevant, as indeed judges point out to juries, reading out the legal definitions and emphasizing that they should 'note that "might be". There need not be evidence that anyone was actually upset' (case 93).

Since the offence presupposes a specified offender and eyewitnesses, there is nothing left at issue but the credibility of the police versus the accused. In Scotland corroboration is required, but since the police (as a result of this legal requirement rather than the hostility of the natives) invariably go around in pairs, this is rarely a problem.

The magistrate who sums up, 'I see no reason to disbelieve the police' (case 8), is not informally ignoring his right to sanction police behaviour but recognizing that there is at law nothing to sanction. The openness of the law means that there are few grounds for judicial control in such marginal cases. It is hardly surprising then that they dominate police work and, since less marginal cases requiring harder proof are more likely to be dropped in the early stages (Mack, 1976) it is not surprising that trivial cases dominate the courts even more. In petty offences judicial control of the police is abrogated by the law.[7]

The holding charge

The significance of police powers on such petty offences, however, does not stop there. Defining as arrestable offences behaviour as indeterminate as these examples gives the police wide powers of legal detention, and these powers may be used to establish evidence for a different suspected offence, which the policeman is really interested in but has no evidence on which to charge and therefore arrest. Once arrested, the person, and the premises he is in, can be legally searched, and if evidence relevant to another charge is unearthed, the search is quite lawful and the evidence admissible. This is despite the principle that such search should not take place until there are grounds for charging on a specific offence. Even in more general instances of search, urgency excuses the police from the principle, 'urgency being widely interpreted in favour of the police' (Renton and Brown, 36; *Bell* v. *Hogg*; *Hay* v. *HM Adv.*).

Indeed, even the seizure without warrant of perfectly legitimate goods has been deemed acceptable in English law. In *Chic Fashions*, 1968, Lord Justice Salmon pointed out that the police had reasonable grounds to suspect that the goods seized might be stolen, and since in the law of arrest 'reasonable grounds to suspect' legitimizes seizure of the *person*, he could scarcely hold that the same did not apply to mere *property*: 'If a man's person is not so sacrosanct in the eyes of the law, how can the goods which he is reasonably suspected of having stolen or received be sacrosanct? Only if the law regards property as more important than liberty and I do not accept that it does so.'

Thus did common law justify illegally invading personal liberty to recover property by the principle that personal liberty is more significant in law than property. In doing so of course it set up a new precedent that reversed its own justification, making the right to recover *possibly* stolen property outweigh the right to individual freedom from interference from the police.

It is not just search that is opened up by the holding charge. Although

[7] This is not to say that the rules of evidence have no effect on police decisions to arrest or prosecute. Mack (1976) has pointed out that cases, ironically major cases rather than the petty ones mentioned here, are frequently dropped because the evidence would not stand up in court. Major criminals *are* major criminals exactly because they can keep themselves clear in strict legal terms. That does not, however, detract from the points made here on what the courts *do* allow.

interrogation is forbidden after a charge, questions regarding a different charge are quite legal. The holding charge thus allows a suspect to be questioned in private and in custody until a confession is elicited. In the 'touching cars' case, according to the evidence of the defendants, it was exactly this motivation that prompted the police to invoke the General Powers Act to arrest them. The boys, defending themselves, tried to use this point to lend credibility to their story that they were lifted for nothing, that they 'were not touching cars' but 'playing football and he came up and asked us about a tv set'. However, because this referred to another offence on which they had not been charged it was deemed legally inadmissible:

Magistrate	(to policeman) Did you apprehend him on another charge of stealing a television set?
Policeman	No sir.
Magistrate	(to accused) Then he can't answer that.

When the second accused brought in the same point the magistrate stopped him:

Magistrate	I'm sorry. I'm not prepared to listen to information about a television.
Accused	But he said he didn't ask us about a tv set and he did.
Magistrate	It's irrelevant to this charge.

When he pursued it further:

Magistrate	Look, this charge is nothing to do with a stolen television. You're doing yourself no good telling me you're involved in another charge. Understand?

But, of course, the suspicion of involvement with a stolen television set might have had everything to do with the use of the holding charge and be absolutely relevant to the defendant's alleged innocence. The police may indeed drop both the holding charge and the other case so that the chance to raise the matter in court at all is denied unless the defendant takes out a suit for wrongful arrest.

The Judges' Rules specify as an overriding principle and fundamental condition that only voluntary statements are admissible, with a veto on questioning after charge precisely in recognition of the unreliability of 'confessions' in such circumstances. So the holding charge is quite contrary to the whole underlying spirit of the Rules. But it is perfectly legal. Indeed, Renton and Brown (1972, 32) point out: 'The police could presumably arrest an offender on this charge and hold him until they obtained a warrant on the charge in which they were really interested.'

Lord Simonds declared in the House of Lords that, while a man should be told the charge against him, it could not 'be wrongful to arrest and detain a main upon a charge, of which he is reasonably suspected, with a view to further investigation of a second charge upon which information is incomplete' (*Christie* v. *Leachinsky,* 1947 AC, 593). Indeed, he went on to assert: 'It is not an essential condition of lawful arrest that the constable should at the time of arrest formulate any charge at all, much less the charge which may ultimately be found in the indictment.' Holding charge practices do not then require abuse but simply use of the law. They are not informal subversions of due process: they are due process as defined by common law and statute.

Lawful arrests and legitimate police treatment of citizens under arrest are therefore defined very much more broadly in legal procedure than the principle of legality might suggest. What is more, an *unlawful* arrest does not of itself damage a police case if it can be justified after the event. Likewise, evidence acquired by an unlawful search can itself be legally admissible, since there is no equivalent in Scots or English law of the American doctrine that the fruit of the forbidden tree is itself forbidden – inadmissible (*Mapp* v. *Ohio* US, 1961).

Scots law on exclusion of evidence is sometimes described as clearer and fairer to the accused, much more geared to disciplining the police via the power of exclusion than English law. Heydon (1975, 230) suggests this, citing in support Lord Justice General Cooper's exclusion of unwarranted search evidence in *Lawrie* v. *Muir*. But the same judge has regularly admitted illegally obtained evidence, for example, because it was taken 'in good faith' (*Fairley* v. *Fishmongers of London,* 1951, JC), although he had ruled out good faith as a good reason just the year before. Indeed, Lord Justice General Cooper has made it clear that the evidence he declared inadmissible in *Lawrie* v. *Muir* was defined as such mainly because it was *not* the police who obtained it:

> It is especially to be noted that the two inspectors who in this instance exceeded their authority were not police officers *enjoying a large residuum of common law discretionary powers,* but the employees of a limited company acting in association with the Milk Marketing Board, whose only powers are derived from contracts between the Board and certain milk producers and distributors, of whom the appellant is not one. Though the matter is narrow, I am inclined to regard this last point as sufficient to tilt the balance against the prosecution (1950, JC, my emphasis).

This is hardly a raising of the standards of civil rights against illegal police activity. However, the image of Scots law as fair and operating tight controls on the police, may be understandable if it is compared with the extremes in English law. In *Kuruma*, a 1955 case of illegally obtained evidence (the evidence itself being rather dubious anyway), English judges went so far as to justify their decision by citing a judicial opinion of 1861, effectively declaring that anything goes: 'It matters not how you get it; if you steal it even it would be admissible.' Ducking the inadmissibility issue means that even the principle of post hoc control of police behaviour via the courts' power to exclude evidence is avoided.

In short, according to case law the police may with impunity make an arbitrary arrest, arresting not on a charge based on some kind of proof of specific implication in a specific offence, but arresting in order to acquire that proof or find out if there has been any activity that could be defined as an offence. ('That could be defined' is important. Remember we are not always talking about finding sacks marked 'Swag' but, for example, left-wing posters and pamphlets.) Authoritative common law thus unceremoniously turns the basic principle governing arrest on its head.

Judicial reasoning and arrest

Prohibitions on interrogation after charge and the right to a solicitor are similarly interpreted at common law in such a way that the police can ignore the principles of the Judges' Rules where they conflict with the practical purposes of crime control. And, indeed, it is exactly with this reasoning that police behaviour deviating from the spirit of legality is justified by the judges themselves. Implicit or explicit in court decisions, textbooks, legislation and commissions on criminal procedure lies a recognition of the dilemma between the liberty of the citizen embodied in the rhetoric of legality and the effective control of crime. We are back to due process and crime control not just as a dichotomy for *explaining* the law but as a dilemma in the law itself, summed up, for example, by Lord Wheatley in *Milne* v. *Cullen* in 1967:

> While the law of Scotland has always very properly regarded fairness to an accused person as being an integral part of the administration of justice, fairness is not a unilateral consideration. Fairness to the public is also a legitimate consideration, and in so far as police officers in the exercise of their duties are prosecuting and protecting the public interest, it is the function of the court to seek to provide a proper balance to secure that the rights of individuals are properly preserved, while not hamstringing the police in their investigation of crime with a series of academic vetoes which ignore the realities and practicalities of the situation and discount completely the public interest.

Lord Wheatley explicitly used this case as 'an opportunity for clearing up certain misapprehensions which may have arisen in the minds of the legal profession, the police and the public' to the contrary.

In short, it is not just the police who informally point to the practical needs of crime control to justify ignoring the principles of legality: that same justification is writ large and indeed offered as guidance for the police, in the cases, textbooks and government reports which formulate the law itself. Police justifications may be a distortion of the spirit of legality but they are an exact replica of the spirit of the law.

Conclusion: law, legality and dominant ideology

In conclusion, this review of the law on arrest suggests a first simple point. There is a clear gap between the rhetoric of legality and the actuality of law in both the procedures laid down and the reasoning behind them.

Legality requires equality; the law discriminates against the homeless and jobless. Legality requires that officials be governed by law; the law is based on post hoc decisions. Legality requires each case be judged on its own facts; the law makes previous convictions grounds for defining behaviour as an offence. Legality requires incriminating evidence as the basis for arrest and search; the law allows arrest and search in order to establish it. Legality embodies individual civil rights against public or state interests; the law makes state and the public interest a justification for ignoring civil rights.

Any gap between how the police should behave according to democratic principles and how they do is not simply a by-product of informal abuse and non-legal motivations among the police themselves, the administrators of justice; it exists in the law as defined in court decisions and statutes by the judicial and political elites of the state. Deviation from legality is institutionalized in the law itself. The law does not need to change to remove hamstrings on the police: they exist only in the unrealized rhetoric.

Indeed the police are in a sense the fall guys of the legal system, taking the blame for any injustices in the operation of the law, both in theory (in the assumption like Skolnick's that they break the rules) and indeed, in the law. The law holds the individual policeman personally responsible for contraventions of legality that are successfully sued, while at the same time refusing to make clear until after the event exactly what the police are supposed to do. It is no coincidence that the police themselves asked for the Judges' Rules.

Coming back to Packer's two polar types for describing law enforcement – due process and crime control – empirical analysis of the process reveals them as a false dichotomy. The law on criminal procedure in its current form does not so much set a standard of legality from which the police deviate as provide a licence to ignore it. If we bring due process down from the dizzy heights of abstraction and subject it to empirical scrutiny, the conclusion must be that due process is *for* crime control.

It is, however, a conclusion that implies a whole complex of further issues. If the contradictions between rhetoric and practice in law enforcement cannot simply be explained away as the unintended consequences of petty officials, then we are faced with contradicitions within the core of the state between the ideology and structure of the law. Why does such institutionalized deviation occur? It might just, of course, be an example of a crude ideological disguise for dominant interests. But that's an answer that needs to be posed in turn as a question and analysed. It might also involve something rather more complex, contradictions within dominant ideology itself. There are 'how' questions too: how is the gap between legality and law managed and legitimized? And questions of change: why does the gap vary? For it does. All I have described is the law in its current form. It is endemic in judicial discretion that cases *can* be used in court, and have been (by reinterpreting or even defying the evidence), to sanction the police. Indeed it is endemic in common law that it changes, swings away from crime control to legality – and back again. The swings are patterned, of course, and historically located. Why do they occur and how are they accomplished within the concept of a single body of law?

Finding that the law does not live up to its rhetoric, then, is not just the end of a piece of indignant exposé research (Taylor, Walton and Young, 1975, 29) but the beginning of a new series of questions. Far from implying that the rhetoric should simply be dismissed as necessarily empty, it implies rather that the rhetoric (and the relationship between the state and the rhetoric) requires analysis too. This has implications beyond the bounds of the sociology of law. Probing how and why notions like legality and justice are constructed currently and historically provides a case study in the wider issues of the sources and mechanics of dominant ideology.

This chapter takes a first step towards these wider issues, introducing a perspective on the police which tries to bridge the gap between interactionist studies of law enforcement and structuralist theories of the politics of law by locating routine police action in its legal context.

[5]
A Right to Silence?

The idea of a suspect's right to silence is one that turns up repeatedly in discussions of criminal procedure, particularly from police and prosecution. The Criminal Law Revision Committee of 1972 made a major issue of it, while the 1978 Royal Commission has had its share of evidence on this theme. Cases sometimes refer to the right to silence too—though they put it in inverted commas (e.g. *R.* v. *Chandler*, 1976), a stylistic reflection of the view of strict jurists that the idea of a right to silence is not a legal concept but a perversion of the legal privilege against self-incrimination. The law puts it in more negative terms: one is *not bound* to incriminate oneself; there is *no duty* to answer police questions (*Rice* v. *Connolly*, 1966). Popular rhetoric—and one might add particularly prosecution rhetoric—thus turns a negative privilege into a positive right. To lawyers the distinction is significant, with the negative statement carrying much less protection. But whichever way you look at it, the principle is contradicted by legal procedure. Having a right to silence might suggest it cannot therefore be used against you; having a privilege against self-incrimination might suggest that the very act of taking that privilege up could not therefore be used to incriminate you. Yet that is exactly what can happen in law.

For a start it depends on when you choose to exercise the right or privilege. If you refuse to answer questions before being cautioned that you need not, your silence can be taken in law to mean guilt. Lord Diplock in *Hall* v. *The Queen* (1971) confronted this by suggesting that everyone had a common law right, even before being cautioned, to stay silent on being accused of or questioned about a crime *without* the conclusion being drawn (with the inevitable qualification of exceptional circumstances) that silence means guilt. In *R.* v. *Chandler* (1976 1 W.L.R.) the trial judge reiterated this right but suggested a neat loophole in his summing up to the jury:

> You must ask yourself whether he declined to answer questions in the knowledge that he was exercising his common law right to remain silent or whether he remained silent because he might have thought if he had answered he would in some way have incriminated himself.

In short it is not a protective right if you actually use it to protect yourself and it is certainly not a right if you don't know about it. This is not only a strange piece of logic in itself but contrary to the normal legal assumption that ignorance of the law is no excuse. Knowledge of the law is simply assumed if you break it but not if you exercise your rights. The case went to the Court of Appeal where Lord Justice Lawton refuted the logic but also refuted any notion of a basic legal right to silence. Lord Diplock's notion that everyone had a right to remain silent without guilt being inferred was simply 'not in accord with the commonsense of ordinary folk'. Silence could mean guilt:

> The law has long accepted that an accused person is not bound to incriminate himself; but it does not follow that a failure to answer an accusation or question when an answer could reasonably be expected may not provide some evidence in support of an accusation. Whether it does will depend on the circumstances.

This rested on *R.* v. *Christie* (1914) which established that a person's reaction to an accusation against him could incriminate him if, by his conduct or demeanour, he seemed to accept the validity of the accusation. Scots law would seem from *Lewis* v. *Blair* (1858) to have traditionally taken the same line. When one accused person made a statement to a policeman on arrest, and the other stayed silent, the judge agreed it was relevant to propose an inference of guilt from the silence.

These cases refer to questioning by a policeman, but silence in the face of accusations by someone who is not 'in authority' is taken even more readily as indicative of guilt. In *Parkes* v. *The Queen* (1976) it was concluded that where a person is accused of something.

> it is reasonable to expect that he or she will immediately deny it and that the absence of such a denial is some evidence of an admission on the part of the person charged and of the truth of the charge.

The basis for this is that the parties concerned are 'on even terms', as opposed to being an individual versus the power of the state in the guise of a policeman. But *R.* v. *Chandler* (1976) allowed the same reasoning in police-accused encounters so long as the accused was brought onto even terms by having his solicitor present. This is a nice example of a pattern that occurs repeatedly—adding protection for the accused with one hand and taking it away with the other, the factor introduced to try and add to the accused's protection becoming the very thing that legitimises reducing it.

How these rulings operate in court can be demonstrated by Case 103. The accused was found on the same floor of a multi-storey car park as a car which had been broken into and goods stolen. His car was on the same floor. Some of the stolen goods were on the ground beside the burgled car but others were not on him or found in the vicinity. The accused said another car had driven past him from that floor as he was approaching. Nonetheless he was incriminated by three things. First because he was there; second because he was looking at the stolen car with its boot open and the remaining contents on the ground beside it; third, and this was what the judge fixed on, because when the owners of the burgled car arrived and asked what he was doing he walked away towards his own car *without answering*.

He explained he just wanted nothing to do with it. The judge intervened.

Judge:	It might be suggested that the obvious answer you'd make if you'd been doing nothing is 'nothing' [and here the well-spoken judge lapses into Glaswegian dialect] 'ah'm gaun fur ma caur'. Was that not to invite suspicion?

In cross-examination the prosecutor, again with the active involvement of the judge, made a big issue of this lack of response.

Prosecutor:	Why did you not say—you were the only person in the world who knew—'a minivan just

went down past me. Hurry, if we're quick we might get him'?

The accused tried to explain that he was anxious about being blamed and did not think so clearly, but the judge, who was taking what in effect was an active cross-examination role, interrupted.

Judge:	Look it's a simple question. Answer it.
Accused:	I didn't know that van had done it. [A point absolutely accurate in law.] It could have been done hours ago for all I knew.
Judge:	[angrily] Let me finish. Why did you not say . . . [repeating the point].

The accused replied he had not had time to think so clearly. The prosecutor took his turn:

Prosecutor:	Come, come, come, what kind of story is this you're trying to tell the ladies and gentlemen. You're frightened of being accused but you're so soft you don't blame anyone else, Mr McG.? . . . Why did you not say instead: 'Look, old chap, there's my insurance. There's my driving licence, I'm a window cleaner, look in the boot' like you did to the police? 'Leave me alone. You've caused enough trouble'?

The accused maintained he did not know who the real culprit was, it was not his business and in any case he panicked, he was shocked. The judge seized on this:

Judge:	You see if you got a shock it might be suggested that was all the more reason for saying it because you 'hadnae time to think aboot it.' It would just bubble out spontaneously.
Prosecutor:	But you were content to walk away.

The accused was found guilty and sentenced to nine months in prison. The accused's silence in the face of pre-caution questioning by the police—and even more readily by someone else—may be construed as evidence against him—only 'in certain circumstances' but since these circumstances are not specified in advance but assessed after the event this is not a right on which one securely bases a case.

Sometimes, the circumstances are specified to an extent indeed where they effectively mean the accused has to prove his innocence and can be presumed guilty if he does not answer police questions. In specified cases of suspected theft or receiving where the accused is found in possession of recently stolen goods and remains silent when accused, it is quite legal for the police to infer guilt from his silence and charge him and for the judge to instruct the jury they may infer this too (*Cryans* v. *Nixon*, 1955). But the accused is not warned of this. Indeed this is exactly how the gap between rhetoric and actual procedure may itself facilitate conviction. The generalised rights of justice—to be proved guilty, to remain silent, to see a solicitor—are not just the property of philosophers; they are publicly coined phrases. People may even believe they have these rights, to be used with impunity, and act upon them. So one gets examples like Case 91.

According to the doctrine of recent possession (shared by England and Scotland), when someone is found in possession of stolen goods, theft or receiving can be presumed without proof of the offence being committed unless the accused positively raises a reasonable doubt against it, so long as two additional conditions are met. First the goods must be recently stolen and second there must be other incriminating circumstances. In this case, the driver of a car stolen some weeks before in another part of the country was stopped by the police, a case of recent possession. The prosecutor produced as his other incriminating circumstances two points. First, the accused's attitude on being stopped was cool and collected, 'couldn't care less' according to police evidence, whereas the innocent citizen would, he suggested, be indignant. Second he refused to produce his log book or answer questions, and asked to see a solicitor. The defence of course refuted this interpretation. Remaining silent was not an incriminating circumstance but a constitutional right. His defence rested on

> . . . a matter fundamental to our law. . . . You may think when the evidence is over so quickly it is all clear. But something central is involved—the right of the individual to remain silent. . . . I do not suggest that a person who stands on his constitutional rights is necessarily innocent but I do suggest that where a person takes up his constitutional rights he is not to be criticised and it is not to be taken by you as an indication of guilt. . . .

The defence counsel argued on the grounds of the rhetoric of justice but the prosecutor won on the grounds of the law. For what the rhetoric overlooks is the statutory requirements of the 1968 Theft Act that it is up to the accused found in possession of goods that have been stolen to explain himself if he is not to be assumed guilty. So the prosecutor could point out 'He had every opportunity to clear the matter up and he failed to do so.' The judge, in his summing up, focused on the accused's reply that he would not answer until he had seen a solicitor and asked: 'Is this the remark of an innocent man?' (Case 91). Accepting the right against self-incrimination offered in the rhetoric of justice thus itself becomes an incriminating circumstance which allows for presumption of guilt.

But what about after the caution? After all it explicitly informs the accused that he need not answer charges or questions and indeed warns that statements may be used against him. It does not, however, warn that silence may also be used in evidence against him. Nor indeed would one expect it to in the same breath as telling him he has a right not to answer. And a whole line of cases like *Robertson* v. *Maxwell* (1951) in Scotland and *R.* v. *Naylor* in England make exactly this point:

> We do not think that the words of the caution can be properly construed in the sense that the prisoner remains silent after being cautioned at his peril and may find his silence made a strong point against him at his trial. (*R.* v. *Naylor* 1933)

Yet cases of this being allowed do occur, with the narrow subcategorisations of legal knowledge to legitimise them. According to Heydon's text on evidence (Heydon, 1975) a judge may always inform a jury that silence even after caution *strengthens* the prosecution case, though it does not *corroborate* it. A judge may invite the jury to take into account in the weight of the evidence that by not mentioning his story to the police, he has deprived them of the opportunity of investigating it (*R.* v. *Littleboy*, 1934). Lord Justice Stevenson, in *R.* v. *Ryan* (1966), distinguished the inference of guilt from allowing silence to affect credibility:

> It is we think clear. . . that it is wrong to say to a jury 'because the accused exercised what is undoubtedly his right, the privilege of remaining silent, you may draw an inference of guilt'; it is quite a different matter to say, 'this accused, as he is entitled to do, has

not advanced at an earlier stage the explanation that has been offered to you today; you, the jury, may take that into account when you are assessing the weight which you think it right to attach to that explanation.'

This distinction—and indeed that between corroboration and adding weight—may be philosophically accurate but the impact is the same. Indeed Lord Justice Salmon in *R.* v. *Sullivan* noted:

> The line dividing what may be said and what may not be said is a very fine one and it is perhaps doubtful whether in a case like the present it would be even perceptible to the members of an ordinary jury. (1967)

Indeed in the appeal on *Chandler* which began this discussion, Lord Justice Lawton's rebuke of the trial judge was not so much over the net result, inferring guilt, but over the style of reasoning used, to 'short circuit the intellectual process which had to be followed.' In short, such distinctions superficially uphold the rhetoric but boil down to little more protection than taking two logical steps instead of one. So judge and jury *may* infer guilt from the exercising of the right to silence; the accused *may* incriminate himself by exercising the privilege against self-incrimination.

But both statements and silence are of course only responses *as reported by the police*. They are unlikely to have been witnessed and they may never have happened. Even the fact that they are rarely challenged by the accused does not mean they actually happened. The defendant may not remember or may not think it worthwhile contradicting the police—there are after all always two police witnesses in Scotland to provide corroboration and in both systems that authoritative notebook—on something he cannot prove or indeed which may rebound on him if he happens to have a previous record.[12] Evidence of the accused's replies, confessions, silence, and demeanour therefore has to be set in context: neither the methods used to produce statements, nor indeed the validity of police reports, is subject to any effective controls.

CONTROLS

There are four potential checks in the present legal structure, legal advice for the suspect, an independent witness at the police station, governmental directions, and judicial sanctions. The structure, substance, and practice of the law make them all too weak.

There is no systematic on-the-spot check in the police station on advice given, methods used, or the validity of statements read out in court, and without that there is no way of enforcing *at the time* the prohibition of 'bullying, pressure or third-degree methods' to secure answers to questions. It is hardly surprising then that cases of 'verballing' arise, like the infamous *Challenor* case[13] or that Cain should find policemen saying, for example: 'I must say I've never told a lie in court myself but I have often said things that were not quite the truth' (1971, p. 91).

Judges and official committees and inquiries have recognised that police malpractices or errors may occur in the privacy of the police station. The Fisher Report recognised this. Lord Devlin has observed:

> Statements have sometimes been put in evidence which have been said to be the prisoner's own unaided work as taken down by the police officer and with which the prisoner has recounted in the stately language of the police station (where, for example, people never eat but partake of refreshment and never quarrel but indulge in altercations) the tale of his misdeeds. (1960, p. 39)

Lord Cooper showed the same suspicions in the *Rigg* case (inauspiciously named, one cannot help feeling):

> I am bound to say that I have viewed with growing uneasiness and distaste the frequency with which in recent years there have been tendered in support of prosecutions alleged voluntary statements said to have been made to the police by persons charged then or subsequently, with grave crime. . . . To my mind, it is quite incredible that such a statement could have been taken from any person, least of all from a person of the age and apparent experience and condition of the accused, as a truly spontaneous and voluntary statement in the sense in which that expression has been used in the decision, or without such interrogation as would in common experience be indispensable to the taking of such a detailed precognition. (*H.M.Adv.* v. *Rigg*, 1946)

It is the sense of a need for some witnessing of what happens at the police station that has led both the Thomson Committee on Criminal Procedure in Scotland and the Criminal Law Revision Committee to recommend the use of tape-recorders (though not just to protect the accused but 'also to protect the police against unjustified allegations'—Thomson Committee, 1975 p. 38). This is one reason too why Fisher has recommended that there should be a clearer right to a solicitor at the police station and a public defender system to make this a real right for everyone, and why Thomson has proposed that in the post-charge situation an accused who wants to make a voluntary statement should be offered an interview with a solicitor. The other reason, of course, is to make legal advice obtainable to someone at the police station so that he knows what rights he has anyway.

But for the moment the accused is alone with the police and the formal structure creates an informal situation of unilateral power. The police are in the position to define what may be an ambiguous situation for the accused with no contradictory expertise to challenge it. Arrest, search, fingerprinting, questioning, being charged are all part of a degradation ritual which constructs an atmosphere of guilt. Alone with the police the accused is exposed to only one version of how the law defines his behaviour or alleged behaviour, how the evidence looks against him, be he innocent or guilty, and what his chances are in court. Given their own involvement, interests, and indeed beliefs in the case the police are likely to create, with the best will in the world, a sense of pending conviction which makes co-operation, not silence, the only sensible reaction. Indeed American police manuals, and English Police Review editorials (Release, 1973, p. 9) provide lists of techniques designed to produce precisely this effect. The first technique of interrogation listed in Inbau and Reid's manual is: 'Display an Air of Confidence in the Subject's Guilt' (1974 pp. ix).

Lord Justice General Cooper has noted:

> In the eyes of every ordinary citizen the venue [the police station] is a sinister one. When he stands alone in such a place confronted by several officers, usually some of high rank, the dice are loaded against him . . . (*Chalmers* v. *H.M.Adv.*, 1954)

Yet though this was the summing up in a full bench case with all the force of common law, he made no recommendation for some check to be introduced, not even the most obvious one of having a lawyer at hand.

This whole issue might seem a bit odd given that the 1887 Criminal Procedure (Scotland) Act laid down that prisoners should have access to 'a law agent' before and during any police examination:

> where any person has been arrested on any criminal charge, such person shall be entitled immediately upon arrest to have information sent to any properly qualified law agent that his professional assistance is required by such person, and informing him of the place to which such person is to be taken for examination; and such law agent shall be entitled to have a private interview with the person accused before he is examined on declaration and to be present at such examination . . . (s. 17)

Indeed it specified there should be forty-eight hours' delay if necessary to ensure the attendance of the lawyer.

The 1887 Act in short would appear to establish unequivocably the accused's statutory right to a solicitor on arrest and during questioning. But the judges have interpreted it differently. The abstract right has been qualified and the mechanics for putting it into operation have quite deliberately *not* been introduced. The judges have qualified the statutory right by refining the definition of the point at which it comes into play. The statute said 'on arrest' but the three-stage model of investigation blurs this. Being charged and being taken into custody were in 1887 the same thing: now there is the limbo of the uncharged suspect in custody but the accused's right to access to a solicitor is only when he is charged. This reasoning thus legitimises not only questioning in custody but questioning without access to, or the presence of, a solicitor. This was clearly established by 1926 when it was noted in the *Aitken* case as one of the disadvantages of the suspect *vis-à-vis* the charged prisoner.

What is more the judges have failed to control violations. In *Cheyne* v. *McGregor* (1941) the Lord Justice Clerk decided that, although it was 'altogether wrong' according to statute to refuse private consultation with a solicitor and that such consultation was 'a very important and valuable right—I should not object to it being described as a constitutional right', he was nonetheless:

> not prepared to assent to the view that in every case where a mistake is made, and the accused person is wrongly refused an

> interview, the effect of that must be to bring the whole proceedings both at that time and forever to an end.

Violating the constitutional right need not therefore be sanctioned.

In England the Judges' rules demonstrate the knack of reiterating the rhetoric but qualifying it in a way that can negate it:

> . . . every person at any stage of an investigation should be able to communicate privately with a solicitor, *provided that in such a case no unreasonable delay or hindrance is caused to the process of investigation or the administration of justice by his doing so.* (Principle(c); my emphasis)

This is exactly the opposite of the provision of the Scottish 1887 Act whereby a delay in proceedings, far from constituting reasons for *not* calling a solicitor, was seen as a necessary measure to be instituted in order to ensure one was present. The police themselves decide whether 'unreasonable delay or hindrance' will be caused—that is to say, those who are supposed to be checked by the presence of a solicitor decide whether a solicitor should be present, an odd state of affairs to say the least. There is one check on them of course, the view of the High Court judges should the case be appealed. But they have elected to sit on the fence on this issue. The Court of Appeal has said it is 'unsatisfactory' to interpret 'delay or hindrance' as meaning simply that the accused might not confess with a solicitor there, but with the nice skill High Court judges have of both having their cake and eating it, they also refused to prohibit this or treat it as grounds for appeal, since it was a matter for the discretion of the trial judge (*R.* v. *Lemsatef*, 1977).

Duty solicitor schemes in Scotland and parts of England have to be set in this context. Studies[14] have indicated that the value of such schemes can be more symbolic than real, given not only police failure to encourage prisoners to contact solicitors, but also the reluctance of solicitors themselves to provide a twenty-four hour service. Generally they meet prisoners for the first time just before their first court appearance. But however the practices of police and solicitors might be 'reformed' the legal context would still impose a barrier. So far as interrogation before charge is concerned there is no clear right to a solicitor at all.

Nor is that a situation which has, as it were, crept in inadvertently or been overlooked by officialdom. Rather proposals to reform it have been rejected outright by Lord Widgery in England: 'Any rule requiring the presence of the suspect's lawyer during interrogation is quite unacceptable' (Zander, 1972), and by the Thomson Committee (1975) in Scotland:

> We recommend that a solicitor should not be permitted to intervene in police investigations before charge. The purpose of the interrogation is to obtain from the suspect such information as he may possess regarding the offence, and this purpose might be defeated by the participation of his solicitor (p. 34)

—a statement that echoes the more direct objection by the police who do not want a solicitor at the police station because he would tell the accused to exercise his right to silence.

Judicial 'clarification' of the statutory right to a solicitor thus denies it at the time it is most needed and defines its value as a check on the interrogation of a suspect out of existence.

As to the mechanics of operating such right to a solicitor as there is, the police are under no obligation, contrary to the American ruling in *Miranda* v. *Arizona* (1966) to tell the accused of his rights. There is a contradiction in the 1887 Act to which the Scottish textbook, Renton and Brown (1972), draws attention. It 'imposes no duty upon anyone to inform the accused of his right to summon professional assistance but this should always be done.' (p. 3). It is not really a contradiction, of course, merely an omission to specify the mechanics to bring the right into operation—an omission which itself contributes to the gap between rhetoric and reality by offering symbolic rights but no instrumental access to them, just as the Factory Acts did (Carson, 1973). However it is an omission which case law could readily have tackled. But the judges have taken the opposite line. They have used the lack of specified enforcement mechanism in the Act to legitimise the police failure to inform the accused of any right to see a solicitor.

They do this by focusing on the word 'entitled' in the statutes and interpreting this as meaning entitled *if he asks* for a solicitor, *not* entitled to be told he may. He is not, in short, entitled to be told what he is entitled to. Again, by decontextualising the word from the apparent intention of the Act, the intention is nullified by judicial reasoning. Parliament is overruled by the judges, and the statute becomes a source for the general principles that constitute the rhetoric of justice, while the interpretation of case law becomes the very different legal reality.

How this operates in court may be demonstrated from observation.[15] The defence counsel was arguing that the accused had a right to a solicitor at the police station. The judge ruled that he was wrong—a suspect's right to be allowed to consult a solicitor did not of course mean that the policeman was under any obligation to tell the defendant of this: 'allowed means what it says'. The young barrister incidentally tried to get over this by telling the jury in his summing up that his argument was not just concocted by himself, someone who might be thought to be wet behind the ears but was the view expressed by someone who was definitely not wet behind the ears, Sir Henry Fisher, in his official report. However, the judge dismissed this. The view he said was not a statement of current law but a recommendation as to what it should be, and he added 'of no authority' anyway, being merely the opinion of an *ex*-High Court Judge! More important than judicial snideness, however, is the demonstration here of how structural contradictions influence the process and outcome of cases. The confidence of both counsel and judge that their interpretations were each correct though apparently contradictory is once again understandable if set in the context of the legal structure. The counsel's argument is based on statute and rhetoric, the judge's on the very different legal reality of case law. One cannot help but conclude from such examples of judicial interpretation of statutes that the ideology of the separation of powers leaving the judges free to protect the citizen from the government can be rendered somewhat ironical by what the judges do.

Indeed this point is supported further still. The Home Office has issued a circular (31 May 1966) instructing that attention should be drawn to a notice at the police station displaying the accused's rights. But the sanction, as we have seen, lies with the judges, and the judges have ruled that failure to do this 'is not necessarily fatal to the case'.

Finally there are ways in which a person who does wish to see a solicitor may be discouraged from—or punished for—doing so. The first is based on observation in court which suggests that asking for a solicitor may be treated as incriminating evidence. In Case 91, as already demonstrated, the accused's response, refusing to produce a log book or answer questions and requesting to see a solicitor was commented on by the judge to the jury: 'Is this the remark of an innocent man?'

The second is more clearly a product of the legal structure as opposed to the interpretation of law by a lower court judge. It is financial. The Duty Solicitor scheme has been the norm in Scotland for some time but it is not general in England. Of course there is legal aid but Sir Henry Fisher notes limitations on the funding of legal advice at the police station with the implication that the accused would have to pay legal costs himself if the police drop the charge, and that the police are more likely to drop the charge if a solicitor is present—a vicious circle with the accused losing out either in freedom or finance.

The law thus explicitly prohibits at some stages, implicitly denies or discourages at others, access to a solicitor. Zander (1972) has shown that 74 per cent of a sample who asked to see a solicitor at the police station were refused, while Baldwin and McConville found that 70 per cent of defendants did not ask to see a solicitor while being interrogated and of those who did six out of seven were told they were not allowed to (1977, p.105). Given the legal context this is hardly surprising.

Enforcement is thus left to the *post hoc* decisions of the courts. And so for that matter are the rules to be enforced. Certainly there is a code of government directions for police conduct with suspects, the Judges' rules, drawn up by High Court Judges and issued by the Home Office to the police. Their impact may be suggested by Sir Henry Fisher's finding in his inquiry into the *Confait* case that some policemen did not know, understand or at any rate obey the rules. He therefore recommends better publicity. What is more important, however, is that whether they are known or not, abided by or broken, there is no machinery to enforce them, *not even* the judicial sanction of exclusion of evidence in court—inadmissibility.

Inadmissibility is the major weapon available to the court to control police practices. The Judges' Rules are the most explicit statement of controls on police practices. But the rules and the machinery for punishment do not cohere. Breach of the Judges' Rules does not automatically lead to inadmissibility. Indeed according to *R.* v. *Prager* (1972) it is not even clear that a judge is *allowed*, at his discretion, to exclude information that has been obtained by methods that breach the rules unless it is also proved to have been involuntarily given.

There is a simple enough reason for this. The Judges' Rules are not law, just administrative directions, and not enforceable in court. As Lord Devlin (1960) puts it:

> It must never be forgotten that the Judges' Rules were made for the guidance of the police and not for the circumscription of the judicial power. (p. 39)

Indeed it has been held in the *Prager* case that a voluntary confession made in breach of the rules could not be made inadmissible exactly because that 'would exalt the Judges' Rules into rules of law'. So while the Judges' Rules are often referred to in court, while they are judge-made and in part based on common law, and while they may give rise to questions of inadmissibility, they are of themselves rules without teeth.

The underlying cause of this situation interestingly enough is the democratic ideology of the separation of powers, whereby judges shall not be the lackeys of the government, in order to prevent political manipulation and protect the civil liberties of the citizen against the state—interestingly, because it is precisely protection of civil liberties that the Judges' Rules might claim to be providing. So a state structure geared to the dominant ideology of democratic rights prevents specific rulings to preserve those democratic rights from being enforced. The structure behind democratic ideology thus ironically legitimises the failure to enforce it.

We must therefore look to judicial sanctions in the courts for control on the collection and presentation of evidence. Judicial sanctions rest on the notion of inadmissibility, on the judge's right to exclude evidence obtained by illegal means. Police conduct in collecting evidence is controlled by the possibility of losing their case if their conduct does not meet legal standards. This *means* of control severely limits its value as a control.

First it can by its nature affect only those cases actually brought to trial (or indeed to appeal) and of course the vast majority of defendants plead guilty, partly because of what happens in their encounter with the police, while the structural barriers to appeals are such that few are allowed. As a control over routine police behaviour in *all* cases, whether they actually end up being brought to trial or not, this method is really a non-starter. What is more, it depends on a case being made out by the defendant on the methods used, and there we are back to square one: no witnesses at the police station, the problems of proof and credibility, a trial in itself involved in raising the issue for control. Indeed when such questions arise in trial by jury, the jury is sent away and 'a trial within a trial' is held to decide how to continue. The police are therefore controlled only by the defendant successfully making a case against them in the course of his own trial.

Second, since inadmissibility involves a *post hoc* decision, the rules themselves are never clear until they are tested in the courts after the event. Indeed it was the police themselves, after two contradictory decisions by judges on the legitimacy of their conduct, who asked for the first Judges' Rules in 1912. Since the rules are still subject to common law decisions, however, the situation has altered little in practice. If rules that lack enforcement make feeble controls, rules that are not known till after they have been broken are feebler still.[16]

Third, inadmissibility is not an absolute control. Even where the conduct of the police is declared illegitimate by the judges, the evidence acquired by that conduct is not necessarily excluded, and the case can still be won by the prosecution regardless. There is no equivalent in Scots or English law of the American doctrine that the fruit of the forbidden tree is itself forbidden—inadmissible (*Mapp* v. *Ohio* 1961). Scots law on exclusion of evidence is sometimes described as clearer and fairer to the accused, much more geared to disciplining the police via the power of exclusion than English law. Heydon (1975, p. 230) suggests this citing Lord Justice General Cooper's exclusion of unwarranted search evidence in *Lawrie* v. *Muir* in support. But the same judge regularly admitted illegally obtained evidence, for example, because it was taken 'in good faith' (*Fairley* v. *Fishmongers of London*, 1951), although he had ruled out good faith as a good reason just the year before. Indeed Lord Justice General Cooper had made it clear that the evidence he declared inadmissible in *Lawrie* v. *Muir* was defined as such mainly because it was *not* the police who obtained it:

> It is especially to be noted that the two inspectors who in this instance exceeded their authority were not police officers *enjoying a large residuum of common law discretionary powers*, but the employees of a limited company acting in association with the Milk Marketing Board, whose only powers are derived from contracts between the Board and certain milk producers and distributors, of whom the appellant is not one. Though the matter is narrow, I am inclined to regard this last point as sufficient to tilt the balance against the prosecution. (1950; my emphasis)

This is hardly a raising of the standards of civil rights against illegal *police* activity. However, the image of Scots law as fair and operating tight controls on the police, may be understandable if it is compared with the extremes in English law. In *Kuruma* v. *R.*, a 1955 case of illegally obtained evidence (the evidence itself being rather dubious anyway), English judges went so far as to justify their decision by citing a judicial opinion of 1861 that effectively declared anything goes: 'It matters not how you get it; if you steal it even it would be admissible.' Ducking the inadmissibility issue means that even the principle of *post hoc* control of police behaviour via the courts' power to exclude evidence is avoided.

Fourth, as this chapter and indeed this whole study demonstrates, the line drawn between the admissible and the inadmissible by the judges in exercising control over the police has been far from rigid. But in drawing that line they are not just exercising control in a specific case, they are also making the rules for the future. The judges have not chosen to use their powers to exclude evidence to offer clear-cut protection of the accused's alleged rights. Rather, with every questionable practice that is admitted and so legitimised, case law has whittled these 'rights' away.

Notes

1 *The Times*, 15 June, 1978; *Guardian*, 8 January 1979.
2 The Director of Public Prosecutions: *Guardian*, 8 January 1979.
3 This and the following section are based on and developed from a previous article, McBarnet, 1978(a).
4 See, for example, Dell, 1971; Baldwin and McConville, 1977.
5 In Scotland there is a duty solicitor scheme which was extended for the first time to the district courts (the nearest equivalent in what is rather a different court structure) in 1975.
6 See Chapter 4.
7 See Chapter 2 and Chapter 6 for further details on corroboration.
8 Sir David McNee, Metropolitan Police Commissioner, *The Times*, 15 June 1978.
9 See Chapter 2.
10 See this chapter, on 'The Right to Silence?'
11 A random sample from a Glasgow court's files.
12 Baldwin and McConville, 1977; and see Chapter 4.
13 See Cox, 1975.
14 For example, Mungham and Thomas, 1976.
15 In England. Full details are being written up by the author in a separate study of the jury.
16 See Chapter 8 for a discussion of the implications of the *post hoc* nature of case law.

Part Three

Legal Form, Legal Ideology, Legal Actors

[6]

Magistrates' Courts and the Ideology of Justice

Magistrates' courts have frequently attracted comment for their role as a conveyor belt for the guilty pleas which constitute 95% of their caseload. Far less attention has been paid to their contested trials, even though, as a recent research study for the Royal Commission on Criminal Procedure notes, by far the majority of contested trials are heard before magistrates.[2]

This article draws on observational research into contested trials in magistrates' courts,[3] to consider two very different levels of sociological problem. First there is the plight of the unrepresented defendant, the focal point of most sociological and social policy studies of the courts. This article tries to offer a fresh approach by locating the problem not just in the social class of the defendant or the informal games played by courtroom personnel, but in the structure of magistrates' justice.

Second, there are the ideological problems posed by the departure of the magistrates' courts from central tenets of the rhetoric of justice. This article seeks to locate this departure not just in the practice of magistrates but in the institutional basis of magistrates' justice. It tries to demonstrate the problems posed for the ideology of justice and the legitimations by which they are resolved.

The research on which the article draws was done in Scotland. Legal institutions in Scotland and England do vary and any problems of generalisability are discussed where they arise.[4]

The Unrepresented Defendant

The conviction rate in magistrates' courts is extremely high. According to 1978 statistics, it is 95% for non-indictable offences in English magistrates' courts, 93% for indictable crimes. In Scottish summary courts the rate is 95%.[5] These figures of course include, indeed are mainly made up of, guilty pleas. But the decision to plead guilty is itself partly a product of people's expectation that they have little chance of being found not guilty if they opt for trial by magistrates. Guilty pleas cannot in short be isolated from the expectations of magistrates' justice in general. In any case, a recent Home Office Study shows 75% of contested trials resulted in conviction, ranging, according to the offence, from 60% to 100%.[6]

This high conviction rate, and the associated problems for the defendant in winning his case, are usually put down to the fact that the defendant is normally working class and normally unrepresented. Hence Dell's description of unrepresented defendants never getting their case across in court, because they remain *silent in court*, silent through working class inarticulateness or fear.[7]

Carlen would put the defendant's problems down to the games played by courtroom personnel, whereby the accused is the only outsider, the only one who does not know what is going on, what the cues passing between magistrates and policemen or social workers mean.[8] But it is not just a matter of the defendant's class or indeed of informal rules and games that poses him problems in court. In fact the sociological focus on these as the issues has distracted attention from the role of legal policy and formal legal structure. Both of these have to be examined to understand first, why defendants in the magistrates' courts *are* usually unrepresented; second, why being represented professionally is, in the current legal structure, so important.

In Scotland there has been a duty solicitor scheme available at all courts since 1975. But duty stretches only to those in custody and stops at the point of plea — legal advice is available of right only to answer a charge, not to contest it. In England the defendant in the magistrates' court only exceptionally has a lawyer: Bottoms' and McClean's Sheffield study found only 19% represented throughout compared to 99% in the higher courts.[9] The reason for this is simple enough: legal aid, though virtually a right in the higher courts, is not available in any but exceptional cases in the lower courts. Nor do the recommendations of the Royal Commission on legal services augur well for any significant change.[10] Discretion is retained in the award of legal aid in cases triable only by magistrates, and although there is a change of emphasis from the need to find grounds to *award* aid to the need to find grounds to *deny* it, the same basic criteria set down by the Widgery Committee in 1966 still stand.

The reasoning in the Widgery Report was clear enough. It denied that a professional lawyer was normally necessary in the lower courts, implying that points of law, tracing and interviewing witnesses or engaging in expert cross examination were not normally involved. Yet the same report insisted that a professional lawyer *was* necessary for the higher courts:

> 'A layman, however competent, can rarely be relied on to possess the skill and knowledge necessary to put forward the defence effectively tried *on indictment* without the guidance of a lawyer.'[11]

Were the structure and rules of procedure in the two levels of courts essentially different, this distinction might be valid. Differences there are, as we shall see, but not in the proof of a case. The trial, and with it the method of proof and the criteria of proof remain exactly the same. There is the same adversarial structure, the same structure of proof by examination, cross-examination, the same requirement of direct witnesses to provide that proof, the same rules of evidence *and the same requirement that the procedures be rigidly adhered to.* In terms of their structure and procedure these are *not* laymen's courts but highly legalised proceedings.

Carlen underestimates this when she talks of the informal rules of interaction as more significant than the formal procedures and refers to the rules of time, place and order being invoked only to suppress challenges to the court.[12] Procedural pedantics are not just emergency measures: they are what make a trial a trial, and the result is that the accused in the magistrates' courts is not just prevented from challenging the court but is *routinely prevented from participating effectively in his own trial.* In short, from my own observation, the accused is often not so much *silent* in court — inarticulate, afraid or outside the game — but *silenced* in court for not obeying the rules of legal procedure.

Silenced in Court

The trial is organised into a quite definite order of events and at each stage different rules pertain:

(1) the defendant makes his plea
(2) the prosecutor calls his witnesses — usually policemen — and examines them
(3) the defendant can crossexamine each witness, immediately after the prosecutor has examined him — at this stage the rule is that he can only ask questions of the witnesses not make statements on his own behalf
(4) the defendant can, though he need not, move from the dock to the witness box to give his evidence
(5) he is crossexamined in turn
(6) if he has any witnesses he can examine them (again ask questions only) to elicit support for his story
(7) each witness is in turn crossexamined by the prosecutor
(8) each party may sum up.

The defendant's first admissible opportunity to make a statement is at stage 4. But repeatedly he takes up the first invitation to speak, at stage 3, to deliver a statement to the magistrate, only to be rebuffed on procedural grounds. He is likewise interrupted or silenced with each witness until, when it comes to his turn to enter the witness box (and often he starts his statement again in the dock only to be rebuffed or moved), he often rejects the chance or is quite taken aback to have a say. When he does speak he may well find his story interrupted and what seem to be crucial points excluded by the rules of evidence.

Some examples from observed cases demonstrate this quite clearly. Hence Case 29:

Magistrate: How do you know what they (the police) said to Pauline (co-accused)?
Accused: She told us
Magistrate: That's hearsay

Or Case 1:

Accused: Sir I'd left before closing time to go to another pub.
Magistrate: That's an alibi defence. You didn't intimate that.

(In his summing up later the magistrate declared the defence inadmissible because no warning had been given). In Case 27 the accused's defence depended on his having good reason to use a police phone:

Magistrate: Would you like to ask the officer any questions Mr. McC?
Accused: Do you know why I was on the phone?
Prosecutor: He can't answer that.

Without an understanding of legal procedure, the layman-defendant can find it extremely difficult to actually present his case in court at all.

Of course proving a case usually involves not just stating one's own version of events but undermining one's opponent's. And the conventional means of doing this is via cross-examination. The Widgery Report sees professional cross-examination as rarely needed in summary cases.[13] Yet cross-examination is one of the essential weapons of the adversarial trial. With no cross-examination there is in a sense no trial and with no professional lawyer there tends to be no cross-examination, as observation in court demonstrates.

The defendant's desperate eagerness to get his version of what happened before the court as quickly as possible has two consequences. Making a statement at stage three, when he should be cross-examining not only gets him into a procedural tangle which threatens his chance of making a statement at all, it also gets in the way of his ever cross-examining. The opportunity is not taken up at the procedurally correct time, and is therefore lost for good, as in Case 1:

Magistrate: Would you like to ask any questions?
Accused: All I said was "what's happening?"
Magistrate to policeman:
Are you in any doubt that this man was committing the offence?
Policeman: No
Accused: I never opened my mouth except to ask what was happening.
Magistrate: You can't deliver a peroration at this point. Have you (moving on to Accused 2) any questions?

Or case 35:

Magistrate: At this time you may ask the officer questions from the evidence he's given. Have you any questions?
Accused: We were just standing talking.
Magistrate: (To policeman) She says they were just standing talking. Is this so?
Policeman: No.

Magistrate: That's the answer to your question. You may not like it but that's it. Move on to the next question.
Accused: There's nothing else.

Case 29:

Accused: We were playing football and he came up and asked our name and about a TV.
Assessor to policeman:
Did you say this?
Policeman: No
Magistrate: There's your answer. Any other questions?

Case 5:

Magistrate: Any questions?
Accused: I was only violent because I was being punched.
Magistrate: Was he being assaulted?
Policeman: No. We put him on the floor when he entered to await assistance.
Magistrate: That's your answer. Any more questions?

Case 25:

Accused to magistrate:
Well all I can say is
Magistrate: It's him you ask the questions
Accused: No questions then.

And so on. There are dozens of examples from the data — these are not peculiar but *typical* cases, as indeed the Lord Chancellor's office recognises in a series of lectures to magistrates:

> cross-examination and re-examination are difficult matters for unrepresented parties, and the help of the court is often necessary, just as it is necessary in most cases for the court to conduct the examination-in chief.[14]

Magistrates are, in short, expected to help the accused with procedure and indeed to help him cross-examine. And this expectation is often used to justify the lack of legal representation in the lower courts. The defendant's interests are said to be "safe in the hands of the presiding judge"[15] and the assumption is made that the "court will usually be able to turn his statements into questions on his behalf".[16] The problem is that this is *not* cross-examination.

For a start it is too late: once the statement is put the surprise is lost. What is more, once the translated direct question is put, it creates an impasse, a categorical denial, with nothing to pursue further. A competent professional advocate would never take this route. Professional cross-examination proceeds by quite different means, by indirect approaches, by a series of questions on apparently peripheral matters, with a crucial issue casually dropped in en route, by a series of questions leading the witness to an accusation which the witness cannot logically deny without discrediting his previous answers.

For the magistrate to turn a statement into a question does not therefore help the unrepresented accused conduct his cross-examination as a professional might, it simply ensures that his amateur non-cross-examination both terminates and fails. The magistrate's "help" is therefore no substitute for defence advocacy. Nor indeed could it be.

The magistrate can, as all judges can, ask questions, but his *role* remains that of independent judge, he has no involvement in the preparation of cases and he may not take sides. And of course he does not know the defendant's version beforehand, so the questions he asks are necessarily coloured by the only version he has heard, the prosecution's. With the best will in the world he is not in the *structural position* to do the job of defence advocate.

Neither, ironically, is the defendant. Indeed the unrepresented defendant is truly in a dilemma. Without exercising the skills of the advocate or knowledge of the law he cannot participate in his trial, and there is no defence, but if he does demonstrate such skills he is caught in the double bind that he is not supposed to.

Underlying the defendant's inadequate self-defence is not only lack of knowledge and skill but the fact that the expected role of the defendant almost *requires* that he behaves like that, that he rushes in his moral indignation to tell his version rather than coolly making a case. The result is that the accused who does cross-examine rather than make statements invites interruption and criticism, even though he is often pursuing only, if perhaps a little more agitatedly, the same lines that the professional would.

It is, for example, a normal technique of advocates to cross-examine on matters which appear to be peripheral as a way of catching the witness on a crucial matter unawares, or indeed to make something significant of a matter which may not seem so to the witness. Either way the crucial elements are surprise and a continuity of flow in the questioning and a judge would be unlikely to intervene. Unrepresented defendants are not so readily accorded this privilege:

> Magistrate: What's that got to do with it? Next question. (Case 1)

Repetition, near repetition, or persistence with a particular line, normal enough advocacy styles invite termination:

> Assessor: I think you've covered that. I think we've got the picture. (Case 21)

It is not therefore just as simple as lawyers being able to do things that laymen cannot. Even among defendants competent in the art of self defence, it is harder for the unrepresented defendant to *get away with* the same methods as a lawyer. Indeed to be too au fait with law, procedure and advocacy can mean inviting not just ridicule or interruption but suspicion:

Magistrate: It seems strange a young girl like you should know all this jargon if you've not been in trouble before. (Case 29)

One defendant who set about cross-examining the first police witness against him with some gusto, was invited drily to cross-examine the second with the quip:

And remember, we don't want a breach of the peace here. (Case 6)

When one of the accused in Case 1 caught out the police witness on a detail of location, exactly the kind of detail advocates rub their hands over, he was interrupted by the magistrate (who after all had to decide his fate) with the comment:

I wish you wouldn't be so aggressive — you're slightly offensive.

Another, in Case 29, was admonished for his approach:

Magistrate: You're still a cocky young whippersnapper. When's your bubble going to be burst? You're a very confident self-opinionated young man.

Dell may point to nerves as a problem for defendants but it would appear from such comments that confidence fares them little better. Defendants *may not* play the role of the confident punch-pulling advocate not only because it clashes with the incompetence and deference routinely demanded of the lower class people who dominate the courts, but because it clashes with the role expected of the *defendant.* The defendant may be diffident, nervous, excited, contrite; he may not be confident, aggressive, cool, calculating, tricky — unless of course he is that rarety, an unrepresented middle class defendant in the lower courts. The inherent characteristics of the competent defendant and the competent advocate make it structurally difficult to get away with playing both roles at once. The accused is thus put in an absurd double bind — damned if he is knowledgeable in the rules, competent in advocacy, damned if he is not.

The problems of the defendant in either getting his case across or undermining his opponent's cannot, then, simply be put down to working class inadequacy or the games played by courtroom personnel. The structure of the trial, in terms of both procedures and roles, itself inhibits the making of a case and leads to the accused being silenced in court.

Underlying all this is a structural paradox. The trial is predicated upon professional knowledge, expertise and adversarial advocacy — but legal policy denies access to it.

The answer, in policy terms, seems simple — provide lawyers. But there are some fundamental reasons why that would not be likely to work. The chances are that even with a lawyer, the defendant in the magistrates' courts would still have the odds weighted against him. The structural paradox is not only a cause but a symptom of a deeper structural and ideological distinction between higher and lower court justice. The magistrates' courts deal in a kind of justice which is in its source, nature and ideology, quite different from the higher courts. They deal in summary justice.

The Structure of Summary Justice

Summary justice is what most people going through the courts — some 98% in both Scotland and England — *experience* as justice, but it clashes violently with the traditional *images* of justice. Other commentators have noted the chaos, casualness and rapidity of the proceedings in magistrates' courts. Few students in my experience emerge from their first visit to the public benches anything but shocked. Certainly the image of justice carried into the court is quickly shattered, and not just by the conveyor belt of guilty pleas. The trials too run counter to all the expectations of a solemn, skilful adversarial joust. Magistrates' justice seems to be another world from the legal system we have learned about in books and films and television.

The statistics, as we have seen, tell the same story. Credibility in the ideology that the scales of justice are tipped to acquitting ten guilty men rather than convicting one innocent man is stretched to breaking point by the work of the summary courts. And not just by its work but by its structure. Examining the legal foundations of summary justice indicates that if the rights of the defendant do not obstruct the conviction process in magistrates' courts too much it is not just because they are not known about or not enforced but because in large measure they do not exist.

Though common law and trial by jury claim a heritage going back to Magna Carta, summary justice is a statutory creation which only came into widespread use in the nineteenth century. It is characterised precisely by its *lack* of many of the attributes of the ideology of law, legality, and a fair trial. The Oxford Dictionary defines summary justice as "proceedings in a court of law carried out rapidly by the omission of certain formalities required by the common law". The lack of representation is but one of many omissions. The judicial definition in Scots law is a procedure:

> without induciae and without indictment and further without any notice to the party of the names of the witnesses that are to be called against him and without the accused being represented by legal adviser unless he chooses to provide himself with one.[17]

The judge might have added, without a record of the proceedings and of course without a jury. Summary justice is thus characterised legally not by positive attributes but by negative ones: it negates many of the procedures held to be necessary in the traditional ideology of due process.

In all sorts of ways the formality of the higher court is abandoned. The indictments by which prosecutions are launched in the superior courts require absolute precision — even the size of the paper and margins were specified in the 1918 rules — but the "information" which initiates the lower court prosecution has no set form, it need not even be written, though it usually is, and not all the elements of the offence need to be stated. Nor as English law puts it can any objection be raised to an "information" on the grounds of defect of substance or form or because the evidence given at the trial varies from it, while the Scottish text, notes generally and succinctly: "No proceeding will be invalidated through a defect which is merely technical".[18]

Hence the administration of the lower courts is often presented favourably — as less formal and legalistic than that of the higher courts, and as more accessible, as a result, to the lay-defendant. But that is hardly borne out by research. In fact, the defendant's *task*, as this article has already tried to show, is still governed by formal procedures, but the defendant's *rights* are greatly reduced.

If the lower courts seem to present a different world from the image we carry in our heads of the higher courts then, it is hardly surprising; in law that is exactly what they are. The law has created two tiers of justice, one which is geared in its ideology and generality at least to the structures of legality,[19] and one which, quite simply and explicitly is not.

This differential structure is of course legitimised. Indeed the same two legitimations occur over and over again. First, both the offences and the penalties involved in magistrates' justice are too trivial for the strictures of due process; second, the issues and processes are such that the niceties of law and lawyers are irrelevant.

The remainder of this paper sets out to analyse these legitimations, to demonstrate their ideological nature, their impact on those who work in the courts, and their ideological accomplishments.

The ideology of triviality

To read law books for information on the magistrates' courts is to come away with the clear impression that what goes on in them is overwhelmingly trivial. They deal with "minor offences", "everyday offences", "the most ordinary cases", "humdrum" events.[20] Legal academics even go so far — rare event — as indulging in jocularity. Coull and Merry's text gives the Scottish police courts, very much the lowest tier of justice, seven lines, largely taken up with the fact that they are empowered,

> inter alia to impose a fine of 50p for 'allowing a chimney to catch or be on fire' or a penalty of £2 for throwing 'any snowball, to the danger or annoyance' of any person.[21]

This dominant image of the triviality of the work of the lower courts is shared by the press. The press benches in magistrates' courts are rarely occupied. The column of offenders and penalties that every local paper carries is the result of a phone call for results. The proceedings themselves are of no interest, except perhaps to provide this week's funny stories for the Diary column. And why not? Much of what happens in the court is funny or pathetic or absurd, and so very trivial, too trivial to attract any serious attention from the press.

Nor indeed from the public: so rare is it for a member of the public to attend summary courts that the public benches are often used as a waiting room for the morning's batch of defendants, from which they can observe their predecessors' fate and shuffle along to each newly vacated space till their turn comes for the dock. To go to these courts as a member of the public is to become an object of curiosity; to sit there taking notes is to invite paroxysms of paranoia.

In the course of the research I have been asked by one police officer on duty if I was "from one of those radical papers" by another if I was "just here to practice your shorthand, dear?" I've been called before the bench to explain myself, had a policeman sent by the magistrate to ask me what I was doing there, been advised not to take notes by a policeman on duty and told by another that taking notes was illegal. The 'public' in the lower court is an unusual phenomenon, and the purveyors of magistrates' justice are somewhat sensitive to anyone seeing their particular brand of justice being done.

More than that, some were just genuinely concerned that I should be wasting my time at the lower courts when I could be watching "juicy cases" and "real judges" elsewhere. *Their* assumption was that the work of *their* court was too trivial to be of interest. So the image of triviality that pervades the lowest ranks of criminal justice has the consequence of removing yet another requisite of due process: that the administration of justice should be public.

One of the objections of the eighteenth century judges to summary justice[22] was that it was "in a private chamber" behind closed doors. The doors were opened in 1848 but the dominant image of triviality helps ensure that the public benches remain empty. It is, after all, difficult to work up a moral panic over, to cite observed cases, taking lead worth 20p from a rubbish tip, "touching cars", or my favourite, "jumping on and off a pavement in a disorderly manner". And however hard the penalties are to those on the receiving end, they can hardly match the salacious fascination of the life and death decisions in Hay's eighteenth century courts.[23]

More specifically it is the relative triviality of the *penalties* that provides the crucial legitimations in law for the lack of due process in summary justice. Due process of law is required in the ideology of democratic justice before a person's liberty may be interfered with. The reasoning which legitimises reducing due process in the lowest courts is based on this premise, but with a refinement. "Liberty" ceases to be an absolute and becomes subject to a measuring rod. The limited penalties available to magistrates means they can interfere less with one's liberty than the higher courts, so defendants in these courts need less due process. The less one's liberty is at risk the less one needs protection. This is perhaps most explicitly stated in the criteria for awarding legal aid. One important condition is where the defendant is "in real jeopardy of losing his liberty or livelihood or suffering imprisonment".[24]

More generally this is in many ways a strange argument. 'Trivial' offences after all still involve state intervention in the citizen's liberty. Indeed if the same due process is not to be awarded to all defendants, it might seem a bit illogical to minimise the legal rights for those who have allegedly infringed least on law and order and maximise them for those who have infringed most. Perhaps it is just that the more unusual the crime and the larger the penalty the more public interest is likely to be aroused and the more justice will be willy-nilly on display. The more criminality in the offence, the more legality in the proceedings might be an odd equation. The more *publicity*, the more legality, is in ideological terms, perfectly understandable. Publicity is not, however, an issue that need trouble lower court justice, closetted from the public eye by its own triviality — or, more accurately, by its own ideology of triviality. Triviality is not just a description but an interpretation, an assessment, and the work of the lower courts could be viewed quite differently.

For a start, offences and penalties may seem trivial from the outside but far from trivial from the perspective of the accused. The James Report rejected the perspective of the defendant as a way of categorising which offences and penalties were serious and which were not, on grounds which stressed its significance but its bureaucratic inconvenience:

> It would be impracticable ... since that importance varies according to his character and position in society.[25]

The same reasoning was, however, used in the Widgery Report to do the opposite, that is, to use the defendant's perspective, *as it varied according to his social status*, to justify discriminating in favour of the middle class in the award of legal aid:

> the seriousness of the consequences likely to result from loss of employment will also differ widely in different circumstances. A young labourer who loses his job in conditions of full employment will obviously not suffer to anything like the same extent as a middle aged black-coated worker who in the loss of his job, sacrifices career prospects, pension rights and may have the greatest difficulty in finding other comparable employment.[26]

One is tempted to conclude from such careful exceptions that the ideology of triviality may ultimately derive less from the triviality of the offences or the penalties but from the triviality in authoritative eyes of *the people*, the lower class, the unemployed, homeless, feeble, who provide the fodder for the lower courts — an implication indeed which is supported by the fact that the only time the lower courts become news is when, for example, Mark Phillips is charged with speeding.

Nor is it just a question of perspective but a question of focus. There is an inherent paradox in the very idea of prosecuting trivial offences. They are too trivial to interest the public but not too trivial for the state to prosecute in the name of the public; too trivial to merit due process of law but not too trivial for the intervention of the law. The ideology of triviality focusses on the offences and penalties, not on the question of prosecution itself. It is these trivial offences after all which are, first, most open to the direct intervention of the state in the sense that the police are often the *only complainants*. A recent Home Office study notes that for offences against public order 86.8% of prosecution cases comprise direct police evidence, and 13.2%

circumstantial evidence. Civilians evidence accounts for precisely 0.0%.[27] Second, they are most open to the imposition of a criminal label on "marginal" behaviour like loitering, and third, most open — because the definitions of offences are so open — to post hoc law-making.[28] In short, it is exactly in the area of minor offences that the operation of the law, in terms of democratic justice, becomes most suspect. If the behaviour involved in the offence is not intrinsically interesting, perhaps the law's processing of that behaviour into an offence is. But contemporary official discourse is more concerned with the quantity of crime than the quality of justice and the lower courts remain something to be laughed at or yawned over for the pettiness of their crimes, not watched with care for the marginality of their legality.

Legal Relevance

The second justification for reducing the strictures of due process — a view that is indeed given some endorsement by socio-legal writers like Mungham and Thomas[29] is that the offences dealt with in the lower courts do not involve much law or require much legal expertise or advocacy. They can therefore be safely left to be dealt with by laymen — by lay magistrates and by the defendants themselves, with lawyers seen as normally unnecessary in the lower courts. According to the Widgery Report, legal aid is rarely necessary for summary offences since:

> The large majority of cases are straightforward and the facts are uncomplicated and clear-cut.[30]

But this view of the lower court is inaccurate in two ways. First empirical study, as already demonstrated, shows that the lower courts are permeated by legalistic and professional consciousness. Second, it is logically confused — it confuses cause and effect — verges indeed on tautology. It might just as readily be argued that minor offences are characterised by simple facts and straightforward cases because there are so rarely lawyers involved.

The 'case' is a construct from an event, not a reproduction of it.[31] The construction of a case as straightforward or as involving points of law is very much the product of the advocate's trade. Case law, after all, develops exactly because advocates present cases which draw subtle distinctions and shades of meaning, in short, complicate the simple, in arguing for the treatment of the case in hand as different from previous precedents. What is more, case law and the development of complicated and difficult legal issues in specific types of offence and case, is predicated largely on the right to appeal on points of law, and both the nature of the appeal procedure in the lower courts and the lack of lawyers to formulate an appeal on a point of law, means that there is little opportunity to develop difficult and complex case law on minor offences.

It is not in the nature of drunkenness, breach of the peace or petty theft to be less susceptible than fraud, burglary or murder to complex legal argument; it is rather in the nature of the procedure by which they are tried. Indeed the James Report implicitly recognises this when it notes that:

> trial on indictment takes longer than summary trial even for a case of similar gravity and complexity.[32]

The "straightforward cases" of the lower courts are themselves legal constructions.

The same is true of the "simple facts". The facts of a case — a case of any sort — are not *all* the elements of the event, but the information allowed in by the rules, presented by the witnesses, and surviving the credibility test of cross-examination. The facts of summary cases may not be simple because of the nature of the offences but because of the lack of professional expertise in manipulation of the rules, persuasive presentation of one's own case and destructive cross-examination of the other side's. It is not that complex facts need lawyers but that lawyers can make 'facts' complex. That is exactly their trade.

Or the facts may be 'simple' not because of the nature of the offence but because of the *definition* of the offence. The openness of the legal definition of what constitutes an offence, and consequent scope for wide police discretion, along with the fact that these offences are normally the result not of citizens' reports but of police-accused encounters, with only the accused's word against the policeman's constituting the case, means that it is extremely difficult to establish a defence. In short, the facts are simple only because they are legally so difficult for the defendant to contest.

Indeed it might be suggested that the openness of the laws defining summary offences argues not for less legal expertise but for more. If the police can legally define almost anything as an offence, then the facts cannot be in dispute and the only way to establish a defence is on a point of law. Consider case 20, the "jumping on and off a pavement in a disorderly manner" case.

One reaction to being charged for that, even if one *was* doing it, might be total disbelief and a defence on the basis of it being absurd to be taken to court for such behaviour at all. But that of course is not a legal defence, just a cut and dried admission of guilt. The accused in this case, the only one of the group charged who pleaded not guilty, defended himself by saying he was not doing anything disorderly, that indeed he had just crossed the road to talk to the others and that he didn't run away because he "didn't expect to be lifted". That was his mistake. The prosecutor even noted in his summing up that

> he may think he wasn't misbehaving as much as the others *but he stayed with them.*

And that was all that was necessary *in law*. The prosecutor had to prove no more than that the defendant was part of a disorderly crowd which he could have left, not that he was actually disorderly himself.

There was therefore no legal defence in denying his behaviour was offensive, not only because that was difficult to maintain against two policemen but because in law it was irrelevant. A relevant defence would have been to take on the meaning of the law, for example, contending that to be "part of a disorderly crowd" requires not just one's presence but active participation. But that would be a point of law: it would require a more sophisticated knowledge of law and legal reasoning than this layman had, and of course, as we've already seen, might require presentation by a lawyer to be given a hearing at all.

The irony is then that because of the openness of the law in minor offences, kept open because there is so little case law to specify meaning, the best route to a defence is to challenge on a point of law. This of course could *establish* that missing case law, but it can't be readily done because no need for lawyers is perceived and the means to raise a point of law are denied. The image of the lower courts as not needing lawyers, which justifies not providing lawyers, is itself a *product* of their absence. The defendant is thus caught up in the vicious circle that lies behind the image of "simple facts" and "straightforward cases".

But, and this is why situational analysis needs to be set in its deeper structural context, providing lawyers would not necessarily make any difference: the ideologies of non-law and triviality pervade the origins and structure of the lower courts and so pervade the attitudes of those who work in them. Remember the police official who helpfully suggested I go to the higher courts for "juicy cases" and "real judges". And lawyers themselves often operate with a different style in the lower courts.

Indeed they are different lawyers. The non-law ideology has its structural expression in the idea that only barristers can act in the higher courts but only solicitors can usually be provided on legal aid in the lower courts. This is not to suggest invidious comparisons between the skills of solicitors and barristers, but merely to indicate that whatever the personal attitudes or competence of the solicitors who do appear in the lower courts the standard of advocacy *required* is pre set as second class.

Likewise there is a structural expectation that lower courts do not need cases that are well prepared or indeed prepared beforehand at all by either side. With no committal proceedings the defence has no advance warning of the prosecution case it will have to face anyway, while Arguile's book on criminal procedure notes that if a matter arises in the defence evidence that takes the prosecutor by surprise he may call evidence in rebuttal of it *afterwards*:

> This is permitted because summary trials usually owe very little to advance preparation of the case, and the prosecution is therefore more likely to be surprised by unexpected defences.[33]

Lack of skilled preparation or presentation is certainly borne out by observation in courts.[34] and indeed by the criticism of the level of advocacy in the magistrates' courts made to the Royal Commission on Legal Services by the Association of Magisterial Officers. The concern here however is less with assessing the level of performance and attitude of lawyers per se than with teasing out what that demonstrates about the professional lawyer's ideology of the lower courts. On that score, the reply by the Law Society is as telling as the criticism, describing, as it does, the offenders, offences and work of the court in general as "relative trivia" and "the dross of the criminal courts".[35] What these comments suggest is that the profession too is imbued with the dominant images of the lower courts as neither serious enough nor legally relevant enough to need lawyers. To simply prescribe lawyers on tap for the lower courts as a solution to the defendant's dilemma is thus to ignore the much more fundamental structural and ideological realities which lie behind the courtroom situation.

The Accomplishments

These images of the court are not just ideological accomplishments; they also accomplish ideological functions themselves. Carlen points to the marginality of the offences, the lack of ceremony, lack of lawyers in the lower courts, as a problem for the magistrate in presenting the court's work as justice.[36] But the situational problem is in fact resolved structurally. The very same factors are transformed into images of the court as trivial and non-legal: and the effect of those images is that the court never actually has to account for its work anyway. The magistrate may have an existential problem in portraying his work as justice but he rarely has a social problem. For the magistrates' court is a theatre without an audience.

Legal policy has established two tiers of justice. One, the higher courts, is for public consumption, the arena where the ideology of justice is put on display.[37] The other, the lower courts, deliberately structured in defiance of the ideology of justice, is concerned less with subtle ideological messages than with direct control. The latter is closeted from the public eye by the ideology of triviality, so the higher courts alone feed into the public image of what the law does and how it operates. But the higher courts deal with only 2% of the cases that pass through the courts. Almost all criminal law is acted out in the lower courts *without* traditional due process. But of course what happens in the lower courts is not only trivial it is not really law. So the position is turned on its head. The 98% becomes the exception to the rule of "real law" and the working of the law comes to be typified *not* by its routine nature, but by its *atypical*, indeed *exceptional* high court form. Between them the ideologies of triviality and legal irrelevance accomplish the remarkable feats of defining 98% of court cases not only as exceptions to the rule of due process, but also as of no public interest whatsoever. The traditional ideology of justice can thus survive the contradiction that the summary courts blatantly ignore it every day — and that they were set up precisely for that purpose.

NOTES AND REFERENCES

[1] Though much abridged and modified, this article draws on Chapter 7 of D. McBarnet: *Conviction: Law, the State and the Construction of Justice* (1981). It was presented to the Sociology Society, University College Cardiff, on February 3rd, 1981.

[2] J. Vennard, *Contested Trials in Magistrates' Courts*. Royal Commission on Criminal Procedure Research Study No. 6 (1980).

[3] This particular piece of research was part of a larger study of courts in general. See McBarnet, *op.cit.* For the purposes of this article only cases in magistrates' courts are considered. Observed cases are numbered and cited by number.

[4] The Scottish court structure is more complex than the English. Scottish Magistrates' courts are presided over by a single magistrate, lay or stipendiary, laymen sitting with a legally qualified "assessor". More especially, magistrates' courts constitute only one section of Scottish summary justice, much being conducted not by a magistrate but by a sheriff sitting without a jury. Magistrates, however, especially in major cities like the one where this work was done, still deal with a very large number of cases.

[5] Criminal Statistics, England and Wales, 1978 (1979, HMSO Cmnd. 7670) Criminal Statistics, Scotland, 1978 (1979, HMSO Cmnd. 7676).

[6] Vennard *op.cit.*

[7] S. Dell, *Silence in Court*, Occasional Papers in Social Administration, 42 (1971).

[8] P. Carlen, *Magistrates' Justice* (1976).

[9] A. E. Bottoms and J. D. McClean, *Defendants in the Criminal Process* (1976).

[10] Report of the Royal Commission on Legal Services (1979; Cmnd. 7648) 58.

[11] Report of the Departmental Committee on Legal Aid in Criminal Court Proceedings (1966; Cmnd. 2934) 46.

[12] *op.cit.* p. 104.

[13] *op.cit.* p. 47.

[14] Lord Chancellor's office: Lectures for Magistrates (1953) 38.

[15] Widgery Report, *op.cit.* p. 2.

[16] Lord Chancellor's office, *op.cit.* p. 38.

[17] *Lamb* v *Threshie* (1892) 3 White 261.

[18] R. Arguile, *Criminal Procedure* (1969). 55; R. Renton and Brown: *Criminal Procedure according to the law of Scotland* (1972) 278.

[19] Note the reference to "*ideology and generality at least*". There are all sorts of ways in which the higher courts too routinely contravene the rhetoric. See McBarnet *op.cit.*

[20] The issue of triviality is one point where it might be thought that the generalisability of the Scottish data is in question. The magistrates' courts in Scotland are a lower rung than those in England in that much of the work that would be done by magistrates in England is done by sheriffs in Scotland and the assumption is often made that the Scottish magistrates are only allocated the most trivial offences to deal with. There could therefore be an *overstatement* in Scottish magistrates' courts of the triviality of the offences involved compared to England. However, two points should be borne in mind. First the data used here were collected in stipendiary as well as lay magistrates' courts and though lay magistrates may well tend to be allocated very trivial cases, there is less evidence that the stipendiaries are. Secondly, the *descriptions* of magistrates' work just quoted are from English as well as Scottish sources. The first is taken from Arguile *op.cit.* the second from the Lords' Debate on the Magistrates' Courts Bill (1953 Hansard), the third is Scottish (Walker). In short, the *image* of triviality, which is the concern of this article, is the same in both jurisdictions.

[21] J. W. Coull and E. W. Merry, *Principles and Practice of Scots Law* (1971). 25–26.

[22] See McBarnet *op.cit.* ch. 7, Section: 'State struggles and the two tiers of justice'.

[23] D. Hay, 'Property, authority and the law' in *Albion's Fatal Tree* (1975, eds. D. Hay *et. al.*).

[24] Widgery *op.cit.* p. 190.

[25] (1975; Cmnd. 6323) 20.

[26] *op.cit.*p. 46.

[27] Vennard *op.cit.*

[28] See McBarnet *op.cit.* ch. 3.

[29] 'Advocacy and the solicitor-advocate in magistrates' courts in England and Wales' *International Journal of the Sociology of Law* (May 1979).

[30] *op.cit.* p. 17.

[31] For a more detailed analysis see McBarnet *op.cit.* ch. 2.

[32] *op.cit.* p. 13.

[33] *op.cit.* p. 164.

[34] From my own observation, and see P. Darbyshire, *The Role of the Justices' Clerk and the Court Clerk.* Ph.D. Thesis (1978 Birmingham).

[35] Quoted in *The Times* 23 August 1977.

[36] *op.cit.* p. 38.

[37] In appearance at least, see note 19.

[7]
Criminal Justice and the Ideology of the Rule of Law

This study set out to analyse the role of legal forms, powers, privileges, limitations, and rulings on the process of constructing conviction in court—conviction in both the subjective sense of how a judge or jury comes to be convinced beyond reasonable doubt of its verdict, and in the legal sense of a finding of guilt; for that, statistically, is the likely outcome of a foray into the criminal courts. The problem for the sociologist is how that is possible when all the rhetoric of the democratic ideology of justice proclaims that in the battle between the state and the accused the system is heavily biased in favour of the latter. By examining the law not just in terms of the general principles of its own ideology, but in terms of the details of its specific structures, procedures, and decisions, this analysis has tried to show that the law governing the production, preparation, and presentation of evidence does not live up to its own rhetoric.

The rhetoric of justice requires incriminating evidence as the basis for arrest and search; the law allows arrest and search in order to establish it. Justice requires that no-one need incriminate himself; the law refuses to control the production of confessions and allows silence as a factor in proving guilt. Justice requires equality; the law discriminates against the homeless, the jobless, the disreputable. Justice requires each case be judged on its own facts; the law makes previous convictions grounds for defining behaviour as an offence and evidence against the accused. Justice places the burden of proof on the prosecutor; the law qualifies the standard and method of proof required and offers the prosecutor opportunities for making a case which the accused is denied. Justice proclaims the right to trial by one's peers; the legal system ensures that 91 per cent of all defendants plead guilty, and of the rest most are tried without a jury.

If, then, the process of conviction is easier than the rhetoric of justice would have us expect—and easier still the lower the status of the defendant—it is hardly surprising. A wide range of prosecution evidence can be legally produced and presented, despite the rhetoric of a system geared overwhelmingly to safeguards for the accused, precisely because legal structure, legal procedure, legal rulings, *not* legal rhetoric, govern the legitimate practice of criminal justice, and there is quite simply a distinct gap between the substance and the ideology of the law.

This conclusion has two direct and immediate implications. First it places the contemporary policy debate over law and order in a new light. The police demand for more powers, for the removal of the hamstrings of the right to silence, the limitations on arrest and search—and indeed the civil liberties camp's agitated response that the legal checks of British justice must be upheld—begin to appear rather odd. *Both* sides of the debate are framed in terms of the ideology of civil rights, not in terms of the realities of legal procedure and case law which, as I hope this analysis has amply shown, have all too often already given the police and prosecution the very powers they are demanding. The law does not need reform to remove hamstrings on the police: they exist largely in the unrealised rhetoric.

Second, more theoretically, this analysis has implications for the explanation of law-enforcement and its outcomes. A whole range of excellent sociological studies has pointed out situational, informal, non-legal factors in police–citizen encounters and courtroom interaction to explain *who* is arrested or convicted, and to explain why the system so often seems *in practice* to be weighted against the accused. Their answer lies essentially in the complex nature of social interaction and motivation; in the fact that people do not merely administer the law but act upon and alter it as they do so. This study offers a supplementary perspective, making the law rather than the activities of its administrators problematic. The conclusion is quite different. Given the formal procedures and rules of the law and the *structure* of arrest, investigation, plea and trial, one could not—even if human beings acted entirely as legal automatons—expect the outcomes to be other than they are. If the practice of criminal justice does not live up to its rhetoric one should not look only to the interactions and negotiations of those who put the law into practice but to the law itself. One should not look just to how the rhetoric of justice is subverted intentionally or otherwise by policemen bending the rules, by lawyers negotiating adversariness out of existence, by out-of-touch judges or biased magistrates: one must also look at how it is subverted *in the law*. Police and court officials need not abuse the law to subvert the principles of justice; they need only use it. Deviation from the rhetoric of legality and justice is institutionalised in the law itself.

Coming back to Packer's two polar types for describing law-enforcement, due process and crime control, empirical analysis of the process reveals them as a false distinction. The law on criminal procedure in its current form does not so much set a standard of legality from which the police deviate as provide a licence to ignore it. If we bring due process down from the dizzy heights of abstraction and subject it to empirical scrutiny, the conclusion must be that due process is *for* crime control.

This perspective offers quite a different ideological gloss on the nature of criminal justice and a shift of focus for its study. Focusing on the subversion of justice by its petty administrators, on the gap between the law in the books and the law in action, in effect whitewashes the law itself and those who make it. Front-men like the police become the 'fall guys' of the legal system taking the blame for any injustices in the operation of the law, both in theory (in the assumption like Skolnick's that they break the rules) and indeed, in the law. The law holds the individual policeman personally responsible for contraventions of legality that are successfully sued, while at the same time refusing to make clear until after the event exactly what the police are supposed to do. It is no coincidence that the police themselves asked for the original Judges' Rules. Shifting the focus to the substance of law places responsibility for the operation of criminal justice—and the need for the spotlight of study—squarely on the judicial and political élites who make it.

Tracing a gap between the rhetoric of justice and the substance and structure of law is not, however, just the end of a piece of indignant exposé research (Taylor, Walton, and Young 1975, p. 29). It opens up a whole complex of further issues. If the contradictions between rhetoric and practice in law-enforcement cannot simply be explained away as the unintended consequences of the action of petty officials, then we are faced with contradictions within the core of the state between the ideology and substance of the law. Why does such institutionalised deviation occur? How is the ideological gap managed? What implications does it have for the idea of the rule of law? Though these are major issues which each require a full-scale study in themselves, the sections that follow offer some speculative beginnings.

RHETORIC AND LAW: WHY THE GAP?

It is too simple to discuss the gap between the rhetoric of justice and the substance of law as unproblematic, as the inevitable and self-evident consequence of a class society in which the rhetoric of justice is necessarily mere illusion. Some more sophisticated analyses have been suggested. Hall and his colleagues (1978) have tried to offer a materialist explanation of a particular move in the 1970s to a more repressive crime-control oriented use of law and steady erosion of civil liberties by relating it to a crisis in the hegemony of the bourgeois state, and that in turn to economic crisis. At another level of contextual analysis a series of sociologists,[1] including indeed Hall *et al.*, have demonstrated how a moral panic and campaign for the repression of a particular social problem—mugging, football hooliganism, drugs, mods and rockers—can lead to more crime-control oriented judicial decisions, and so help explain why particular swings in the orientation of law to or away from the rhetoric of justice take place. It might also be possible, however, that a tendency one way or the other exists in the law itself. From examining the legal structure it would seem that there are also forces *within* the law which might well lead *routinely*—when there are no moral panics in either direction—to a development of case law that favours crime control rather than due process.

Case law and judicial discretion could as readily be used—and indeed have been—to condemn police practices as to condone them. But case law emanates, to state the obvious, from particular trials. There is no public interest law in Britain, no way in which a point of law can be brought to court as an abstract issue of public concern. A point of law can only be clarified in the context of a dispute in a real case, either directly at a High Court trial from the decision taken by the judge on a dispute over a point of law, or indirectly via appeal from the trial court to the Court of Appeal or House of Lords. Locating the dispute over law in the facts of a concrete case might well, despite the distinction drawn in legal theory between issues of fact and issues of law, mean that the facts of the case affect the finding in law by providing the context in which the decision has to be made. What this whole study has suggested is that that context, if the point of law is being raised in the course of a trial, is one in which the accused is likely to look guilty. If it is being raised on appeal, then he will already have been *found* guilty since, in the main, only defendants can appeal, and only defendants with a grievance—that is, those who have been convicted.[2] What is more, because re-trials of fact, or the introduction of new evidence, are rarely allowed on appeal, that defendant's case is often of necessity based on technicality rather than equity, on the means by which the evidence was acquired rather than the misleading or inaccurate nature of the evidence itself. Judges making case law on appeal are thus faced in effect with a guilty defendant trying to argue his way out of his due deserts through legal technicalities. Who would blame them for closing the escape route by removing the technicality, by seeing rights as loopholes that should in the name of justice be removed? If these hypotheses are correct, one can readily see why in particular cases judges may be likely to decide against the accused.

The problem is that judges are exercising a dual function in reaching their decision. They must not just ensure that justice is done in the sense of the accused getting his deserts; they must also ensure that the technical checks on *how* criminal justice is executed are upheld. They must not just uphold the substantive criminal law but the procedures of legality. They must think not only of the apparently guilty man before them but of the protection of the innocent in the future. But this duality of function sets up an impossible contradiction. The decision is a finding for *either* one party *or* the other. It has *either* to declare the methods illegitimate, the evidence inadmissible and quash the defendant's conviction, *or* uphold the conviction, but in doing so, inevitably legitimise the questionable methods—inevitably because of a second duality in the function of decisions. The judicial decision does not just resolve the particular case but sets a precedent for future cases. Provisos in civil rights introduced in the context of a particular case become abstracted and available for argument in all cases. Rejecting a technical defence may be quite understandable in the context of the black-and-white cases constructed through advocacy and procedure, but with every rejection of a technical defence case comes an extension of police and prosecution powers. Civil liberties cease to be legal rights and the control of crime is safeguarded at the expense of legality.[3]

In short, from the structure of trial and appeal, and from the functional dualities in the judicial decision—deciding on both the individual case and the law; upholding both substantive and procedural law—one can plausibly hypothesise a structural trend in case law towards crime control and away from due process. While contextual analysis is obviously vital, the legal system itself may also help explain why substantive law might routinely be upheld at the expense of procedural law and the rights of the rhetoric of justice gradually whittled away.

MANAGING THE IDEOLOGICAL GAP

The gap between the rhetoric of justice and the substance and structure of law raises not only 'why' questions but 'how' questions. How is it possible for the law to deviate from the rhetoric, and how does the rhetoric survive the deviation? Much has been made of the tension between due process and crime control but the law seems to achieve crime control while keeping the ideology of due process in play;[4] it seems to achieve in some measure at least the impossible task of maintaining two contradictory ideas at once. How are the ideological gap and the ideological contradictions managed?

Part of the answer lies in the mystique and inaccessibility which protects the detail of law from the mass of people. It is the rhetoric rather than the law that is public knowledge. Indeed one can observe defendants losing their case precisely because they are arguing it on the basis of the rhetoric rather than the law. One needs a knowledge of both law and rhetoric before the gap between them becomes evident. What is more, a good deal of what occurs in the courts, as argued in Chapter 5, may appear to fit the rhetoric of justice only because the organisation of the facts into not only black-and-white cases but into black-and-white cases that are likely to persuade ordinary people of guilt has taken place *out* of the public eye. The ideological shutters around the magistrates' courts (Chapter 7) and the difficulties attached even to getting leave to appeal, have the same effect. The division of the process into public and private faces helps in itself to maintain the ideology.

Part of the answer lies too in the techniques of judicial reasoning. Judges deciding a point of law routinely reiterate the rhetoric in resounding prose, yet decide the case in such a way that the rhetoric is, for this individual, effectively denied. Throughout we have seen examples of how this apparent contradiction is calmly and routinely accomplished. Judges may draw literal distinctions which re-iterate the principle but make it simultaneously irrelevant or indeed uphold the principle but give such specific reasons that it cannot be generalised, as in *Lawrie* v. *Muir* or *H. M. Adv.* v. *Aitken*.[5] They may avoid the applicability of the rhetoric by redefining the situation in such a way that it is no longer covered by the principle; for example, creating the limbo of the 'suspect' who was thus not protected by the rhetoric or law on arrest and interrogation.[6] They may uphold the rhetoric by expressing dissatisfaction with the questionable means used to acquire evidence, but simultaneously allow that evidence to be used to convict on other grounds, maintaining that the trial judge has discretion in such matters as to precisely how it should be applied as in the *R.* v. *Lemsatef* case,[7] or deciding—on no rational empirical grounds at all—that the conviction by the jury did not depend on that piece of evidence anyway. All kinds of techniques of reasoning allow the rhetoric to be both eulogised and denied.

But structural factors also provide some of the means of bridging the ideological gap. The doctrine of the separation of powers provides a multi-headed state and with it the potential to extol the rhetoric in one sector and deny it in another. Statutes may provide rights in general terms—the 1887 Act, for example, made provision for a defendant to consult a solicitor—only to have the judges refine the right out of existence.[8] The rhetoric lives on in the statute but is routinely negated in the courts by judicial reasoning.

Beneath judicial reasoning itself structural factors are also at work. Just as the techniques of advocacy are themselves only adaptations to a particular form of proof, so the techniques of judicial reasoning are themselves significant only in a particular form of law. Law is made through the case law method both in the development of common law and the application of statutes. The rhetoric of justice in the form of general abstract rules is quite simply incompatible with the notion of case law. Levi notes that a general overall rule is useless in law because:

> It will have to operate at a level where it has no meaning. . . . The legal system does not work with the rule but at a much lower level. (Levi, 1949, p. 9)

A legal system based on case law (and even the states that boast codified law also use case law in a modified form) operates at the level of the concrete case: is highly particularistic. Hence the justification of excepting the specific case from the application of the general rule without destroying the general rule *per se*. The rhetoric and the law operate at two different levels, the abstract and the concrete, and the contradiction is operationally negated and a clear clash prevented by each being pigeon-holed out of the other's realm of discourse. The rhetoric is rarely actually denied, it is simply whittled away by exceptions, provisos, qualifications.

Law in this form is rather like a Russian doll. You begin with the rhetoric and a single, apparently definite, condition which on closer inspection turns out to contain another less clear condition which in turn opens up to reveal even more ifs and buts and vaguenesses, reducing so often to the unpredictability of 'it all depends on the circumstances'—what criteria we use in your case depends on your case. This form provides an extremely potent way of maintaining the facade of civil rights ideology—the first doll—while in fact allowing extensive *legal* police powers. Cases can readily accommodate both statements of general principle and the exceptions of particular circumstances. Thus an appeal on the grounds of abuse of a legal right can be rejected because of the circumstances of the particular case, while at the same time a grand statement reiterating that right is made. The conflicting rhetoric of due process and practical demands for crime control are thus both simultaneously maintained and the gap between rhetoric and practice is managed out of existence. Lawyers may boast of the flexibility and individualised treatment afforded by case law but it also plays a potent role in maintaining the ideology of justice.[9]

This has implications for policy for it sets parameters on any possibility of lasting reform. Recommendations for changes in the law made by the Royal Commission on Criminal Procedure, the Fisher Report, committees on law reform, or whatever, must be seen as themselves subject to future change, future change which if the hypothesised development of case law noted in the previous section is anything to go by, all too often means a whittling away of the original principle. The spirit lingers in the rhetoric of justice but the qualifications and provisos of case law render it rather less effective. Lasting reform cannot be possible without some deeper change in the form of law itself.

But the nature of case law has implications not only for policy but for sociological understanding of the role of law in society, for the operation of dominant ideology and the democratic state. It has implications in particular for one area in which these three coalesce, in the idea of the rule of law.

THE CASE LAW FORM AND THE RULE OF LAW

The principles of justice are part of the ideology of the democratic state not only in their substance but in a much more fundamental way, in the very idea that there should be principles at all, that those who wield the power of the state should not do so arbitrarily but should themselves be governed by law. The idea of legality itself is an essential ideological form of the democratic state; its rule is the rule of law.

The idea of the rule of law is central not just to the arena of criminal justice, perhaps the most explicitly coercive aspect of state–individual relations, but to sociological theories of law in general in capitalist society. One strand, epitomised by Weber (1954) and Neumann (1957) emphasises dependability or certainty as its one essential element; the rule of law is the rule of *known* law. Concerned more with civil than criminal law, they relate the development of law in capitalist society to the need for commerce to operate in a situation of certainty, in the knowledge that contracts could be relied on to be fulfilled or enforced. Second, E. P. Thompson has sparked off debate by challenging the crude Marxist notion that the rule of law is merely a mask for the rule of the dominant class. Though he qualified his argument as being only certainly applicable to eighteenth-century England, it has been generalised in debate to the question of the function of law in capitalist society in general.[10] He argues that the ideology of justice is no mere mask but also a potential for genuine transcendence of class interests: 'The law may be rhetoric but it need not be empty rhetoric'. (E. P. Thompson, 1975, p. 263).[11] There are two reasons for this. Class relations are expressed in law '*through the forms of law*' (*ibid.*, p. 262). These are independent of class interests and Thompson implies, a constraint upon them. What is more, people are not, says Thompson, mystified by the first man to put on a wig. The principles of justice, once declared, take on a force of their own in that they have to be lived up to if their ideological functions are to succeed. The rulers thus become 'prisoners of their own rhetoric' (*ibid.*, p. 263). The essential issue here is the *autonomy of law*, the idea of the rule of law above man as of theoretical as well as ideological validity.

For both these strands of theorising and debate on the rule of law the form of case law must raise serious questions, questions which have indeed been raised at various historical moments in the politics and ideology of Common Law.[12] Certainly one can find quotations from judges on the need for certainty in the law. In 1754 Lord Hardwicke noted: 'I think authorities established are so many laws and receding from them unsettles property; and uncertainty is the unavoidable consequence' (cited in Holdsworth, 1934, p. 188). But such statements jar so clearly not just with the practice of judges but with the *form* of the case law method, that one cannot help but speculate that Weber's description of a move to 'rational' law for the sake of certainty traces the development of an ideology of law rather than a description of either its practice or its form.

Case law is discretionary and particularistic; it does not operate at the level of general rules. What is more, as noted in Chapter 3, it only operates *post hoc*—it does not make law until *after* a dispute has made it into an issue. Of course there are precedents to constrain judgements. But they need only constrain the justification of the decision rather than the decision itself. Indeed the discretion invested in judges, and the fact that the case comes before them only after dispute, only because 'informed lawyers disagree' and can make out a case for both sides, means 'a judge's decision either way will not be considered a failure to perform his judicial responsibilities' (Greenawalt, cited in R. Cross, 1977, p. 221). What Hart (1961) calls the open texture of law allows wide scope in the use and application of precedent. Indeed precedents can be employed to do the exact opposite of their original use, as examples in this study show. The meaning attached to precedent deserves attention too. Holdsworth argues that the method of making law by precedent was only accepted historically by the judiciary on condition that it was *not* an overbearing constraint (Holdsworth, 1934, p. 180). This was accomplished by developing their own ideology of law. Coke, Hale, and Blackstone were all firm exponents of the view that decisions and precedents were *not law* but merely 'evidence of what the law is'. The result is that: 'The courts must decide what weight is to be attached to the evidence in different sets of circumstances'. Holdsworth concludes:

> The manner in which they have decided this question has left them many means of escape from the necessity of literal obedience to the general rule that decided cases must always be followed. (*ibid.*, p. 185)

Structurally indeed there *could not* historically have been a systematic following of precedents quite simply because there was no systematic reporting of cases until the end of the nineteenth century, a matter which provided further justification for the judges to ignore precedent on the basis that reports were not authoritative.[13] Cross suggests that with more systematic law reporting and restructuring of the courts, by the nineteenth century the idea of binding precedent had become more rigid (R. Cross, 1977, p. 23). But it did not last long, for he also observes that the English doctrine of precedent is *currently* in a state of flux (*ibid.*, p. 6). Though the Court of Appeal is still in theory bound by its own and the House of Lords' decisions, there are several well-known cases in which it has not followed them,[14] while in 1966 the House of Lords stated quite explicitly it need not be bound by its own precedents. This is not to say that precedent is never followed in the making of case law; it may even *usually* be followed. It is merely to say that it *need* not be a rigid constraint. Indeed the very degree of constraint involved is, it would seem, subject to the changing decisions of the judges themselves, the people it is supposed to constrain. The doctrine of precedent may thus be placed more aptly in the rhetoric rather than the actual procedure of justice. The doctrine of precedent may tell us where the ideology of the rule of law is grounded and how it is maintained, but it tells us very little about the practice of case law—not just because of judicial techniques to use and avoid precedent but because of the nature of the ideology of precedent and the *post hoc* discretionary particularistic form of the case law method.

The result is that the law is so far from being certain as to be almost impossible to pin down. This study would never have taken the shape it has if I had been able, as an observer in courts unread in law at all, to get a precise answer from the lawyers I eagerly asked what the law of search, or arrest, or the right to silence, actually was. The answer was a list of cases all with different specific lines—'in *R.* v. *Green* the decision was X but of course in *R.* v. *Brown* it was Y'—and so on. The textbooks offered the same, noting sometimes that the law on that point *may* be so and so. And soon it became clear that it was not my lack of legal learning that made the law so elusive: that was the nature of the law, a will-o'-the-wisp pausing but a moment before the next decision, and then only 'clear' for the particular circumstances of that particular case.

When law takes such a form, there *can be* no fixed or certain rule of law. The Weberian thesis of the bourgeois need for certain law must be challenged by even a perfunctory analysis of the form of law, especially in the common law systems of both the first capitalist society, Britain, and the most advanced, the United States, which illustrate the case law method *par excellence*. But it is not just common law that is based on cases; modern law *per se*, however codified in general, comes down in the end to application to concrete situations, to case law. Law in modern society,[15] far from being certain, is as elusive and as adaptable as a chameleon.

This elusiveness also plays its part in the mystique of law. What can be more mystical than a statement of what the law is which is not only veiled by the need to know where and how to look for it, but which turns out when you find it to be provisional, particular, and only really ascertainable for your specific question if you take it to court? The portrayal by Thompson—and others—of the mystique of law is too simple. People may not be bamboozled by the wigs and ceremony and jargon of the law, but they are quite likely to be bamboozled by the law itself. It is not just that they are in their ignorance puzzled by the law, it is also quite simply that the law *is* a puzzle. Its particularistic *post hoc* form inevitably makes it so.

But analysing the form of law undermines Thompson's argument in deeper ways. Thompson discusses the 'forms of law' by which he means procedures, but not the basic '*form*' of law, the nature of law itself. Nor does his analysis really distinguish between the general rhetoric and specific rules of law[16]. He equates them—'the law may be rhetoric . . .'—but he is really talking only of the ideology of justice. On that level his point on the ideological availability of 'justice' to *all* of society is beyond reproach. Of course 'justice', 'equality', and 'liberty' have all been banners for all classes: it is the meaning they are invested with that ties them to one, and it is in the specific rulings of law that those meanings are defined and refined into the particular shape endorsed and enforceable by the state.

It is at that stage that Thompson would see class interests constrained by the need to abide by the rhetoric for ideological purposes, and by the 'forms of law', its logic, procedure, and rules. But the theory is too simple. It is not enough to say the rulers are 'prisoners of their own rhetoric', that the law cannot seem just 'without upholding its own logic and criteria of equity'. Studying the content of the law shows this is not necessarily what happens. The logic, rules, and procedures of the law, as this study has shown, far from being fixed constraints, are highly malleable. The question that must arise is rather: how is it possible for the ideological function to be fulfilled *without* overly constraining the rulers? What this study has tried to show in examining the management of the ideological gap between the rhetoric of justice and the content of law is precisely how judges can *both uphold*, even eulogise, the rhetoric yet simultaneously deny its applicability. The '*can*' is important, since they can also do quite the opposite, as the brief discussion in this study of the eighteenth-century judges, or the fuller one in Hay's of the eighteenth-century courts (Hay, 1975) shows. But the opportunity is always there, and it is there not just in the hypocrisy or reasoning powers of rulers but in the structure of legal procedures and the form of law. The 'forms of law' not only *express* constraints, they include methods for negating them.

This has a further implication. General theories of law too often analyse the role of law as though it were an ideological monolith. What this study underlines is the need to analyse the different aspects and levels of law with greater precision. If we separate out the rhetoric, substance, and—much deeper than Thompson's 'forms'—the basic form of law, we find not only that they are different elements but that the articulation of the different elements helps explain how the ideology *can* operate successfully *without* making the rulers of the state too extensively the prisoners of its rhetoric.

Returning to the debate between Thompson and a more directly economistic Marxism as to whether law is a mere mask for class interests or not, or indeed to any of the polarised conceptualisations of law posed in the sociological debates over law, one can perhaps conclude that the polarities lie not in the theoretical perspectives so much as in the law itself. The question may be less a matter of which of two alternative theories of the role of law in society is right, but of how it is possible for the law to present itself plausibly in such opposing ways, how it is possible for the contradictory theories to be posed in the first place. To examine the form of law in relation to the ideology of the rule of law is to gain some insights into *how* the law is able to contain—in both senses—internal contradictions. It may help us understand not only how the legal system can simultaneously maintain both due process and crime control, the prime concern of this study, but more broadly, how it can reproduce the ideology of justice while denying it, and *how* the state through law can give class-based ideas 'the form of universality' (Marx and Engels, 1965, p. 66).

There have been criticisms of the uncertainty of the case law method. Bentham likened it to making law for a dog—'You wait till he does it and then beat him.' The contemporary police lobby—just like that in 1912 seeking guidance over exactly what powers were available to the police in doing their job after two contradictory decisions in the courts—echo this, for it is in a sense seeking not so much *more* powers (they so often do have them *de facto* in case law) but *certain* powers. Academic lawyers still analyse specific areas of law and express anxiety over the gaps, loopholes, and uncertainties they find there. Ashworth (1979), for example, criticises loose phraseology in the law; he describes ambiguities in the operation of criminal justice, traces them to ambiguities in the conceptualisation of what criminal justice is for, and implies they must be made explicit, discussed, and resolved. For the policeman and the lawyer ambiguity in law is an anomaly to be cleared up. From a sociological perspective, however, such gaps and uncertainties are not contingent or anomalous but the inevitable product of the form of law—these are not weak points in the system but a source of *operational strength*—a crucial means by which the legal system is able to work at all—and of ideological strength—precisely what allows the law to be all things to all men, to contain contradictions, to manage the gap between what it does and what it should.

The rhetoric of law in capitalist society can thus safely extol the principles of legality or the rule of law, of a concept of justice geared to safeguarding the citizen from the state, of an impartial and universal classlessness in the idea of the equal legal subject. It can do so safely not only because the rhetoric of criminal justice is routinely subverted in practice by its practitioners, whether through the non-legal motivation of the policeman on the beat or through the reasoning powers of the High Court judges. Nor indeed only because the rhetoric of equality is negated by the economic structure, by the disconsonance between legal ideology and social reality epitomised in Anatole France's much-quoted observation that the law equally forbids rich and poor to sleep under bridges and beg, by the fact that the law *cannot* allocate equal rights in an unequal society (Marx, 1875, p.16; Corrigan and Sayer, 1979, p. 12).

The disconsonance can also exist *and be resolved* within the law itself; the ideology can also be managed out of existence within the law's own institutional structure.[17] It is certainly true that the law or any other ideology must not be dismissed as merely empty rhetoric; it must be taken seriously as a set of ideas with its own complex structure, substance, and methods. The operation of dominant ideology must be studied not only in terms of how it is put into practice in social interaction, not only in terms of its interrelationship with the social and economic structure of society, but also in terms of its own internal form and dynamics.

Notes

1 Taylor *et al.* (1971); Young (1971); Cohen (1971).
2 The inevitable exceptions are: in England, the prosecutor's right of appeal from a magistrates' court where the magistrate has dismissed a case on a point of law; in Scotland the prosecutor may not appeal against the decision of a High Court or Sheriff Court with a jury but may appeal by stated case against a summary acquittal. In addition, Andrew Ashworth has kindly pointed out that the Criminal Justice Act 1972 s. 36 introduced an opportunity to clear up disputed points of law even if the accused was acquitted, though he also notes that this is statistically insignificant.
3 Developed from a discussion in McBarnet 1978(b).
4 Surveys may not suggest any overwhelming belief by the British public at large in the impartiality of justice, but there is sufficient indignation expressed by middle-class liberal camps, when crime control or *raison d'état* too explicitly steamrolls over civil liberties, to suggest a belief on their part at least that the law is, or should normally be, geared to civil rights. Witness not just the liberal reaction to the law and order campaign of the 1970s but to specific incidents like the Hosenball affair (in 1977) or jury vetting in 1979.
5 See Chapter 3, p. 46.
6 See Chapter 3, p. 47.
7 See Chapter 3, p. 63.
8 See Chapter 3, p. 62.
9 See McBarnet, 1978(b); Kinsey, 1978; Picciotto, 1979.
10 See National Deviancy Conference/Conference of Socialist Economists proceedings, 1979.
11 This echoes Carson, 1974.
12 For example see Horwitz, 1977, Chapter 1 on early nineteenth-century American criticisms of the unpredictability of Common Law, or Bentham (discussed later).
13 T. Ellis-Lewis, 1930–32; Holdsworth, 1934.
14 R. Cross, 1977, pp. 105, 118.
15 At least on the basis of this analysis of *criminal* law.
16 Despite separating them before he actually engages in discussing them (1975, p. 260).
17 This is not of course to deny in any way that the structure and form of the law need themselves to be explained and related (though on the basis of two-way interaction rather than economic determinism) to their material base. (See for example Pashukanis, 1978.) It is merely to pose a supplementary issue.

[8]
Law and Capital: The Role of Legal Form and Legal Actors

Introduction

In the early days of radical deviance theory the links between law and capital seemed self-evident. Law was made by the state; the state was run by the ruling class; and law was obviously in the interests of the class which made it. Law which at first sight did not quite fit with the model, such as health and safety regulation or pollution control could be readily dismissed as merely ideology, ineffective in practice, or in the 'real' interests of the capitalist class — if not in the short term, in the long term, if not in their financial interests, in their ideological interests, if not in the interests of individuals nonetheless in the overriding interests of the survival of the class [1].

Capital*ists* were much in evidence. Did not big business lobby parliament for law in its interests, subsidize the parties that worked in its interest, use the threat of economic crisis to blackmail governments that imperilled its interests? The dominant picture was of an omniscient ruling class bulldozing its way through history intent on the pursuit of its own self-evident good. Law was simply an instrument to this undisputed end.

The model was exciting but, with the wisdom of hindsight, oversimple. Law, state and capitalist interest too often became interchangeable elements in an unholy trinity with little thought of the possibility of autonomy or conflict. Likewise the possibility of intra-class conflict was lost in the preoccupation with *inter*-class clashes and in the taken-for-granted absolute of a dominant interest so widely defined as to be irrefutable. Law was equated with statute, and with politics in the narrowest sense, with the apparatus of the courts relegated too readily to the role of enforcing rather than making law. Outcomes of forays into the courts were explained away by the biases of an upper class judiciary rather than by raising any deeper questions on the structure of law itself. The idea of law and rule by law were mere masks for realpolitik.

In more recent shifts to sounder theoretical ground, law and the state have come to be taken more seriously. The relative autonomy of the state has become an issue. Analysis has moved from concern with the relationship between specific laws and specific capitalists to the question of a deeper structural relationship between law and capital in its abstract forms [2]. More sophisticated analysis, especially of the form of law, has resulted. But in the concern to go back to theoretical basics the active human element which once provided such a central focus has been lost; and without it structural analysis remains a mere abstraction. In this context, probing the links between law and capital also means forging theoretical links between the structures of law and capital and the empirically observed human action which makes them work. This article suggests that one key link between the two is legal form, not as a conceptual abstraction, but as a facilitative structure available for *use* by legal actors.

Legal actors

Both the simple instrumental notion of law and the state and the structural approach can suggest too positive, re-ordained and easy a picture of the legal advantage of capital. Any notion that law, by the time it reaches the statute book or the enforcement agency, will inevitably be in the interests of the economically powerful, is belied by a close, empirical look at the real life operations of the individuals and institutions of capital. Far from happily accepting law and letting it run its course inexorably in their interests, the individuals and institutions of business and private capital in fact employ armies of City or Wall Street law firms, in-house corporate lawyers and accountants to work on the law on their behalf. The profession's task is to make the law fit the interests of its clients or employers, to seek ways of maximising any advantage in the law, even if it was intended for quite a different purpose, to avoid, without blatantly breaking, any disadvantageous law by careful manipulation of activities to fall just outside the law's ambit, or by careful interpretation of what the law might arguably mean. In short, if law is in the interests of capital it is not simply because it is handed over on a plate by predetermined structures, however complex, or by a captive state, but because of continuous work upon it on a day to day pragmatic basis to try to make if fit the specific, dynamic and sometimes conflicting interests of the moment.

The legal profession is an essential element in this from-the-ground-up perspective on the relationship of law and capital. Yet its role in determining the practical meaning of law — and whose interests it serves — has attracted remarkably little attention. Sociology has tended to be concerned more with the 'official' side of things, with the creation and imposition of law at the level of legislation and enforcement than with the underbelly of routine legal practice. Moreover, its approach to the profession has been largely in terms of access to dispute resolution — which segments of society are able to have their problems translated into legal terms, and professionally presented in court. The concern is with the availability of the profession rather than its role, concentrating on the *lack* of services to the lower class rather than the *nature* of services to capital, private and institutional. But lawyers are not significant simply for translating factual disputes into clearcut legal terms, for bringing ready-made law to some and not to others. Law, indeed is not so clearcut precisely because there is a second tier to lawyers' work. The lawyer's role is also to work *on the law*, to interpret it, to seek loopholes in it, to *make the law fit the facts* of the client's activities and interests. Lawyers are not just translators but transformers and transcenders of law [3].

What is more they are legal entrepreneurs, routinely 'making law' by establishing legal practice. Often the value of standard legal practice is precisely that it slips nicely between legislative or case law definitions of what shall or shall not be done, thus avoiding proscription, regulation or liability; or that it *uses* substantive law for purposes for which is was never designed. Ireland's study in this issue of the use of the legal device of incorporation demonstrates this nicely. As the utility of specific devices is recognized in the profession — via practice books that run into many editions — they may become standard legal practice, and indeed may eventually be endorsed in statute or case law. But it would be misleading to ascribe such law only to legislators or judges. Their role is one of endorsement. The origins of the law lie rather in the pragmatic practices of legal entrepreneurs serving their clients' interests.

Note the pragmatism involved. In its nature the legal profession does not act in a vacuum, in a world of merely intellectual problems; practical lawyers are always working in someone's interests. Law made from the ground up via established legal practice is inevitably law in the specific interests of the lawyer's clientèle. Given market forces, and despite exceptions such as organised labour and the limited mediation of legal aid, that clientèle is dominated by private and corporate capital. Hence the readier access of capital to the translation and construction of law in its interests rather than the mere translation of its disputes into law.

The questions of whose interests does the law serves and why, cannot then be answered merely by looking at the activities of legislators, enforcers or even the political processes and lobbying behind statutes. Law must be recognised as an ongoing, renegotiable phenomenon open to being worked on constantly from the ground up by those formally subject to it and by the mediating force of the legal profession. This helps provide one more perspective on *how* law can be made to work in the interests of capital. But it raises deeper issues too: why is such manipulation of the law possible? Underlying the operations of legal actors lie the permissive structures of legal form.

Legal form

The notion that law in the books is not always in the interests of capital can be amply demonstrated simply by noting that corporations, for example, regularly break the law, although it would be added in haste that they rarely meet their deserts in the way that non-white collar criminals do — the rich get richer and the poor get prison. Levi's paper in this issue neatly demonstrates the criminal law in *inaction*. What is of particular interest here however is not *crime* but the skill of manipulating the meaning of law or modifying activities regulated by it in order to maximise one's own interests by emasculating the law while still, literally at least, complying with it. The issue is the legitimate use of law not its abuse, the legitimate avoidance of law not its violation. The question is how is it possible for such manipulation, use and avoidance to be both possible and legitimate? Some beginnings of an answer can be found in the nature of law, in the institutional forms of law and in the overriding concept of the rule of law.

Law tends to be formulated in general statements which are neither all-inclusive, nor all-exclusive [4]. Hence the opportunity for those whose interests are in conflict with the law to devise methods of organising their affairs — or legal categories for describing the organization of their affairs — to keep them outside the ambit of the statutory clauses, or indeed to bring them *inside* their ambit if that is advantageous. Further legislation may seek to amend the situation, but it cannot in its nature cover all contingencies, so the game of legal leapfrogging goes on.

Devices to use or avoid the law can also be tested in court, but that process is far from automatic. Although sociology has tended to concentrate on criminal or other public law, much law is in fact private, that is to say initiated by private parties rather than state officials. The state provides the apparatus of the courts, legal procedure and substantive law but does not actively initiate their use. Since case law takes the form of dispute resolution, a device will only be tested if an interested party, actively involved in a legal dispute, has sufficient motivation and resources to challenge it. Until successfully challenged it may continue and indeed, as we have seen, extend to become standard legal practice.

Indeed, the combined forms of common law and private law provide a potent mechanism for manipulation of the law by those with adequate resources of finance and expertise. Cases — at least at the higher levels — do not merely resolve specific disputes but set legal precedents for the future. Hence the more general significance of judicial decision-making, and where any class advantage is detected, the tendency to explain it in terms of the social background and political leanings of judges. But judges also operate in a context. They do not initiate cases; interested parties do that, and their lawyers shape cases from the start by setting the agenda for decision-making. Again active subjects and their agents, the legal profession, have to be taken into account as the *initiators* of case law, and again where access to such services is governed largely by market forces this entree to *lawmaking* by the citizen may in practice be more readily available to corporate capital. Not of course that authoritative legal rulings on their affairs are necessarily what the institutions of capital want. The preference for autonomy is a point that sociologists of law should bear in mind in keeping the relationship of law and capital in perspective [5]. The form of private law is pertinent here too. Even if the validity of a specific issue is raised in a dispute, law can be manipulated by resourceful citizens or corporations in their own interests negatively as well as positively by a generous settlement out of court. This may be a small investment to avoid the risk of a dangerous principle being institutionalised in law, or to keep some convenient practice from being challenged.

Even in the realm of public law, with enforcement agencies available to take the intiative, there are obstacles to successfully challenging avoidance practices which slip the net of the law. These are not after all practices which *break* the law and clearly open the way for official intervention. The more skilfully constructed the device, the more difficult it is to challenge it on grounds of legitimacy. This is especially so where canons of literal interpretation are followed by the judges as, to draw on my own current research, in UK taxation cases for the last century or more. Literally millions of pounds saved by tax avoidance devices have been left in the taxpayer's pocket by judges operating on the principle that "if the ... Crown cannot bring the subject within the letter of the law, the subject is free, however apparently within the spirit of the law the case might otherwise appear to be" [6]. Of course judges do not always find themselves so tied to the words of the law [7] and there are no doubt deeper reasons for their tendency to literalness in some situations and not others. Nonetheless the point might be worth bearing in mind as a context for regulatory agencies' general tendency to negotiation rather than litigation. More generally, however, both the use and avoidance of law and the difficulties in challenging it stem from a much more fundamental aspect of legal form — the idea of the rule of law.

The notion that the rule of law can operate *for* citizens and against the state has, of course, become a familiar refrain since E.P. Thompson's sanctification of the ideology of the rule of law as operating at a real and not just an illusory level (1975). If the idea of the rule of law is to survive, rulers must be seen to some extent at least, to live up to it. The principles of law are not therefore mere empty rhetoric but a standard under which the working class has fought and won. The idea of the rule of law has thus been embraced by critical sociology. But perhaps the deeper message is not so much that the standard of the rule of law can fly over working class batallions but that it can fly over anyone. Indeed it may be that the rule of law is appealed to and used even more readily and routinely by the upper echelons of society.

The first response of the tax avoider in justifying activities or complaining about measures taken against them, is to invoke the rule of law. Tax avoiders — or avoiders of any law — carefully and deliberately operate in the grey areas of the law, in the no man's land of practices *not* specifically prohibited by law. Their activities are legitimate because there is no law against them. If *post hoc* anti-avoidance measures are introduced — and particularly when as has happened in recent months in the UK [8] a practice *is* declared illegitimate in case law, years after its carful construction within, it seemed, the letter of the law — the immediate response is a surge of letters to the press asserting the breakdown of the rule of law. The spectre of retrospective law is invoked, of state officials operating outwith the proclaimed law of the land and thus flagrantly flouting the principles of democracy and the rule of law. Ironical as it may be, manipulation and avoidance of the law is based firmly on and legitimated by the ideology that law rules.

The rule of law is not merely available to the underdogs as a stick with which to beat the top dogs' state. It is a stick used to good effect by the top dogs *against* the state, and of course often against the underdogs, who find their employers or landlords or suppliers have successfully avoided liability for compensation, slipped the net on rent control, or gone into liquidation with the consumer's money in their pockets — all through activities quite irreproachably within the letter of the law [9]. Though the rule of law has been embraced by critical sociology then, the irony is that with access to the law largely governed by market forces, it is in fact the wealthy who are more likely to successfully harness the rule of law to their cause.

Implications

Contemporary sociology has tended to concentrate on the oppressive side of law but it can be facilitative too and not only in its substance but in its form. Focussing on the *facilitative form* — and its *use* allows intellectual space for a more complex relationship between law, state and class. It allows for the possibility of the relative autonomy of the state by demonstrating how law can be manipulated *after the event, despite* rather than because of laws made and enforced by the state. Legislators and enforcers do not need to have been captured by big business, their intentions need not be underhand, for law to be ineffective in practice. The subjects of law and the profession that serves them can quite legimately make it so regardless.

This focus also requires something less than an omniscient all powerful ruling class, but allows for trial and error adaptation after the event. We have had historical pictures of farseeing individuals, the large capitalist lobbying *for* safety regulations, patently not in his immediate interests, because he could see it serving his longterm interests by wiping out smaller competitors who could not afford to comply. But we can also draw a picture of a multitude of less gifted and farsighted owners and managers of capital — or more often their professional advisers — looking less to their longterm interests than to immediate solutions to practical problems. Aware that new law does not suit them, they may well lobby against it but at the same time they will be working to construct loopholes which will seek to make it irrelevant anyway. The success or failure of pressure groups in the political process is not the end of the story. It is merely the beginning of lawyers' work to secure the same end by quieter means.

This focus suggests too that law is not the monopoly of the state. The tendency for sociology to concentrate on criminal law — even its forays into the world of big business tend to concentrate on fraud, anti-trust and other proscribed activities — has been at the expense of recognising the significance of civil and private law and of the entrepreneurial role of legal practitioners. The conventional notion that law lags behind business practice may well be totally misconstrued. It may be less that law lags behind business practice and more that businessmen and their lawyers make very sure they keep one step ahead of the law's proscriptions, that they keep literally outside and ahead of the law. Hadden's paper in this issue on corporate group management demonstrates this nicely. Quite contrary to the image of the state handing businessmen the law they want on a plate, one can draw just as powerful an image of the state in constant pursuit of the practices of capital, whether in business, the management of wealthy estates, trusts or taxation, and never quite catching up. The interests of state and capital can be in conflict; taxation again is a good example. But the history of taxation has been the history of loopholes with the well advised leapfrogging over each new tax hurdle before it has even passed through the legislature. In October 1983 the U.K Chancellor of the Exchequer announced plans to curb the avoidance device of offshore roll-up funds — a means of reducing tax liability from up to 75 per cent down to 30 per cent less inflation allowance, and indeed zero if the gain was less than £5000. Estimates indicate that over £2000 million was invested in this way in a single year, and this is only one tiny device among many. But when the announcement was published, the same newspaper pages that carried the story also carried an array of advertisements for new and better methods to achieve the same ends. The avoidance industry was one step ahead again.

More generally this notion of the facilitative form of law suggests one meeting point for structural theory and empirically observed human action. It is the *use* of legal form by active subjects and their lawyers which gives it effect;

it is the specific forms of law which permit and legitimise such use. Structure and action are intertwined.

Finally, this focus calls for less reification of the law. Indeed perhaps the instrumental metaphor of law and capital should be refined a little. Law is less a tool than a raw material to be worked upon. The tools are legal form and legal ideology, the artisan is the legal profession, the dominant client, capital.

Notes

1 For a good contemporary overview see Carson (1974).
2 For an original approach to this see Mott and Kay in this issue.
3 See Cain (1979).
4 See Picciotto (1979); McBarnet (1981, 1983) Ch. 8.
5 See Ferguson and Page in this issue on self regulation and Hadden on autonomous management structures.
6 *I.R.C.* v. *Barclays Bank* (1951) AC 421, p. 439.
7 McBarnet (1981, 1983).
8 *Furniss* v. *Dawson* AC 9th February 1984.
9 See Plett and Gessner in this issue for the fate of employees in bankruptcy cases.

References

Cain, M. (1979) The general practice lawyer and the client. *International Journal of the Sociology of Law* **7**, 331–354.

Carson, W.G. (1974) The Sociology of Law. In *Deviance and Social Control.* (Rock, P. & McIntosh, M., Eds). Tavistock: London.

McBarnet, D. (1981, 1983) *Conviction.* Macmillan: London.

Picciotto, S. (1979) The theory of the state, class struggle and the rule of law. In *Capitalism and the Rule of Law.* (NDC/CSE). Hutchinson: London.

Thompson, E.P. (1975) *Whigs and Hunters.* Allen Lane: London.

Part Four

Law, Class and Labelling

[9]

It's Not What You Do but the Way that You Do It: Tax Evasion, Tax Avoidance and the Boundaries of Deviance

The publication of the official crime rates every year routinely stimulates outcry over the breakdown of law and order. Large-scale white-collar crime has increasingly become front page news. Yet law and order may be undermined just as much, and quite routinely, by activities which are quite immune from any hint – or possibility – of criminal stigma. These activities are committed by people who, far from breaking the law, go to great lengths to ensure they abide by it, yet while abiding by the law they also escape its impact. They are both immune to legal requirements and prohibitions, *and* immune to any threat of penalty or stigma. This chapter explores this paradox in the context of a study of tax evasion and tax avoidance, and argues that social control through law is challenged not just by those who abuse the law but also, and perhaps more fundamentally, by those who *use* it.

THE RESEARCH PROJECT: BEYOND WHITE COLLAR CRIME

This research project was undertaken in the wake of increasing public discussion of the 'black economy', the scandal over large-scale tax evasion among casual workers on Fleet Street and the 'lump'[1] in the contracting industry, an estimate by the Chairman of the Board of Inland Revenue of 7.5 per cent of gross domestic product (or £3–3.5 billion) being lost to the revenue through tax evasion, and the exposure of large-scale VAT fraud. The Inland Revenue had been reorganised with the aim of greater enforcement efficiency; and the Keith Committee had been set up to explore the enforcement powers of the Revenue departments. In short, the effectiveness of tax law and enforcement was being defined as a problem.

There are several standard routes for research into an area like tax. One is the criminological route: why don't people comply with the law, why do they break it? Or the enforcement agencies are studied. Those enforcing the law are seen as having inadequate powers or resources, organisational pressures are seen as directing attention to some sorts of contravention of law rather than others. In studies of regulation, agencies are seen as 'captured' by those they are regulating, penalties are seen as too low to deter, establishing proof as too difficult to secure conviction, judges as too readily swayed by white-collar status. The institutional treatment of 'white-collar crime' as different from conventional crime, being dealt with by regulatory agencies rather than police, by regulatory law rather than criminal law, may be seen as undermining deterrence by removing the threat of criminal stigma. The substance of the legislation itself may be scrutinised, and seen as reflecting the interests and values of economic and political élites, because of lobbying or basic economic power. Law, class and state are seen as in alliance. Law apparently against the interests of economic élites is seen as merely symbolic; if legal control or legal regulation of white-collar activities fails, it does so because it was not, or not wholeheartedly, intended to do otherwise.

This research project set out with a different approach to the problem of legal control of white-collar activities. It suggested another model of law and another relationship for law, class and state. It treated law not merely as substance, a body of requirements and prohibitions served up on a platter to be accepted or rejected (often with the implication that for economic élites it could be accepted since it would inevitably be in their interests). Rather it approached law, *after* legislation, as a 'raw material to be worked on' (McBarnet, 1984), as something which might be used, manipulated, crafted to suit one's own interests. The approach focused less on the content of law – of legislation and case law – and more on exploring its methods, structures and ideologies, its 'facilitative form', and how it could be actively used.

From this model flowed several changes of perspective, framing theoretical issues in new ways. Law need not be a monopoly of the state (however constituted or influenced) but might be available to others to use *against* the state. Loopholes in the law might well be written into law as a matter of underhand policy, the product of symbolic law, but they might also be constructed after the event by active legal work. Legislation might be the end-product of a process of lobbying and subtler means of exercising power, but it might also be a starting point for a process of legal manipulation and creativity, *turning it, whatever* influences the lawmakers had sought to reflect or constrain, to the service of specific interests. In short, the primary concern of the project became the craft of law itself, the *post hoc* use and manipulation of law. The focus was on those subject to the law, on their role in actively constructing law in their own interests, and on the professional and financial advisers involved in the process. Indeed, the role of the professions as mediators working on the law for economic élites, to make it fit their interests, emerged as a key part of the research.

Our particular interest lay not in petty moonlighters (those who evade tax by failing to report income, often paid in cash) but in economic élites, on big business and on what our interviewees referred to as 'high net worth individuals' – people and organisations subject to redistributive taxes, who could afford expert professional advice and commission creative legal work; people and organisations for whom tax involved large sums of money, who had a strong economic motivation to escape it, but also (perhaps) a strong motivation to escape any risk of criminal stigma. One question for the research was whether and how both goals could be simultaneously achieved. If law was a 'material to be worked with', was it possible to use and manipulate law and legal institutions to achieve the same goals as crime – escaping legal prohibitions or requirements – without its risks of penalties or stigma? Studies of the politics and enforcement of law had shown some of the ways in which white-collar activities could escape the criminal label. What could a study focused on the 'craft of law' add?

As a result of these perspectives, the project took a rather unconventional approach. It did not look just at crime, nor even just at 'law-breaking', whether dealt with under criminal law or administrative law, as tax violations often are. Nor was it confined only to grey areas where law might or might not have been violated. We also went further and studied activities which were indisputably lawful, activities which did not merely escape investigation or labelling by enforcers, but which *could not* be defined as violations of law, which were indisputably on the right side of the boundary of deviance – yet which deliberately escaped tax payments just as surely as crime. Crime was thus set in a wider context, in which it became just one of several ways to escape social control.

Tax appealed as a good area to explore these issues – if a daunting one, in terms of its legal complexity and breadth (touched by many areas of law beyond the Finance Acts and tax cases), by its constant state of flux, by the moral ambivalence surrounding it, by its hybrid role between regulatory requirement and policy incentive, not to mention its decidedly boring image! It appealed as a good area to consider the relationship of law, class and state, since here, on the face of it at least, state interests in collecting tax and the interests of economic élites in non-payment could be at odds. It appealed because of the institutionalised recognition in tax law of a halfway house – tax avoidance – between full compliance with legal policy and the outright violation of the law represented by the category of evasion. It appealed because, along with the publicly expressed concern in the early 1980s over evasion and enforcement were other concerns over tax *avoidance* as a social problem.

Tax avoidance is neither criminal nor a regulatory offence. All the legal textbooks stress this. Yet the 1980s saw increasing discussion of an 'unacceptable' side of tax avoidance. Judges, seeking to develop a 'new approach' in the hope of controlling the unacceptable, referred to it as tax evasion. Inland Revenue and police acted together using techniques normally associated with large-scale criminal fraud to garner evidence for a case against the Rossminster operation,[2] which presented itself as selling not evasion but avoidance. The Keith Committee, in the few pages of its report devoted to tax avoidance, noted concern over 'schemes where the line between avoidance and evasion may have been crossed' (1983, p. 156). The hybrid term 'avoision' had been coined (Seldon, 1979). The relationship between tax evasion and tax avoidance thus offered a provocative case-study for exploring the boundaries between law-breaking and law-abiding activity.

Yet the area was not one which had attracted much empirical study. If tax evasion is still an under-researched area in the UK, it has at least attracted some study (see for example Cook, 1989). But the topic of tax *avoidance* was virtually virgin territory, having attracted little sociological attention and virtually no empirical research. In the United States, although there has been a recent burst of research on tax evasion and non-compliance, the issue of tax avoidance has been neglected, and this lacuna continues; for example, the major agenda for tax research set by a recent US task-force has neglected the issue of avoidance (Roth, Scholz and Witte, 1989). The area, in short, called out for empirical and conceptual attention.

The research, conducted with Dr Graham Mansfield, was based on in-depth technical interviews with 105 accountants, city solicitors, barristers, judges, merchant bankers, insurers, Inland Revenue officers, tax consultants and scheme promoters, along with contextual interviews, participation at professional conferences, observation of key cases in court, and legal and documentary analysis. Quotations from interviews in the text are referred to by the category of the source – solicitor, officer of the Inland Revenue, and so on.

The research explored how the boundaries are drawn between criminal and non-criminal means of escaping tax. It described the 'grey areas' at the boundaries, where the boundaries are transgressed without discovery, and the blurred edges of law-abiding and law-breaking activities where the two interlink. It looked at the process of labelling activities 'evasion' or 'avoidance', showing how 'labelled' taxpayers or their advisers could take not a passive but an active role in the process, ensuring, by a range of techniques involving what we called 'non-disclosing disclosure', that even in grey areas, a criminal label was made impossible (McBarnet, 1991). The taxpayer could also seize the initiative and pre-empt labelling altogether by using the letter of the law and the institutions, forms and methods of the law to construct alternative routes for escaping tax that were immune from social control. Just as the criminal label has been seen as a construct of enforcement decisions, so legitimacy was seen as a construct of taxpayer strategy.

Tax-avoidance devices were investigated and the legal techniques on which they were based analysed. We explored the role of the professions in relation to avoidance and evasion. We studied the construction and marketing of devices designed to escape the law and showed that marketed artificial tax schemes were not confined to a few 'unacceptable' marketeers, as media coverage of and judicial approaches to the Rossminster team might suggest, but that a central role was played by City institutions and the professions. We studied the manipulation by taxpayers of the institutions of law, showed how they sought to manage what we called the 'politics of case law' (McBarnet and Mansfield, 1986), or shopped around for barristers' opinions and used them as 'fraud insurance' (McBarnet, 1991) where there were doubts about the legal status of transactions, a technique which later came to light and may have been put in doubt by the County NatWest affair.[3]

The research analysed the problems for enforcers in dealing with dynamic and creative use of law, describing the cat-and-mouse games between regulators and regulated. Recent judicial attempts at a 'new approach' were researched and analysed (Mansfield, 1989), and more fundamental contradictions, dilemmas and problems for enforcement in the deeper structures of law were explored (McBarnet, 1988; McBarnet and Whelan, 1991a). The research raised serious doubts about the feasibility of effective legal regulation of economic élites with access to sophisticated legal skills.

Some of these specific areas of empirical research and analysis have been published elsewhere, others will be. This chapter is inevitably much more narrowly focused, drawing on the larger project to explore the boundaries between deviant and legitimate behaviour, how they are managed, and to touch on some of the problems raised for social control through law.

ESCAPING TAX AND ESCAPING SOCIAL CONTROL

Faced with income or a capital gain on which a tax bill will be due, there are four possible responses. First, taxpayers can declare the deal to the Inland

Revenue and pay the bill. Secondly, they can haggle over the bill or over what might count as allowances to set against it – an option open more readily to those with large bills or complex businesses than to the mass of taxpayers whose tax is deducted at source. Thirdly, they can opt to evade tax: not declare the deal to the Revenue; keep cash under the mattress; pack it in a suitcase and smuggle it offshore; or divert it through chains of companies, trusts and middlemen, through 'black holes', as one consultant called them, such as Luxembourg or Panama, to a Swiss bank account. Fourthly, they can put lawyers, bankers, accountants, consultants to work on dreaming up a scheme which will escape tax legally, utilising the techniques not of tax evasion but of tax avoidance.

Tax evasion and tax avoidance are both designed to escape payment of tax. Both are complex terms covering a range of activities on a spectrum from the indubitably lawful to the fraudulent. Tax evasion is illegal, subject to civil or criminal penalties. It may range from failure to make a return on time through to fraudulent understatements or claims. Deliberate fraud may be dealt with through criminal prosecution. In practice, the Inland Revenue prefers to negotiate a settlement, and prosecution is rare. But it is also Revenue policy to prosecute some cases of all classes of tax law for deterrence purposes. Tax evasion with intent to defraud the Revenue is thus vulnerable to criminal prosecution and the stigma of criminal labelling. Even if dealt with under administrative rather than criminal law, evasion carries the risk of civil penalties of up to treble the amount overdue, and although these may be negotiated downward, penalties are charged (according to the Keith Report (1983), in 73 per cent of investigations by the Special Investigations Office). What is more, although the risk of being caught may be low for sophisticated evaders, the risk of prosecution if caught may be higher. Witness Lester Piggott's three-year prison sentence for income tax and VAT fraud of over £3 million.

Tax avoidance, by contrast, attracts no legal penalties, criminal or civil. Avoidance ranges through a spectrum from the 'acceptable', sometimes distinguished as 'tax planning', to the 'unacceptable', which might be challenged in the civil courts, but in neither case is it criminal or a violation of regulatory law. On the contrary, the use of legal techniques to avoid tax has been upheld repeatedly in the courts as not only lawful but as a right, an entitlement, even (in the context of company directors' obligations *vis-à-vis* shareholders) a duty. Tax evasion thus escapes tax but not the threat of social control, carrying the risk of criminal stigma or penalties; tax avoidance escapes both tax *and* any risk of stigma or legal penalty. One is law-breaking activity, one law-abiding. One is on the right side, one on the wrong side of the boundaries of deviance. Legal textbooks refer repeatedly to the 'sharp distinction' between evasion and avoidance. What is the difference between them?

The answer from the legal textbooks is that tax evasion is characterised by deceit, misrepresentation and concealment. Criminal tax evasion might involve deliberately understating profits or other income with intent to escape tax, deliberately overstating expenses, fabrication of invoices, or making false claims to allowances. It would be fraudulent to give a false description of the legal status of a payment or person; or to deliberately fail to disclose income.

Yet tax *avoidance* schemes and devices have been constructed and used routinely by large companies, banks and the stock market, by nationalised industries and 'high net worth' individuals to achieve just these ends by legal means. Such devices have involved double charging of the same interest costs twice against profits; artificial creation of losses, not actually sustained, to set against capital gains, or of expenses to set against profits; transferring allowances from a taxpayer who would be entitled to them but cannot use them to offset against tax, to a taxpayer for whom they were not intended; legal laundering of interest into tax-free capital gains, or of capital assets into revenue expenses. We have analysed elsewhere some of the techniques for achieving these ends (McBarnet, 1988; 1992). A wide range of schemes is explored in the research project as a whole. The examples detailed below may give some flavour of what can be involved.

Double-Charging Interest: the Delaware Link

In 1985, according to Revenue estimates, £700 million in double-charged interest was set against the profits of multinational companies to escape due tax, and without legislation there was not a thing the Inland Revenue could do about it. How can you quite deliberately double-charge interest, that is, charge one interest bill twice over, without risking criminal stigma? If it is done by falsifying documents to produce two bills when you have really only paid one, or by passing expenses incurred by one taxpayer and used to offset tax to another to do the same, it is illegal evasion. But it could, via the 'Delaware link' scheme, be done legally.

The trick here was clever use of jurisdictional loopholes between different countries. In this case there was a clash of legal definitions on company residency between the USA and the UK, which the scheme exploited. The US definition depended on where the company was registered. The UK test was a matter of where the company's management and control were exercised. A company could therefore be registered in the US, usually in

Delaware with its particularly favourable company laws, hence the name, but be managed from the UK and meet the requirements for residency in both countries. Being defined as resident means a company is subject to that country's tax regime. However, double-tax treaties stop double-charging of tax on the same income. In the Delaware link scheme, dual residency, immune from double tax, was none the less used for the opposite purpose, to use one set of expenses to escape tax twice.

Dual resident companies were set up and used by multinational groups specifically and deliberately to create expenses which could be claimed in both jurisdictions by borrowing money from one of the other companies in the group, thus creating interest payments as an expense. The tax-allowance value of the expenses could be used, under group relief provisions, to offset against profits in the rest of the group – but it would be used twice: once in the United States, once in the UK.

Artificiality permeated the device. The money borrowed would not necessarily be used for any commercial purpose. The dual resident company might borrow to acquire a company already owned by another member of the group. 'It would have been more palatable if it had involved real fresh investment as opposed to just shunting debt around the group to restructure it for tax avoidance' (Inland Revenue). It was important that the dual resident company did not have taxable profits itself or the interest would simply be set against those, instead of being used twice for the rest of the group, so the money to pay for the interest would be carefully injected into the dual resident company in a form which did not give rise to taxable profits. Indeed a *double* dual resident structure might be used to separate interest going out from dividends coming in.

Of course, the interest which created the double-charged expense would be paid to another company in the group and tax might be payable on it as income. Indeed, internal movements of money within a group would, without tax-avoidance devices, be likely simply to cancel each other out. In this case, however, even if tax was paid on the interest received from the dual resident company, the double-charging of the interest in the two countries meant a bonus since tax would only be paid once but expenses would be charged twice. Not content with this bonus, however, some corporate tax planners would create structures which not only allowed double charging of the interest as expense, but avoided tax altogether on the interest received as income. This might be done by using a conduit company in a tax haven. The Inland Revenue stated that it did not in practice receive tax from the interest payment income. The group might therefore achieve double tax relief on an artificial interest charge which was itself received free of tax.

Expenses were thus manufactured and double-charged to offset against tax and cut the tax bill. But the scheme was not evasion, just clever avoidance. It did not break the law; it used the law. The group complied with the rules of both UK and US tax law and in doing so quite legally charged the same expenses twice.

Manufactured Losses

Claiming losses to offset against gains is another way to cut the tax bill. Where real losses are sustained this is just as intended by legal policy. Where losses are faked, perhaps by false invoices, this would be evasion. But 'losses' which are not actually sustained can also be used to cut the tax bill via tax avoidance.

If shares rise in value, the gain, above a specified exemption level, is subject to capital gains tax. If some lose in value and some gain, the loss is offset against the gain in calculating the net gain to be taxed. One way to save tax is to sell shares at a time when they are making a loss. But this would be rather pointless; people buy shares to make gains, not losses. The investor would normally want to hold on to the shares until they rise in value, and sell them at a gain. But what if there was a tax-avoidance scheme which allowed you to have your cake and eat it, to sell your shares at a loss *and* keep them to rise in value? This is what the technique known as 'bed and breakfasting' (discussed in more detail in McBarnet, 1992) achieved. Shares showing a current loss would be sold on to a broker to crystallise the loss and produce a legal document to prove it. But they would then be repurchased the next day at virtually the same price so that they could be retained until they rose in value. By the time they were sold, the gain might in turn be cancelled out by other paper losses, current or stockpiled. The Stock Exchange's 'Black Monday' in October 1987 was seen by tax advisers as an ill wind, since mass bed and breakfasting was seen as a way of cancelling out capital gains for years to come.

There have been many attempts at using legal means to create artificial but allowable losses to reduce tax bills. A series of transactions might be set up to produce a self-cancelling effect for tax purposes, or produce a paper loss in an exempt area to offset a real gain and eliminate the tax on it without actually sustaining the loss. One which was challenged by the Inland Revenue in a celebrated case was the 'exempt debt capital loss scheme', one of many tax-avoidance schemes created and marketed in the 1970s by the Rossminster team.

The nub of the exempt debt capital loss scheme was to produce an artificial loss to offset against a real capital gain to produce a zero tax situation. One of these clients, whose case was to reach the House of Lords in 1981, was a farmer, Ramsay. Ramsay has sold land at a substantial capital gain. The Rossminster scheme created a loss of £175,000 – it could have been any figure, as required by the client – to neutralise it. The scheme required two companies and a subsidiary controlled by the taxpayer, and two companies controlled by the scheme promoters. It involved two loans, one share issue, the exercise of options on interest levels (the interest rate on one loan was changed from 11 per cent to 22 per cent, on the other from 11 per cent to zero), the sale of the 22 per cent loan to a company controlled by the scheme promoter, which then sold the loan to the subsidiary of taxpayer company B, two liquidations, loan repayments, and exchange of shares for loanstock in another promoter-controlled company. The result of all this shuffling around was that a paper gain and an equivalent paper loss were created out of nothing. As Lord Templeman put it, it was a 'circular game in which the taxpayer and a few hired performers act out a play; nothing happens save that the Houdini taxpayer appears to escape from the manacles of tax' (*W. T. Ramsay Ltd* v *Inland Revenue* [1981]).

The object of the exercise, however, was that something should happen, not in the world of real money, where the taxpayer should be no worse off for all the transactions except for the cost of the fees to the scheme's creators, but in the world of legal status. The aim was to create an unreal but legally recognised loss. The mesh of deals aimed at establishing, first, an artificial gain which would not be taxable, since the claim was that it fell into the exempt category of a debt, and, secondly, an artificial loss. This artificial loss would not simply be offset against its mirror-image artificial gain because that gain was not taxable anyway. Instead, it would be left as a free-floating loss to offset against the real gain which had brought the client to Rossminster in the first place.

Schemes to create artificial losses were themselves usually highly artificial, involving specially created companies which were never intended to trade, and based on transactions within a network of companies or trusts or banks or charities often controlled by the people selling the scheme and never intended to be more than temporary, paper-only deals. Those involved in buying and selling the scheme might then sit around a table and, wearing different hats as board members of the different companies every few minutes or every few days, sign cheques from one company to the next. Despite the large sums of money apparently being signed away, there were, other than the promoters' fees, no real costs. 'No one let go of the corner of the cheque', as one Revenue officer put it. The transactions and cheques went round in circles. But the object of the exercise was not simply to go round in circles. The objective was rather to set up a magic circle which would make a real capital gain vanish, not by fraud, not by non-disclosure of gains, not by fabrication of false invoices, but by the creation of an artificial but legally recognised loss, by legal avoidance.

EVASION AND AVOIDANCE: WHAT IS THE DIFFERENCE?

As *avoidance* a scheme may or may not succeed. Successful avoidance, accepted by the Revenue – as in the case of the Delaware link – or by the courts despite a Revenue challenge, is, by any definition, criminal or civil, a lawful method of escaping tax. The exempt debt capital loss scheme, outlined above, eventually failed in the House of Lords. The example was selected deliberately. Avoidance can fail. But so long as the companies used are properly constituted, the laws on the transactions complied with, the panoply of *legal propriety* met, the scheme is on the right side of the criminal line. It is an unsuccessful attempt at *legal avoidance* not evasion.

What then is the difference between tax evasion and tax avoidance? The simple answer may be: it's not what you do but the way that you do it. The motivation behind both approaches is the same: to escape tax. The effects are the same; public funds are depleted. In substance the activities – double-charging interest, claiming losses not actually sustained – may seem indistinguishable from false claims and declarations. In law, however, they are very different and the key difference lies in the means employed. Tax evasion methods simply ignore or break the law. Tax avoidance devices *use* the methods of law to neutralise its impact. Sometimes evasion is quite explicitly converted to avoidance; one solicitor discussed advising the use of a non-resident trust to escape tax rather than his client's proposal of a 'dummy – non-existent – relative'. By using rather than abusing the law, taxpayers can achieve precisely the same end as evasion without any of the risk of criminal stigma or regulatory penalty which evasion entails. Indeed, tax avoidance has a double purpose: escaping tax *and* doing it legally.

Thus Delaware link companies did not fraudulently present themselves as claiming interest in one country only. They claimed in both because the law of both countries allowed it. They went to great lengths to take advantage of the situation. It was very far from simply being a take-up of allowances explicitly intended for them. Nor was it simply a matter of slipping into an accidental but convenient loophole. Highly complex and artificial structures and transactions were contrived in order to exploit fully the opportunity which the gap between jurisdictions presented. The loophole was stretched far beyond its immediate scope by creative legal engineering. But no rules were broken, no transactions were hidden, no fraudulent claims or misrepresentations made. On the contrary, part of the reason for the rise in the use of the device between 1983 and 1985 (from 50 companies claiming £400 million in relief to nearly double) was the public statement by a reluctant Inland Revenue that it was, in the present state of the law, quite lawful. What the multinational companies involved were doing was not prohibited by law; on the contrary, the device was constructed *from* the law. They had not broken the law but worked creatively on its fabric and turned it to their advantage.

Likewise the artificial losses created by the exempt debt scheme involved no misrepresentation. The fictional loss claimed was not a forged or fake invoice, but a legal fiction, neatly crafted from the raw materials of law. The hallmarks of criminal evasion are misrepresentation or concealment; the hallmarks of legal avoidance are legal transformation of one thing into another: income into capital, equity into debt, and so on. Law is full of fictions – the legal distinction between companies and their owners, for example, or trusts and their beneficiaries; legally recognised fictions do not constitute fraud; only misrepresenting, forging or concealing them does. Receiving money in the name of non-existent people – the Mickey Mouses of Fleet Street – constitutes evasion; using specially created legal personae – companies or trusts – to receive money constitutes avoidance. As one Revenue officer put it: 'If it's make believe and you tell us, it's OK. It's only if you tell us it's real when it's not, that it's evasion.'

Getting the form right effectively provided what I have discussed elsewhere as 'fraud insurance' (McBarnet, 1991). Criminal acts require proof of intention – '*mens rea*' – and although in some areas of law that has proved less of a burden than it might seem, it is difficult to sustain proof of intention to break the law, when the whole strategy of avoidance is to do it legally. Often there will be counsel's opinion to back up the taxpayer's interpretation of his legal obligations, and this may be enough in itself to distinguish avoidance from evasion. Law, after all, is arguable; getting it wrong is not of itself an indication of evasion if you can provide evidence that you tried to get it right. You may, as it happened, have had to go to rather a lot of trouble to get it right. Interviewees referred to the practice of 'opinion-shopping', going to not one but a number of barristers for an authoritative opinion on the legality of a scheme until one provided the 'right' opinion – the one the customer wanted to hear. Barristers' opinions might be managed too (McBarnet, 1991). The fraud insurance supplied by 'trying to get it right' might itself be the product of a process of manipulation. Even getting the procedures *wrong* need not of itself constitute evasion unless there was intent to break the law. As one Inland Revenue officer put it: 'If it's sloppy technically it doesn't mean there was intent to evade. In fact it means there was intent to do it properly.'

So those interviewed tended to lay great stress on getting the form right, getting the procedure right, keeping precisely within the rules: 'getting funds in the right place at the right time' (City solicitor); recommending only 'technically impeccable schemes' (barrister). Some schemes were particularly admired for their 'beautiful carpentry' (barrister); or distinguished from less-marketable products by their 'technical elegance' (accountant). The Keith Committee discussed schemes which 'typically involved a complicated series of transactions prepared with full legal formalities' (1983, p. 159). Some of these schemes could involve 250 legal documents (consultant). 'Avoidance is perfectly legal,' said one Inland Revenue officer. 'I'm not against it. But if they do it they must do all the steps for real.'

This ideology of strict adherence to form, legal technicality, doing it properly, was contrasted with those who slipped over the line into the fraudulent: 'the insurance salesman, backdating documents, who has a blind spot, doesn't see the difference between right and wrong' (barrister); the standing insurance joke about backdating to beat the midnight deadline before the change of rules on controlled company pensions in 1988 – 'It's been a funny week, Tuesday the 13th, Wednesday the 13th, Thursday the 13th . . . .' Inland Revenue officers talked of the move into fraud coming where taxpayers do not go through all the proper steps but say they have. Evasion came into play when taxpayers got the form wrong and pretended they had got it right.

But drawing the line in this way left some Revenue officers bemused:

> One problem has always bothered us – the genuineness of documents. Where a scheme involves three hours of meetings with a specified order of events and cheques passing round at appropriate moments, they would be foolish if they didn't get it right and it seems an insult to their intelligence to ask for the documents. But sometimes they do forget to minute, say, a commercial motive. If we ask for the minute they'll manufacture it, and why not, they'd say, let's keep the silly Inland Revenue happy, we just forgot to minute it at the time. But the manufacture of evidence is criminal. Yet morally, if they just forgot it, is that worse than the whole business of creating a circle of artificial transactions in the first place?

The perplexity stemmed from the fact that it was the technicality and not the pervasive avoidance intent that breached the law. Getting the form right kept the device on the right side of the boundaries of deviance even where in substance, purpose and effect it did not differ from evasion. The means justified the end.

GREY AREAS AT THE BOUNDARIES

It would be quite wrong to slip into any assumption that economic élites always opt for tax *avoidance* rather than evasion. It takes only a glance at the front pages of newspapers in the last year to underline the reality of outright white-collar *crime*. And for every deviant activity that is discovered there may be many more which are not. Despite being based on interviews, which would hardly seem a medium for uncovering the 'dark figure' of evasion, this research project found instances where avoidance transgressed the boundaries into evasion, overlapped with evasion, or was interlinked with it.

In practice the line between evasion and avoidance may be hazy. 'Offshore invoicing', for example – a means of moving money out of Britain to a low-tax or no-tax jurisdiction – might range from the genuinely commercial to the fraudulent. It might involve a genuine invoice from one company to another (related) company for actual and precise services rendered at market prices. It might be an invoice from a real offshore office for vaguer management charges by staff based there. It might be an invoice issued from an office which is no more than a brass plate to show company registration. It might be an invoice on neat headed paper from a non-existent company. Where, asked the Revenue officer who gave this example, do you draw the line? The first is clearly legal but what of the others? In his terms of legitimate and non-legitimate 'make-believe', the first, entailing real expenses, is clearly legitimate; the fourth, entailing a fake invoice, clearly criminal; but what of those in between? There is a spectrum of greys at the boundaries of legality and criminality. Sometimes, as another Revenue officer observed, what begins as avoidance slips in practice through the spectrum into activities that border on or constitute evasion. An offshore company may be set up in a legally impeccable way for the initial purpose of avoidance, technically within the rules, but then become 'a vehicle for criminal extraction', for example via the issue of completely spurious invoices.

Avoidance and evasion may also interlink. The link may be distanced and indirect, akin to receiving stolen goods, perhaps unwittingly but none the less receiving the benefit of someone else's crime. Interviews suggested that this kind of interlinking can creep into bona fide avoidance schemes.

One example occurred in the context of selling-on tax-shelter leasing businesses.

In the late 1970s and early 1980s, companies making profits, and therefore incurring corporation tax bills, could reduce their tax by going into the leasing business. At the time, as an incentive to investment in equipment, the government allowed 100 per cent of the value of capital equipment to be set against profits in the first year of the purchase, thus dramatically reducing or eliminating the tax bill otherwise due. Many large companies which did not themselves want equipment but did want to wipe out their tax bills, bought equipment and leased it on to others, first of all taking advantage of their legal ownership of the equipment to take 100 per cent capital allowances to wipe out the tax due on profits in their other businesses. Capital allowances were only intended to defer tax, however. Once the 100 per cent allowances were gone, the income from the leases would be taxable. This moment was delayed by writing more and more new leases to keep up the allowances, but then a change in law removed 100 per cent capital allowances, and with them much of the tax appeal of the leasing business. The deferred tax started to catch up. If the business was sold on, its value would be reduced by the fact that tax would now be due on the income.

But what if tax were not due? If the business could be sold on to a loss-making company, it would be able to continue taking the leasing income without having to pay tax since its existing losses would wipe them out. Such a company could afford to pay higher prices for the business than the value of the leasing company otherwise (in terms of due income *less* tax) would justify. The result was a strong market for leasing companies and a tax-free escape for those companies who could no longer get tax benefits and wanted out. So far so good – for everyone except the Revenue at least, who had seen capital allowances claimed without ever getting any tax back on the resulting income. But the market was perfectly lawful.

Our interviews suggested, however, that purchasing companies paying higher prices were not always genuine loss-making companies, that the techniques employed to make above-market-price 'dicky bids', as one City solicitor termed them, slipped sometimes into evasion, as when the ultimate buyer escaped tax, not by offsetting against genuine losses but by simply 'doing a bunk out of the country'. A solicitor coming up against such offers when acting for a leasing company vendor might sniff a 'smell of fraud' about them, but would, according to this solicitor, 'need immense foresight to advise against the higher offer'. Vending companies would be likely to insist on indemnities from the purchasing company against any tax that might arise, and thus keep their own heads off the block of tax or opprobrium. But the implication is that tax avoidance might sometimes depend on *someone's* evasion.

Sometimes, what is in general an avoidance scheme depends at some point on something just a bit more akin to evasion. One key criterion used to distinguish evasion from avoidance is disclosure: if the techniques used are legal it should be possible to disclose them openly with impunity: 'you must feel you are no worse off if you have to lay all your cards on the table', as a representative of the Law Society put it.

None the less interviewees described to us examples of complex tax-avoidance schemes where the assumption was that the scheme might *not* work 'if all the cards had to be laid on the table'. One complex deal, for example, depended in part for its tax-efficiency on neglecting to disclose at the time clearance was given (Inland Revenue clearance in advance of a deal that, in the form proposed, it will not be taxable) that a third-party bid was anticipated. This was 'the sensitive bit', as the interviewee describing the deal put it, which might affect the tax consequences of the deal. Tax avoidance, then, cannot always be taken at face-value. What are apparently clever and strictly legal avoidance schemes may need careful scrutiny. It may be that, at one point or another in the complex chain of events, avoidance breaks down, with legal cleverness replaced by simply hiding key facts, and dependence on legal rules replaced by a dependence on not being caught. A complex scheme which is largely avoidance may sometimes *incorporate*, however fleetingly, elements rather more akin to the techniques of evasion.

Indeed, subtle concealment is rather more characteristic of routine dealings over tax than the disclosure distinction might suggest. In 1978 the Chancellor of the Exchequor criticised a 'new form' of tax avoidance 'accompanied by a level of secrecy which amounts almost to conspiracy to mislead'. It emerged in our interviews that the promoters of the schemes referred to here required their clients, and the professional advisers who brought them there, to sign pledges of secrecy. This was an extreme measure of concealment. Our research suggests, however, that tax is routinely escaped simply by using techniques which prevent the Revenue from realising the real nature of transactions, not just by 'ghosts' or 'moonlighters' who evade tax by failing to disclose their existence or their earnings, but by subtler methods of information control, by a range of techniques of information management, which we have termed 'non-disclosing disclosure' (detailed in McBarnet, 1991). The relevant information *is* disclosed, keeping the taxpayer on the right side of the criminal line, but it is presented in way that will not attract tax simply because it will not attract attention. Key information might be buried, noted inconspicuously in passing; hidden in a welter of irrelevancies; spread between pages 12, 119 and 164, when their tax significance depends on being related to each other. Activities might be 'redescribed' (accountant). The *method* echoes, however subtly, the techniques of concealment associated with evasion, rather than the open disclosure supposed to typify avoidance; and the maintenance of legitimacy may be more a tribute to the manipulability of the criminal boundary than to a clear distinction of approach. Providing a legal definition of the line between evasion and avoidance – disclosure – simply leads to manipulation of behaviour to fit the definition in form but not in substance.

Evasion and avoidance may interrelate in another way. The very fact that a concept of legal avoidance is officially recognised may serve to *disguise* outright evasion and perhaps even foster it. Techniques employed in legal tax avoidance are so complex, circuitous and artificial that they may accustom tax inspectors and investigators to the normality of *deviousness* and so make it harder for them to spot actual *deviance*.

MANAGING THE BOUNDARIES OF DEVIANCE

Studying the boundaries between tax evasion and tax avoidance shows, first, that the difference between deviant and legitimate behaviour may be more blurred than the legal textbook presentation of a 'sharp distinction' suggests. The Keith Committee on the enforcement powers of the Revenue departments noted concern over 'schemes where the line between avoidance and evasion may have been crossed' (1983, p. 156); and Inland Revenue officers interviewed observed that 'some of the avoidance cases now seem very near the line'. Our data suggest that sometimes the line is crossed, and that sometimes the distinction between evasion and avoidance can be very blurred indeed. Far from there being a 'sharp distinction' between evasion and avoidance, then, there is a complex interrelationship between the two in the grey area at the boundaries.

Secondly, the research shows that where clear lines are drawn to distinguish evasion from avoidance, these lines can in practice be used and managed by taxpayers and their advisers. The Keith Committee assumed as a basic principle that 'as a general rule, particular consequences should follow particular acts or omissions in every case. In this way everyone knows where they stand and compliance is likely to be improved' (1983, p. 9). But the compliance secured by clarity and certainty in enforcement may only be compliance in form rather than substance, as in disclosure which does not disclose. Policy recommendations need to take account of the scope for active manipulation by those allegedly 'subject' to the law, who are, on the contrary, often subjecting the law to their own uses. Focusing on how the boundaries of deviance are managed may also offer a new perspective on the concept of 'labelling'. The process by which people are labelled deviant or not is usually approached from the perspective of those enforcing the law. Focusing on those 'subject' to the law, and on how they can play with, or work on, the boundaries of deviance, suggests that the 'labelled' can in fact be in control of the labelling process.

Thirdly, this chapter shows that law can be not just a mechanism of social control but a mechanism for escaping it. What is being used in the management of boundaries is the law, its rules, institutions and forms. Law can be used to construct techniques which escape tax but also provide immunity from control. In defining what is a violation, law also defines what is not. In defining what is to be taxed, law also defines what is not to be taxed. In defining what is to be controlled, law also defines the limits of legal control. Boundaries mark the point for keeping out as well as for keeping in. Enforcers are not always limited by the law, but neither are those 'subject' to it. If law is a 'material to be worked on', these rules can be used and manipulated. The rules can be changed, the boundaries can be moved to catch the escapees. Loopholes can be plugged, as happened eventually with the Delaware link. But the solution is not always simple. Avoidance is dynamic and creative. If the boundaries move, so do the guidelines; and the activities may simply be adapted to the new rules. When rules were introduced to catch bed and breakfasting, by cancelling out the overnight sale and purchase against each other before calculating the tax due, the consequence was 'weekending': getting round the new rules by spreading the deals over two different stock exchange periods and using two brokers. More complex adaptations are also commonplace, and where specific devices are successfully stopped, new schemes are soon on the market aiming to replace them. Changing the rules may affect only the specific form of avoidance, not the scope for avoidance *per se*.

Of course, one way to stop manipulation of the boundaries is to remove them, or at least to refuse to map out where they are. This indeed is exactly what happened in the *Ramsay* case (and in *Furniss* v. *Dawson* which followed it). The judges reinterpreted the boundaries by looking beyond the form of the transaction to its real tax-avoidance purpose, and, despite the fact that each step in the transaction was technically correct, despite the fact that the forms employed were recognised legal forms, they refused to accept that the schemes could lawfully escape tax. What is more, instead of setting up clear precedents for the future, they explicitly stated that the law was still evolving. The result was a storm of protest, a powerful lobby, a curtailment of the new approach and a new set of guidelines. The factors involved in this process, the ambivalence of the judges, even in the new approach, and the issue of whether its demise was inevitable, are major questions tackled in the research but beyond the scope of this chapter. However, the tale, even told in brief, does indicate another level in the use of law to avoid control; in this case the ideology of the rule of law was invoked to argue against retrospective law and to argue for certainty and clarity; in short, to argue for clear boundaries. We are back full circle to clear boundaries and scope for boundary management.

This scope is not, however, equally available to all. This is partly because people dependent on payments made by others and taxed at source – most wage-earners – have little scope for juggling the declared figures. The choice then is between evasion (say, by 'moonlighting' – working for cash and not declaring it) and paying tax (which has been, in fact, already deducted). But avoidance may not be an option anyway because creative legal services do not come cheaply. Indeed, the most successful schemes are unlikely to be the popular 'mass-marketed' ones cited here (interviews suggested that it was in part the off-the-peg nature of the Ramsay scheme that provoked reaction), but the one-off, tailor-made schemes, cost-effective only for tax bills which one City solicitor, disdaining figures, described as 'more than you could possibly contemplate', evidently considering the sums beyond the sociological imagination. Even in tax *avoidance* there are strata and stratified success.

POSTSCRIPT: THE CHALLENGE FOR CONTROL

Avoidance poses a different kind of problem for control from evasion. Evasion and 'grey areas' play on problems of enforcement. The 'sensitive bit' in the 'grey' deal mentioned above would be problematic if it was discovered. Another interviewee discussed a transaction where a key factor in assessing whether or not it would succeed in escaping tax was the calculation that the Inland Revenue would not spot it. Indeed, there was concern lest the accounting practice of making provision for a tax bill which might have to be paid would 'make the Revenue wake up'. This was not seen as verging on evasion, but as 'capitalising on the real world' of, in this case, likely Revenue policing problems. The Inland Revenue faces a wide range of problems which impede enforcement, some familiar in any enforcement agency, some peculiar to white collar crime, some unique to tax. The research project describes and analyses the problems involved. In theory, however, one could conceive of an enforcers' ideal world with the requisite resources, powers and expertise to make enforcement, and with it social control of evasion and the grey areas, more effective.

Pure avoidance presents a different challenge altogether. It does not rely on concealment but on confrontation. Though, in practice, even techniques of avoidance that are assumed watertight are not 'shouted from the rooftops' (solicitor), they should escape tax and control even if they are discovered. Hence the Law Society representative's rule of thumb: 'you should feel you are no worse off if you have to lay all your cards on the table'. More tax inspectors with more motivation, training, experience, resources, might help control tax evasion and the grey areas, but would not prove the panacea for dealing with avoidance. Although discovering avoidance can itself be a problem, it is not the fundamental one. The fundamental problem is how to stop it once you've found it. How do enforcers enforce the law when the law has not been breached? How do they use strategies to secure compliance when the literal requirements of law are already being met? It may be argued that the issue is more one of prevention than *post hoc* control. Aren't laws free of loopholes possible? But this may be to take too reified a view of loopholes and of law. Tax-avoidance devices do not just depend on finding loopholes built into particular clauses of legislation; they are also complex creative constructions using basic legal forms and drawing on many statutes, cases and jurisdictions. So long as the professions – and other dealers in law – can work creatively on the fabric of law in their clients' best interests, it is difficult to see how every potential device could be foreseen and prevented.

Tax avoidance thus poses a major problem for social control, not only, in the narrow sense of this chapter, of escaping both tax and the potential penalties or stigma of evasion, but also in the wider sense of challenging the limits of civil as well as criminal law. Does this challenge to control extend beyond tax? Tax is in many ways a peculiar branch of law and some problems may be unique to it. The challenge to control posed by using rather than abusing the law, by legal avoidance, needs to be studied in other contexts, and we are already engaged in follow-up work in the area of finance.[4] However, the implication of this research, with its emphasis on the manipulability of law, and on the scope of bending it to specific interests regardless of the intentions behind it, is that economic élites with the resources to buy legal creativity can also buy immunity from law.

NOTES

1. Tax enforcement problems are created by the system of labour-only subcontracting in the construction industry, colloquially known as the 'lump'. The subcontractor does not supply any materials but only labour, with payment usually on a piecework basis. This allows workers to become self-employed and avoid Pay-As-You-Earn tax, with a real problem arising in collecting tax later if evasion practices are used. For more detail, see Smith (1986). The tax evaded was reported for the year ended 1985 at £35 million (Cook, 1989, p. 46).
2. Roy Tucker and Ronald Plummer set up an organisation specialising in creating and marketing tax-avoidance devices which attracted a good deal of adverse publicity in the late 1970s and early 1980s. See Tutt (1985) for details.
3. County NatWest Bank was investigated by the Department of Trade in 1989 for failing to disclose shareholdings. Among the resulting arrests was that of a solicitor from one of the advising firms.
4. A study of off-balance-sheet financing (McBarnet and Whelan 1991a, 1991b).

REFERENCES

Cook, D. (1989), *Rich Law, Poor Law* (Milton Keynes, Bucks.: Open University Press).

Keith Committee on the Enforcement Powers of the Revenue Departments (1983), *Report* (London: Her Majesty's Stationery Office) Cmnd. 8822.

McBarnet, D. (1984), 'Law and capital: the role of legal form and legal actors', *International Journal of the Sociology of Law*, August.

McBarnet, D. (1988), 'Law, policy and legal avoidance', *Journal of Law and Society*, **15**(1) Spring; special issue edited by R. Cotterrell and B. Bercusson.

McBarnet, D. (1991), 'Whiter than white collar crime: tax, fraud insurance and the management of stigma', *British Journal of Sociology*, **42**(3).

McBarnet, D. (1992), 'Legal creativity: law, capital and legal avoidance', in M. Cain and C. Harrington (eds), *Lawyers' Work* (Milton Keynes, Bucks: Open University Press).

McBarnet, D. and Mansfield, G. (1986), 'The politics of case law', paper presented at the Law and Society Association Conference, Chicago.

McBarnet, D. and Whelan, C. (1991a), 'The elusive spirit of the law: formalism and the struggle for legal control', *Modern Law Review*, **54**(6).

McBarnet, D. and Whelan, C. (1991b), 'Creative compliance and the defeat of regulation: a case study in corporate finance', forthcoming.

Mansfield, G. (1989), 'The new approach to tax avoidance', *British Tax Review*, (1).

Roth, J., Scholz, J. and Witte, A. D. (1989), *Taxpayer Compliance* (Pittsburgh, Pa: University of Pennsylvania Press).

Seldon, A. (ed.) (1979), *Tax Avoision* (London: Institute of Economic Affairs).

Smith, S. (1986), *Britain's Shadow Economy* (Oxford: Clarendon Press).

Tutt, N. (1985), *The Tax Raiders* (London: Financial Training Publications).

CASES

Furniss v *Dawson* [1984] 2 WLR 226.
Ramsay, W. T. v *IRC* [1981] 2 WLR 449.

[10]

Whiter than White Collar Crime: Tax, Fraud Insurance and the Management of Stigma

ABSTRACT

Based on an empirical study of tax evasion and avoidance, this article explores the boundaries of deviant and lawful activities and shows how those boundaries are manipulated to ensure that tax payers can both try to escape tax *and* stay on the legal side of the boundary. It describes techniques of 'non-disclosing disclosure' and 'fraud insurance', to show how the labelling process can be managed. It concludes that labelling theory should take account of the scope for self-labelling and the management of stigma. It suggests a rethinking of the classic debate over the definition of white collar crime.

Tax evasion is a term usually reserved for non-payment of tax by means of criminal fraud or other violations of law. Tax avoidance involves minimising or eliminating a tax bill legally. On the face of it the first is a subject appropriate to white collar crime research; the second is not. It is a legitimate activity, whiter than white collar crime. It falls on the right side of the boundary between lawful and deviant behaviour.

The boundary between lawful and deviant behaviour, however, is not as clear as it might sound. In the first place transactions themselves may straddle the boundary, avoidance slipping into evasion, or being permeated by it. Second, the location of a transaction on the right or wrong side of the boundary depends on how those enforcing the law decide to label it – classic labelling theory. Third, the boundaries can be stretched not just by regulators but also by the regulated. What classic labelling theory does not take into account is the scope for those apparently subject to the law to turn the tables on law enforcement, to actively take the legal initiative and 'launder' activities into a non-taxable form. By using rather than breaking the law, however, they definitively label their activities legitimate and themselves as beyond the reach of criminal law enforcement.

The research project* on which this paper draws, explores techniques of legal tax avoidance and how they work. It shows *how* the law can be used – by individuals, small firms and especially big business – to gain all the benefits of evasion – escaping tax – without the potential costs – penalties and stigma. It shows how sophisticated taxpayers – or non-taxpayers – can eschew fraudulent fake expenses, false representation of deals or non-declaration of interest or dividends, and opt instead for achieving the same results by legal techniques. Such well-tried devices as the 'Delaware Link', 'bed and breakfasting' or 'bondwashing' have, in their time, allowed, without any recourse to criminal law, double charging of the same interest costs twice against profits, the artificial creation of losses, not actually sustained, to set against capital gains, and the legal laundering of interest into tax-free capital gains, all for the purpose of quite deliberately escaping tax.[1]

This paper is also concerned with manipulation of the boundary between lawful and deviant activity, but here the focus is on the enforcement process and some of the ways in which this process is managed by taxpayers and their advisers, or by tax scheme promoters, in their own interests. Drawing on interviews with 105 accountants, city solicitors, barristers, judges, merchant bankers, insurers, Inland Revenue officers, tax consultants and scheme promoters,[2] along with contextual interviews, and legal and documentary analysis, the paper examines how the boundary is drawn between tax evasion and tax avoidance, how it can be manipulated to ensure immunity from criminal stigma, and what implications this has for the study of white collar crime and labelling theory.

THE BOUNDARY BETWEEN EVASION AND AVOIDANCE: DISCLOSURE

Drawing a line between tax evasion and tax avoidance is not easy. Offshore invoicing, for example, might range from the genuinely commercial to the fraudulent. It may be a genuine invoice from one company to another (related) company for actual and precise services rendered at market prices. It may be an invoice from a real offshore office for vaguer management charges by staff based there. It may be an invoice issued from an office which is no more than a brass plate to show company registration. It may be an invoice on neat headed paper from a non-existent company. (Interviewee 94, Inland Revenue) Where, asked the Revenue officer who gave this example, do you draw the line? The first is clearly legal but what of the others? In his terms of legitimate and non-legitimate 'make-believe', the second is legitimate in *form* though possibly make believe in terms of the sums claimed. The third is make believe in all but form. Yet only the fourth is clearly *fraudulent* make believe. There is a spectrum of greys at the boundaries of lawful and deviant behaviour. For practical enforcement purposes, however, there has to be some way of drawing a line between what may be treated as deviant and what may not. The criterion currently employed is disclosure.

Faced with a tax bill there are four general responses to tax liabilities. First, one can pay the bill, second, one can pack the money in a suitcase and smuggle it offshore, third, one can negotiate over how much to pay, and fourth, one can technically launder the deal into a non-taxable form. Options two, three and four all escape paying tax: but only the second is criminal. The essential distinction between option two and options three and four is *disclosure*. In option two, the money packed in the suitcases and the transaction which produced it are never declared. In option three enough of the deal is disclosed to negotiate over tax liability. In option four the transaction is repackaged into a form which technically escapes tax liability and, *in its new form*, can be disclosed. If the techniques are clever enough there may be nothing to hide since the key lies not in secrecy but in the legal repackaging. In short, avoidance may be disclosed and still succeed. Evasion by contrast necessarily involves lying about a transaction or hiding it – it is characterised by 'misstatements, omissions or false declarations'.[3]

Disclosure emerges repeatedly as the rule of thumb for distinguishing avoidance from evasion in law, professional codes of practice and the working rules of practitioners and Revenue officials. Textbooks on tax law routinely draw a distinction between tax evasion and tax avoidance with concealment and disclosure as the key issues

> Tax avoidance is legal in that it incorporates no wrongful concealment of relevant facts. [Evasion by contrast involves] fraud or concealment.[4]

> Tax evasion . . . occurs where a taxpayer . . . ignores or conceals his liability.[5]

Where tax evasion[6] 'is treated as fraud it is dealt with under the general criminal law via the common law offence of defrauding the public revenue, the Theft Acts 1968 and 1978 and the specific offences of false accounting, forgery or perjury.[7] Deception and falsehood are the key aspects of these offences. The Roskill Committee, noting that fraud is not a clearly defined term, described its 'main ingredients' in law as 'dishonest practice, deception, false disclosure, concealment of assets, etc'.[8]

There are two routes to tax evasion. It might involve doing something which is in itself illegal – such as forging documents to claim allowances. That would be clearly fraudulent. Or it might simply involve engaging in some moneymaking activity which is in itself perfectly legal, but failing to disclose it to the tax authorities. In this case, it is not the activity but the failure to disclose it which constitutes the offence, and the question then becomes one of whether the omission was a product of criminal intent or honest error.

Failure or unwillingness to disclose information thus becomes a key issue in determining whether an activity is tax evasion or not, and *continuing* failure to disclose on investigation becomes *prima facie* evidence of criminal intent, and enhances the likelihood of prosecution.[9] The Keith Committee saw 'sustained failure to provide information' as a major offence[10] and noted that 'the concealment of material facts, leading to an under-assessment, marks the point at which avoidance crosses the borderline and becomes evasion'.[11] In law, evasion is characterised by deception and concealment: avoidance by honest disclosure.

Most direct dealing with the Revenue is done by accountants on behalf of their clients and the accountancy bodies' professional codes also emphasise the importance of disclosure. In distinguishing tax evasion from avoidance the Institute of Chartered Accountants [12] notes

> It is particularly important that in all tax matters the member should be in a position to assure himself that no relevant information has been or will be withheld from the tax authorities. It follows that the highest standards of disclosure should be observed by members.

The ability to disclose with confidence was noted repeatedly in interviews with tax practitioners as the litmus test for whether a scheme constitutes evasion or avoidance

> . . . you must feel you are no worse off if you have to lay all your cards on the table. (Interviewee 28, solicitor)

> . . . as a rule of thumb, a tax-saving proposal is likely to be on the right side of the line if, after it is carried out, a full disclosure of all the documents in the case can be put before the authorities without any concealment.[13]

The same rule of thumb is used in the Revenue as a matter of working practice: 'If it is not full disclosure it it evasion'. (Interviewee 95, Inland Revenue). The guidance note with the annual tax return form reminds taxpayers . . . that it is a serious offence to conceal any part of your income or chargeable gains'[14] while the Revenue's tariff on penalties depends heavily on the degree of disclosure given.[15]

The issue seems clear-cut: suitcases of cash heading for numbered Swiss bank accounts after undisclosed property deals constitute evasion: disclosed property deals with legal arguments over the rights and wrongs of the Revenue's claim to tax on the deal are at worst avoidance. One method is clear, open and legal. The other, dishonest, secretive and illegal. There is 'a sharp distinction' between the two.[16]

Yet the same Revenue officials who accept and use the disclosure distinction, complain that they do *not* normally get full disclosure of information to work with. Interviewed accountants and solicitors tended to take a minimalist approach to disclosure

> I don't subscribe to the belief that you should bare your soul to the Revenue. (Interviewee 44, accountant)

> You don't have to do the Inspector's work for him. (Interviewee 47, accountant)

A senior partner of one of the Big Eight firms of accountants, in a lecture to a group of Inland Revenue inspectors, noted that 'Full disclosure is very hard to achieve in practice, and is not necessarily undertaken by even the big firms'. (Interviewee 47, accountant) The Inland Revenue feels disclosure only comes 'when they think the Revenue are getting onto it' (Interviewee 94, Inland Revenue). One Revenue officer talked of a letter from an accountant to his client which came to the Revenue in error. It noted that 'transactions were really distributions not royalties and the inspector is getting warm. We may have to admit it soon'. (Interviewee 94, Inland Revenue) The Association of Inspectors of Taxes gave evidence to the Keith Committee that 'deliberate attempts are often made to prevent the Inspector being aware of all the transactions in the scheme. Secrecy is often an important part of the scheme'.[17] Respondents talked of the need for full disclosure '*if* we have to lay all our cards on the table' suggesting that they did not always assume they would have to. (Interviewee 28, solicitor) In fact our research indicated that taxpayers and their advisers do *not* tend to 'lay all their cards on the table'. 'Misstatements, omissions and false declarations' have been noted as characteristic of evasion. Yet normal tax reporting clearly misleads, omits and is 'economic with the truth'.

The question is: if disclosure is the mark of legitimate non-payment of tax, non-disclosure the mark of evasion, how can the taxpayer avoid *disclosure* but still avoid the 'taint of fraud'? How can he manage the boundary between legal and deviant behaviour?

Of course one might ask, why bother? In tax evasion, as in other areas of white collar crime, policing is difficult so that one may never be caught: prosecution is rare – only around 6 per cent of all acknowledged evasion cases per year; and settlement is normal. There are still penalties involved, however, and still stigma attached to criminal evasion, however settled, as opposed to avoidance, which, whether it actually succeeds or not, carries no taint of criminality. Major public companies do not want the adverse publicity of a tax evasion case. Even in the greyer areas of avoidance, 'company treasurers get nervous' about publicity (Interviewee 72, tax scheme promoter). There is some incentive, therefore, to stay on the right side of the line.

But at the same time there are numerous reasons why even for avoidance schemes disclosure may be unattractive. Of course, if a scheme is technically impeccable, it should be able to be disclosed in full with impunity. That is the essence of the disclosure rule. But there's the rub. Is an absolutely technically watertight scheme possible? Can there be infallible predictions on how judges will treat it? Witness the shocks sustained over the *Ramsay*[18] or *Furniss v Dawson* cases.[19] For even the best of schemes the law itself may be uncertain and susceptible to grey areas. For those further down the spectrum of technical purity, there may well be acknowledged grey areas within the scheme itself.

There may be other reasons for preferring non-disclosure. Tax scheme promoters may wish to protect their market from competitors. In the heyday of the 1970s off the peg schemes, purchasers – and their professional advisers – were required by some promoters to sign undertakings of secrecy for just this purpose. And for another. The promoters recognised only too clearly that a good scheme was likely to be stopped by law as soon as it was known to the Revenue. They talked of having 'just one season' per scheme (Interviewee 72, consultant/promoter). However confident they were about its present legality therefore they preferred to protect it from both competition and future prohibition by keeping it secret. How then is disclosure avoided without risk of stigma?

NEGOTIATING DISCLOSURE: REVENUE AND PROFESSIONAL PRACTICE

Scope for limiting the disclosure of information arises from the sheer weight of information involved in complex financial deals. Some editing, some decision as to materiality must be made for manageable presentation. This scope is enhanced, despite the emphasis the Revenue places on disclosure, by Revenue policy and practice.

The Revenue is heavily reliant for the assessments it makes and decisions it takes on tax liability on the information provided by the taxpayer. Although it obviously does instigate investigation, receive information from third parties, either by law, as in the statutory obligation of banks to inform the Revenue of bank interest received, or from 'grasses', and keep an eye on the press for unusual events, it is dependent, for the vast bulk of its job of raising taxes, on the information disclosed by the taxpayer simply to get a starting point for a case. This, combined with the special difficulties of policing, is one of the sources of pressure to negotiate.

But there is a vicious circle involved here – negotiation in turn discourages too much disclosure. Minimal disclosure is in fact exactly what one would expect in an enforcement environment based on negotiation. To negotiate the tax liability on a deal one must obviously disclose the deal, as opposed to packing the proceeds in a suitcase bound for Switzerland and never mentioning it. One need not, however, disclose all the nuances and subtleties of the deal, its context or the processes behind it. Indeed it would be a foolish negotiator who entered the game with all his cards exposed. Beginning from a strong position, bluff, manipulation are the essence of negotiation. There is no place for a starting position of full disclosure. Is there, therefore, a contradiction between the criterion used by enforcers and their methods of enforcement?

In fact procedural law and Revenue policies can leave considerable scope for negotiating *disclosure* as well as negotiating tax. For a start one need not disclose everything. Enquiry Branch has tended to prosecute if 'subsequent investigation shows that the disclosure was incomplete in a *material* degree'[20] but this begs the question of materiality. Evasion more generally requires '*wrongful*' concealment of 'relevant' facts.[21] What is 'relevant' and whether concealment was 'wrongful' themselves become issues for negotiation.

The 'wrongful' element is difficult to prove and the Revenue has the power to accept 'incorrect information' as having been supplied 'neither fraudulently nor negligently'.[22] It can be accepted merely as 'innocent error'.[23]

A window for negotiating how far one has to 'lay one's cards on the table' is also provided by the rules allowing late disclosure when defects in the information come to the attention of the tax practitioner or taxpayer, or indeed the Revenue.[24] Indeed full disclosure from the start is not really expected by the Revenue, who even treat subsequent disclosure or unforced disclosure after challenge as grounds for negotiating penalties. 'A reduction of up to 20% (or even 30% for voluntary disclosure)' is made.[25]

Evidence to the Royal Commission on Criminal Procedure indicated that in Enquiry Branch policy, it was not failure to disclose *per se* that led to prosecution but failure to 'make a proper disclosure within a reasonable time'.[26] Deane's research suggested that in practice this was softened further to not so much continued non-disclosure, but continued *fraud* after the Revenue investigation has begun. Of the 98 criminal prosecutions studied by Deane only 29 were concerned with incomplete disclosure.[27] Our own recent research indicated there was a recognised limbo in the period of inquiry and adjustment that takes place before any hardening of attitudes to the activities involved. 'It's not evasion because they don't tell us', one tax officer put it, 'But it is stepping over the boundaries if they lie when we ask.' (Interviewee 94, Inland Revenue) Enforcement policy and practice thus create a window for trying bluff and minimal disclosure before shifting position if necessary and laying one's cards on the table.

Much tax negotiation takes place through professional advisers. Yet the professional approach to disclosure is also less clear-cut than its rhetoric suggests. For a start, all advisers would claim a contractual obligation of confidence to their client as a limit on how much they should disclose. For the legal profession this is written into law via the idea of privilege – the right to withhold from a court evidence about a client, and this legal privilege is written into provisions denying the Revenue access to certain documents held by lawyers.[28]

These obligations are seen by the professions as setting limits on their legal obligation to disclose information relating to their clients. The ICA code, for example, notes situations where an accountant may be obliged by law to disclose information about his client, e.g. by a court order. But unless that happens he need not do so. He is *free* to disclose an intended criminal offence, civil wrong or a past arrestable offence. But even then 'the fact that there may be no bar to disclosure does not necessarily mean that a member should disclose'.[29] Indeed the code goes on to say 'Council therefore recommends that members even though free to do so, should *not disclose* past or intended crimes or civil wrongs . . .'[30] Even in the extreme criminal situations where ethically the accountant should, according to the guidelines, stop acting for his client and tell the Revenue he is doing so, he is not to tell the Revenue why. Professional confidentiality thus set limits on or provide legitimations for straying from full disclosure.

The structural role of the Revenue is also taken as an argument against full disclosure. A Revenue officer is not an impartial judge but the adversary in a dispute. Indeed the American Bar Association explicitly takes this as good reason for there being less of a duty of disclosure to the Internal Revenue Service than there is to the courts.[31] The Revenue is therefore in an ironic structural situation. As an adversary it is not entitled to full disclosure of information. At the same time, however, it is not a regular 'party' in the sense that it is not involved in the transaction it has to assess and is therefore *not* party to the information involved in a case. Yet as a 'party' it is not entitled to it in the sense that a court is. Those who have experienced Inland Revenue investigation might of course by quick to say that the Revenue has plenty of legal power and even more practical power in its ability to make life difficult, anxious and expensive for those being investigated. But the point for the moment is the Revenue's structural power *vis à vis* the professions on the issue of disclosure. Disclosure may, in terms of professional codes, be less than total. 'If it's only arguable, it's up to the Revenue to look out for itself'. (Interviewee 37, accountant)

The gap within professional codes only widens when one looks at professional politics. The ICA guidelines make explicit reference to 'the highest standards of disclosure' with 'for example the deduction of an item in respect of which there may be any doubt'.[32] Yet the Keith Committee's proposal, that the tax return should include disclosure if 'the benefit of any doubt'[33] had been taken, was resisted by the legal and accountancy professions. Full disclosure is not in keeping with the way the professions work.

Both Revenue and professional policy and practice thus undermine the rhetoric of full disclosure as a practical reality. It is in this context that strategies for managing disclosure of relevant information without risk of stigma come into play. One strategy is to use techniques of non-disclosing disclosure.

NON-DISCLOSING DISCLOSURE

Non-disclosing disclosure involves disclosing the relevant facts but doing so in a way which makes it difficult or impossible for the reader to recognise the presence or extent of a taxable transaction. The sheer complexity of business makes it less difficult than it might seem for 'big corporations as a matter of routine (to) deliberately stop the Inland Revenue from seeing the full picture'. (Interviewee 47, accountant) The Keith Committee report talked of taxpayers showing 'only a minimum amount of information', so that 'the complicated background to the transactions forming part of the scheme would be omitted in the hope that the inspector would not attack the scheme'. The scheme would be 'partly visible' but the full facts suppressed.[34] This is the case both generally and as a specific tactic in specially constructed avoidance schemes.

Avoidance schemes are rarely simple and they usually involve a number of stages or separate transactions with a total view being necessary to recognise the sum of the parts as avoidance. A scheme may involve several companies, trusts, transactions and jurisdictions. The different corporate entities may have different tax returns and different tax districts. Deals may be spread across several different tax years and tax returns, and some parts of the deal may be in other countries with lower disclosure requirements and therefore not in the disclosure net at all. It is therefore extremely difficult for the Revenue to fit together the jigsaw puzzle and spot the scheme, even if all the relevant parts that should by law be disclosed, are.

Some accountants also suggest that the Inland Revenue's lack of commercial experience makes it difficult for officers to spot the significance of a deal: 'they're on a different wave length so you can sometimes get something past them because of that'. (Interviewee 48, accountant) Having provided the jigsaw pieces one need not disclose how to put them together. 'You needn't display the nature of the transaction'. (Interviewee 47, accountant) The jigsaw puzzle has to be tackled without the cover picture as guidance.

Revenue officers complain of professional ambivalence to disclosure

> You send a lot of questions out and you get a lot of answers – and they can be truthful, but not full. They answer the question but don't provide the natural extension to it. (Inland Revenue)

Practitioners support the view that there should be disclosure in *response* to questions but not necessarily to provide the information to make the questions possible. A barrister and solicitor gave the hypothetical example of a client, at his lawyer's suggestion, adding his seventy year-old mother to the payroll of his company in return for a few hours work a month, in order to make his support of her a tax deductible expense. It was recognised that the client would probably overpay. However they suggested that the probable approach of the UK profession would be to 'put it forward as a deduction and let the Inland Revenue argue if they thought fit'.[35] Again it was recognised that the Inland Revenue would be unlikely to question 'the reasonableness of the mother's compensation' unless they were aware of the relationship, but observed that 'UK lawyers would not volunteer the existence of the relationship'. Internal correspondence in accountant's files sometimes contains queries such as 'The Inland Revenue inspector hasn't asked to see this, shall we show him?' with the response 'No, since he hasn't asked'. As the accountant describing this concluded, 'ask and it shall be disclosed, but not otherwise'. (Interviewee 47, accountant) The problem of course is that of chicken and egg: without facts it is difficult to ask the questions necessary to acquire them.

The mere fact of there being a middleman – the professional practitioner – between the person best informed on the facts - the taxpayer - and the authorities, helps limit disclosure in a way that does not constitute a breach of the rules. The practitioner may present in good faith information which is, none the less, not an accurate representation of the client's activities. Revenue officers feel taxpayers 'may not do it technically correctly, but they tell their accountants what they *intend* to do and accountants don't check but present it as though it was properly done'. (Interviewee 94, Inland Revenue) This was not just a Revenue gripe since instances cropped up in interviews with accountants too, e.g. where a Channel Island company was reported – not necessarily deliberately – as offshore when in fact its management and control were in the UK, bringing it in law *within* British jurisdiction. (Interviewee 34, accountant).

Professional bodies advocate full disclosure between client and professional adviser, but at the end of the day practitioners argue that they can 'only act for people on the basis of what they tell you. It would be impossible otherwise'. (Interviewee 21, solicitor) It is not quite so simple however. Practitioners are not always anxious to hear every dubious facet of a client's business, and techniques can be employed to positively suppress disclosure rather than encourage it.

> You frequently say you don't want to know over small things. This is a coded message to the client to stop telling you. (Interviewee 41, accountant)

The classic strategy of asking questions with care to elicit acceptable answers may be employed, with happy encouragement when the client fills the bill: 'you've given just the right answer'. (Interviewee 46, accountant) Sometimes only the taxpayer can know what was really going on, for example, the real purpose of travel claimed against a business. Reporting this to the practitioner may be less a matter of disclosure than a way of testing the plausibility of any particular version of events.

More specific tactics may also be employed. One may *bury* the salient point on p.195 of a 300 page document and leave tax inspectors to spot it and its significance if they can. (Interviewee 49, accountant) One may spread salient points which only take on avoidance significance when read together, between pages 12, 119 and 164, or hide crucial facts in a welter of irrelevances in the 'extended disclosure approach'. (Interviewee 42, accountant) Full disclosure can in fact hide, rather than reveal. One may 'tuck away details in masses of schedules then use the *Olin* case to argue that the case cannot be reopened'. (Interviewee 94, Inland Revenue) or mention salient information in the director's report but not include it in the computations.

One may lay false scents. 'Presentation is all important: how a return strikes an inspector in the first instance can easily send him in the wrong direction'. (Interviewee 41, accountant) One may use words with care. Accountants will 'redescribe' the activities outlined by their client into a more innocuous form. 'I say don't use these words in the accounts, use these, they're less likely to excite the inspector'. Or, 'It'll be an uphill battle for me if you describe it like that. Try this'. (Interviewee 43, accountant). One may direct attention from a big issue to a little one: 'leave something for the Inland Revenue to find'. (Interviewee 41, accountant) One may also create evidence in one's favour for future disclosure. At a time when commercial purpose is an important criterion for the acceptability or otherwise of an avoidance technique, company minutes may well record a decision on business grounds without recording the discussion of tax advantages which took place before. Or one may merely highlight the business grounds in a way one would not have otherwise done. 'Careful minuting' may be important. (Interviewee 49, accountant)

A whole range of techniques is available. Far from promoting disclosure,

> the taxpayer builds a tax-proof castle and presents it to the inspector who tries to see inside it. If he could he would see the weaknesses. But the accountant and the client try to stop him seeing inside the castle. (Interviewee 94, Inland Revenue)[36]

In short, information is presented in a way that will not attract tax simply because it will not attract attention. Non-disclosing disclosure plays on the problems of policing complex financial areas, the low risk of being caught, the scope for settlement if one is challenged, and the protection from stigma involved in *having* disclosed however obscurely. Non-disclosing disclosure minimises the chances of being caught while providing 'fraud insurance'[37] if one is.

STRATEGIC USE OF COUNSEL'S OPINION

A more legalistic approach may be taken to the game of avoiding disclosure – and tax – while simultaneously avoiding the evasion label. One method is to use the legal profession and legal institutions, specifically to make strategic use of counsel's opinion.

Counsel's opinion – the assessment by a barrister of the legal status of a transaction – may simply be used in a game of bluff or as a negotiating counter. One accountant cited the example of a problem over an already completed sale of capital losses. The barrister consulted offered a possible get-out put merely in terms of 'consider trying this strategy, with lots of ifs and buts and maybes, but there was nothing to lose so it was worth a go'. (Interviewee 37, accountant). It was worth a go partly because of the negotiating power produced by going to counsel. If a questionable transaction is disclosed or emerges, the fact that counsel's opinion has been taken may be used as a technique for putting the Revenue off further investigation. 'It shows you're treating it seriously.' (Interviewee 42, accountant)

Because of legal privilege, the Revenue has no right to see counsel's opinions. Even if an opinion is volunteered as evidence in support of an interpretation of tax liability, Revenue officers 'don't know the precise facts presented to counsel to get that opinion' (Interviewee 92, Inland Revenue). One barrister talked of vital information being omitted. 'A £100,000 loan was involved but counsel was not told it had been tranched up'. (Interviewee 1, barrister)

There can also be 'a subtle change between what's presented to the Bar and what is actually done'. (Interviewee 92, Inland Revenue). In short, reference to counsel's opinion may make a case appear stronger than it is in the game of bluff with the Revenue.

Counsel's opinion may be more than just a negotiating counter, however. It may provide another means of non-disclosing disclosure; it may even provide a means of pre-empting disclosure altogether.

Even if Revenue officers suspect the existence of an undisclosed transaction they may not be able to find out enough about it to assess or challenge it – not just because of policing problems but because of avoidance techniques. This may be done in an extreme way by careful use by the taxpayer of the profession's legal privilege. Professional privilege means that a solicitor or barrister cannot be asked by the Revenue to hand over documentation on a client's case. The Revenue *may* enforce disclosure of the same information from taxpayers themselves, thus neatly avoiding professional privilege. But the avoidance spiral goes on. Professional privilege can in turn be used even to avoid this. The Revenue Bar Association in evidence to the Keith Committee cited instances where

> 'commercially formulated tax avoidance schemes have been committed to writing only in instructions to counsel'[38]

as a way of withholding factual information from the Revenue altogether. The taxpayer could not be forced to hand over documents he did not hold. The lawyer who did hold them was protected by legal privilege.

Fear of complete non-disclosure was also claimed by the Revenue in its request for more power to gain information on the purchasers of off the peg avoidance schemes.[39] The concern was that the sponsor of a tax avoidance scheme which has subsequently been established as 'not legally effective', may have told his clients that there is no tax liability on the profits covered by the scheme and no need to include them in their tax returns. There may, therefore, be reason to believe that there are large amounts of income which are liable to tax, but which have not been reported.'[40] The sponsor would almost certainly have based his advice on counsel's opinion.

More routinely, use of counsel's opinion can operate as another, legalistic, means of non-disclosing disclosure. The precise legal status of a transaction, its definition as falling into one legal category or another, is often arguable. Different categorisations may, however, attract different levels of tax; some may attract no tax at all. On the basis of counsel's opinion a transaction may be defined by the taxpayer as falling into one legal category or form, which is not taxable, rather than another, which is taxable. The transaction is then disclosed, but is disclosed in its non-taxable form, when the Inland Revenue, given all the facts, might categorise it quite differently and claim a tax liability. The Revenue could, of course, challenge the taxpayer's legal interpretation of the nature of the transaction. However, to do so they would first have to smell a rat, be prompted to suspect the innocent declaration, so confidently presented. Where there is something odd about the transaction, or where a pattern of oddity begins to emerge, the Revenue may well investigate. But in a one-off, well presented case, the chances are that they may simply never realise there is a grey area open to challenge.

As already noted the Institute of Chartered Accountants explicitly states in its guidance notes for members that 'the highest standards of disclosure should be observed' including 'the deduction of an item in respect of which there may be *doubt* as to its allowability for taxation purposes'.[41] Yet when the Keith Report suggested that tax returns should explicitly ask whether taxpayers had taken the benefit of any doubt in completing their returns, there was an outcry of protest from both accountants and solicitors.

In practice the issue is resolved by the use of counsel. A practitioner may not disclose too early that counsel is being used: 'it may suggest you're worried'. (Interviewee 43, accountant) Taking an issue to counsel indicates very clearly that there is a doubt involved. Acquiring a favourable opinion, however, provides licence to discount the doubt. Disclosure of the grey areas is thus effectively pre-empted.

OPINION-SHOPPING

If a scheme has been declared authoritatively to meet the criteria of legal acceptability, does this matter? The problem is that if disclosure is not so clear-cut as it might seem, neither is counsel's opinion. First, law is always arguable anyway and any party need only argue in its own interest. This is basic to the adversary system of law. Disclosure does not require volunteering that 'you could argue X and that would cost more'. (Interviewee 47, accountant)

Second, there is the issue of opinion-shopping. The opinion on which the taxpayer decides a deal need not be disclosed, may be not just one opinion among many possible opinions, but one opinion among many possible opinions which the taxpayer has received. Taxpayers need not stop after one counsel has given the opinion that the deal *is* taxable. The taxpayer can 'opinion-shop' until the appropriate answer is received. The decision as to which to go by is not democratic: it is not a question of counting the opinions and going for the majority view. The only opinion that counts is the one the client wants. Of course, going on the basis of one opinion out of six might not look terribly convincing if it is discovered. So the matter is usually approached more subtly. Counsel's general attitude to particular topics may be known so that one may 'shop on a horses for courses basis'. (Interviewee 41, accountant) Psychology may be involved, calling counsel in early at the correspondence stage so 'he can't do a lukewarm case, since he's been in on front'. (Interviewee 42, accountant) Preliminary discussions with counsel before formally seeking an opinion can also serve to test the water on how an opinion is likely to shape up: 'If you don't like the way the opinion is developing you drop him quickly and go on to the next'. (Interviewee 21, solicitor)

The really well-organized scheme promoters of the 1970s fragmented their deals into component parts and fragmented the legal issues that went with them. These fragments were then taken to a range of different specialist counsel and validated in their fragmented form. 'We used six or seven barristers in putting a scheme together' (Interviewee 71, consultant/promoter) A master set of instructions to one final counsel was then constructed by the scheme creator from these fragmented opinions to attain the 'marketing opinion' (Interviewee 71, promoter/consultant) One commentator equated the instructions for opinion on some schemes with 'a driving licence application'. (Interviewee 1, barrister) The legal issues were so carefully constructed on the basis of the preceding opinions that any equivocation, indeed, anything other than section by section validation, was unlikely. Any general opinion of the law was discouraged and indeed one barrister who insisted on commenting on the 'wood not the trees' was quickly dropped.

These were extreme tactics from the 'bad old days' of the 1970s. But our interviews indicate that counsel's opinion is still used for marketing devices (Interviewee 24, city solicitor; Interviewee 75, consultant), that opinion-shopping continues, as does the expectation that with careful preparation one can have one's scheme validated without too much difficulty. Barristers may tailor the 'robustness' of their advice to the client. A barrister can also only respond to the facts provided. 'You have to assume the facts you are told are truthful and honestly disclosed.' (Interviewee 1, barrister) But the opinion may be given on the basis of less than full information.

In the County NatWest affair – not over non-disclosure of taxable deals but over non-disclosure of share holdings – Allen and Overy, solicitors to stockbrokers Phillips and Drew, gave evidence to DTI inspectors that they did not have all the relevant facts available when crucial legal advice was given. Had they been instructed of the full intentions, 'I doubt our advice would have been the same.'[42] Opinion shopping was also at work. When Allen and Overy's opinion proved slightly ambivalent, Phillips and Drew went ahead on the basis of the more robust opinion of Travis, Smith Braithwaite. In the County NatWest affair, legal opinions were used mainly to persuade the board to follow a particular course of action, but the incident demonstrates quite clearly that use of legal opinions, opinion-shopping and the manipulation of legal institutions extend beyond the confines of tax.

Some tax advisers are genuinely seeking opinions when they go to counsel 'I want them to give the seal of approval or tear it apart'. (Interviewee 73, tax consultant) But others want not opinion but endorsement. Before counsel is approached, issues will already have been sifted into black and white rather than grey issues.[43] 'The instruction of a solicitor can become simply a request for a second opinion'. (Interviewee 3, barrister) 'We use counsel for a second opinion once the scheme has been refined'. (Interviewee 53, insurer) 'If your instructions are properly drafted you shouldn't get a surprise'. (Interviewee 21, solicitor) There will be preliminary discussions, even several conferences with counsel before the instructions are written, so that the 'right questions' emerge. (Interviewee

21, solicitor) Authoritative endorsement rather than opinion may be what is being sought. 'Carbon copy opinions' was the phrase used by one respondent. (Interviewee 41, accountant)

FRAUD INSURANCE

The use of counsel can also provide 'fraud insurance'. As respondents put it

> Yes, it's fraud insurance, and it's cheap insurance at that. (Interviewee 16, solicitor)
>
> The client needed to be comforted they what we were doing was proper and not fraud. But if anyone was concerned we were able to show evidence that everything was fully investigated and produce the barrister's opinion. (Interviewee 71, consultant/promoter)
>
> You are known by your advisers. That's your insurance policy. We use the bar all the time. (Interviewee 70, banker)

The assumption was that acting on legal opinion would pre-empt any possibility of tagging the activities involved criminal.

There are in fact various methods of taking out fraud insurance. Disclosing information via non-disclosing disclosure helps, allowing the taxpayer to claim disclosure however disguised as we have seen. So does the use of a professional firm as a buffer. The Keith Committee accepted the evidence of an international accounting firm that 'the participation of two sets of persons in the process of preparing and submitting a return opens up more possibility of error' – innocent error as opposed to negligence or fraud.[44] 'Honest error' is both more likely and easier to argue. The Inland Revenue's Technical Division itself may also be used. Accountants and solicitors ring up 'on a no-names basis' and sketch out a possible scheme. Would Technical Division accept it? Informally negotiated clearances of this sort are helped along by the networks of ex-Inland Revenue officers in the tax planning world who can ring old colleagues on a friendly basis. Revenue officers complain that the discussion may then be used out of context, or the scheme marginally but crucially modified, and clearance still claimed. According to one Revenue inspector, if the Revenue officers then reject the scheme they may be accused of 'deliberate intention to mislead'. (Interviewee 95, Inland Revenue) Another talked of the practice of carefully noting on file that the tax office had been phoned and had given clearance. (Interviewee 87, Inland Revenue) Fraud insurance will certainly be claimed by the fact of having involved the Revenue in a clearance procedure, however informally. What is more, interviews with major accountancy firms indicated internal intelligence systems for obtaining information on clearances (Interviewee 35, accountant). Informal clearances therefore quickly become informal precedents for a very large constituency of cases. There is room too for devices in creating fraud insurance via clearances. One merchant banker talked of the 'sensitive bit' of a scheme being 'how far the Inland Revenue is informed' and suggested a covering device

> You must tell everything you intend to do to get a clearance. But if a third party mucks it about later, there is no withdrawal of the clearance. (Interviewee 68, banker)

Another litmus test for fraud insurance is the press. A dubious scheme may be leaked to the press and if it's not expressly stopped 'the city will treat it as OK to use it'. (Interviewee 62, banker) Fraud insurance can be had in another rather odd way. One may disclose all the facts – even 'highlight them' so that it is up to the inspector to 'disagree if he thinks fit'[45] – so providing fraud insurance, but make a quite unfounded *legal* interpretation of these facts and hope it sticks

> Although it is difficult to find a legal reason to support it, there is a fairly generally held view that so long as all the facts are disclosed one may in practice take a quite unreasonable legal position.[46]

Indeed the Keith Report obliquely supports this by suggesting a no fault, no penalty approach if a taxpayer discloses that he has taken the 'benefit of the doubt'.[47] So one respondent talked of 'getting the Inland Revenue to accept the liability as Capital Gains Tax, when it was arguably Income Tax (taxed at a higher rate at the time). The Revenue now realise their mistake but it's too late'. (Interviewee 23, solicitor)

But a major method for acquiring fraud insurance is to seek counsel's opinion. Any accusation of evasion requires proof of intent. Though the legal rules on intent or *mens rea* are not always as difficult to meet as they might seem,[48] proving intent in the area of white collar or economic crime *is* notably difficult.[49] This is an area of immense technical complexity – legal, financial and commercial – and often of organisational complexity with culpability difficult to fix. When a charge is made it is never quite clear whether the accused is culprit or scapegoat – the vice president responsible for going to jail, hired specifically to be the fall guy.[50] White collar crime literature abounds with examples of the difficulties of proving intent, and tax evasion is no different

> When we find reality is different from the picture presented on paper, it doesn't necessarily mean it is deliberate. It might not be evasion but just technically sloppy. Evasion needs intent. If it's sloppy technically it doesn't mean there was intent to evade. In fact it means there was intent to do it properly. (Interviewee 94, Inland Revenue)

Difficulties however become impossibilities if fraud insurance is taken out, particularly via leading counsel. Tax schemes can hardly be described as intentionally illegal if *expert* legal opinion on their legality was sought.

Whether the recent arrest of a lawyer in the County NatWest affair – an unexpected action which has shaken both City solicitors and their City clients – heralds an end to the safety net afforded by legal opinion remains to be seen. In the past, however, the judiciary has attached considerable weight to counsel's opinion in assessing whether a tax scheme constitutes evasion or avoidance. When the transfer to Jersey of £20.5 million of the assets of the estate of Sir Charles Clore came to light in 1982, the Court of Appeal suggested there might have been a criminal conspiracy to evade tax. The money had been transferred to a company set up in Jersey and owned almost wholly by an offshore trust. It was set up in September 1978. In May 1979, 3 months before Sir Charles' death, he transferred ownership of his Herefordshire estate to the Jersey company and instructed that the estate be sold. He died before the contract was completed and the Jersey company completed the deal and received the money. The Inland Revenue assessed a tax liability of almost £22 million plus interest. The Court of Appeal noted of the various dealings that 'there is a grave possibility that the object . . . was to *evade tax* of £20 million'.[51]

This view of the deal as evasion not avoidance was based explicitly on the fact that 'no evidence has been produced that the advice of English counsel was sought'. The court therefore recommended that the Director of Public Prosecutions should investigate. When it emerged that in fact the advice of two English counsel had been obtained and followed, the case was dropped. The Financial Times, commenting on this new evidence noted that 'legal opinion is that this fact alone (acting "on the independent advice of a leading tax barrister") would be enough to dispose of any suggestion that (the company's) directors or solicitors took part in a criminal conspiracy'.[52]

This case suggests an inclination to treat taxpayers who seek legal opinion as acting in good faith, and thus as safe from accusations of deviant behaviour. What this paper has suggested, however, is that counsel's opinion may also be used strategically to avoid or manage disclosure of relevant information – and therefore tax – while simultaneously providing fraud insurance in the event of challenge.

MANAGING THE CRIMINAL LABEL: WHITE COLLAR CRIME AND LABELLING THEORY

The susceptibility to manipulation of the lawful-deviant boundary has implications for two conceptual classics of criminology: the concept of white collar crime and labelling theory.

This paper has analysed some of the methods used to construct immunity from both legal control and the deviant label in the area of tax. The emphasis has been on the active role of taxpayers, their advisers, and the promoters of tax avoidance schemes, in managing the legitimation of their methods of escaping tax. The tax system is not heavily geared to criminalisation. There is, as already noted, a preference for settlement or for use of non-criminal sanctions. There is, in short, an institutional tendency to 'decriminalise' tax violations. Dee Cook has shown too how the ideologies surrounding tax help 'decriminalise' the lawbreaking activities of 'valuable' citizens.[53] But what this paper has tried to demonstrate is that activities can also be decriminalised by the active strategies of taxpayers and their advisers themselves. Not everyone is merely processed by the agents and institutions of the law for pragmatic, ideological or any other reasons; some actively manipulate the enforcement process, the institutions and (as I have shown elsewhere[54]) the substance of law to their own ends. They do so after engaging in criminal activity and being caught.[55] But they also do so *pre-emptively* – managing legitimation and disclosure of information in such a way as to both minimise investigation and avoid any danger of invoking criminal procedures, or other deviant labelling, at all.

Labelling theory in the context of white collar crime should therefore be reviewed: it may be not so much a matter of others defining the individual or organisation as deviant but of individuals or organisations managing the labelling process to pre-empt the possibility of stigma. 'Neutralising' techniques are used not to neutralise one's own self-image of criminality but to neutralise the public label itself.[56]

This in turn suggests the need to rethink the concept of white collar crime. White collar crime research slipped, some criminological generations ago, into an arid definitional debate. Sutherland argued that the concept should include 'legally defined social injury' even if administered not by regular criminal but by special procedures which blur their criminality and eliminate stigma.[57] Tappan responded that only behaviour outlawed by criminal law could be properly called crime; taking a wider view was unscientific value judgement.[58] Levi talks of the subsequent dilemma for researchers, of walking a tightrope between being attacked for accepting uncritically the legal definitions of crime or alternatively for providing mere propaganda.[59] He cites Orland's critique of Clinard, whose claim for the prevalence of white collar crime was criticised on the basis that 'less than 1% of these violations involve accusation of crime'.[60]

Fear of being accused of polemics has driven many criminologists to focus research only on out and out crime. But it is not helpful to close off thinking by saying X is a subject worthy of white collar crime research, Y is not. It is not helpful precisely because definitions are manipulable, not just by enforcers of law but by those subject to the law and the labels themselves. Instead of frowning on research on activities which cannot be defined as violating law, we should be researching just *why* those activities cannot be defined as violating law. This paper suggests that the explanation lies not only in an institutional or ideological bias in the treatment of white collar activities – in the definitions applied from above – but in the active manipulation of institutions and definitions from below, by economic elites and their advisers themselves. How legitimation is achieved, how non-deviant status is accomplished, are questions worthy of research too.

These questions can be addressed at a more general level too. This paper has analysed some of the specific techniques employed by the 'labelled' in managing the enforcement process. But the research project as a whole is concerned at a more general level with how tax *avoidance* differs from deviant tax *evasion*, finding that it differs in form rather than substance, purpose or effect.[61] In analysing the role of law and crime in society it is worth exploring just how economic elites organise their activities in ways which escape legal control yet remain legitimate, how, at this more general level, 'whiter than white collar crime' status is accomplished. To ignore such issues as beyond the remit of criminology would be to stultify research and theory.

'White collar crime' in its wider approach was grasping at a real problem. To turn aside from it on definitional grounds and focus only on legally defined crime is to miss the whole point and skew the answers. To limit white collar crime research to out and out crime is to overlook a vital issue. Forget the terminology. The issue remains. Legal control of the activities of economic elites, of big business, frequently fails. That it fails because of something that is *not* crime does not mean we should not study it. On the contrary it means we have to widen our thinking, just as Sutherland advocated, beyond crime. But the way to do this is not to redefine everything dubious as crime. It is to redirect the question. We need to focus research not just on crime but on the subtler phenomenon of legal avoidance, not just in tax but generally. We need to explore how economic elites actively use the institutions, ideologies and methods of law to secure immunity from legal control.

(Date accepted: January 1990)

NOTES

* This paper is based on research conducted by Doreen McBarnet and Graham Mansfield and funded by the ESRC, award numbers E0625033 and R000231235.

1. D. McBarnet, 'It's not what you do

but the way that you do it: tax evasion, tax avoidance and the boundaries of deviance', in D. Downes (ed.), *Unravelling criminal justice: eleven British studies*, MacMillan 1991. D. McBarnet 'Law, policy and legal avoidance: can law effectively implement egalitarian policies?', *Journal of Law and Society*, 15, vol. 1 (winter 1988), pp. 113–121.

2. The source of quotations from interviews used in the paper is referred to by the appropriate category.

3. J. Chown, *Taxation and multinational enterprise*. London, Longman, 1974, p. 8.

4. Simon's *Taxes* 3rd edition, London, Butterworth, 1988, Al. 117.

5. CCH Editions, *British Tax Guide*, Bicester, CCH Editions, 1987, p. 85; 100.

6. There is no specific crime of tax evasion. The proposal by the Keith Committee to introduce a specific Revenue offence for dishonesty has since been dropped. Inland Revenue *Keith: further proposals*. IR, 1988, p. 27.

7. A. Arlidge and J. Parry *On Fraud*, London, Waterlow, 1985, p. 261.

8. Roskill Committee *Report* London, HMSO, 1986, p. 39.

9. Inland Revenue's evidence to The Royal Commission on Criminal Procedure, *Report*, London, HMSO, cited in K. Deane, 'Tax evasion, criminality and sentencing the tax offender '*British Journal of Criminology*, vol. 21, no. 1, 1981.

10. Keith Committee, *Report* Vols 1 and 2, Committee on enforcement powers of the Revenue Departments, London, HMSO Cmnd 8822, 1983, p. 421.

11. Keith Committee *op. cit.* p. 162.

12. Institute of Chartered Accountants *Guidance for members in practice: professional conduct in relation to defaults or unlawful acts* (V12) 1.306, paragraph 31.

13. Chown, *op. cit.*, p. 8.

14. Keith Committee, *op. cit.*, p. 27.

15. Inland Revenue, *Inland Revenue Investigations: how settlements are negotiated*, IR 73, 1987.

16. P. G. Whiteman and D. C. Milne, *British Tax Encyclopaedia Whiteman* and *Wheatcroft on Income Tax*, London, Sweet and Maxwell, 1976, p. 9.

17. Keith Committee, *op. cit.*, p. 159.

18. Ramsay (WT) *Ltd v IRC* (1981) 2 WLR 449.

19. *Furniss v Dawson* (1984) 2WLR 226.

20. Inland Revenue evidence to Royal Commission on Criminal Procedure, *op. cit.*

21. Simon's Taxes, *op. cit.*, Al : 117.

22. Taxes Management Act 1970, S97 (1).

23. Keith Committee, *op. cit*, p. 417.

24. Taxes Management Act 1970, S97.

25. Inland Revenue 1987, *op. cit.*

26. Inland Revenue, Deane, *op. cit.*

27. Deane, *op. cit.*

28. Taxes Management Act 1970 20 B (8). Proposals by the Keith Committee to limit lawyers' privilege and extend it to accountants failed. (IR 1988, *op. cit.* pp. 44–5.

29. ICA, *op. cit.*, paragraph 11.

30. ICA, *op. cit.*, paragraph 12.

31. American Bar Association, *Opinions on Professional Ethics*. Chicago, ABA, 1967.

32. ICA, *op. cit.*, paragraph 31.

33. Keith Committee, *op. cit.*, p. 162.

34. Keith Committee, *op. cit.*, p. 159.

35. F. Corneel, S. Bates and J. Avery Jones, 'Tax payer compliance'. *Justice for a generation*, papers presented at the American Bar Association conference, London, July 1985, p. 277.

36. Keith Committee, *op. cit.*, p. 161.

37. M. J. Graetz, J. Reinganum and L. Wilde, 'The tax compliance game', mimeo, September 1985.

38. Keith Committee, *op. cit.*, p. 541.

39. Finance Bill (2) 1988, Section 118.

40. Law Society Gazette, No 15, 20 April 1988, p. 41.

41. ICA, *op. cit*, paragraph 31.

42. Department of Trade and Industry *County Natwest Ltd*, London, HMSO, 1989, p. 100.

43. D. McBarnet, *Conviction*, London, Macmillan, 1981.

44. Keith Committee, *op. cit*, p. 149.

45. Corneel *et al.*, *op. cit*, p. 275.

46. Corneel *et al.*, *op. cit*, p. 283.

47. Keith Committee, *op. cit.*

48. McBarnet, 1981, *op. cit.*

49. M. Levi, *Regulating Fraud*, London, Tavistock, 1987. Keith Committee, *op. cit*, ch. 8.

50. J. Braithwaite, *Corporate Crime in*

the pharmaceutical industry, London, Routledge and Kegan Paul, 1981.

51. IRC v Stype Investments (Jersey) Ltd Re Clore (1982) 3WLR.

52. Financial Times 8 December 1982.

53. D. Cook, *Rich Law, poor law*, Milton Keynes, Open University Press, 1989, p. 7.

54. McBarnet, *op. cit.*, note 1.

55. K. Mann, *Defending White Collar Crime*, New Haven, Yale University Press, 1985.

56. D. Matza, 'Techniques of Neutralisation' *American Sociological Review* Vol. 22, 1957, pp. 664–70.

57. D. Sutherland 'Is "white collar crime" crime?', *American Sociological Review*, Vol. 10, 1945, pp. 132–9.

58. P. Tappan, 'Who is the criminal?', *American Sociological Review* Vol. 12, 1947, pp. 96–102.

59. Levi, *op. cit*, p. xxiv.

60. L. Orland, 'Reflections on corporate crime', *American Criminal Review*, Vol. 17, 1980, pp. 501–20.

61. McBarnet, *op. cit.*, note 1.

Part Five

From Regulator to Regulated: Creative Compliance

[11]

Law, Policy, and Legal Avoidance: Can Law Effectively Implement Egalitarian Policies?

This special issue of the journal tackles the question of law, democracy, and social justice: to what extent do legal forms and institutions help or hinder the implementation of egalitarian policies? Can legal regulation effectively promote social justice and democracy?

The effectiveness of the regulation of business has been the subject of extensive socio-legal research and analysis. Laws have been introduced ostensibly to provide individual rights for the less powerful in society or to protect collective interests against the absolute rights of property or the absolute right of business to pursue profit maximisation. Health and safety codes, pollution regulations, rent control, and anti-discrimination legislation are good examples. Yet research on the effectiveness of the regulation of business has not been optimistic. Although the tendency to critical assessment in the social sciences may often *under*play the measure of real progress achieved by legal reform, it is nonetheless the case that research has tended to highlight the limitations of regulation rather than its success.

The failure of egalitarian regulation has been largely ascribed to four factors: the failure of the law makers, the failure of the law enforcers, the failure of the drafters, and the failure of the whole cumbersome apparatus of law itself, destined always to lag behind dynamic business.

Those who make the law have been criticised for succumbing to powerful lobbies and fatally weakening legislation as a result, or for being necessarily a "captive state" by virtue of social networks, economic powerplay, or the blackmail of multinational business able to threaten to damage the economy by turning elsewhere if regulation is overdone. The substance of the law itself is thus often seen as an inadequate compromise riddled with exemptions and loopholes and lacking the teeth to give it any chance of effectiveness.

This in turn affects the enforcers. What can they do with inadequate powers? How successful can bluff be against sophisticated violators?

This paper draws on the research of the author and Graham Mansfield in a project funded by the E.S.R.C. on tax evasion and avoidance.

Enforcers also are seen as "captured". There is a trade between regulators and regulated; regulators are often insiders from the regulated industry. Organisational pressures intrude. There are too few enforcers, too many people and organisations to be policed. Negotiation, compromise, and underenforcement result.

At a more technical level the drafter is blamed. How can law be implemented effectively when it is overcomplex, unclear, and riddled with loopholes? At the most general level of all is the notion of lag: law is just too slow to keep up with the pace of changing economic reality.[1]

But there is another problem which has been ignored in the analysis of why egalitarian regulation fails – not how the law makers *make* law, not how the regulators *enforce* it, but how those on the receiving end *use* and manipulate it. Political lobbying over the content of law is one way in which the potentially regulated can actively influence the effectiveness of law. But the active role of those subject to regulation does not stop with the passing of an Act. Rather, legal techniques are brought into play to create strategies for weakening the law by legally *avoiding* it. Even if one could imagine a legislature so committed to egalitarian policies that it would not compromise in its law-making, armed with an enforcement agency with the commitment and powers fully to control violations, effective regulation may meet yet another barrier.

Enforcers cannot enforce laws unless they are violated. What regulation studies have underplayed is the extent to which the regulated do not violate but merely avoid the law. Responses to law are not just a matter of breaking it (crime) and obeying it (compliance). It is also possible to use legal techniques to achieve non-compliance with the *intent* of the law without technically violating its *content*. The law is not broken but it is, nonetheless, entirely ineffective in achieving its aims. *Despite* the legislature, *despite* the enforcers, law becomes merely symbolic.

This focus requires re-examination of the two other factors conventionally blamed for the failure of regulation: drafting skills and time lag. Faulty, hasty, and excessively complex drafting may well create problems for regulators. But much of the complexity of law and the convoluted style of its wording is not the cause but the result of avoidance. Specific devices to avoid law result in more law and more verbose law in the attempt to close the loophole. As for the notion of lag – the inevitable inability of the rusty apparatus of law to keep up with thrusting dynamic business practice – it may also confuse cause and effect. It may be less a matter of law lagging behind business practice than business practice quite deliberately moving out of reach of law. Regulation is not so much lingering behind business practice as a major motivation for its change. Business adapts to law not necessarily by complying with its aims, but by changing to keep outside its ambit. Those allegedly subject to the law can turn the law upon itself and render it ineffective.

AVOIDANCE IN ACTION: TAX AVOIDANCE

Consider two examples of avoidance in action – tax avoidance and the avoidance of rent regulations. Both are particularly relevant to the issue of law and social justice in that they are attempts to use law to limit absolute private property rights. Taxation impinges on private property rights for the *collective* 'good', rent legislation impinges on private property rights in order to establish counter-rights for *individuals* in a less powerful market situation. To the extent to which the tax system claims to be progressive (perhaps less and less), tax law is also aimed at the redistribution of private wealth.

But the world of taxation is riddled with avoidance devices. Indeed, there is a whole sophisticated tax avoidance industry specialising in the creation, marketing, and dissemination of legal methods to minimise or avoid tax. Take capital gains tax, for example. In 1965 the Labour Chancellor of the Exchequer introduced capital gains tax in the interests of greater equity. It was to be an effective tax on the rich, "an attempt to make speculators, property developers and well-advised financiers pay a fair share of tax on their profits".[2] But creating effective law that impinges on the interests of the "well-advised" is a difficult task. Being well-advised includes being well-advised on how to avoid tax. Capital gains tax has been successfully avoided over the years by a series of devices which have rendered it "the most legalistic and least cost-effective major tax in the Government's armoury" according to specialist commentators.[3]

One can, of course, avoid tax simply by taking property out of the jurisdiction altogether by going off shore to one tax haven or another. Or, indeed, one can evade tax by criminal action, by simply not disclosing assets – the world of secret money, numbered Swiss bank accounts and safe deposits. But there is the less drastic option – though it involves transaction costs – of taking advantage of one device or another to *avoid* the law in a way which may break the spirit but does not break the letter of the law, and thus leaves the avoider immune from either the necessity of compliance with the law or the risk of punishment. Specific devices popular at various stages over recent years have included such esoteric-sounding but utterly routine methods as 'bed and breakfasting' for avoiding capital gains tax on shares; 'bondwashing' for avoiding tax on gilts; or, on a rather different tack, 'offshore rollup funds' for 'legally laundering' income into capital to take advantage of the differentials in tax rates between the two.

Bed and breakfasting traditionally refers to a way of creating artificial capital losses to set against real capital gains and thus reduce or totally avoid paying capital gains tax. This involves taking shares which are currently at a lower value than when they were purchased, and which the owner actually intends to continue to hold in the hope that they will rise in value again. In the meantime the shareholder can crystallise the paper loss by selling the shares one evening and buying them back (by pre-arrangement with the dealer) the next morning. As long as they are out of the shareholder's hands for 'bed and breakfast' the paper loss will count against real gains and avoid tax. The introduction of indexation meant that a loss in relation to index-linked value (even though there was none in relation to actual cost) could be crystallised in this way too. This method is continually practised on a large scale, seen as "a staple of investment practice",[4] and indeed was widely recommended as a way of cutting the real costs of the Stock Exchange's 'Black Monday' in October.[5]

Bondwashing and offshore rollups use the law by manipulating the legal definition of income and capital. Bondwashing, in addition, depends on two exemptions: the exemption of government bonds (gilts) from capital gains tax if held for over a year, and the tax-exempt status of particular categories of investment and market actors, notably pension funds and market jobbers.[5]

Gilts realise income twice a year with a dividend. The practice was to sell the gilt, just before the next dividend was due for a price which reflected the value of the coming dividend. The dividend would have been subject to income tax but, by selling the gilt at a value that included the dividend rather than actually realising the dividend, the dividend value became a capital gain rather than income. The capital gain was exempt from tax. The security was sold to a tax-exempt organisation which took the income without paying tax and resold the security so that the process could begin again. Therefore no tax was paid at all.

Offshore rollup funds enjoyed a heyday in 1983-4, when some £2,000,000,000 was invested in them. Again, the interest (subject to income tax) on deposited funds was 'converted' into capital by taking it to a fund off shore (out of United Kingdom jurisdiction), 'rolling up' the interest due by adding it to the capital sum and re-importing the money as capital rather than income. At the time, higher rate income tax was seventy-five per cent compared to thirty per cent capital gains tax, so that for the higher rate taxpayers who normally used this device the tax savings were enormous.

Tax avoidance schemes attained a certain notoriety as employed by the Rossminster Group in the 1970s. For example, a major specific capital gain, perhaps resulting from a once-only transaction such as the sale of land for development, would be offset by a paper loss artificially created by a paper marketed scheme. These schemes were often inordinately complex, using devices relating to several areas of law – for example, different corporate entities constructed solely for the purpose of playing some role in the scheme, trusts, charities, and offshore elements. Financial transactions never intended to be fulfilled would cancel each other out in substance but in legal form would stand to create a situation where effectively 'nothing' became $+x\ -x$. A positive paper gain was created but fell into an exempt category, and was therefore irrelevant. A corresponding paper loss was left and this could be used against the gain in the real world which the scheme was designed to offset.[6]

All of these devices have now provoked legal action of some sort in an effort to control them. But many standard devices also have long histories of such attempts to control them without great success. The specific form of the device aimed at by the law may cease to be used, only to give rise to another remarkably similar but formally different method which technically escapes the law. Bed and breakfasting, for example, was the subject of regulatory measures in 1982. But it merely became 'weekending'. Instead of one transaction, there were two, carefully timed to fall into two accounting periods and thus avoid the rules. Old-style bed and breakfasting is in fact legal again. Bondwashing has been the subject of regular legislation and litigation since 1927 and has featured in every Finance Act since 1965. Its history demonstrates sixty years of careful adaptation of the device to meet new controls without essentially losing its effect. The announcement on 15 September 1983 that offshore rollup funds were to be subject to new methods of assessment was followed in the financial press within two days by advertisements for rollup alternatives, at least some of which have proved effective.

What we are seeing here is a positive and manipulative response to the attempts by law both to establish measures geared to greater social equity and to make those measures effective. Both types of law have met with active avoidance techniques which undercut the law by technically legal means.

Such techniques, though perhaps most notable and blatant in the area of tax, crop up across the range of law. Rent legislation can be taken as another example.

AVOIDANCE TECHNIQUES AND THE RENT ACTS

Nelken's study of landlords, law, and crime describes the harassment techniques used by landlords to exploit tenants despite the legal rights established by the Rent Act 1965. He points to the scope provided by the Act, which sought to "encourage as a priority 'freely negotiated' agreements between landlord and tenant",[7] and underlines that many of the methods used by landlords, such as 'winkling' (offering financial inducements to leave tenancies) were quite legal. Therefore, the substance of the law is seen as allowing, whether by policy or by silence, the practices which made it ineffective.

It is vital to recognise that the ineffectiveness of regulation is often written into the law itself.[8] But the law has also been used, in much more subtle and technical ways, in an endeavour to create loopholes where there is no positive policy encouragement at all. In short, even where the law-makers do positively seek to make law unambivalently effective, legal avoidance techniques can be brought into play to try to undermine it. The crucial technique is the manipulation of definitions. Exceptions to rules seem to be inevitable on equity grounds. Yet, as soon as an exception is recognised in law, the way is open for those whose activities the law is seeking to bring within the ambit of its control to redefine those activities to fall within the exempt category. Just as in tax law a more favourable rate of capital tax over income tax has spawned devices to redefine income as capital, so the distinction between tenants and licensees created the "potential for wholesale avoidance" of the Rent Acts by redefining ordinary tenancies in terms of licences.[9] Indeed, precedents soon became available for "judge-proof licences", achieved, for example, by renting through a company specially created for the purpose with memorandum and articles of association which permitted the company only to licence and not to lease. By definition, anyone renting accommodation from the company could be only a licensee and not a tenant.[10]

Likewise, exemptions in the Rent Acts for holiday lettings or lettings with board led to a rash of "holiday lettings in sunny Kilburn"[11] or the provision of board "consisting perhaps merely of a sandwich".[12]

To some extent judges do look through the legal form of the activity to its substance. For example, in an effort to uphold the spirit rather than the letter of the law, the judges in *Street v Mountford*[13] and *Ramsay v I.R.C.*[14] recognised the need to look through the form of devices to their substance, and see them as merely means of evading the Rent Act in the former and taxation in the latter case.

But as new criteria are established for what *is* acceptable, devices are adapted to fit these criteria and stay on the right side of the fence between illegitimate and legitimate practices. The emphasis in tax law on a need for commercial purposes as well as merely tax avoidance if transactions are to be held to result in reduced tax has, for example, led to tax planners advocating that commercial purposes should be built into schemes. Regulation founders on adaptation.

Legal avoidance techniques are routine and permeate the range of law. Current research on insolvency law shows how financial institutions have constructed devices to secure priority for their claims over the scarce resources of insolvent companies.[15] In the face of statutory attempts to ensure basic equality among creditors, or indeed priority for particularly weak creditors such as employees, devices such as the floating charge have been adopted to keep lenders in the most powerful position. Even in areas such as health and safety regulation one can see examples of avoidance in action. For example, Braithwaite's study of multinational pharmaceutical companies mentions in passing a company in the United States of America involved in its eleventh lawsuit over a drug declared by the enforcement agencies to be in contravention of the Food and Drugs Act. Each time the drug was banned its ingredients were minutely adapted to make up a "new" drug, and it was marketed until successfully challenged again.[16]

What makes avoidance possible? To understand this we must look at the role of the legal profession and the nature of law itself.

THE ROLE OF THE LEGAL PROFESSION IN AVOIDANCE

Research on the legal profession has tended to focus on access to it rather than what it actually does. Lawyers offer two classes of service – off-the-peg and tailor-made, or routine and creative. Access is a vital aspect of the issue of legal avoidance, but it is not so much access to lawyers as access to the *creative* role of lawyers that is at issue. Lawyers are not simply means to the implementation of statutory or other ready-made rights, but creators of legal techniques, definitions, and devices. Indeed, far from being means to the implementation of rights, it is lawyers who create the devices which *obviate* them and render them ineffective.

The legal profession, in short, is as much geared to the avoidance of law as it is to its implementation. Nelken, observing the legal advice necessary for some of the Rent Act avoidance strategies he describes, sees them originating in the readiness of "tame solicitors, barristers" and others to participate in shady dealings.[17] But avoidance is not just the prerogative of a few marginal "tame" members of the legal profession: it is a normal, routine part of the legal profession's role. Indeed, it is the creative side of the lawyer's job that is its most prestigious aspect and attracts the highest fees.

It is important to give due emphasis to the active and creative role of lawyers in working *against* the spirit of the law. There is little point in merely laying the blame for loopholes in the law at the door of the legislators and those who draft the law. Exemptions or faulty drafting may provide scope for legal creativity – these may leave the chink open for the thin end of the wedge. But it takes the active hammering of the profession to split the law apart. Lawyers may not, of course, see themselves as working against the spirit of the law. Their role is merely to interpret, apply, and work with the law as best they can in the light of their client's interests – any client's interests. But the nature of law allows considerable scope for legal creativity, and the nature of access to the law means that that creativity is more likely to be used to avoid than to implement egalitarian law. So long as there is unequal access to the creative role of lawyers, avoidance techniques are bound to be available only to those with the resources to buy legal expertise to tailor-make law to fit their own interests.

If, then, law tends to be less than effective in promoting egalitarianism, it is not simply because it is handed over on a plate by pre-determined structures, by a captive state, or by incompetent drafting. It is because of the *post hoc* creative work upon the law by the legal profession on a day-to-day, pragmatic basis to meet the interests of clients who can afford to buy its services in creating or avoiding law.[18]

AVOIDANCE AND THE NATURE OF LAW

How can the law be used to avoid the law? This may seem rather a contradiction in terms. But law is a multifaceted phenomenon and one facet can often be used to contradict another. Within the concept of law we can distinguish the ideology *of* law (as in the rule of law), legal ideology (the ideas expressed in law), legal policy (the purpose of law), the *content* of law (the actual wording of statutes and cases), legal forms and institutions, the legal professions, and legal techniques.[19]

Avoidance devices use the legal *techniques* of the legal *profession* to work on the *content* of statutes and cases, to produce a method of literally complying with the words of the law while nonetheless defeating its purpose. This is done in a way which meets the requirements of the *forms* and procedures of law, may even use the *institutions* of law for endorsement, and justifies the whole process via the *ideology* of the rule of law.

This special issue of the journal is not just about law and social policy, but also about democracy. The ideology of the rule of law in a democratic state requires that citizens be governed according to law, not by the whim of governors. Law should therefore be pre-stated, not *post hoc*. This, of course, assumes a degree of certainty in the content of law which is, in fact, elusive. It is elusive because the content of law cannot include every possible variant which it is intended to cover, or would be intended to cover if it had been foreseen. Indeed, one of the reasons every variant cannot be foreseen is that, in order to create a legal loophole, a good deal of legal brainpower is being put into *finding* a variant – however outlandish – which has *not* been foreseen.

Law seems to fall between two stools. In attempting to formulate effective regulations it can either be very general or very specific. In either case the rule of law can be called on to criticise and undermine it. If it is very general it necessarily operates with wide discretion in its application and this is resisted and lobbied against in the name of the rule of law. If it is specific, the very fact that it specifies the circumstances in which it should apply leaves it open, again in the name of the rule of law, to circumvention by carefully defining one's activities to fall outside its ambit.

Much law in Britain has tended to the latter approach – to literal interpretation and to only literal compliance – and thus to avoidance. Indeed, when in *Ramsay v I.R.C.* the judges abandoned literalism and looked through formal compliance to the substance of the activities involved, this resulted in something of a furore, with explicit criticism in the name of the rule of law. For example, a long-running series of letters in the press saw the "new approach" as "usurping the authority of Parliament", "infringing the provisions of the European Convention for the Protection of Human Rights"[20] and as a "clear infringement of individual freedom and a support for the state".[21]

The ideology of law can, in short, be called upon both to lobby against or challenge broadly framed law and to justify using the forms, techniques, and institutions of law to defeat its more specific content and purpose. And, although the rule of law has been looked to as a source of support for the underdogs of society,[22] in fact it is much more accessible to the top dogs of society with the resources to articulate and use it.

CONCLUSION: LAW AND AVOIDANCE

Law is, in its nature, multifaceted, contradictory, and manipulable, and it is the legal profession's role to take maximum advantage of the contradictions to manipulate the law in the interests of its clients. As the law, the legal profession, and access to both stand, it is hard to see how avoidance can be avoided. One problem is unequal resources; the other is endemic in the tensions and contradictions within the law itself.

Before the inevitability of avoidance is assumed, however, much more detailed analysis of law and its avoidance across a range of areas and styles of jurisdiction is necessary. As well as degrees of success and failure, it may be that there are areas where avoidance has *not* succeeded. It may be that some regulatory approaches are more effective in limiting avoidance than others. For example, one argument in response to avoidance of the law is to call for laws framed in terms of general principles and purposes and for wide discretion in their application.

But perhaps a word of caution is necessary here. For these are the very approaches which those who call for effective regulation of the rich criticise in the law governing the poor. Too much discretion, too little accountability in welfare law or policing, for example, are criticised precisely in the name of the rule of law. Those anxious to tackle the issue of whether the institutions of law in Britain today can foster egalitarian regulation *and* democracy are faced with the fundamental question of what is *law*? How far down the road to discretion can law go and still be *law*?

NOTES AND REFERENCES

1 J. Braithwaite, *Inegalitarian Consequences of Egalitarian Reforms to Control Corporate Crime* (1980); C. Stone, *Where the Law Ends: the Social Control of Corporate Behaviour* (1975).
2 *Financial Times*, 2 May 1985.
3 id.
4 *Financial Times*, 20 April 1982.
5 *Financial Times*, 30 October 1987.
6 G. Mansfield, "Techniques of Tax Avoidance" presented at the Law and Society Association Conference, Washington, 1987.
7 D. Nelken, *The Limits of the Legal Process* (1983) p. 56.
8 D. McBarnet, *Conviction* (1981).
9 D. Yates and A. J. Hawkins, *Landlord and Tenant Law* (2nd ed. 1986). See also J. Farrand and A. Arden, *Rents Acts and Regulations* (2nd ed. 1981); J. T. Farrand "Rent Act Roundup" (1978) 42 *Conveyancer* p. 379; M. Haley, "Avoiding the Rent Act: *Street v Mountford* and Beyond" (1985) 135 *New Law J.* p. 1053.
10 J. E. Adams, "Licences Made Easy" (1976) 40 *Conveyancer* p. 5.
11 Shelter Housing Aid Centre, *Annual Report 1974-75* (1975).
12 *R. v Battersea etc. Rent Tribunal ex p. Parikh* [1957] 1 W.L.R. 410.
13 [1982] 2 W.L.R. 877.
14 [1981] S.T.C. 714.
15 D. McBarnet and C. J. Whelan, "The Development of Priority in Insolvency" presented at the Law and Society Association Conference, Washington, 1987.
16 J. Braithwaite, *Corporate Crime in the Pharmaceutical Industry* (1984).
17 D. Nelken, op. cit., n. 7, p. 56.
18 D. McBarnet, "Law and Capital in the Role of Legal Form and Legal Action" (1984) 12 *International J. Sociology of Law* p. 233.
19 D. McBarnet and H. F. Moorhouse, "Business Law and Business Ideology" (an unpublished paper presented at the Social Stratification Seminar, Cambridge, 1977, and liberally used in *Economy and Society* (1984; eds. D. Sugarman and G. R. Rubin) pp. 49 and *passim*).
20 *Financial Times*, 5 July 1984.
21 *Times*, 3 March 1984.
22 E. P. Thompson, *Whigs and Hunters* (1975).

[12]
International Corporate Finance and the Challenge of Creative Compliance

6.1 REGULATION AND THE INTERNATIONALISATION OF CAPITAL MARKETS

Internationalisation of capital markets has underlined two key inter-related issues in the regulation of corporate finance. First, demands for access to reliable financial information have escalated as international financial risks have grown. The sums involved in corporate deals grew exponentially in the 1980s. The leveraged buyout of RJR Nabisco in 1988 cost $25.08 billion, resulting in borrowings for the new RJR of $22.08 billion, more than the combined national debts of Bolivia, Uruguay, Costa Rica, Honduras and Jamaica.[1] The need for transparency in financial reporting has been further highlighted by recent major corporate and banking crashes, such as the Bank of Credit and Commerce International, British and Commonwealth, Rush and Tompkins, Polly Peck, Bond Corporation and Maxwell Communications Corporation.

Subsequent analysis of some of these has revealed that the reliability of

* This chapter is based on research in the UK, France, Germany and Brussels. We are grateful for the funding contributions of the European Commission, French Commissariat du Plan, and Jacob Burns Socio-legal Fund.

[1] *Sunday Times*, 4 September 1988.

the financial information disclosed prior to collapse was suspect while the transparency of corporate financial activity was undermined by the use of 'havens' throughout the world where secrecy rather than disclosure is the norm. The suddenness, at least as far as the public was concerned, of many of these crashes, as well as the 'mega' sums involved, both testify to the fact that, in practice, investors are not always properly informed of the real financial risk to which they are exposed.

Secondly, calls for international harmonisation of the rules governing disclosure have increased as markets have opened up to international capital. The demand is for harmonisation which allows the players in capital markets to genuinely compare the financial results disclosed by different companies in different countries, and creates a 'level playing field', in which all the players are subject to the same rules. In an international capital market, the argument runs, there are dangers in differences in national rules, dangers, for example of creating what has been called a 'Delaware effect'. In the USA, the advantageous rules of the state of Delaware attract corporate registration of companies which actually operate elsewhere — at the time of our research only one major US corporation operated out of Delaware but 56% of the top 500 US corporations, and 45% of all companies whose shares were listed on the New York Stock Exchange, were registered there.[2]

Concern has been expressed that in an international market, different national rules can likewise create competitive advantage. Companies in one country might attract investment on the basis of high profitability or net value which is a product of advantageous rules on financial reporting and disclosure rather than genuine superiority of performance. The Securities and Exchange Commission recently announced a review of US accounting standards to determine whether they were 'adversely affecting the ability of US companies to compete internationally with foreign companies whose home country's accounting rules may be less stringent than US standards'.[3]

Different rules in different regimes may well distort the level playing field as when UK accounting rules have given UK companies an edge in takeovers, allowing them to offer higher bids for acquisitions than otherwise equally placed competitors. So, for example the spate of takeovers in the 1980s of US corporations by UK companies, often large US companies by smaller UK companies, has been put down in part to the comparative advantage given to UK companies by rules on accounting for goodwill. When Blue Arrow acquired the US corporation, Manpower, it could, under UK accounting rules, project annual profits of $30.1 million. A US bidder operating under US rules would have had to deduct at least $30 million each year from profits to write off goodwill, allowing a projected profit of only

[2] W Landau (1989), 'The Federal and State Roles in Regulating US Business Corporations', in B Wachter et al., *Harmonisation of Company and Securities Law*, Tilburg University Press.

[3] 22 Sec Reg and Law Rep (BNA) 1111, July 27, 1990.

$1.1 million. This could make it harder to sell the bid to shareholders and to raise finance.

How advantageous this competitive advantage was, might with hindsight be questioned, where overbidding and major financial difficulties have resulted.[4] However differences in rules have provided fuel for complaints and for the rhetoric of the need for harmonised rules and a level playing field in international capital markets. Can harmonisation and comparability, and the perhaps more fundamental goals of transparency and reliability, be achieved? This chapter addresses the issue by drawing on our research on law and accounting in the Single European Market.[5]

The creation of the Single European Market (SEM) provides us with a case study in regulation aimed at harmonisation. Fundamental to its idea of a free competitive market is the removal of those rule-based competitive advantages which act as prohibited trade barriers and their replacement with single community rules. The harmonisation programme of the SEM is a regulatory response to the problem of divergent rules within an international market. The tool being used in this strategy is European Community law. The SEM is thus a prime example of an attempt at using law to achieve international integration into a single market based on a level playing field. How successful has it been? How successful can it be?

In practice there have been major problems in the EC's programme of integration and regulation. Some are familiar problems with any regulation, although they are exacerbated by the international context. We will explore these in the specific context of the regulation of the financial reporting, briefly reviewing the familiar problems of legislation and enforcement, then focusing on the particular challenge we identify as 'creative compliance'.

6.2 CONTROLLING COMPETITIVE ADVANTAGE: THE CASE OF THE SINGLE EUROPEAN MARKET

Harmonisation of disclosure of financial information in the SEM has been tackled via the company law directives, particularly the fourth directive on company accounts and the seventh directive on group accounts. It has been no easy task.

The process of political compromise which has marked EC legislation generally has led to problems. There is the problem of settling for the lowest common denominator in standardisation. While the playing field may then be level, the EC rules are too weak. Worse, they may have been substituted for strong national regulations. Thus, fears have frequently been expressed that high standards of protection — for investors, employees, consumers,

[4] *Sunday Times*, 7 October 1990.

[5] Based on analysis of law and financial techniques and interviews with leading practitioners and regulators in the UK, France, Germany and Brussels.

etc. — in particular member states will be 'jeopardised in pursuit of economic integration.'[6] Then there is the tolerance of options within apparently harmonised rules. This can take the form of permission for member states to derogate from or to choose whether to implement certain terms of the measure. It seems, for example, that only the UK has implemented the option in the Seventh Directive which declares a parent-subsidiary relationship to exist where there is a participating interest and the actual exercise of dominant influence (discussed further below).

Compromise can also lead to gaps. It has been argued that a mergers regulation has been possible only on the basis that it concentrates on the competition aspects and ignores the social effects of mergers.[7] There is also the problem of delay with the result that by the time old problems are sorted out new ones have appeared. In an accounting context, the new practice of transferring goodwill to intangibles such as brands is possible 'as a result of the absence of any requirement to the contrary within EC directives'.[8] Such problems of the political and legislative process have undermined the quality of the rules themselves and their value as an instrument of genuine harmonisation. In short, while EC Directives are binding on all member states as to the end to be achieved and uniform standards may be mandated, significant deviations in the actual rules of member states remain in practice.

In the particular context of the disclosure of financial information, the European Community was confronted with marked differences in the basic purposes and philosophies of accounting in different countries. Indeed, even after the implementation of the fourth directive there remain considerable variations between member states, as Touche Ross's recent study[9] indicates.

This study demonstrated how a hypothetical company's performance could be reported in line with the national rules of different European Community countries. The reported profits for the same company undertaking the same transactions in the course of a year could vary from a lowest achievable ECU 27 million under German rules to a highest achievable ECU 194 million under UK rules. The most likely German result was only two thirds of the UK's (ECU 133 million in Germany, compared with ECU 192 million in the UK). Yet this was the same company reporting exactly the same business. This is a striking example of the difficulties involved in making international comparisons of company performance on the basis of disclosed financial information when the rules governing that disclosure are so diverse.

The Touche Ross study attributed a key role in this to the different orientations of member states to accounting for the capital market or accounting for tax. Where UK and Netherlands accounting separates tax and market

[6] See, e.g., A. McGee and S. Weatherill (1990), 'The Evolution of the Single Market — Harmonisation or Liberalisation', 53, *Modern Law Review*, p.578, p.585.

[7] Ibid. p. 591, n.90.

[8] Touche Ross (1989) *Accounting for Europe*, Touche Ross, p. 18.

[9] Ibid.

accounts, in other countries, such as Germany, ta . and market accounts are the same so that companies wishing to claim tax allowances must present the market with accounts with the appropriate claims deducted from profits. This leads to an inbuilt conservatism in German accounts which distorts comparability.

One can see just how difficult comparison can be by considering the accounts of German motor manufacturer BMW at the time of our research of Germany. BMW was taking full advantage of tax benefits such as the 100% first year allowances for investments in West Berlin, involving accelerated depreciation, which appeared as such on the accounts. The result is that one could not even sensibly compare a Berlin company's financial accounts with those of a Hamburg company. Yet even for the international market, BMW did not (and was not required to) disclose the effect this had on profits, noting merely that 'full advantage is taken of tax concessions regarding depreciation charges'[10]. As one (then) Big 8 accountant observed: 'this tells you they are extremely prudent but does not tell you much else'. How then are investors to compare BMW's performance with that of companies based elsewhere in Europe, or for that matter in the world? Continued variation in rules, and in accounting purposes and philosophy, undermines comparability.

This situation has been compounded by problems of enforcement and non-compliance even with compromised rules. Enforcement of law is a perennial problem even within the nation state. Effective enforcement is constrained by organisational problems, by lack of resources, by problems in detecting violation or non-compliance. Enforcing *international* regulation is more complex still.

In the European Community there are policing problems at two levels. First there is the problem of ensuring member states who have agreed to the substance of specific directives in fact implement them. European Community law comes in different forms. While 'regulations' are directly applicable in member states, the more frequently used 'directives', have, for the most part, to be implemented into their own domestic law by member states before they take effect. The organisation of the European Commission has been focused more on making than on enforcing legislation.

Then there is the problem of how closely member states themselves police compliance among companies falling under new regulations. Politics can play a part here too. Implementing law, but failing to enforce it, can result in the 'law in the books' bearing no relation to actual practice, and reduce the appearance of regulation and harmonisation to the merely symbolic.

In Germany, for example, the fourth directive was extremely unpopular. Many small and medium sized companies had not hitherto been required to produce public accounts. The implementation of the fourth directive meant

[10] BMW annual report to December 1987.

340,000 companies would now have to do so for the first time, this in a country where in 1985 there were only about 6,000 and in 1990 only 12,000 qualified auditors (Wirtschaftsprufer and Vereidigte Buchprufer).[11] Germany was five years late in implementing the directive and has throughout lobbied (successfully)[12] for a change in the directive to exempt many of these companies. In the meantime enforcement appears to have been somewhat ineffective. Less than 10% of German companies complied with the requirement to register company accounts in the prescribed time.[13] Harmonisation of member state legislation did not necessarily mean harmonisation — or transparency — in practice.

What are the solutions to such problems? The routine reaction is to demand a regulatory response, calling for better rules, better enforcement to achieve more effective rules and real compliance. Yet even if they could be achieved, better rules, better enforcement may not produce transparency or comparability. A great deal of effort — in policy- making, enforcement and research — is expended routinely on the objective of securing compliance. But even achieving this objective may not solve the problem. Securing compliance may not be enough.[14]

Formal compliance by those subject to regulation with even tough rules, cannot necessarily be equated with effective achievement of declared regulatory goals. Compliance far from being a solution to a regulatory problem may itself pose a regulatory problem. This is what we see as the paradox of compliance. Regulatory problems have been defined for too long as problems of non-compliance. The problem we focus on is the problem of compliance, and particularly the problem of 'creative compliance'.

Focusing on compliance as a problem involves a switch of perspective, from the regulatory response, to the response of the regulated. After all, those on the receiving end of rules do not simply receive them passively; they react and respond. They can respond by lobbying for change or by non-compliance, taking the risk of sanctions if law is enforced.

But the regulated can also respond in another way, setting lawyers and other advisers to work to develop responses to regulation, which do not simply accept the impact of the rules but which circumvent them. This involves using the rules themselves in innovative ways to avoid and manage regulation. This is why we have to switch perspective in another way too, from issues of politics and enforcement, to closer scrutiny of the nature and role of law and regulation. Law and regulatory rules are amenable to use not only as instruments for implementing regulation but as instruments for

[11] *The Wirtschaftspruferkammer* (1991), Wirtschaftspruferkammer, Dusseldorf.

[12] 90/604/EEC.

[13] Senior official, German Ministry of Justice.

[14] D. McBarnet (1992), 'The Construction of Compliance and the Challenge for Control: The Limits of Non-compliance Research,' in J Slemrod (ed.), *Who Pay their Taxes and Why?*, Michigan University Press.

resisting it. Such resistance to law through law is epitomised in the strategy of 'creative compliance'.

6.3 CREATIVE COMPLIANCE

Creative compliance means complying with rules in form without complying in substance, meeting the letter but not the spirit of the law. This is not an enforcement problem. On the contrary enforcement is pre-empted because control is avoided without breaking the rules. Creative compliance means operating within loopholes in the law, beyond the reach of the law, or using the fabric of the law itself to create loopholes or innovative techniques which comply totally with the requirements of the rules but nonetheless completely undermine the policy behind it.

So for example when Germany implemented the fourth directive requiring disclosure of financial information for many companies for the first time, one response for the companies concerned was to lobby for change; another was simply not to comply. These strategies posed practical enforcement problems and political problems for regulators. There was, however, another response possible, and it posed a more fundamentally legal problem. That was to change the legal structure of the business to remain outside the ambit of the law, and so avoid disclosure by creative use of law.

In Germany there are a number of different legal forms available for the conduct of business. Those affected by the 1987 implementation of the fourth directive were mainly GmbHs. However, those who wished to escape the requirement of the directive to disclose financial information could reorganise into a different legal form, into a GmbH & Co or a GmbH & Co. KG, often via highly complex legal routes.[15] The advantage lay in the fact that the GmbH & Co and GmbH & Co.KG were commercial partnerships which were not required to disclose financial information like other German corporate structures (Aktiengesellschaft, Kommanditgesellschaft auf Aktien, and GmbH). Disclosure could thus be escaped without non-compliance, via legal lateral thinking, via creative compliance.

This particular loophole has been closed by new rules[16], not least because of EC fears that what was defined at the time as a local German problem might be used more widely, fear, indeed of a Delaware effect, despite apparent legislative harmonisation by regulators. As a senior European Commission official put it: 'It would be iniquitous and contrary to the spirit and aims of the Fourth and Seventh Directive to allow those particular kinds of partnerships and unlimited companies to evade the accounting requirements

[15] Strobl, Killius and Vorbrugg (1988), *Business Law Guide to Germany*, 2nd ed., CCH Editions Ltd, Bicester.

[16] Directive extending the scope of the Fourth Directive on annual accounts and the Seventh Directive on companies, adopted Nov 1990. Implementation date is 1 January 1993, but it need not apply until 1995: 90/605/EEC.

applicable to other undertakings having limited liability.'[17] The regulatory response was not enough; the regulated could respond in turn to find new sources of rule-based competitive advantage, requiring further regulatory response in a cat and mouse game which is repeated in tax avoidance, the regulation of financial institutions and elsewhere.[18] And the game is not yet over. European Community law has itself provided other business structures which, we would suggest, might in turn be used to avoid disclosure. Certainly, even where such structures are set up for other reasons, non-disclosure of financial information is one consequence.

So, when Airbus criticises British Airways (BA) for being anti-European by buying its engines from America and even hints that 'sweeteners' may have underpinned its decision-making,[19] BA cannot easily retaliate. Airbus is a French Groupe d'Intêrets Economique (GIE). As such it does not have to publish accounts. Its liabilities, its sweeteners, government subsidies or whatever are hidden, legally, from view.

The GIE is only available in France. But it was the model for the new business structure available since July 1989, throughout the EC known as the European Economic Interest Grouping (EEIG).[20] The EC Regulation on EEIGs was designed to facilitate cross-border business cooperation within the Community by removing the need to operate in an unfamiliar system of law. But the EEIG is not only freed from legal obstacles, it is also freed from the obligation to disclose financial information. An EEIG has the advantage of flexible forms of funding. There is no capital requirement and liabilities can be hidden. The EEIG may thus offer route to escape from harmonised disclosure rules.

It is paradox enough that the 'strongest' form of EC law, a Regulation[21], can be used as a means of escaping from EC Directives, but there is more. While the Regulation provides for a uniform framework throughout the EC, it leaves to national law a number of matters it could not cover without seeking to impose a uniform system of private law. EEIG members are free to register it in any member state where it has a business presence or where it has its central administration. It will then be subject to the law of that state. The perceived and actual differences in national law, such as tax provisions, and in national legal systems — common law/adversarial versus civil/inquisitorial — re-emerge then as factors in determining where to register the EEIG. The effect of the Regulation may thus be that the choice of location will be distorted, 'Delaware' fashion, to the most favourable state.

[17] K Van Hulle, (1987), *Developments in Financial Accounting and Reporting of the European Community*, p.14, (KPMG, Amsterdam).

[18] D. McBarnet, (1988), 'Law, Policy and Legal Avoidance', *Journal of Law and Society*, Spring; and see E. Kane on the 'regulatory dialectic' e.g. in 'Impact of Regulation on Economic Behaviour', *Journal of Finance*, Vol.xxxvi no.2, May 1981.

[19] *The Times*, 27 November 1991.

[20] Regulation 2137/85.

[21] That is, it is directly applicable in member states.

This may be the least regulated. Whether this will pose a significant problem remains to be seen.

Escaping disclosure requirements altogether is one way to throw transparency and comparability, but of course if a company wants to enter the market it may have to disclose information. Indeed, in practice there may be more harmonisation than the formal rules would imply. French companies often voluntarily produce accounts following US GAAP (Generally Accepted Accounting Principles) for the simple reason that they want to enter the US market. Companies may produce multiple accounts for different markets or show how accounts prepared under one set of rules would have to be adjusted in another context.

But that is where we come to the underlying issue of the reliability of the information that is being disclosed. Creative compliance affects the reliability of financial information and, in doing so, it also affects its comparability. One area of creative compliance currently attracting regulatory attention is that of off-balance sheet financing (OBSF). This refers to the raising of finance in ways which do not appear in the accounts at all or do appear in the accounts but fail to make clear the real exposure involved.

OBSF can take many forms. It can involve the creation and use of complex and innovative financial instruments, which have posed a challenge for accounting rules worldwide. It is often unclear just how they should be accounted, measured or categorised, and this provides an opportunity for creative accounting. But OBSF can also involve the use of legal structures which avoid disclosure of awkward information. One UK example which has stimulated extensive regulatory response is the 'quasi-subsidiary'.

In the UK, and with the implementation of the seventh directive throughout the European Community, groups of companies are required to produce consolidated accounts showing the assets and liabilities of the group as a whole. However the techniques known as the non-subsidiary subsidiary, quasi-subsidiary or orphan subsidiary, have been used to avoid the requirement to consolidate financial information, thus hiding liabilities, manipulating performance indicators such as earnings per share, and, according to the reported figures, making the company stronger on the market, more creditworthy to lenders, and more powerful in the takeover market, in short, creating a potential competitive advantage based on manipulation of rules rather than performance or value.

The form used depends on the rules in play. In the UK under the rules of company law prior to the 1989 Companies Act, a subsidiary's accounts had to be included in the group's accounts (subject to some exceptions) if the parent company owned more than 50% of the shares and controlled more than half of the board of directors. A number of legal structures were created with varying degrees of complexity to retain control of a company while avoiding meeting those two requirements and so avoiding the need to include the quasi-subsidiary in the group's accounts. With the quasi-subsidiary safely off the balance sheet it could be used to carry debts or other awkward financial information in *its* accounts without affecting the balance sheet or earnings per share ratios of the group.

Such vehicles were used for many purposes by many household name companies including Cadbury Schweppes, Dixons, Burton, Storehouse, Habitat, S & W Berisford and Beazer.[22] Maxwell Corporation's acquisition of Macmillan and the Official Airlines Guide (OAG) for $2.6 billion and $750 million respectively, in 1988, used off-balance sheet structures. Macmillan was bought through shell company Mills Acquisition. OAG was bought by Pergamon, which as a private company, was not included in Maxwell Corporation's balance sheet. If the companies had been bought directly by MCC and included in the group's balance sheet there would have been seriously adverse effects on the earnings per share ratios of the group with possible knock on effects on share prices. The interest costs involved in servicing the enormous debt incurred would also have affected MCC's pre-tax profits.

Purchasing through an off-balance sheet structure provided a window in which to try to sell off assets to reduce the enormous burden of debt before bringing the acquisitions onto MCC's accounts. MCC's broker was reported in the press offering reassurance that the timing of the transfer of ownership of MacMillan would ensure there was no dilution of group earnings per share.[23] In reality, neither the debt nor the interest costs went away. But they were kept off MCC's reported assets and profits, even though MCC remained ultimately exposed to the financial risks involved.

The quasi-subsidiary in the particular forms constructed in the 1980s is no longer possible. These have been caught by new rules in the Companies Act 1989. However, the form employed is dictated by the rules in play at any given time. New rules can simply mean adaptation and new techniques. Even before the 1989 Act was on the statute book, the practitioners we were interviewing claimed to be constructing new techniques with the express purpose of meeting the requirements of the new rules yet still avoiding consolidation of riskier ventures in group accounts.

The deadlocked joint venture is one of several current techniques, carefully designed in a bid to escape the new law. The criteria for consolidation of a company's results in the larger group's accounts moved in the 1989 Act towards broader criteria, aimed more at capturing the economic substance of corporate relationships and not just their formal legal structures.[24] The new criteria were, first, participating interest (which was broadly but clearly defined) and second, control defined more vaguely in terms of 'actual dominant influence'.

The deadlocked joint venture is geared to avoiding this criterion of

[22] For a detailed analysis of Bearer's use of a quasi-subsidiary for the acquisition of Koppers, see McBarnet and Whelan (1992). Law Management and Corporate Governance, in J. McCahery, S. Picciolo and S. Scott (eds), *Corporate Control and Corporate Accountability*, forthcoming.

[23] *Financial Times*, 5 November 1988.

[24] See McBarnet and Whelan (1991), 'The Elusive Spirit of the Law', *Modern Law Review*, November.

control, being based on a 50-50 partnership with neither partner controlling. Deadlocked joint venture companies have been used as vehicles for property development, and the discovery, after its sudden collapse, of a claimed £700 million of debt in joint ventures involving construction/property development group Rush and Tompkins clearly reveals how the joint venture can work to hide liabilities. The receivers at Rush and Tompkins have suggested many of its 50 joint ventures were joint in name alone with Rush and Tompkins carrying most of the risk.[25]

The regulatory response continues with the accounting profession's efforts to produce a new accounting standard to ensure the reality of risks and rewards is disclosed. But the approach is controversial. The standard has been in process since 1987 and is still at draft stage, in Exposure Draft 49 (ED49).[26] There must also be doubts as to the feasibility of effectively and sustainedly enforcing the 'spirit of the law' rather than ensuring merely formal or creative compliance.[27] Off balance sheet financing is not a UK phenomenon nor even just a European phenomenon, but a regulatory headache in the corporate sector and in banking internationally.[28]

Such creative compliance has relevance for both transparency and comparability in financial reporting. A company which can raise finance in ways which protect its balance sheet and earnings per share ratios may not only distort its own financial image but may create for itself a competitive advantage over those who offer fuller disclosure of debt and risk.

6.4 THE CHALLENGE OF CREATIVE COMPLIANCE IN A COMPETITIVE MARKET

When issues arise perceived as requiring a regulatory response, then, however powerful that regulatory response may be, it may still be rendered ineffective by the response of the regulated. Even if we could achieve harmonised rules and formidable enforcement it would not be the end of the regulatory story but the beginning of the next chapter, the regulated's response. In the context of international capital markets, variation in the stringency of different nation's laws and regulations has been pointed to as a source of competitive advantage. Indeed there are often powerful economic incentives for governments to promote a 'Delaware effect' so long as they are benefiting. But law can provide a means of competitive advantage in another way, less dependent on governments or regulators. Law must be

[25] Christopher Morris of Touche Ross, *The Times*, 30 April 1990.

[26] Accounting Standards Committee (1990), ED49: Reflecting the Substance of Transactions in Assets and Liabilities, Accounting Standards Committee.

[27] See McBarnet and Whelan (1991) op cit., note 24.

[28] For example, Bank of International Settlements (1986), *Recent Innovations in International Banking*, BIS.

recognised not just as a means of regulatory control but as a raw material[29] with which the competitors themselves can create rule-based advantage.

Indeed there is a paradox in using law or other forms of regulation to remove rule-based competitive advantage and create a level playing field for fair competition. The situation needs to be viewed from the perspective of the players in the competition. From this perspective the level playing field may well be something seen as an unqualified good—*for one's competitors*. For oneself, there may be other ambitions, such as the vantage point of a little molehill of competitive advantage in the middle of that level playing field. In the competitive environment which is the goal of the SEM, there may be every incentive to use creative compliance to stay one step above levelling law.

Paradoxically, regulation, intended to remove artificial competitive advantage can also create opportunities to gain competitive advantage. A legally based level playing field opens up new sources of competitive advantage, with some more able than others to creatively escape even harmonised regulatory restrictions. The rules of the level playing field themselves become obstacles to some but not all. Regulation in effect becomes a further stimulus for innovative use of law both to defeat unwelcome regulation and to secure advantage over competitors.

This produces a dilemma for regulatory authorities, bent on a policy of free competition. How are they to encourage companies to take advantage of a competitive environment while at the same time discouraging them from gaining a competitive edge by getting round the restrictions of the rules themselves? One irony of the Single European Market is that the European Commission uses law to establish a level playing field for competitive market activity, producing, indeed, 'an immense corpus of law'.[30] But in a competitive market law may become just one more market obstacle to be overcome by the legal creativity of the regulated. The same paradox is likely to be repeated in regulation of international capital markets more generally. As one of the then Big 8 accountants we interviewed put it: 'What we are seeing is competition based on comparative creativity rather than on financial strength or traditional business links.'[31]

The significance for the international capital market is not, however, just a matter of a level playing field, perhaps always something of a holy grail. It is also a matter of risk. Global markets imply bigger deals, more volatility and more risk. The reality of the risk that was there in the creativity of the 1980s is under the spotlight in the recession of the 1990s. Creative compliance poses a challenge not just for a competitive market but for the exposure to, and indeed creation of, risk in that competitive market. It also poses a major

[29] McBarnet (1984), 'Law and Capital: Legal Form and Legal Actors', *International Journal of the Sociology of Law*, August.

[30] P. Sutherland, 'Address by Mr Peter D. Sutherland', in Irish Centre for European Law (ed.), *The Legal Implications of 1992* (1990), p.4.

[31] Head of Treasury Practice Group, International Accounting firm, London.

challenge for regulation, with no easy solution in sight. Yet unless the challenge of creative compliance can be effectively met, there can be little realistic prospect of achieving comparability in the market or of ensuring adequate disclosure of financial risk.

[13]

Transnational Transactions: Legal Work, Cross-Border Commerce and Global Regulation[1,2]

The topic of law in a global economy is commonly framed as a problem. It is framed as a problem for the *regulation* of transnational business, in the absence of unified norms and global authorities to enforce them. It is also framed as a problem for the *transaction* of transnational business in the face of the conflicting demands of multiple jurisdictions, or in the face of massive 'gaps' in the commercial law of, for example, emergent markets. This chapter focuses on the second of these issues, the legal aspects of *doing business* transnationally, but it has significant implications for transnational *regulation* too.

The research on which this is based was prompted by an apparent paradox. The dominant discourse on global business law is couched in terms of the major problems posed for business by cross-border legal gaps and clashes, and the urgent need to resolve them. Resolution is seen as a matter for international policy and institutional development, in particular by constructing, or constructing further, a global framework of laws or pseudo-laws.[3] In the meantime, however, the global economy appears to be thriving. The empirical reality is that business goes on. Cross-border deals are proceeding, on a massive scale, with or without cross-border law – and they are proceeding as *legal* constructs.

How are these deals legally accomplished in the absence of a fully developed framework of global law? The key to this lies in *legal work*, and the role of legal work in transnational transactions. The term 'legal work' is used here to mean technical work, with and on the law, undertaken usually but not necessarily by

1 This chapter draws on a paper presented as 'Legal work in a global economy' at the Law and Society Conference, Miami, May 2000 and written up during a period of sabbatical leave at Edinburgh University Law Faculty, to whom many thanks.

2 Doreen McBarnet is Reader in Socio-Legal Studies at Oxford University and Senior Research Fellow at the Oxford Centre for Socio-Legal Studies. Her main area of interest for some years has been business and the law, in terms of both business practice and its regulation, and, more generally, in the nature of law, legal work and the rule of law. She directs the Centre's research programme on *Business, law and lawyers*, and her own projects have included work on tax avoidance, financial reporting, company law, the Single European Market, and the role of lawyers. Major publications include *Conviction*, and (with Chris Whelan) *Creative Accounting and the cross-eyed javelin thrower.*

3 See eg, Goode (1991); Bonnell (1992).

lawyers, in specific transactions for specific clients. This is a remarkably under-researched aspect of law, whether global or domestic.

To focus research on legal work in a global economy is to adopt a rather different perspective from the main body of transnational research, since it homes in on legal and business practice at the micro level. There is a good deal of debate and research on the need for, or construction of, shared global norms and global institutions to make or enforce them.[4] The focus here is on the macro level and on collective action, whether by states, business associations, legal firms or non-governmental organisations to produce legal, or pseudo-legal, structures.[5]

The writer's research, by contrast, focuses on action at the level of the individual business deal, on the law firm's work for its individual client in specific global transactions. It looks at technical legal work at the micro level.[6] But it also has implications for macro-level analysis. It shows how problems at the macro level are resolved at the micro level. Legal work produces micro-solutions for macro-problems. At the same time, demonstrating how the micro can affect the macro suggests some less benign consequences. If legal work can produce micro-solutions to macro-problems, it also has the potential to undermine the macro-solutions of painstakingly constructed global norms and institutions.

Focusing on legal work means we can not only try to understand the macro through the micro, but to elide analysis of both commercial deals and regulation, and as suggested in the opening paragraph, to draw out the implications of one for the other. Though conventionally commercial law, on the one hand, and regulation, on the other, whether at international or domestic levels, fall into two separate categories – private and public law – and legal academics tend to specialise in one or the other as distinct concerns, the reality is that at the level of legal practice, public and private law are intertwined. Focusing on legal work shows how private law in action affects public law in action and vice versa. Both in terms of solving problems and in terms of creating them, the workings of transnational regulation and the workings of transnational commerce cannot be properly understood in isolation from each other, or from legal work.

This chapter, then, turns the spotlight on the legal construction of global deals, on transnational transaction work. It looks at problems and problem-solving in the context of global business and the law. But it approaches 'problems' not from a policy perspective but from the pragmatic perspective of practising lawyers working for specific clients, and it analyses problem-solving at a micro rather than a macro level. It focuses not on how the problems posed for business by the current state of law in a global economy *should* be resolved in normative or institutional terms in the future, but on how they *are* being resolved in practice now. In this analysis, however, lie some lessons for policy and for the future. For it not only shows how legal work can solve problems; it demonstrates how solving problems for some can create problems for others. It suggests that law in a global society – whether commercial or regulatory – may face more endemic problems than the challenges involved in constructing uniform norms and enforcing them.

4 Eg Gessner and Budak (1998).
5 Teubner (1997).
6 Flood and Skordaki (1997) analyse the role of lawyers and others in a specific case, but with an interest in the collective creation of norms to deal with a cross-border dispute rather than the initial construction of a cross-border transaction.

BUSINESS, LAW AND COMPETITIVE ADVANTAGE

The problems posed for global business by the lack of global law are generally presented, in terms of the substance of law, as:

- clashes between jurisdictions, in terms of basic legal concepts as well as their interpretation and application;
- multiple requirements being imposed. The classic example is the range of different accounting rules to be met if a company wants to be listed on different stock exchanges; and
- gaps, where there are emergent markets, for example, but no legal infrastructure within them appropriate to market dealing.

These are also seen as leading more generally to uncertainty, and uncertainty is underscored by concerns over cross-border enforcement.[7]

Variability in substance has been addressed by numerous strategies of harmonisation. This may be by way of international treaties between states, such as the Vienna Convention on the International Sale of Goods, or by the more ambitious harmonisation of domestic law envisaged by the EU based on the inter-state Treaty of Rome. It may be by way of the work of international organisations such as UNCITRAL or UNIDROIT. It may be addressed by judges, lawyers and accountants working together in specific cases to create special hybrid rules for cross-border contexts.[8] Or it may be initiated by business associations such as International Chambers of Commerce.[9]

The role of business associations themselves has led to the view that global law or pseudo-law is being constructed by business for business as a new lex mercatoria.[10] Business has also been active in setting up its own institutions for international arbitration to deal with disputes.[11] Business can therefore be seen in this sense to be solving its own problems and finding ways to unify the patchwork of varying national laws that obstruct its global deals via collective action at the macro level, the level of shared structures.

This is a macro perspective however. At the micro level, business is also doing it for itself, but by individual rather than collective means, and with a more immediate pragmatic and individual business agenda in mind.

Businesses are responding to the 'global problem' through transactional legal work by their legal advisers. If a desirable cross-border deal is being obstructed by clashing or inadequate laws or enforcement structures, these are no longer policy problems to be solved by negotiating agreed structures for the future but practical problems which management expects its lawyers to solve now. And solving them is exactly what its lawyers do. Indeed solving obstructive legal problems is exactly what legal work – at its most sophisticated level – is all about.

These are, however, individual solutions for individual clients and individual transactions. Often these solutions disseminate to become standard practice. Lex mercatoria is constructed from below, bottom-up from the legal work done to solve problems for individual clients, as well as top-down through standard-setting

7 Gessner and Budak (1998).
8 Flood and Skordaki (1997).
9 Goode (1991).
10 See eg, Mertens (1997); Banaker (1998).
11 Dezalay and Garth (1995); Banaker (1998).

bodies. None the less they are solutions that originated in private legal work for private clients, through 'the pragmatic practices of legal entrepreneurs serving their clients' interests', as the writer phrased it many years ago in setting out the concept of law in practice as a 'raw material to be worked upon'.[12]

It should scarcely come as a surprise to find that businesses (and lawyers) operate at the individual as well as the collective level in addressing global problems. Not only do they have to resolve problems in the here and now in order to pursue global business pending future collective developments, but their role in relation to other businesses is not essentially one of collective action. Businesses may have common interests in working together to solve common problems, but they are also in competition. Associates in a sector are also rivals, bent on finding competitive advantage vis-à-vis each other.

Uniformity has the advantages of simplicity and of fostering a sense of certainty and enforceability, and even individual creative solutions can benefit from a wider use that legitimises them.[13] But from a competitive perspective uniformity is a disadvantage. Discussions of global business and the law are often framed in terms of a level playing field. In fact a level playing field is a mixed blessing. From the perspective of any given business, a level playing field is exactly what is wanted – for its competitors. For itself it would prefer to find a nice little molehill of competitive advantage rising above it.[14]

Legal work is one means of securing such competitive advantage. Law is not just an obstacle to business, but a material which can be worked on to its advantage. If creative means can be found to overcome legal obstructions to global deals then those obstructions – still in existence, at least for a time, for others – become not an obstruction but an opportunity, and a route to competitive advantage. There is therefore a constant drive for new legal constructs to solve the global problem, not just at a collective level but at the level of the individual business, the individual deal. That background should be borne in mind as we go on to look in some detail at one example of legal work in a global economy.

GLOBAL LEGAL WORK IN ACTION

The role of legal work in a global economy can best be illustrated through a case study drawn from ongoing research.[15] This particular example concerns the legal construction of cross-border investment in emergent markets, and focuses specifically on a series of deals set up in the late 1990s – and still[16] in play – to

12 McBarnet (1984) at 233.

13 See Frankel (1998) for an interesting elaboration of this.

14 For examples in the context of the Single European Market, see McBarnet and Whelan (1994).

15 The project as a whole draws on data on legal transaction work collected in the course of research conducted over several years in the areas of tax, corporate and banking law and practice (all of which inevitably involved transnational deals), along with new work on the specific issue of transnational transactions. The research has involved documentary analysis, including analysis of contracts and transaction structures, participant observation and especially in-depth technical interviews with individuals from major international law firms, international accounting firms, senior in-house legal counsel for multinational corporations, barristers, bankers, regulators and government agencies. Funding sources include the ESRC, the Jacob Burns Foundation and the European Commission.

16 Writing in 2000.

initiate foreign investment via international capital markets in a major company in the Russian Federation. The analysis that follows presupposes no knowledge of Russian law or international finance, but simply an interest on the part of readers in how lawyers work for clients, and work *with* law, in the context of a global economy. The focus, in short, is on the perceptions and legal accomplishments of transnational actors – and particularly international law firms. This chapter looks at some of the problems posed by Russian law for cross-border investment – as perceived by the international firms acting as intermediaries and advisers in these deals – and how they were resolved by legal work, specifically by the legal work of the international law firm acting for the Russian company.

Cross-border legal risk

The Russian Federation example was chosen in particular to explore the issue of jurisdictional variability, as a result of the absence of global law, and especially the resulting issues of 'gaps' in law and legal clashes. Finance now works via global markets, and societies such as the Russian Federation are seen as new openings for financial markets. They are, however, 'emergent' markets, and one of the reasons they are 'emergent' rather than emerged is the fact that they are developing from a different social, political and economic context. Their legal infrastructures are likewise 'emergent'. They are not yet seen by global market players as providing the legal requisites of a market economy. Even where legal provisions have been made there may be concern about their reliability in practice. In short, the economic opportunity for cross-border dealing is there, but there are deemed to be 'gaps' in the legal framework.

At the macro level the question is: How should an appropriate legal infrastructure be created to facilitate investment in emergent markets? How can capitalist legal structures be effectively transplanted? The focus is on development, on changing the legal structures of emergent markets as quickly as possible (though that is fraught with difficulties). At the micro level, however, the question is different. The question here is how *do* transition economies attract investors who are seeking reasonable legal security in a legal infrastructure that does not, in their view, provide it? How *is* global finance, cross-border investment, functioning in such circumstances? The fact is that foreign investment in transition economies does take place on a large scale. Partly this is because investors entering such markets are willing to take more risk – political and economic as well as legal – because of the potential for very high returns. But it is also because legal risk is mitigated through legal gaps and legal clashes being tackled and overcome by technical legal work.

For any Russian company wanting to attract investment from abroad in the late 1990s (and still), and, in this case, for the US/international law firm advising it, there were two general problems posed by the Russian Federation's legal structure. One problem was posed by the lack of legal protections for investors normally available in western capital markets. The other was posed by the existence of special regulatory obstacles in Russian law which meant conventional instruments used for cross-border investment would not work in the Russian legal context. This is then a classic example of both legal gaps and legal clashes, or indeed legal barriers, posing problems for cross-border transactions.

These problems were resolved through legal work: partly through spotting problems and negotiating and drafting contractual solutions; and partly through technical transaction work, some routine, some far more complex, tortuous and creative. We will look first at the more straightforward, at how legal work dealt with regulatory gaps.

Dealing with regulatory gaps: contractual regulation

The first general problem was the lack of standard Western legal protections for investors in the Russian regulatory structure. As the prospectus for one of the share offerings warned:

> 'Russia is still in the process of developing the legal framework required by a market economy.'[17]

Similar problems pervade the 'transition' economies of Eastern Europe in general. In a recent survey conducted in relation to Kazakhstan, 91.6% of respondents saw the legal infrastructure and pace of change in its development as a barrier to trade. Half of those respondents saw this as the major barrier.[18] In our case study, the strategy adopted was to write in, as contractual obligations, requirements and arrangements normally provided by western regulatory systems, so that what was lacking in Russian regulation was provided for by private agreement. In short, private law substituted for what state law had failed to provide; legal work created private or contractual regulation.[19]

This can be illustrated by two examples, two matters judged particularly important for potential investors: the regulatory structures for share registration and financial reporting. The first was basic. It concerned legal recognition of a shareholder's ownership of the shares he or she had purchased. The second is also seen as fundamental to capital markets. It concerned reliable representation of the company's value and prospects to prospective shareholders, and meaningful accountability to shareholders after purchase.

Establishing ownership: share registration

The first problem for the architects of the securities offerings was evidence, and therefore security, of ownership. Under Russian law, ownership of shares in a company was established solely by reference to the company's shareholder register or the records of a depository. The shareholder's rights were therefore entirely dependent on the accuracy of the company's register or the depository's record. Unless the shareholder was recorded on the register he or she would not have any legal basis for claiming ownership of shares in the company. There is an obvious paradox in being totally dependent for legal rights to the profits and assets of a company on records under the control of the company itself, and one lawyer recounted instances of foreign shareholders simply being struck off the register and so losing the basis of any legal claim to ownership.

17 The analysis that follows quotes from some of the documentation studied in detail as part of the research.

18 Kazakhstan Survey, May 1997.

19 Teubner (1997) p xiv also observes relationships between the public and the private in the global context, although in his case in the context of norm creation by non-governmental organisations – 'private governments' with 'a public character'.

At the time of the offerings under analysis, a regulated registration system was just about to come into play. However, there were still concerns over how the system would work in practice. For example, the writer was told that brokers sometimes held shares in their own names, which not only implied continuing risks for the shareholder who was still not registered in person, but which could also produce all kinds of knock-on effects in terms of adverse tax implications.

There were concerns that there was not yet a sufficient infrastructure of independent registrars, especially outside the main urban centres such as Moscow and St Petersburg. There was also concern, expressed in the prospectuses, that even with the new rules –

> 'many Russian companies are unlikely to be in compliance with the share registrar rules'

by the due date. What is more, a close look at what is legally allowed, even for the 'compliant', raises questions about just how independent of companies the new registrars would be. Under the new laws, companies could quite legitimately own up to 20% of the company registering their shares. Indeed, our case study company (which had hitherto owned and controlled its registrar) intended to comply with the new rules by joining with several other companies to set up (and each partially own) their new registrar.

Such a situation was unlikely to encourage investors. Measures to address this regulatory situation were therefore incorporated into the contractual arrangements for the offerings. The company undertook as a matter of contractual obligation, to –

> 'take all and any action as may be necessary to assure the accuracy and completeness of all information set forth in the Share Register.'

What is more, the company agreed to provide the intermediary institutions involved in the deal with 'unrestricted access to the Share Register' to check registration 'regularly (and in any event not less than monthly)', along with committing to a whole list of specific duties in specific circumstances.

The company was also to be held liable, under the contract, for any failures on the part of the registrar. This might be seen as converting from disadvantage to advantage the scope under even the incoming Russian law for continuing control of the registrar by the company. The regulatory failings of Russian law, from the perspective of investors, were therefore addressed privately by the introduction of contractual obligations.

Information and accountability: financial reporting

In established markets such as the UK or US, companies are required, as a matter of statutory obligation, to provide public information on their financial status, both in terms of their performance and their assets and liabilities. Lawyers advising the Russian company on foreign capital-raising were faced with a different situation under Russian Federation law. As the prospectuses noted:

> 'While the Securities law contemplates that any company that issues securities to the public will provide periodic reports to the market, regulations implementing this requirement have yet to be adopted. As a result public information about Russian companies is extremely limited.'

– or, more bluntly, as one lawyer put it –

'company accounts in Russia are absolutely useless.'

This is of course scarcely surprising since the regulations governing them were drawn up for a completely different economy with completely different criteria of accountability. But the net result is that what is seen by capital markets as appropriate information for assessing risk and reward was simply not required in the Russian legal and regulatory structure at the time of the offering.

However, it was required *contractually*. The information given to would-be investors – the offering memorandum – included financial statements drawn up by the company and its subsidiaries not under Russian accounting procedures but under US Generally Accepted Accounting Principles (US GAAP). These were drawn up for the full period of the company's privatisation, resulting in two full annual accounts, and interim half-year accounts for the period prior to the share issue. The annual accounts were audited by a 'Big 5' international accounting firm under US GAAP rules.[20]

The company also undertook –

> 'in connection with the Global offering, to publish audited consolidated financial statements in respect of its future financial years ... and to publish unaudited consolidated half year financial statements in respect of financial periods ... in each case in accordance with US GAAP.'

It undertook, in short, to comply with the standard legal requirements of western capitalist states, specifically, in this case, US federal law. The company did not even make available to its global shareholders the accounts it prepared under Russian regulations, and the prospectus expressly warned that they –

> 'should not be relied on by anyone who is unfamiliar with RAR [Regulations on Accounting and Reporting of the Russian Federation] and how they differ from US GAAP.'

So US law is transposed into the Russian deal by private legal agreement. It does not merely supplement Russian legal requirements, but replaces them completely for the purpose of the global deal.

None of this is very complex technically. Rather, it is legal work evidenced in spotting regulatory gaps and filling them by private contractual arrangements, though of course it also involved persuading the Russian company voluntarily to undertake obligations not imposed on it by its own law. This is the more significant when one realises that the state – or at least a vehicle set up to represent it – was itself still the largest shareholder in the company, with a 40% holding of the charter capital, including a 'golden share' with special powers. The state had not yet managed to establish an indigenous regulatory framework satisfactory to foreign investors. None the less, here it was, under another hat, privately contracting to abide by what was in effect a series of imported foreign regulations.

In a sense the state had no choice of course; it wanted foreign investment both in the company and in Russia. The first of this particular set of global offerings was particularly significant. It was to create a marker in the market. There was express reference to this in the prospectus:

20 Not that this alone guarantees reliable reporting. 'Creative accounting' as well as enforcement issues remain a problem even where there are established rules. See Griffiths (1986) and McBarnet and Whelan (1999).

> 'The Global Offering is being conducted in part in order to establish an active international trading market in [the company]'s shares and thus to facilitate access to the international capital markets in the future.'

What is more, the hope was that this would open the markets to other Russian companies in the future. This company had to succeed to forge a path for others. There was therefore a strong motivation to do what was necessary to make the deal acceptable in the global capital markets. But it also required effort, a point the lawyer in charge was keen to emphasise, to persuade the company to agree.

It is not the lawyer's power of persuasion that is of particular interest here, however. It is the lawyer's technical skills in problem-spotting and problem-solving through contract drafting. In particular, it is the way contract is used to tackle what are perceived, from a cross-border perspective, as regulatory lacunae. The result is legally binding controls constructed through contracts to compensate for regulatory gaps.[21] Legal work creates public law surrogates through private law – it constructs 'private public law'.

Mechanical and functional transplants

In the context of law in a global economy, what we see, in effect, is the problem of regulatory variations across borders being overcome in transnational transactions through legal work, either by transplanting, lock, stock and barrel, ready made protections from established regulatory regimes abroad, as in the financial reporting example – we could think of this as a *mechanical transplant* – or by transplanting an established regulatory function and satisfying it by constructing functionally equivalent rights, duties and liabilities appropriate to the specific situation, as in the share registration example – we could think of this as a *functional transplant.*

Mechanical transplants may be particularly attractive as a means of transplanting *legitimacy.* Teubner[22] suggests that –

> 'contractual rule-making ... is either seen as non-law or as delegated law-making which needs recognition by the official legal order.'

But by using rules already recognised by an 'official legal order' elsewhere, indeed, by the leading market economy, and recognised in practice in the international capital markets this company – and country – were seeking to enter, the issue of legitimacy may be mitigated. The mechanical transplant of established rules may therefore be a less risky strategy, de facto at least, than the invention of new ones.

Transplanting of legal systems, or elements of them, is often discussed at macro level as a policy for global regulation. But cross-border transplants are also the stuff of cross-border deals, accomplished at micro level through private law, and through private legal work by lawyers for private clients. Indeed, what is being accomplished is a kind of private harmonisation. Private treaties may be accomplishing more readily at the micro level what, at the macro level, is still being striven for through public international law or the work of international organisations.

21 How legally binding *in practice* these are depends, of course, on the efficacy of cross-border enforcement. This issue is beyond the scope of this chapter but is addressed in McBarnet (2002).

22 Teubner (1997) p xiii.

This is, however, harmonisation with a spin. Indeed it is perhaps more a matter of legal imperialism, with the law of established markets – in this case the US – transplanted privately into the emergent market.[23] There is, after all, a body of international accounting rules, constructed by the International Accounting Standards Committee (IASC). It was not IASC rules that were written into the contract, however, but US GAAP.

From substance to structure: cross-border obstacles and the passport deal

Constructing a cross-border transaction, whether with emergent markets or not, usually involves more than just filling legal gaps. It also means dealing with legal clashes and, indeed, with legal obstacles to what have, in other jurisdictions, become established as standard legal forms in business practice. Such clashes and obstacles are also overcome through legal work – legal work of a different nature to that discussed in the contractual examples given above. This legal work is concerned less with the substance of the deal than with its underlying structure.[24]

Primary and secondary contracts: substance and structure

The contractual work illustrated above, dealt with the *substance* of the deal – the sale of securities. But underpinning this was a body of deeper transactional work, which dealt with its *structure*. Legal work often involves both what we might think of as the *primary* deal, which is the original objective, and a network of *secondary* deals which serve to establish the optimal structure for it.

It is important to distinguish these two levels of legal work. Where socio-legal research refers to commercial law in action it has tended to focus only on what the writer sees as *primary* contracts. But transaction work is about more than primary contracts. The primary contract is, in sophisticated legal work, just the tip of the iceberg, with an often massive, but largely invisible, substructure beneath the surface that needs to be researched too. Researching the primary contract alone would oversimplify the nature of the legal work involved in complex cross-border transactions and understate its subtlety, creativity and technical complexity.

In our case study this deeper structural work was crucial for making the deal work across borders, and in a way deemed commercially, as well as legally viable. Indeed, it was this deeper structural work rather than the surface contractual work that earned the transaction its nickname among those constructing it – the 'passport deal'.

What kind of legal clashes and obstacles were met in the course of constructing these cross-border deals, and how were they resolved? A brief look at one of the underlying structures from our case study may help demonstrate the legal work involved.

The passport deal

An established instrument used these days for cross-border securities (*now* established – but itself a product of creative legal work in the past) is the Eurobond.

23 For a more detailed analysis of the nature of legal work at this level, see McBarnet (2002).
24 See Dezalay (1992).

One advantage of the Eurobond form is that it does not attract withholding tax. This maximises yield and makes a security sold in this form an attractive option for investors.

Russian law, however, allowed no exceptions to the payment of withholding tax. This meant that the established advantages of the Eurobond structure would not work for Russian shares. This would reduce their attractiveness vis-à-vis other global offerings. The task for advisers, then, was how to construct a structure that would transfer the advantages of the Eurobond across Russian borders despite the obstacles posed by Russian law.

This was what the construction of the underlying passport deal accomplished. The prospectus for this particular offering could proclaim on its front page:

> 'Payments on the Notes will be made without deduction for or on account of taxes of Ireland or the Russian Federation.'

How does Ireland suddenly come into the picture? In fact, not just Ireland but Luxembourg and Germany – or at least corporate structures and financial institutions in them – became involved in the underlying structure that was finally devised to provide a 'passport' for what in business terms would be seen as a tax-efficient and therefore commercially viable offering.

In the course of construction, other obstacles were met in Russian law. One solution to the withholding tax barrier, involving loans and interest payments between the company and a specially set up foreign subsidiary, which would have worked in other cross-border contexts, would not work in Russia because of its particular rules on VAT, charged (at 25%) on inter-corporate loans. Another barrier concerned Russian rules erected to protect the country from flight of capital abroad. Russian companies wishing to set up an offshore subsidiary company to hold finance abroad could do so only with the permission of the Central Bank.

The solution finally settled on to overcome these barriers involved interpolating a series of legal relationships between the Russian company and its potential investors, involving an Irish subsidiary along with a German bank and its Luxembourg subsidiary.

The role of the Irish company was to issue the securities, Ireland being chosen for its particular tax advantages. The money would not stay in the foreign subsidiary, however, but come back into the Russian company. How would it come back in without attracting tax? Here the foreign bank became important. A German bank would (though only indirectly as we shall see) receive the money paid for the securities and pay it on to the Russian company. This would be paid to the Russian company, however, in the form of a commercial loan. As such it would attract neither withholding tax nor, since it was a bank loan as opposed to a loan between parent company and subsidiary, would it attract VAT.

Finally, as noted above, the securities were issued from Ireland because of tax advantages. However, these particular tax advantages were available only under particular conditions, including the purchase of assets on the secondary markets. Introducing the extra step of the Luxembourg subsidiary between the German bank and the Irish company effectively created a secondary market and so allowed these conditions to be met.

The whole structure involved a network of guarantees, pledges of indebtedness on two levels of priority, certificates of indebtedness and, of course, the aforementioned loan agreement, each of these also transnational, between the Russian company, the Irish company, UK, US, German and Austrian underwriters, the German bank and its Luxembourg subsidiary.

On the face of it then, we have a sale of Russian securities to, primarily, US and UK investors, and this primary deal incorporates a number of contractual safeguards, the product of legal work, to provide safeguards that the law of the transitional society does not yet provide for itself. This contractual legal work fills gaps.

There is also, however, an invisible substructure of secondary deals underlying this primary deal. This too is the product of legal work, highly creative legal work, and itself of a transnational character. The main task of this structural legal work is to overcome barriers posed to a transnational deal by differences in national legal structures. Under the particularities of Russian law the offering, even with the introduction of contractual safeguards, would not have been attractive. Contractual legal work would have helped temper the legal risks, but, to the business world, the impact of Russian-specific tax would have made the deal insufficiently rewarding vis-à-vis other offerings where no tax was involved. The offering would, in short, not have been competing on a level playing field in the global market.

The job of structural legal work was to find a way to make the deal commercially viable through legal means. In this case that meant finding a way to replicate the advantages of a Eurobond-type form across borders despite domestic laws that at first sight made this impossible. From the business perspective, its job was to level the playing field for the Russian offering and allow it to participate in the global market.

That these transnational deals were made both legally and commercially viable in a global market was therefore the product of active legal work at both primary contractual and structural levels, legal work which was often highly technical, complex and creative, and which itself involved a further network of secondary multi-transnational deals in support of the primary cross-border contract.

IMPLICATIONS: LEGAL WORK, CROSS-BORDER COMMERCE AND GLOBAL REGULATION

What does all this mean for the global law enterprise? Does it mean there is no need for global norms and institutions to facilitate cross-border commerce, since legal work can do the job without it? If shared global law is being accomplished, a level playing field established, from the ground up through practice, is there such a pressing need to establish it from the top down through international agreements on policy?

Cross-border commerce and harmonisation

In fact there will still be a drive at institutional level towards uniformity. There is value in standardised mechanisms, and tailor made legal work of the kind described here is expensive – although, of course, what begin as tailor-made mechanisms tend to percolate to become standard practice.[25]

Legal work, as noted earlier, contributes to a growing lex mercatoria.

That said, business has a complex attitude to harmonised law. Although there is a standard rhetoric among businesses complaining about variations between

25 McBarnet (1984); Powell (1993); Frankel (1998).

legal regimes, and calling for harmonisation, in practice variation between regimes is routinely exploited by business to its own advantage. This occurs at the level of politics, in negotiations over what kind of legal regime will be acceptable to multinationals operating (in theory)[26] under it, with one regime being played off against another. It occurs too in private legal constructions designed to take full advantage of cross-border variations in a sort of regulatory arbitrage. Complex global legal transactions are often only comprehensible if they are seen as artificial constructs designed specifically to take advantage of gaps and clashes between jurisdictions. In short, far from the lack of a harmonised global law posing a problem for business, it can also provide an opportunity that is routinely exploited. Business, in other words, can find advantage in both uniformity and conflict between regimes.

In the context of legal creativity, advantage can also be found in different ways, with different consequences for harmonisation. In a world in which business is hampered by cross-border gaps and clashes, it may be in the interests of business to use legal creativity to overcome them. Indeed, in a context in which competitors remain hampered by gaps and clashes this can produce competitive advantage. A consequence may be a levelling of the international playing field, both for the transaction in hand and, if the practice disseminates, more generally. But that is not the essence of the practice, nor its purpose. Creative legal practice is not about harmonisation but about innovation, and the purpose is simply to optimise client interests. Any resulting levelling of the playing field for others is purely incidental. Indeed, once such levelling occurs that particular source of competitive advantage through legal creativity is gone. Business needs to find its 'nice little molehill of competitive advantage' some other way.

Legal creativity in pursuit of business interest and competitive advantage is, in fact, much more likely to pose problems for harmonisation than to solve them, because it is continually producing new instruments and practices. As these emerge, so do new challenges for any harmonised law. New forms need decisions on how they are to be treated in law, with the danger of a new patchwork of varying treatments emerging, whether from national legislation, courts or simply the informal decisions of those applying or enforcing the law, until, and unless international consensus on treatment can be accomplished. Creative legal work, in short, can lead to a perpetual dynamic with harmonised law constantly lagging behind. In the Single European Market, many years of labour went into trying to produce a level of harmonisation of corporate financial reporting. But the (much compromised) 'consensus' was no sooner achieved than it was outdated by the development and escalation in use of derivatives and other new financial instruments, on which there was no agreed treatment.[27]

In short, in a business context in which competitive advantage can be gained from legal creativity, legal harmonisation is likely to be constantly chasing legal innovation.

This must make us think carefully about the role of lawyers and legal work in a global economy. Gessner has argued that 'legal certainty cannot be achieved globally at the level of programmes' – my macro level of global norms. Rather, he pins his faith in 'roles' – and so in the shared expectations generated by networks of arbitrators, business communities, and international lawyers.[28] But the role of

26 See below: 'creative compliance' is frequently used to escape control.
27 From research by McBarnet and Whelan.
28 Gessner (1998) p 438; see also Banaker (1998) p 382.

lawyers can also be less consensual and collective. Focusing on transnational transactions underlines the more fundamental role of corporate lawyers – working in the interests of clients, often by creative legal engineering. In their role as creative legal engineers, lawyers should be seen as not only having the potential to contribute to harmonisation, but also as having the potential constantly to challenge and undermine it.

Legal work and transnational regulation

Harmonisation is one issue, the effectiveness of transnational regulation, another. And for many the regulation of transnational business is the real concern, with harmonisation merely a potential means to that end. Micro-analysis of cross-border deal-making has implications for this concern too.

The chapter has shown how creative legal work can overcome legal barriers to cross-border deals and create a level playing field, which may seem a benign enough accomplishment. What are 'barriers' from the outside are, however, 'policies' from the inside of the country. They are there for a purpose. They are there to regulate business or to raise tax, and creative legal work undermines those policy purposes.

In the Russian example these policy purposes can be seen as rather more complex than this comment may imply. Indeed, the creative legal work involved could be seen as avoiding Russian law in order to facilitate Russian governmental policy, since it made possible a deal which the Russian government very much wanted to succeed. It was seen as a key step in facilitating the entry of Russian companies into global markets, and in bringing into the country much needed foreign investment. None the less there is a certain irony in the situation. The Federation of Russia was the dominant shareholder in the company in question. Under one hat, then, it stood for the laws of the land, under another it was not only agreeing to US laws overriding its own, but was party to a deal carefully designed to avoid Russian laws.

The point should be considered more generally, however. Creative legal work can undermine or quite simply defeat legal control. This is not a trait confined to cross-border legal work but to legal work more generally. Elsewhere, my own work or work with colleagues has demonstrated how creative legal structuring of deals can facilitate the circumvention and avoidance of regulatory law of all sorts, with knock-on effects for those intended to be protected by it.[29] In short there is a sting in the tail of creative legal work. Legal work involves overcoming legal obstacles, and those obstacles are very often regulations intended to protect others.

This has implications for those concerned not just with the facilitation of global business, but with its control. One long-term concern in globalisation has been the ever-increasing power of multinational corporations and the issue of how to establish effective global regulation of their practices. Since it is recognised that companies currently take advantage of countries with weaker regulations, hope is vested in enhancing and harmonising regulations – and their enforcement – at global level. But this ignores the potential impact of creative legal work.

Creative legal work is not just about playing with the different laws of different jurisdictions, finding tax – or regulatory – havens, set up precisely for that purpose.

29 McBarnet (1988); McBarnet and Whelan (1997).

It is about playing with law per se, even within one jurisdiction. It is about constructing 'creative compliance',[30] finding legal forms which fall outside disadvantageous or inside advantageous legal categories. It is about scrutinising legal definitions and thresholds, and repackaging deals to fall within or beyond them – in form though not in substance – as suits. It is about concocting legal forms as yet undreamt of by legislators and regulators. Creative compliance, the product of creative legal work, is likely to remain a problem for regulation even under harmonised and well-enforced global laws. What is more, since creative compliance so often depends on legal work at the 'invisible' substructural level, its occurrence may not be readily detected.

CONCLUSION

So what does a focus on legal work suggest for those concerned with transnational commerce and for those concerned with transnational regulation?

For those concerned with the problems of legal gaps and clashes obstructing cross-border commerce, the immediate message of our case study may be encouraging, since it demonstrates that private legal work by lawyers for business can overcome such problems. It can accomplish a kind of harmonisation in practice from below.

However, that is not the goal of, or driving force behind, legal work. At the macro level, lawyers and law firms, like businesses, may be working for harmonisation in policy, and it is true that the dissemination of their legal work techniques creates a kind of harmonisation in practice – in time and temporarily. But at the micro level of private legal work, the driving force is not collective policy. The goal is merely to serve the interests of the individual private client and to find or innovate legal ways to accomplish that. Though legal creativity can, in the current context, be a force for harmonisation, the driving force of innovation for competitive advantage is more likely overall to frustrate harmonisation than to promote it.

What is more, the driving force of clients' interests means legal work is not concerned to promote effective control but all too often is concerned to undermine it. So for those concerned with the *global regulation* of business through law or law-like structures, the message is far from encouraging. Work at macro level to construct global norms and institutions may face problems – not always readily discerned – at the micro level of practice. Efforts at global control of business may be set up at macro level, only to be destroyed by stealth through routine private legal work.

Select bibliography

Banakar, R, (1998) 'Reflexive Legitimacy in International Arbitration' in V Gessner and A C Budak (eds), *Emerging Legal Certainty: Empirical Studies on the Globalization of Law.*

Bonell, M J, (1992) 'Unification of Law by Non-Legislative Means: the UNIDROIT Draft Principles for International Commercial Contracts', 40 AJCL 617.

Dezalay, Y, (1992) *Marchands de droit.*

30 McBarnet and Whelan (1991; 1997; 1999).

Dezalay, Y, and Garth, B, (1996) *Dealing in Virtue: International Commercial Arbitration and the Internationalization of Legal Practice.*

Flood, J, and Skordaki, E, (1997) 'Normative Bricolage: Informal Rule-making by Accountants and Lawyers in Mega-insolvencies' in G Teubner (ed), *Global Law Without a State.*

Frankel, T, (1998) 'Cross-border securitization: without law, but not lawless', 8 Duke Journal of Comparative and International Law 2.

Gessner, V, and Budak, A C (eds), (1998) *Emerging Legal Certainty: Empirical Studies on the Globalization of Law.*

Goode, R, (1991) 'Reflections on the harmonisation of commercial law', Uniform Law Review, vol 1.

Griffiths, I, (1986) *Creative Accounting.*

Kazakhstan Survey, (1997) Kazakhstan, May.

McBarnet, D, (1984) 'Law and Capital', 12 International Journal of the Sociology of Law 3.

—(1988) 'Law, Policy, and Legal Avoidance: Can Law Effectively Implement Egalitarian Policies?', 15 Journal of Law and Society 1.

—(2002) 'Legal work in a global economy: micro-perspectives on macro issues', 1 Socio-Legal Studies: an international journal 1.

McBarnet, D, and Whelan, C, (1991) 'The Elusive Spirit of the Law: Formalism and the Struggle for Legal Control', 54 MLR 6.

—(1994) 'International Corporate Finance and the Challenge of Creative Compliance' in S Wheeler (ed), *The Law of the Business Enterprise.*

—(1997) 'Creative Compliance and the Defeat of Legal Control: The Magic of the Orphan Subsidiary' in K Hawkins (ed), *The Human Face of Law.*

—(1999) *Creative Accounting and the Cross-eyed Javelin Thrower.*

Mertens, H, (1997) '*Lex Mercatoria*: A Self-applying System Beyond National Law?' in G Teubner (ed), *Global Law Without a State.*

Powell, M, (1993) 'Professional innovation: corporate lawyers and private lawmaking', 18 Journal of Law and Social Inquiry 3.

Teubner, G (ed), (1997) *Global Law Without a State.*

[14]
Looking for Loopholes

The search for loopholes has traditionally followed a number of strategies. The basic approach is to search the words of statute, standard and, if it exists, case law to find material on which to argue a practice is 'perfectly legal'. What kind of material is sought out and used?

Gaps

The first strategy is to look for what is not there, to seek out gaps in regulation, to point out simply that there is no statute or standard that expressly prohibits the company's approach. This can be summed up as the 'where does it say I can't do that' approach.

The ex-files

Another version of the gap approach is to seek out *express* gaps, what we'll call the 'ex-files' of law and regulation. Lawyers look for express *exclusions* and argue 'the law expressly says this activity falls beyond its remit. It is therefore obviously beyond the remit of regulators.'

Gaps can be found *within* a statute or standard in express *exemptions*. Sometimes there are express rules acknowledging that legitimate *exceptions* may occur. The basic rule is for the 'ordinary', but other rules allow for extraordinary situations too.

A classic avoidance technique, then, is to structure activities in a way that can be *argued* to locate them in excluded, exempt or exceptional categories. We consider how companies might seek out gaps and 'ex-files' in the new regulations in Chapter 8.

Out of bounds

Another strategy is to scrutinise definitions and construct structures that fall beyond the defined reach of the regulation. The classic case in the creative accounting of the 1980s was the orphan subsidiary. In substance it was a subsidiary but in legal form it was not. It fell beyond the statutory definitions of a subsidiary, beyond the bounds of law.

The orphan subsidiary has been a key target of the new regime's new weapons. Is it dead? Or can legal arguments still be constructed to justify off balance sheet corporate structures? (Chapter 9)

Working to rule

The orphan subsidiary and many other techniques of creative accounting have been based on claims of compliance with the letter of specific rules. The new regime hopes to counter this with regulations based on principles rather than specific rules. FRS 5 is a keystone of this approach. But can FRS 5 still be scrutinised for opportunities for 'working to rule'? (Chapter 10)

Literal compliance

Literal compliance is key in working to rule. The question arises: can literal compliance also be claimed in relation to *principles*? Might even the requirement in FRS 5 to report substance be used to justify creative accounting? (Chapter 11)

Brief 'n' Counter

In the chapters that follow we demonstrate how these strategies might be applied in the new regime of financial reporting regulation. We explore bases on which legal arguments might be constructed in a bid to pre-empt or counter intervention by the Panel, to challenge the legal enforceability of the Panel's view, and to claim immunity from control.

Whether they would succeed or fail – with the Panel or in court – is another matter. We look at the factors affecting that – and what it means – in Part V.

Part Six

Law, Power and Control

[15]

Creative Compliance and the Defeat of Legal Control: The Magic of the Orphan Subsidiary

One of the pleasures of working under the Directorship of Don Harris was the unequivocal encouragement he gave to us to research previously unexplored areas in socio-legal studies. The Centre's programme on business, finance, and the law has been one outcome and it has proved a most fruitful area of study. Yet, at the time it began it was a risky strategy for both the Centre and those involved in the programme. For the Centre it meant a long-term commitment was being made to an area whose 'researchability' was untested, and indeed frequently doubted. For us and others, it involved a major investment in the acquisition of new skills and knowledge as well as a willingness to move beyond research 'origins'—in our case criminal justice and labour law. It is no small irony that the research has itself evolved into a study of the regulation of risk (in the context of corporate finance). The research would not have been possible without Don's creation of an environment which fostered freedom of thought, and the pursuit of new lines of inquiry. In this Chapter we shall explore one of the central themes of the research programme—the concept of 'creative compliance'—and the challenge it poses for legal control.

The practice of 'creative compliance' raises significant issues for our understanding of the operation of law and society. One issue of particular concern for both theory and policy is that of securing effective legal control. While many studies in law and society have researched the failure of legal control, focusing especially on the issue of enforcement, there has been little empirical research or analysis of the particular challenge posed for legal control by creative compliance.

[1] This Ch. is based on empirical research on business finance and the law funded by the Jacob Burns Fund for Socio-Legal Studies, the Economic and Social Research Council, and the European Commission. The research was based on analysis of legal and accounting data, the financial press, and on interviews with lawyers, accountants, consultants, bankers, and regulatory authorities. Where data collected from confidential interviews have become the subject of public discussion we have presented references for the reader's information.

Creative compliance involves avoiding law's requirements without actually contravening them. It involves creative use of the 'material' of law (McBarnet, 1984) to construct devices which comply with the letter of the law, while nonetheless escaping from legal control. One strand of Centre research demonstrates and analyses the practice of creative compliance in the context of tax, 'tax avoidance' being a familiar concept to layman and lawyer alike (McBarnet, 1988, 1991, 1992; Mansfield, 1994). But the practice of creative compliance is not confined to tax. Nor indeed is it confined to public law and state regulation; private law, as we shall see, is just as susceptible.

Creative compliance can be an expensive strategy, requiring major inputs in legal technicality and innovation. It is therefore characteristically—though perhaps not inevitably—a feature of the world of economic elites and large-scale corporations, in corporate finance, taxation, takeovers, and bankruptcy, or in battles for market share. In this context legal control—both state regulations and the controls of private law—can become just another obstacle to be overcome in the pursuit of economic and competitive advantage (McBarnet and Whelan, 1992).

In this Chapter we show creative compliance at work in the context of corporate finance. This is a complex and technical area, with many different techniques of creative compliance involved, and our research as a whole deals in detail with a wide range of devices and situations (McBarnet and Whelan, forthcoming). This Chapter will illustrate the role of creative compliance by examining the use of just one device in one specific context, the spate of mega-takeovers in the late 1980s in which astonishing sums of money were raised by sometimes relatively small acquiring companies as accomplishments of 'sheer magic'. It demonstrates how creative compliance provided the magic spell for accomplishing these feats for management. But it also analyses the other side of the coin, the risks that creative compliance can obscure, and the challenge creative compliance poses for effective legal control.

MEGA-TAKEOVERS AND LEGAL OBSTACLES

The late 1980s saw a spate of mega-takeovers with vast sums raised through creative corporate financing techniques, including but extending far beyond the now notorious 'junk bonds'. The corporate debt created was unprecedented. KKR's leveraged buyout of RJR Nabisco cost $25.08 billion, resulting in borrowings for the new RJR of $22.08 billion, more than the combined national debts of Bolivia, Uruguay, Costa Rica, Honduras, and Jamaica (*Sunday Times*, 4 December 1988). A major part of the scene was acquisition of US corporations by UK companies. In

1988, for example, there were 389 such acquisitions (*Accountancy*, October 1990, 66). Some of these were takeovers of very large US corporate groups by relatively small UK companies. While there may have been some regulatory advantages available to British companies in such takeovers against their US competitors, there were also many legal and market constraints; indeed on the face of it, the acquisitions in the late 1980s of US Goliaths by UK Davids seemed to be an achievement of the impossible. Vast sums of money had to be raised—often in excess of the acquiring company's own value.

One remarkable example was the takeover of the second-largest American aggregates (sand and gravel) corporation for $1.81 billion (£977 million) by a relatively small British company whose own total share value was just half that amount (£486 million). 'Unbelievable! Sheer magic!' was how one analyst (Angus Phaure, of County NatWest, *Accountancy*, April 1988, 9) described the deal which the British company C. H. Beazer put together with a British and two American banks to take over Koppers, the Pittsburgh-based corporation in 1988. When its chairman Brian Beazer inherited the sixty-year old, Bath-based, company, in 1983 (from his father, its founder), it was only the fourth largest housebuilder in the United Kingdom. How did the Beazer group manage to raise the finance to take over a US company worth twice its own value?

Raising the money to acquire a company worth double your own value poses a major problem at any time. But there were particular problems for the group at the time of this acquisition. It would have been difficult, if not impossible, for Beazer to have issued shares to raise finance to pay for as large a proposed acquisition as Koppers. This was 1988, just after the October 1987 'crash' of world stock markets. In any case, Beazer may also have been reluctant to raise finance in this way having done so throughout the 1980s when it 'absorbed nine large acquisitions' (*Sunday Times*, 30 June 1991), including French Kier (£144 million—1986), Christian Salvesen (£13 million—1986), MP Kent (£34 million—1984), and William Leech (£25 million—1985) (*Financial Times*, 27 June 1991).

This process of issuing new shares ('*paper*') via rights issues meant that between 1983, when Brian Beazer took over the company, and 1988, the number of shares issued by the company rose from 12 million to 300 million (*Financial Times*, 25 April 1991). In these circumstances the issue of dilution arises—individual share value may fall as the number of shares grows—and this can be a cause for concern among shareholders. This process culminated in the takeover in 1986 of another American corporation, Gifford Hill (a cement producer), for £200 million. But the share issue for this takeover was not entirely successful: it was less than three-quarters subscribed (*Financial Times*, 25 April 1991).

In May 1987, an alternative method of raising finance—an American

Depositary Receipt (ADR)—was attempted in the United States. ADRs are dollar-denominated and dividends are paid to ADR holders in dollars. Through the mechanism of the ADR, American institutional investors were able to hold and trade a bundle of Beazer's shares represented by the ADR. But the ADR issue had to be 'scaled down' because it caused 'uproar' among British institutional investors (*Sunday Times*, 6 March 1988).

This outcry, together with an expression of concern over the Gifford Hill share issue, led chairman Brian Beazer to state that he would not use this method of financing again: 'there would be no more paper' (*Sunday Times*, 6 March 1988). To buy Koppers, Beazer therefore had to use debt rather than equity.

In this the Beazer takeover was not alone. Many major takeovers at this time were also 'highly leveraged', based on vast levels of debt. Maxwell Communication Corporation's takeover of the US publishing company Macmillan for $2.6 billion was also a highly leveraged acquisition. So, on the domestic front, was Brent Walker's takeover of bookmakers William Hill. Highly leveraged acquisitions were a feature of the late 1980s. And this is where the analysts' expressions of astonishment come in. For seeking to raise money on this scale via debt has the potential to introduce a number of major legal and market obstacles to management's goals.

Burdening a company with huge quantities of debt can destroy its market value. It can also trigger public and private legal controls such as restrictive covenants, shareholder rights to consultation or veto or, in the specific context of takeovers, regulatory obstacles to sharebuilding in target companies. The key to triggering many of these market and legal obstacles lies in the company's accounts and in the legal requirement to disclose financial information. Many legal controls over management action, such as shareholder powers or restrictive covenants, are founded on company accounts.

The Regulatory Context

Financial reporting lies at the heart of law governing companies in many countries as a means of protection for third parties, particularly shareholders and potential investors, but also employees and creditors. In the United Kingdom, accounting techniques also come under the regulation of the profession. The Accounting Standards Board (ASB), and its predecessor, the Accounting Standards Committee (ASC)) issues Financial Reporting Standards (previously Statements of Standard Accounting Practice). These are rules of professional conduct applicable to all financial statements: 'authoritative statements on accountancy practice'

(Ernst & Young, 1990, 8). The stated purpose of accounts is, as the law puts it, 'to give a true and fair view' of a company's financial performance and value, or, as the profession has put it more generally, 'to assist the user's understanding of an enterprise's affairs by presenting condensed, structured information on the resources, obligations and performance of the reporting enterprise'. (ASC, 1988)

The UK companies taking over US corporations were regulated primarily by UK company law and accounting standards. The Companies Act 1985 required accounting records to be kept by all companies, to show and explain the company's transactions, and to disclose with reasonable accuracy the financial position of the company at any particular time. There are three parts to company accounts:

(i) a balance sheet—a set of numbers which sets out the company's assets (either fixed assets acquired for use in the business, such as property and machinery, or current assets (cash or cash-related assets such as stock and debtors (money owed)) and liabilities (current and long-term claims against the company's assets) together with any residual interest, that is, the capital and reserves that make up the 'balance' between the assets and the liabilities. This information relates to the *value* or worth of the company;

(ii) a profit and loss account—another set of numbers which sets out the company's results of the last year (including turnover (sales), profit from ordinary activities, income from extraordinary activities, charges, or costs). This information relates to the *performance* of the company and indicates the amount available for distribution as a dividend to the owners (shareholders) of the company;

(iii) notes to the accounts—a combination of words and numbers that provide additional information.

The form and content of company accounts are regulated by the very detailed provisions of Schedule 4 to the Act which sets out the rules and formats to be used in presenting accounts.

The objective that the 1985 Act required (and requires) of accounts was that they give 'a true and fair view': by the balance sheet, of the state of affairs of the company as at the end of the financial year; by the profit and loss account, of the performance of the company for the financial year. The requirement to provide a true and fair view was overriding (Companies Act 1985, section 228(3)): even specific statutory rules could be departed from in order to give a true and fair view. The requirement has been described by leading academic accountants as the 'paramount principle' of accounting (Nobes and Parker, 1984, 82).

Most large and many small businesses operate not as a single company but as a group of companies, comprising a parent or holding company and one or more subsidiaries. A group normally operates as a single economic unit with shared top management and control (EC, 1976, 19) so that, although each subsidiary may be a separate company (with its own individual accounts), the interests of companies in a group are closely linked, and the value and performance of any one company may be affected by its relationship with others in the group. In addition to each company producing individual accounts, therefore, there has been a legal requirement under the Companies Acts since 1947 for the directors of the parent company in a group to produce accounts for the whole group. These are group financial statements which take the form of consolidated accounts: a consolidated balance sheet and a consolidated profit and loss account. The group accounts must include all companies which are subsidiaries (or 'subsidiary undertakings' post-1989) of the main or parent company in order to give a true and fair view of the overall picture of the group's financial status and performance for a particular year.

The Companies Act 1985 not only provides detailed rules on disclosure of financial information, it also regulates the policing and enforcement of the law. It does this in several ways. Company accounts have to be approved by the board of directors and a copy delivered to the Registrar of Companies, who will file them in publicly available files. Company accounts are examined by the company auditors who must make a report. In this they must state whether in their opinion the accounts have been properly prepared in accordance with the Act, and whether a true and fair view has been given. The auditors' role, their rights and duties, their relationship with the company are all subject to regulation by the Companies Acts.

Corporate Governance

The legal requirement to disclose financial information is a fundamental element in corporate governance, the basis of management accountability to the company's owners. It is also the basis of many legal and market controls over management. Market assessment and comparability between companies is based on ratios drawn from the figures in the accounts in order, for example, to assess performance (e.g. via earnings per share), estimate the investment potential via the value of shares and expected future earnings (price earnings ratio), measure the degree to which owners (equity financing) or creditors (debt financing) have financed a company (known as gearing in the United Kingdom, or leverage in the United States), and evaluate the financial condition and liquidity of a company (current ratio).

Massive debt on a relatively small equity base means 'high leverage' or 'high gearing'. In Beazer's case, for example, purchase of Koppers by Beazer taking on massive debt would produce a ratio where the debt would dwarf the equity, with potentially adverse consequences in the market. Existing shareholders may become unhappy if they feel too much debt is being taken on, or their stake is being put at risk. Unhappy shareholders may exercise market power by selling their shares or threatening to do so, thereby reducing share price and the value of the company. We have seen how shareholder concern had already been expressed prior to the Koppers takeover when the number of shares issued by Beazer had risen dramatically to fund acquisitions. As a result, earnings per share, which is important to a company share price, had risen more slowly than it would have otherwise (*Financial Times*, 3 June 1988). But there may be more for management to contend with than the unhappiness, and potential market response, of shareholders. There may also be the matter of their legal rights and powers.

A company's accounts are significant not simply as a means of informing shareholders of the performance and financial status of a company. They also form the basis of specific mechanisms of control over management. The public law requirement to file annual accounts is also a foundation for private law controls, on an ongoing basis. The ratios referred to above are often used in a company's memorandum and articles of association as the basis of shareholder power. For management, at any particular time, to exceed a specified ratio of, for example, debt to equity, it may be legally required by the company's constitution to have shareholder approval.

There are other controls over management based on ratios drawn from the accounts. Existing creditors such as lending banks might well have restrictive covenants in place in the contract of loan to protect themselves by preventing excessive additional debt being undertaken. Specified gearing ratios may be built into these covenants. If the borrowing company goes ahead and takes out more debt, the ratio may be exceeded and the company will be in breach of the covenant. The existing bank lender may then invoke contractual clauses which allow it to commence action to recover the sums lent. This might include placing the company into bankruptcy.

In addition, in the specific context of takeovers, there can be, in general law or in, for example, Stock Exchange listing regulations, other regulatory obstacles to predatory stakebuilding in a target company without public disclosure, or there may be regulations requiring shareholder consent.

There are, then, a number of significant legal obstacles to be faced in raising vast sums of debt or engaging in major takeovers. Yet none of these may affect management at all—*not* necessarily because shareholders, lenders, and the market have given their blessing to management plans, but because the potential legal controls over management are simply kept out of play. Highly leveraged takeovers can in practice be accomplished without upsetting market ratios, without triggering shareholder controls, without breaching covenants, and without breaking the law. How? The answer lies in creative compliance.

CREATIVE COMPLIANCE IN ACTION: THE ORPHAN SUBSIDIARY

There is a whole range of creative devices through which the legal requirements to report financial information, including potential liabilities such as large-scale debt in a company's accounts, can, in practice, be circumvented. One simple but potent device, which was used in a number of highly leveraged takeovers, was one known as a 'controlled non-subsidiary', 'non-subsidiary subsidiary', 'controlled dependent company', or 'quasi-subsidiary'. We will refer to it as an 'orphan subsidiary', for reasons which will become clear below. Using an orphan subsidiary provided an escape route from legal constraints, yet it operated in compliance with them. Indeed it was constructed with legal building blocks.

The device of the orphan subsidiary operates in the context of the requirement to produce consolidated accounts for a group of companies. Without this requirement it would be possible for company A to enhance its own reported balance sheet and performance, by keeping major debts, for example, hidden away in a controlled but legally separate subsidiary company B, whose full liabilities would appear in B's but not in A's accounts.

Although the exposure of each company in the group may theoretically be limited by a corporate structure in which each company in the group is a separate legal entity with limited liability and directors are not entitled to sacrifice the interests of their company to the interests of the group, in practice the interconnection of interests may be such that a parent company may be constrained to rescue a failing subsidiary. Tolley notes that this is assumed to be 'good commercial practice' (Tolley, 1988, 662); the Cork Committee acknowledged that it was common practice for directors to consider the interests of other companies in the group (Cork, 1982, paragraph 1951); it may even be argued that it is the duty of directors of company A to rescue subsidiary company B if their interests are intertwined. In practice, therefore, the risk of losing credibility—and creditworthiness—may force a parent to rescue a subsidiary. In short, the risk-exposure of one company may in practice be affected by others in the group to a greater extent than the principle of limited liability might suggest: the whole picture of the whole group is therefore necessary to be able to make commercial assessments. Likewise, where management controls several dependent companies, management performance can only be fully assessed in relation to the whole picture of the group.

It is this whole picture which group consolidated accounts should provide. It cannot be obtained from the individual accounts of each company on its own. Only through the provision of consolidated accounts, said the European Commission, was it 'possible to obtain a true and fair view of the economic and financial position of the group, and through it, a more complete picture of the position of the individual company' (EC, 1976, 19). The legal requirement to produce consolidated accounts should mean that 'bad news' cannot be hidden away in a controlled dependent subsidiary: the performance of the group as a whole, *all* the assets and liabilities, and *all* the revenue and expenses should be disclosed. But what if 'bad news', such as massive debts, can be housed in a company which is controlled, dependent, but *not,* according to the strict letter of the law, a subsidiary? Debts and risky transactions would no longer appear in the group accounts. They would be 'off the balance sheet' of the 'parent' company, even if the 'parent' should prove ultimately responsible for them; they would be *orphan subsidiaries*. How could this be done?

The Orphan Subsidiary

In the 1980s, the Companies Acts (before amendment by the Companies Act 1989, of which more later) spawned a number of ways of structuring companies which were the offspring of their 'parent' companies, were controlled by and totally dependent on them, but in law were not subsidiaries and were thus conveniently excluded from group accounts. According to the letter of the law, they had no parents. They did not have to be consolidated in the group accounts of the companies that controlled them.

Under the Companies Act 1985 (section 736(1)) provisions, there were two questions to determine if a company was a subsidiary:

(a) does the holding company control more than half in nominal value of the subsidiary's equity share capital; or
(b) is the holding company a member of the subsidiary and does it control the composition of the board of directors?

If a company could be constructed so that the answer to both questions was in the negative then a parent–subsidiary relationship had not been created; the company would be an 'orphan subsidiary' and the debts of the orphan would not therefore have to be disclosed in the controlling group's accounts. A number of legal methods could be used to avoid the creation of this relationship by achieving the requisite negative answers. Some structures were simple, others very complex indeed. Each could be customized to meet the particular circumstances and needs. One of the simplest structures was as follows. First, the subsidiary company would issue share capital combining two types of shares, ordinary shares and preference shares. Preference shares confer preference as to income and capital, or both, over the ordinary share capital of the company. The ordinary shares and preference shares would be issued in equal numbers with an identical nominal value, the ordinary shares to the parent company and the preferential shares to the parent company's bank. Thus, half the shares were held by the parent, half by the bank; the parent did not own more than half.

Secondly, the articles of association (the constitution) of the new company would be drafted to ensure that the parent company and its bank had the right to appoint an equal number of directors. In this way, the parent company did *not* have the power unilaterally to appoint or remove the holders of all or a majority of the directorships of the 'subsidiary', so that control over the number of directors—the composition of the board of directors—was not in the hands of the parent company. Despite lack of control over the composition of the board, the parent company could still have effective control of the decisions of the board by giving directors appointed by the holders of ordinary shares (that is, the parent company's directors) special voting rights, say, two votes, to the preferential shareholders' directors' one vote. Moreover, if the parent company was not a 'member' of the 'subsidiary' (those who subscribe their names, for example, by buying shares, to a memorandum of association: Companies Act, section 22) then it could control the composition of the board of directors without having to treat the company as a subsidiary.

The law, of course, also included more general provisions. It required companies 'to give a true and fair view' of its profit and loss account and balance sheet, and auditors were required to sign off accounts on this basis. If companies structured as orphans were 'really' controlled by a group and dependent on it, should the group not be required, regardless of its compliance with other specific provisions of the Act, to consolidate? In the context of the 1980s this was not, however, how law was being interpreted and applied. Indeed in the *Argyll* case (see Ashton, 1986), directors consolidated a company in its 1979 accounts on the ground that the accounts would be more true and fair as a result of so doing. But they were successfully prosecuted on the basis that the company did not meet the strict criteria for consolidation in the Companies

Act of the time. Moreover the Department of Trade had issued an authoritative statement to back this up, stressing the need for strict compliance with the law (Department of Trade, 1982). We deal with this, why this line was taken, and its consequences, in detail elsewhere (McBarnet and Whelan, forthcoming). One result, however, was that in this context there was a clear basis for claiming that an orphan subsidiary *could not* be lawfully included in a group's accounts, and indeed that directors faced prosecution and conviction if they did so.

In the 1980s a number of structures, from the simple so-called 'diamond' to highly complex multiple-tiered structures (combining different distribution and voting rights, and various types of shares (Tolley, 1988, 648–9)) were created to meet the Companies Act requirements but avoid consolidation and thus disclosure. Through the structure of the orphan subsidiary, massive debt could be created without it being consolidated in a group's accounts. The acquiring company was structured such that it was not part of the group, but was an orphan subsidiary.

The Beazer Takeover

The structure of Beazer's acquisition demonstrates the role of the orphan. With the American banks, Shearson Lehman Brothers and Citibank, and the British NatWest Investment Bank, Beazer set up a financial and legal package 'of mindnumbing complexity' (James Buchan, *Financial Times*, 3 June 1988) but certainly not atypically so in the world of corporate finance. The diagram below sets out the basic structure.

At the heart of this complex structure was an American orphan subsidiary, set up by Beazer, NatWest, and Shearson, as BNS Inc. Beazer held 49 per cent of the shares, a subsidiary of SLB 46.1 per cent, and a subsidiary of NatWest 4.9 per cent. It was BNS that would raise the money and make the takeover. The total consideration required to finance the purchase of Koppers' shares came to approximately $1.81 billion. This was provided by the partners' equity investment in BNS of $50 million (of which Beazer contributed $24.5 million), $241 million 20 per cent redeemable cumulative preferred stock in a BNS subsidiary (provided by Beazer), $97 million loan to a BNS subsidiary (also provided by Beazer), $879 million syndicated bank loan (from Citibank and a syndicate of banks), and the issue of $540 million subordinated loan to a BNS subsidiary subscribed from Shearson Lehman. This financing would be on BNS's balance sheet rather than on Beazer's, and the Beazer Group's accounts would be protected.

Table: Financing the Koppers Takeover

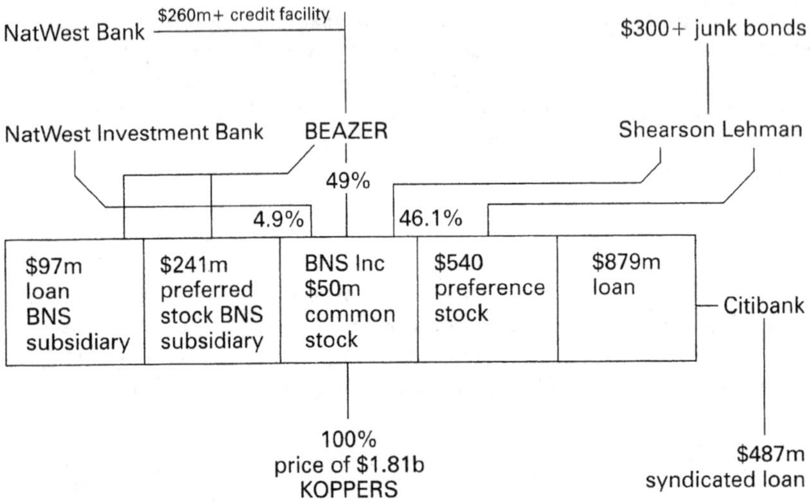

(*Source*: Directors' Report, Beazer Group Accounts, year ending 30 June 1988; table adapted from *Corporate Finance*, April 1988, p. 6)

Legal Obstacles and the Orphan Subsidiary

The orphan subsidiary has been used frequently as a vehicle for raising finance on a large scale. It was the device employed by Beazer, by Maxwell, by Brent Walker, and by many others to make their highly leveraged takeovers in the late 1980s.

Using an orphan subsidiary does not necessarily mean there is no disclosure of information. In many of these high-profile takeovers, including Maxwell's and Beazer's, much was discussed in the press or in announcements made to shareholders or the public more generally, so disclosure in one form did take place. In September 1988, for example, Brian Beazer made presentations to shareholders to reassure them about the company's borrowings. However, such informal disclosure does not always occur.

It is also possible that disclosure may be made, not in the balance sheet or profit and loss account, but in the notes to the accounts. When the tender offer was announced for Koppers, Brian Beazer stated that 'shareholders would be provided with pro-forma balance sheet information over and above that required by statute' (Chairman's Report, Beazer Accounts, 30 June 1988). This was done as promised 'as if the interests of the outside shareholders of BNS Inc had been acquired by the group'. But not all note disclosure is so informative. The Accounting Standards Committee (ASC, 1987) criticized some disclosure in notes as providing only inadequate and 'anodyne' descriptions of the arrangements. What is more, the two types of disclosure may have very different implications, for control and for market assessment. Disclosure in the notes provides information; disclosure in the accounts affects the key ratios which so often form the basis of corporate governance controls.

Through the orphan subsidiary massive finance can be raised without it appearing on the balance sheet, upsetting the ratios, and operating legal triggers. Accounts-based market indicators such as earnings per share and gearing are protected. Potential legal controls which predatory companies might face, such as restrictive covenants and shareholder rights in the memorandum and articles of association, can be successfully managed. The orphan subsidiary provides the magic spell for accomplishing management goals despite a range of potential legal hurdles.

RISK

The magic of devices such as the orphan subsidiary may, however, have a downside. While disclosure and corporate governance hurdles may be bypassed and group accounts may exclude the orphan's liabilities, exposure to risk may nonetheless remain. After all, how does an orphan subsidiary raise money when it has no assets of its own? There are several possibilities with the parent playing a key role. Some of these will have to be disclosed by the parent. For example, if the parent provides a 'guarantee' for the orphan, it will have to be disclosed as a contingent liability. Others, however, will not, or would not in the late 1980s, require disclosure. For example, a parent could 'sell' assets to the orphan while retaining an option to buy them back at a later date at a fixed price. In law, ownership of the assets may have passed; in substance, however, the transaction is not a transfer of ownership via a sale but a loan secured on the assets.

In the Beazer case, other methods were employed. First, Beazer purchased 49 per cent of the common stock of BNS (at a cost of $24.5 million). Secondly, Beazer provided unsecured loans to the subsidiary ($97 million). Thirdly, and most importantly, investment in the orphan by third parties was encouraged by the use of options. Beazer had a 'call' option to purchase the BNS shares held by the banks. If this option was not exercised within five years, the banks could exercise their 'put' option which would require Beazer to purchase their shares at any time between five and a half and six years.

The options provided two advantages, one for the Beazer group and one for the banks. For the Beazer group, they provided a five-year 'window' in which to sort out the takeover, sell off some assets, reduce debt or restructure it with more manageable interest rates, before taking Koppers onto its own balance sheet in a state which would, if all went to plan, have little or no adverse impact on the group's accounts. The banks knew that, after five years, if they still owned BNS shares, they could dispose of them if they wanted to, at an agreed price, regardless of performance. The price of the BNS stock was agreed in advance whether the call or put options were exercised: the banks would get a price equivalent to a 25 per cent *per annum* compound interest equivalent on their equity stakes (*Corporate Finance*, April 1988, 6). In this sense the $25.5 million subscribed by the banks was just like a loan to Beazer.

During the bid Brian Beazer announced that the bulk of the borrowings raised to fund the purchase was not guaranteed by the company and would never be so unless the board wanted to do so: '[t]here is no attempt to hide the figures' he was quoted as saying (*The Times*, 23 March 1988). He also stated that he would have sought shareholder approval had the financing been on a recourse basis by guaranteeing BNS. But there was in practice no need to do this (although it was considered as a way of getting round a US court injunction (*Financial Times*, 1 June 1988)). Using an orphan subsidiary and options rather than guarantees avoided this.

In practice, however, BNS immediately became a *de facto* subsidiary of Beazer. This was recognized by Brian Beazer himself when he stated that the group had 'had management control of Koppers for some 4 months', adding that 'Koppers will prove to be an excellent acquisition' (Chairman's Statement, Accounts for the year ended 30 June 1988). Whether or not the options were exercised, Beazer in effect had both control of BNS and responsibility for its debts. The options provided the legal mechanism for that control and for ensuring that ultimately BNS would become a *de jure* (wholly-owned) subsidiary of Beazer. When that occurred, not only would Beazer have to assume another $25.5 million of investment, but it would then have to consolidate BNS and bring the BNS debts into the Beazer group accounts. In the meantime, however, that requirement was avoided.

The solution to the question of how a company like BNS, with no assets, could raise so much finance, is simple: Beazer, not BNS, carried the risk. Ultimately, of course, the banks carried the risk. If Beazer had collapsed during the five-year window—or walked away from its commercial responsibilities to BNS—the banks would have borne losses—so-called 'bad debts'. But this would hardly improve the situation of Beazer shareholders, creditors, and employees.

In short, whether the acquisition proved profitable or not, the legal reality was that Beazer could still not escape the ultimate requirement to buy out its partners after 1993. The commercial reality was that, while the loans to BNS were not technically guaranteed, commercial risks did fall on Beazer. The use of the device of the orphan subsidiary together with the put and call options, however, meant that these risks were, quite lawfully, off-balance sheet.

The significance may be underlined by the subsequent collapse of another company in which Beazer had an interest. Beazer announced an extraordinary provision of £29 million pounds in its interim results for March 1990 against its involvement in the Australian company, Girvan, which had been placed in receivership (a form of bankruptcy procedure). The involvement was off-balance sheet: it was not incorporated in Beazer's accounts. Shares dropped 4 per cent at the news. One financial commentator observed that a 4 per cent drop 'might seem excessive.... But it is unsettling to hear of the demise of an Australian investment whose existence could not have been inferred from the accounts' (Lex, *Financial Times*, 31 January 1990). Yet, as the law stood, these off-balance sheet vehicles were perfectly legal.

The structure of a deal can therefore involve risks even if, in strict compliance with the letter of the law, they are not written into the accounts. The actual exposure may depend on how well strategies pan out in practice. In the Beazer case developments after the takeover suggest that the $1.8 billion deal in fact proved too big to handle.

A Deal Too Far?

The intention had always been, if the bid was successful, to replace the original borrowings in December 1988 by 'merger finance' of $1.83 billion. This would have included the refinancing of most of the $540 million subordinated loan subscribed by Shearson by the issue of $570 million high-yielding debt securities (junk bonds) by Koppers, thereby reducing the high level of interest repayments required under the bridging scheme, and to pay it off by way of asset sales (disposals of parts of the Koppers group). In other words, the plan was to restructure the debt in order to avoid the high-interest loan notes. Beazer had not expected to complete this task before the summer of 1989 at the earliest (*Corporate Finance*, December 1988, 8).

But this plan still involved refinancing at junk-bond levels of interest—18 per cent plus at the time. This could have undermined the overall earnings of the company. There was an alternative: Beazer could buy out the banks earlier and save on interest charges, but this would undermine the balance sheet.

As it turned out, the latter route was adopted. Restructuring occurred early, following a $2.3 billion refinancing of the debt, in October 1988, underwritten by a syndicate of banks: Citibank, National Westminster Bank, Barclays Bank, and Mellon Bank (*Financial Times*, 15 November 1988). This included $400 million loan finance pending disposals. The funding allowed the call options to be exercised and Koppers to be consolidated on 1 January 1989. As a result, an estimated $25 million a year in interest charges was saved by the Beazer group (Alan Chapple, Beazer Finance Director, *Corporate Finance*, December 1988, 8), but the gearing ratio soared to 150 per cent (a 'healthy' gearing ratio would normally be seen as a low percentage—the lower the better—indicating more equity than debt). Moreover, the attempts to reduce gearing thereafter were not entirely successful.

Disposal of Koppers' assets hit problems. It took longer than expected and Beazer had to support financially some of the purchases. As a result, the heavy interest repayments on the finance to bridge $400 million of expected asset sales continued for longer than anticipated, and some of the sales that did take place were not the absolute disposals that had been sought.

In 1990 and 1991, the Beazer empire began to break up. In April 1991, with interest repayments remaining a problem, Brian Beazer proposed selling off half the group's UK and European operations in order to raise £250 million. By June, with the company debt rising once again from £770 million to £1 billion (as a result of a rising dollar—most of the debt was denominated in dollars), with capitalization at just £236 million and a further sharp fall in profits expected, more radical surgery was attempted, perhaps forced by the banks (*Financial Times*, 17 September 1991). Beazer proposed selling off the entire European operation to pay off £500 million borrowings. This would have led to a US–Europe split in the group, an end to the family control of the company which had lasted for over half a century (described as 'selling a family heirloom' (*Financial Times*, 26 June 1991); 'selling the family silver' (*Independent*, 28 August 1991; *Financial Times*, 25 April 1991)) and the relocation of Beazer's base to the United States.

But by September 1991, with the banks requiring repayment of $600 million (*The Times*, 11 September 1991) and Beazer reporting a 43 per cent drop in pre-tax profits to £60.6 million, Beazer itself was taken over by the Hanson Group, a UK giant industrial conglomerate. Hanson made a successful offer to acquire Beazer, debt and all, for the agreed sum of £351 million. While it was Beazer and its advisers that did all the hard work in the Koppers takeover—and took the risks—it was Hanson that ended up with the 'prize'. Hanson, of course, also acquired the debts but, with its better credit rating, the cost of servicing them was lower than it had been for Beazer.

From the day of the Koppers takeover—the result of innovative financing and creative compliance—Beazer had been on a 'treadmill' (*The Times*, 26 June 1991). Disposals could not reduce the 'horrendous group debt' (*The Times*, 26 June 1991) after 1988. Shareholders saw the share price dip from its peak of around 275 pence in 1987 to 88 pence in 1991. Hanson's bid valued each share at 123.5 pence. Beazer was simply unable to achieve sufficient sums to pay for a level of debt raised to acquire Koppers that turned out to be a 'deal too far'.

It was not the only one. In the case of Maxwell Communication Corporation, the highly leveraged acquisition of Macmillan has been seen as a deal too far. Every year $290 million was needed to repay the interest on the $2.6 billion borrowed (Bower, 1992, 488), more than the business appeared to be producing. The acquisition was blamed as a contributory factor in the collapse of the Maxwell empire and when Macmillan was sold by the administrators in 1993 it fetched only $552 million (*The Times*, 11 November 1993). In many other companies recession has exposed the real risks hitherto obscured in the accounts through devices of creative compliance.

CREATIVE COMPLIANCE AND THE DEFEAT OF LEGAL CONTROL

From the perspective of those on the receiving end of regulation, creative compliance through devices such as the orphan subsidiary can provide a means of removing obstacles and accomplishing goals. It provides legal magic for achieving the apparently impossible. From the perspective of regulators, however, and of those looking to law for protection, it may be seen in more negative terms; creative compliance can mean no less than the defeat of legal control, and of the policies that lie behind it.

The stated objective of financial reporting regulation is that companies provide a true and fair view of their financial situation and performance. This is seen as a means of helping protect creditors, lenders, employees, by providing relevant and reliable information on which market decisions can be made (see, for example, European Commission, 1976, 19; ASB, 1991, 99). Risks may, of course, still be taken, but in theory relevant and reliable information should be provided to assess them. Legal requirements on financial reporting play a key part in corporate accountability and corporate governance, as was underlined in the Cadbury Report (Cadbury, 1992). Yet, if significant potential liabilities can, without any suggestion of contravention of the law, be kept off the balance sheet, accounts are not providing the information necessary for users of accounts to be fully aware—or perhaps aware at all—of the risks involved. Off-balance sheet devices, by keeping vital information out of the accounts, go to the heart of what financial reporting is purportedly about.

In 1987 when we began researching corporate finance from a number of perspectives, the stock markets of the world were still booming, there was little talk of recession, and new financial instruments were being rapidly developed and marketed. There was an explosion of mergers and acquisitions fuelled by an abundance of credit. Since then high interest rates and recession have exposed the heavy debt burden assumed by many corporations. Many of the companies identified in our research as engaging in creative compliance have since faced severe, and in some cases terminal, financial difficulties. Yet the financial risks, and the implications for shareholders, creditors, employees, the economy at large, were not readily apparent from the figures in their accounts. We have referred in this chapter to *known* cases where creative compliance devices, such as the orphan subsidiary, have been used. But one reason for the concern raised by these devices is that their use may not be known, or not known until long after the event, with the bad news eventually emerging only when it is too late to be useful.

Some of the major cases of financial collapse have, of course, involved allegations of fraud, but use of creative compliance devices has also served routinely to obscure the risks to which businesses have in reality been exposed. To the extent that financial reporting regulation is aimed at ensuring that information on such exposure is available through the accounts, that regulation has failed. Legal control has been circumvented, and the policies declared to lie behind it defeated, not just through breach of the law but through creative compliance.

What is more, analysing creative compliance in the context of corporate finance demonstrates that it is not just state regulation which can be overcome in this way. Controls based on private law are just as vulnerable. Contractual covenants, and terms in the memoranda and articles of association through which companies are constituted, can also be sidestepped and basic mechanisms of corporate governance undermined.

Legal control can, of course, fail for many reasons. Companies may get away with non-compliance because enforcement is inadequate. In the context of corporate finance, the finger has certainly been pointed at weak enforcement by auditors (Mitchell, 1995). Professional regulation has been criticized as lacking teeth (Dearing Report, 1988). Laws and standards themselves may be poorly drawn. The rules defining a subsidiary in the 1985 Companies Act (and before) seem like invitations to avoidance, so simple are they—with hindsight—to circumvent. Regulatory strategies may be misconceived or have unintended consequences. Regulation may be compromised, half-hearted, or merely symbolic. All of these factors have played a part in undermining financial reporting regulation. A significant part has also, however, been played by creative compliance.

Creative compliance poses its own special challenge for the achievement of effective legal control. While non-compliance may succeed because of inadequate enforcement, creative compliance effectively pre-empts enforcement, or at least straightforward enforcement. (This is discussed further in McBarnet and Whelan, forthcoming.) The whole point of the strategy of creative compliance is to be able to lay claim to the fact that it does not contravene the law as stated but complies with it, that it is 'whiter than white collar crime' (McBarnet 1992). The problem this poses for enforcement is that, in so far as there is no such contravention of existing law, there is arguably nothing to enforce. Despite the frustration expressed by accounting regulators over off-balance sheet devices such as the orphan subsidiary, we are not aware of any public suggestion that anyone acted unlawfully. On the contrary, there were strong arguments that keeping orphans off the balance sheet was what the law required (Aldwinckle, 1987; see also Law Society, 1990a, 1990b).

Creative devices can be thwarted, at least for the future, by changing the rules. Law is, indeed, frequently amended to close off 'loopholes'. The definition of a subsidiary in the Companies Act 1985 has been amended by the Companies Act 1989. A subsidiary undertaking, the concept now employed, is defined in much more inclusive terms (Companies Act 1985 (as amended) section 258). These definitions would require a structure such as BNS to be incorporated into Beazer's group accounts. As a means of managing accounts, the orphan subsidiary structure of the 1980s is certainly dead. But creative thinking aimed at managing accounts is not. New rules simply invite new structures and techniques to achieve the same result. The structure of BNS was constructed with a careful eye on the 1985 Act. The structure for such a deal today might be adapted to the amendments introduced by the 1989 Act, with an off-balance sheet vehicle achieved by other means, or alternative techniques of managing financial reporting requirements employed.

Even before the rules of the new Companies Act were in the statute book, our interviews (with accountants, bankers, lawyers, regulators) indicated new devices were being dreamed up with the aim of circumventing the new criteria for consolidation of subsidiary undertakings in group accounts. One example of the new generation of creative compliance devices being worked on was the deadlocked joint venture. This aimed at circumventing the toughest—in the sense of being the most inclusive—of the new definitions of a subsidiary undertaking, that requiring consolidation where there was a participating interest in, and actual dominant influence over, another undertaking (Companies Act 1985, section 258(4)(a)).

In the deadlocked joint venture company, companies A and B control half the voting rights and directors' voting rights of company C, which they created together. Company C is also 'deadlocked', that is, the ability of A or B (or any other 'external' agent) actually to exercise a dominant influence over C is restricted since C cannot depart from specified policies. As a result, since neither A nor B controls it, C need not, under the terms of the amended Companies Act 1985, be consolidated in the balance sheet of either A or B. Since there is no 'actual exercise of a dominant influence', there is, in terms of the literal wording of the Act, no requirement to consolidate. Yet the purpose (and commercial effect) of establishing C may have been to remove assets and the loans used to acquire them from the balance sheet of the company or group working through them. Joint venture companies can work to hide liabilities. For example, after the collapse of the property development group, Rush & Tompkins, an estimated £700 million of debt in joint ventures emerged, which had not been on the balance sheet (*The Times*, 30 April 1990). If BNS had been deadlocked, then it, too, could be off-balance sheet in the 1990s.

Creative compliance is directed at, and based on, current law, *whatever* that law may be. If legal control seems to be constantly lagging behind current practice, it is quite simply because current practice is geared to staying ahead of legal control and using the law in creative ways to achieve this. New laws may effectively control old devices, but new laws will also stimulate attempts to find new devices based upon them.

Creative compliance thus poses its own challenge for control. By complying with the letter of the law rather than breaching it, it poses a challenge for enforcement, while its inherent dynamism poses a challenge for those seeking to formulate laws comprehensive enough to capture all possible devices. Yet unless creative compliance can be effectively controlled, legal policies will be constantly vulnerable to being routinely nullified by legal creativity.

The challenge of creative compliance is periodically addressed. Enforcement is not necessarily mechanistic, confined to applying the letter of the law. As we have noted elsewhere (McBarnet and Whelan, 1991), the courts have thwarted some devices, and caught in the enforcement net those using them, by rejecting literal interpretations of the requirements of law in favour of a purposive approach (e.g. *Litster* v.

Forth Dry Dock Engineering Co Ltd [1990] AC 546), or by moving the goal-posts after the event by introducing a 'new approach' (*Furniss* v. *Dawson* [1984] AC 474; *Ramsay (WT) Ltd* v. *IRC* [1982] AC 300). In practice, however, these turning-point decisions tend, like legislation, to generate new criteria on which to base new devices, and constant new approaches may meet resistance.

One reason for our continuing interest in financial reporting regulation is the fact that there has been an explicit acknowledgement there of the particular problems posed for control by creative compliance, and recent developments have demonstrated an explicit attempt to find a means of formulating law and regulations in ways which can not only combat it, but which are immune to it. Our current work is concerned to analyse these developments, the strategies being adopted to enhance control and their prospects for success.

What an analysis of the practice of creative compliance underlines is that law is a double-edged sword. It is not only a mechanism for control, but a mechanism for escaping it. It comprises prohibitions and requirements; but it also constitutes the material for constructing devices to escape them. The orphan subsidiary illustrates how the raw material of law can be worked on to produce a potent device of creative compliance as a mechanism for overcoming legal barriers and defeating legal control. The challenge for regulation is to come up with an approach which can control creative compliance; the challenge for law and society researchers is to explore more fundamentally whether this is possible.

REFERENCES

ACCOUNTING STANDARDS BOARD (ASB) (1991), *The Objective of Financial Statements and the Qualitative Characteristics of Financial Information (ED—Statement of Principles)* (ASB, London)

ACCOUNTING STANDARDS COMMITTEE (ASC) (1987), *Exposure Draft 1487: Accounting for Off-balance Sheet Finance* (Institute of Chartered Accountants, London).

—— (1988), *Exposure Draft 42, Accounting for Special Purpose Transactions* (Institute of Chartered Accountants, London).

ALDWINCKLE, R. (1987), 'Off-balance Sheet Finance—The Legal View', *Accountancy*, June.

ASHTON, R. K. (1986), 'The Argyll Foods Case. A legal analysis', *Accounting and Business Research* 3–12.

BOWER, T. (1992), *Maxwell: The Outsider* (BCA, London).

CADBURY COMMITTEE (1992), *Report of the Committee on the Financial Aspects of Corporate Governance* (Gee & Co Ltd, London).

DEARING COMMITTEE (1988), *The Making of Accounting Standards* (Institute of Chartered Accountants, London).

DEPARTMENT OF TRADE (1982), *The True and Fair View and Group Accounts* (Department of Trade, London, 15 January 1982; reprinted in *Accountancy*, February 1982 and in Tolley's (1988), *Company Law* (Tolley, Croydon), 1377–80).

ERNST & YOUNG (1990), *UK GAAP* (Longman, London).

EUROPEAN COMMISSION (EC) (1976), *Group Accounts: Proposal for a 7th Directive*, Bulletin of the European Communities, Supplement 9/76.

LAW SOCIETY COMPANY LAW COMMITTEE (1990a), *Comments on ED49—Reflecting the Substance of Transactions in Assets and Liabilities* (Law Society, London, September 1990, No 232).

—— (1990b), *Comments on ED50—Consolidated Accounts* (Law Society, London, October 1990, No 236).

MCBARNET, D. (1984), 'Law and Capital: The Role of Legal Form and Legal Actors', *International Journal of the Sociology of Law* 12, 231–8.

—— (1988), 'Law, Policy and Legal Avoidance', *Journal of Law and Society* 15, 113-21.

—— (1991), 'Whiter than White Collar Crime: Tax, Fraud Insurance and the Management of Stigma', *British Journal of Sociology* 42, 323–44.

—— (1992), 'It's Not What You Do but the Way That You Do It: Tax Evasion, Tax Avoidance and the Boundaries of Deviance', in D. Downes (ed.), *Unravelling Criminal Justice* (Macmillan, London), 247–68.

—— and WHELAN, C. (1991), 'The Elusive Spirit of the Law: Formalism and the Struggle for Legal Control', 54 *The Modern Law Review* 848–73.

—— and —— (1992), 'International Corporate Finance and the Challenge of Creative Compliance', in J. Fingleton (ed.), *The Internationalisation of Capital Markets and the Regulatory Response* (Graham & Trotman, London), 129–41; reprinted in S. Wheeler (ed.), *Law and the Business Enterprise* (Clarendon Press, Oxford, 1995) 403–416.

—— and —— (forthcoming), *Law, Creativity and Control* (provisional title).

MANSFIELD, G. (1994), 'Five Ways out of Tax', *Journal of Financial Regulation and Compliance* 2, 133–49.

MITCHELL, A. (1995), 'Oh Dear, Another Huge Dollop of Auditing Whitewash', *The Times*, 4 January 1995.

NOBES, C. W. and PARKER, R. H. (1984), 'The Fourth Directive and the United Kingdom' in S. J. Gray and A. G. Coenenberg (eds.), *EEC Accounting Harmonisation: Implementation and Impact of the Fourth Directive* (North-Holland, Elsevier, Amsterdam).

TOLLEY (1988), *Tolley's Company Law*, (Tolley Publishing Company, Croydon).

[16]

The Elusive Spirit of the Law: Formalism and the Struggle for Legal Control

The struggles for effective legal regulation and control have been charted in many areas of law. Attention has been drawn to political power and compromised legislation, to the issue of law being rendered merely symbolic whether by design or default, and to problems in implementation and enforcement. In our own recent work, we have emphasised the problem of 'creative compliance' — using the law to escape legal control without actually violating legal rules. This perspective[1] focuses on the active response of those subject to the law, not just in political lobbying over legislation but in *post hoc* manipulation of law to turn it — no matter what the intentions of legislators or enforcers — to the service of their own interests and to avoid unwanted control. It emphasises the role of regulat*ees* rather than regulat*ors*; it also emphasises the two-sided nature of law, as a means of controlling *and* a means of escaping control; it underlines both the structural manipulability of law and the means by which — in its many facets — it is actively manipulated. Creative compliance thrives on a narrow legalistic approach to rules and legal control, on a formalistic conception of law. Of considerable interest then to the issue of legal control, particularly of the powerful economic interests most frequently associated with such legalistic avoidance, is the regulatory strategy of 'anti-formalism' recently adopted in both financial reporting and taxation in an explicit bid to restrain creative compliance.

This article analyses the limits of formalism and the retreat from it in current strategies of control but it also shows how formalism is already being reasserted. It assesses how far anti-formalist strategies can be sustained, asks whether formalism is inevitable in law, addresses the issue of legal indeterminacy and questions its practical relevance. At root is the fundamental question of whether effective legal control, particularly of those with resources to resist, is attainable.

Formalism and the Failure of Legal Control

Different approaches to law and control co-exist in legal policy and legal thinking, but formalism is often presented as dominant.[2] Formalism implies a narrow

---

This article is based on our research on corporate finance and on research by McBarnet and Mansfield on tax avoidance. These projects were funded by the Commissariat du Plan, the European Commission and the ESRC, to all of which we are extremely grateful. We would also like to thank Joe McCahery for comments on earlier drafts.

1 See McBarnet, 'Law and Capital: The Role of Legal Form and Legal Actors' (1984) 12 Int J Sociology of Law 233; McBarnet, 'Law, Policy and Legal Avoidance' (1988) J Law & Society 113; McBarnet, 'It's Not What You Do But The Way That You Do It: Tax Evasion, Tax Avoidance and the Boundaries of Deviance' in Downes (ed), *Unravelling Criminal Justice* (London: Macmillan, 1991); McBarnet and Whelan, 'Beyond Control: Law Management and Corporate Governance' in McCahery, Picciotto and Scott (eds), *Corporate Control and Accountability* (1992); McBarnet and Whelan, 'Creative Compliance and the Defeat of Legal Control: A Case Study in International Corporate Finance' (mimeo, submitted for publication); McBarnet and Whelan, *Beyond Control? The Regulation of Financial Risk, Corporate Activity and the Single European Market* (forthcoming).

2 Kelman, *A Guide to Critical Legal Studies* (Cambridge: Harvard University Press, 1987).

approach to legal control — the use of clearly defined, highly administrable rules, an emphasis on uniformity, consistency and predictability, on the legal form of transactions and relationships and on literal interpretation.

Although the term formalism has been used in divergent ways, at its heart 'lies the concept of decision making according to *rule*,'[3] rule implying here that the language of a rule's formulation — its literal mandate — be followed, even when this ill serves its purpose. Thus, 'to be formalistic ... is to be governed by the rigidity of a rule's formulation.'[4] A formalist approach also assumes that law is 'intelligible as an internally coherent phenomenon,'[5] that there is consistency, predictability, logical coherence and ultimately autonomy and 'closure': a systemic isolation of the legal system from such things as politics and culture. This isolation will be reinforced if lawyers are 'legalistic': 'rule-preferrers' and 'rule-followers,' interested in relationships, rights in something and against somebody, in relation to others. Legalism as an ethical attitude has been described as the operative outlook of the legal profession: moral conduct is a matter of rule following, and moral relationships consist of duties and rights determined by rules. As a social outlook, legalism has been described as 'The dislike of vague generalities, the preference for case-by-case treatment of all social issues, the structuring of all possible human relations into the form of claims and counter-claims under established rules, and the belief that the rules are "there".'[6]

Creative compliance uses formalism to avoid legal control, whether a tax liability or some regulatory obstacle to raising finance, effecting a controversial takeover or securing other corporate, or management, objectives. The combination of specific rules and an emphasis on legal form and literalism can be used artificially, in a manipulative way to circumvent or undermine the purpose of regulation. Using this approach, transactions, relationships or legal forms are constructed in order to avoid the apparent bounds of specific legal rules. In this sense, the detailed rules contribute to the defeat of legal policy. Though creative compliance is not limited to law and accounting, accountants are particularly conscious of its potential to reduce the effectiveness of regulations[7] and to avoid tax.[8] Much of the current impetus for a broad, open approach to professional standard setting stems from concern that a 'mechanistic "cookbook" approach ... [which] is very precisely drafted ... will be relatively easy to avoid.'[9]

3 Schauer, 'Formalism' (1989) 97 *Yale Law Journal* 509, 510.

4 *ibid* p 535.

5 Weinrib, 'Legal Formalism: On the Immanent Rationality of Law' (1988) *Yale Law Journal* 949.

6 Shklar, *Legalism* (Cambridge: Harvard University Press, 1964) p 1.

7 Griffiths, *Creative Accounting: How to Make Your Profits What You Want Them To Be* (London: Sidgwick & Jackson, 1986); Report of the Review Committee under the chairmanship of Sir Ronald Dearing CBN, *The Making of Accounting Standards* (London: ICAEW, 1988) p 13 (*The Dearing Report*).

8 Law Society Revenue Law Committee, *Tax Law in the Melting Pot* (London: Law Society, 1985) (hereinafter L Soc Rev Co) p 4, 'The introduction of capital gains tax in 1965, with its detailed and intricate code of statutory provisions, encouraged taxpayers and their advisers to discover and apply avoidance techniques tailored to the new tax.' Shortly before his appointment as the first chairman of the Accounting Standards Board, David Tweedie stated that he regarded detailed prescription as 'undesirable as it can lead to inflexibility and to incentives to conduct an accountancy standards avoidance game analogous to tax avoidance': Tweedie and Whittington, 'Financial Reporting: Current Problems and their Implications for Systematic Reform' (1990) 21 *Accounting and Business Research* 87, 97.

9 Institute of Chartered Accountants of Scotland, Comments on ED 49, on file at the ICAEW Library, London. See also Ernst & Young, Comments on ED 49, 1/10/90: 'The danger of any detailed guidance such as this [ED 49 application notes] is that it may encourage the development of avoidance schemes (there is evidence that financial institutions are already thinking in these terms)'; ICAEW, Comments on ED 49, 'If a strict rulebook approach is encouraged we are unlikely to see in practice situations

Creative compliance is often a prerequisite to a successful 'off balance sheet financing' transaction (OBSF). OBSF is currently perceived as a major problem in the regulation of financial reporting. It is the 'funding or refinancing of a company's operations in such a way that, under legal requirements and existing accounting conventions, some or all of the finance may not be shown on its balance sheet.'[10] Assets or, more likely, liabilities are hidden from the reader of accounts, effectively destroying the purpose of financial reporting. There are many motivations for OBSF, for example to enhance market image, secure competitive advantage, increase credit, circumvent rules of corporate governance, increase management remuneration and avoid employee demands. This is not just a matter of cutting through formalities. In circumventing control, OBSF can also hide large scale financial risk, resulting in sudden insolvency, major creditor losses and redundancies. In recent years, creative compliance in the form of the 'quasi-subsidiary' has underpinned 'the most commonly used and well-known' OBSF transactions.[11] Most major undertakings operate within a group of companies. Since the group is often in effect a single economic entity it is required to 'consolidate' the accounts of all its subsidiary undertakings in one set of group accounts, to give a true and fair picture of economic status. A quasi-subsidiary is a company, trust or other vehicle which is effectively controlled by a parent company and which is 'a source of benefits and risks for [it] that are in substance no different from those that would arise were the vehicle a subsidiary.'[12] Although a parent undertaking has been required under Companies Acts to present in its consolidated or group accounts the activities of subsidiary undertakings in the group, it has not consolidated the quasi-subsidiary because it falls outside the statutory definition of subsidiary undertaking. Creative compliance, using quasi-subsidiaries, was given a boost following the *Argyll* case in 1981, and the formalistic emphasis of the statement by the Department of Trade and Industry (DTI) that followed it. The directors of Argyll were successfully prosecuted for consolidating in their 1979 accounts a company which was managed and effectively controlled by the same people but which was not legally acquired until 1980.[13] The DTI subsequently stated that they considered it 'axiomatic that any emphasis on substance over form must not be at the expense of compliance with the law.'[14]

Creative compliance highlights the limits of formalism as a strategy of legal control. A formalistic approach, which relies upon a 'cookbook' or code of specific and rigid rules and emphasises the legal form of transactions, can 'fail' to control for a variety of reasons. Unless the rules promote the overall purpose of the law, compliance with them and insisting on their literal interpretation or enforcement will not achieve the declared objectives. The letter of the rule may not accord with the spirit in which the law was framed; a literal application of the rules may not produce the desired end, it may be counter-productive; there may be gaps, omissions or loopholes in the rules which undermine their effectiveness. The rules may be out of date and no longer relevant. There may be other problems too. The legal form of a transaction or a relationship may not reflect its legal or its economic or

that exactly match those in the application notes because the originators of such "schemes" will ensure there are differences.'

10 ICAEW, TR 603, *Off-balance Sheet Finance and Window-dressing* (London: ICAEW, 1985) para 5(1).

11 Ernst & Young, *UK GAAP* (London: Longman, 1990) p 647.

12 ASC, ED 49, *Reflecting the Substance of Transactions in Assets and Liabilities* (London: ASC, May 1990) (hereinafter ED 49).

13 See Ashton, 'The *Argyll Foods* Case. A Legal Analysis' (1986) 15 *Accounting and Business Research* 3.

14 Statement of the Department of Trade and Industry, *The True and Fair View and Group Accounts* (London: DTI, 15 January 1982) reprinted in Tolley's *Company Law* (Croydon: Tolley, 1988) p 1380.

commercial substance. The totality of a transaction or relationship may not be reflected in any individual part. There may be a dynamic adaptation to escape rules. Formalistic regulation may increasingly drift from any relationship with the real world and any chance of effectively controlling it.

In both financial reporting and taxation a major recent response to creative compliance and the limits of formalism has been to try to reinstate control by adoption of approaches which reject the closed narrow legalism of formalism. The anti-formalist approach is 'more flexible, open-textured and policy-oriented,'[15] there is an emphasis on the substance of transactions and relationships, on the purposes and 'spirit' of regulation and on the need for dynamic responses. Recent developments demonstrate in effect a 'package' (though with different sources and operating at different levels) of anti-formalist strategies of control. These include broad approaches both to rule-making and interpretation: the formulation of 'catch-all' provisions, which are left undefined or vague to prevent literal avoidance and settled law; an emphasis on the purpose of regulation; an acknowledgement that practices evolve and so must regulation, by avoiding the use of statute and the courts (and the danger of ossification) and using the accountancy profession for guidance and regulation of standards of practice (and achieving flexibility); and reflecting the substance of transactions and relationships, both in regulations and by looking through their legal form.

Anti-formalism is not new. Since the Companies Act 1948, and surviving the introduction of the Fourth Directive's detailed rules on the form and content of accounts in the Companies Act 1981, the 'overriding purpose' of annual accounts and 'paramount principle' of accounting has been the requirement to provide a 'true and fair view'[16] of the state of affairs of the company. Tax law had not been quite so formalistic as the House of Lords implied in their decisions in 1981 and 1984 which they characterised as 'the new approach.'[17] However, recent developments are significant for the sheer number of fronts on which an anti-formalist approach is being adopted, and the explicit debate over the need for anti-formalism for control.

The central aim of this article is to assess whether the strategy of control through a reliance on general principles and general catch-all provisions can be sustained, or whether there is likely to be an irresistible drift — or push — to formalism and cookbook rules. Anti-formalism in taxation and financial reporting is a move away from the limits of narrow rules, rigidity, closure and legalism in the legal system to openness and flexibility, extra-legal regulation and a recognition of economic and commercial realities. Will such a move work in practice? Are there limits to anti-formalism? Our analysis highlights the obstacles to anti-formalism, the problems the policy makers have met and are facing in pressing an anti-formalist approach to control. This analysis is relevant beyond the confines of tax and financial reporting. Strands of anti-formalist thinking permeate other legal contexts. Since the nineteenth century, if not earlier, judges have been willing to depart from the 'literal' effect — the mere words — of legal documents, to 'tear away the mask or cloak,'[18] for example, to determine whether a transaction is, in substance, a sale or a mort-

15 Johnston, 'Uncertainty, Chaos and the Torts Process: An Economic Analysis of Legal Form' (1991) *Cornell Law Review* 297, 342.

16 Nobes and Parker, 'The Fourth Directive and the United Kingdom' in Gray and Coenenberg (eds), *EEC Accounting Harmonisation: Implementation and Impact of the Fourth Directive* (North-Holland: Elsevier, 1984) p 82.

17 See Mansfield, 'The "New Approach" to Tax Avoidance: First Circular, Then Linear, Now Narrower' [1989] BTR 5.

18 *Re George Inglefield Ltd* [1933] Ch 1, 17 *per* Lord Hanworth MR.

gage.[19] Similarly, the 'corporate veil' of limited liability has been pierced, for example where the existence of a company is a 'mere cloak' for an attempt to avoid legal obligations.[20] Much regulatory law is framed as broad standards. In future, the growth in EC law in many areas may foster greater use of purposive rather than literal interpretation and a willingness to depart from or even re-write the letter of the law to further its overall purpose.[21]

There have also been long-standing tensions and swings between broad and narrow approaches to the expression of law,[22] and long-standing debates in jurisprudence over the descriptive accuracy, appropriateness or legitimacy of broad policy-oriented concepts of law as opposed to narrower positivist ideas.[23] In practice, legal systems are likely to combine both approaches. Both narrow 'rules' and broad 'standards' are said to be 'omnipresent'[24] in many areas of law; they are both used to achieve legal control.[25] Indeed, their co-existence in the discourse of law has been described as a 'central contradiction in liberal thought,'[26] although one in which 'rules' are identified by some as having a 'privileged' position.[27] In the Companies Acts since 1981, detailed specific rules on financial reporting have co-existed with the true and fair 'override.' The *Argyll* case revealed the tensions here prior to the 1989 Act. However, in the strategies being discussed in law and accounting at the moment, we see legal policy pulling explicitly and in multiple ways *away from* formalistic rules. In short, current developments in law and accounting constitute an arena of conflict over what law should be and how legal control should operate, providing an ideal case study for exploring empirically this tension in law, and the factors which affect its outcomes.

Of course, it could be argued that the debate over formalism is of little practical relevance. Research and theory, including our own past work,[28] points to an indeterminacy in rules, broad or narrow, and to the scope within law to legitimise

19 In *Helby* v *Mathews* [1895] AC 471, 475 Lord Herschell agreed that it is the substance of the transaction as evidenced by the agreement that must be looked at and not its mere words. See also *Re Curtain Dream* [1990] BCLC 925, 935 *per* Knox J: 'it is the substance of the transaction that has to be looked at and not just the form' in sale, sale and repurchase and charge cases. The cloak is liable to be torn aside for two reasons: (i) the documents are shams; (ii) by analysing the effect of the totality of the transaction and seeing what is the totality of the relationship between the parties.

20 *Gilford Motor Company Ltd* v *Horne* [1933] Ch 935; *Littlewoods Mail Order Stores Ltd* v *McGregor* [1969] 3 All ER 855. See generally Ottolenghi, 'From Peeping Behind the Corporate Veil to Ignoring it Completely' (1990) 53 MLR 338; Blumberg, 'The Corporate Entity in an Era of Multinational Corporations' (1990) 15 *Delaware Journal of Corporate Law* 283; Tolley, *op cit* pp 569–574.

21 See generally Hepple and Byre, 'EEC Labour Law in the United Kingdom — A New Approach' (1989) 18 ILJ 129.

22 See generally Kelman, *op cit*. Johnston's theory suggests a pattern of 'ceaseless oscillation' between rules and balancing, *op cit* p 346. Critical legal scholars argue that there is conflict and contradiction between rules and standards; there is no way to balance them: eg Kennedy, 'Form and Substance in Private Law Adjudication' (1976) 89 *Harvard Law Review* 1685, 1775. This view is criticised by Kress, 'Legal Indeterminacy' (1989) 77 *California Law Review* 283, p 308 *et seq*.

23 See eg Kennedy, *ibid* and references cited p 1687, n 4; Atiyah and Summers, *Form and Substance in Anglo-American Law: A Comparative Study of Legal Reasoning, Legal Theory and Legal Institutions* (Oxford: Clarendon Press, 1987). Hart, 'Positivism and the Separation of Law and Morals' (1958) 71 *Harvard Law Review* 593, 607; Fuller, 'Positivism and Fidelity to Law — A Reply to Professor Hart' (1958) 71 *Harvard Law Review* 630, 663; Fuller, 'The Case of the Speluncean Explorers' (1949) 62 *Harvard Law Review* 616; Johnston, *op cit*.

24 Kelman, *op cit* p 38. See generally Smith and Bailey, *The Modern English Legal System* (London: Sweet and Maxwell, 1984) p 13.

25 See eg Companies Act 1989, Sched 9, para 3(1). Our earlier work, *op cit* n 1 has analysed the potential of narrow rules for effective legal control.

26 Kelman, *op cit* p 3.

27 Kelman, *op cit*; but see also Johnston, *op cit*.

28 McBarnet, *Conviction* (London: Macmillan, 1981); Whelan, 'Military Intervention in Industrial

contradictory decisions. Legal determinacy — the ability to formulate legal rules 'that yield certain or at least predictable outcomes at least some of the time'[29] — is 'one of the central concerns of post-Realist jurisprudence.'[30] Most recently, critical legal studies (CLS) writers have described pervasive contradictions in liberal thought, of which 'rules v standards' is one example, resulting in indeterminacy in legal decision making. There are no 'easy cases, though there may be ones whose outcomes are perfectly predictable,'[31] because the repressed contradictory impulse could govern the decision. The CLS position is that 'no significant legal regime is rule grounded even where there appear to be particular rules.'[32] Economic analysis points to an inherent uncertainty in both *ex ante* private choices and *ex post* legal decisions.[33] Sociologists, too, emphasise how rules are used to construct *post hoc* accounts of decisions rather than actually constraining them; and underline the autonomy in practice of regulatory agents, relying as much on bluff and blunder as on legal rules and powers, or ignoring legal rules altogether.[34]

Although such debates are not necessarily concerned with control in our sense, they have implications for the feasibility of effective legal control of form-based creative compliance. To the extent that judicial or regulatory decision making is indeterminate, and uncertainty therefore endemic, *covert* anti-formalism may be said to permeate the legal system in practice. There may always be scope, consequently, for providing effective control by introducing new interpretations of rules. Indeed, this may be done quite overtly as when well-established rules of statutory construction were overturned in the 'new approach' to tax avoidance,[35] and the judges explicitly underlined the unsettled state of law by referring to an 'evolving' doctrine. Exploring the obstacles to anti-formalism *in practice* may thus help us analyse the significance of the indeterminacy debate for the issue of control and beyond.

Anti-formalist Strategies in Law and Accounting

The move to anti-formalism can be seen in the 'new approach' to tax avoidance and consolidated accounts, in the Seventh Directive, in the Companies Act 1989, and in the accounting profession's proposals to regulate OBSF, which make up some or most of Technical Release (TR) 603 and Exposure Drafts (ED) 42, 49 and 50.[36]

Disputes' in Rowe and Whelan (eds), *Military Intervention in Democratic Societies* (London: Croom Helm, 1985).

29 Johnston, *op cit* p 341.

30 Johnston, *op cit* p 341 and see references p 341, n 1.

31 Kelman, *op cit* p 4; Kress, *op cit*.

32 Kelman, *op cit* p 45.

33 Johnston, *op cit* p 347.

34 Scott and Lyman, 'Accounts, Deviance and Social Order' in Douglas (ed), *Deviance and Respectability* (New York: Basic Books, 1970); Hawkins, *Environment and Enforcement* (Oxford: Clarendon Press, 1984); Skolnick, *Justice Without Trial* (New York: Wiley, 1966).

35 In *Miliangos* v *George Frank (Textiles) Ltd* [1976] AC 443 the House of Lords overturned several hundred years of 'settled practice.' The merits or otherwise of the old, rigid rule compared with the new approach are discussed in Bowles and Whelan, 'Judgments in Foreign Currencies: Extension of the Miliangos Rule' (1979) 42 MLR 452; Bowles and Whelan, 'Judicial Responses to Exchange Rate Instability' in Burrows and Veljanovski (eds), *The Economic Approach to Law* (London: Butterworths, 1985).

36 Seventh Directive of 13 June 1983, 83/349/EEC; OJ No L 193 of 15 July 1983; ICAEW, *op cit* n 10; ASC, ED 42, *Accounting for Special Purpose Transactions* (London: ASC, 1988); ED 49, *op cit*; ASC, ED 50, *Consolidated Accounts* (London: ASC, 1990) (hereinafter ED 50). An exposure draft is a draft accounting standard published for comment.

Creative compliance uses legal forms which hide the reality of relationships, economic status and risk. A key part of anti-formalism is thus the emphasis on capturing and controlling the substance rather than the form of a real life transaction or relationship, and implementing the spirit rather than the letter of the law. 'Substance' implies a reality beyond the mere packaging of a sometimes artificially selected or created legal form.

The concept of substance over form underpinned the approach adopted in the early 1980s by the judiciary in the *Ramsay* and *Dawson* cases involving tax avoidance.[37] The substance of the transaction was arrived at by looking at the transaction as a whole and not as a series of separate parts, and by identifying the real intention of the parties. This was characterised as a 'new approach' after years dominated by the discourse of literalism. The decisions were highly publicised and hailed as a new era to end artificial tax avoidance.

Putting the strategy of anti-formalism into practice involves a number of related methods. One is to stress the purpose of the law. In the Companies Acts there is an overriding requirement that accounts give a true and fair view. Doubts about the operation of the true and fair override raised by the *Argyll* case, the DTI statement and subsequent debates have been tackled in the 1989 Act. This has made the override more readily available. Directors must depart from statutory provisions 'if in special circumstances compliance with any of those provisions is inconsistent with the requirement to give a true and fair view.'[38]

A second anti-formalist method is to use broad criteria, for example to decide which undertakings have a sufficient relationship to require consolidation in group accounts, the issue central to control of avoidance through quasi-subsidiaries. The European Commission originally preferred an 'economic group' or substance approach — consolidation should occur where minority participating interests were used for actual control either by the exercise of a dominant influence or through management on a unified basis. In the event, this approach was retained as a member state option; compulsory consolidation was required only when a parent has a legal power of control.[39] However, the UK government decided to introduce it 'in a very broad form which is based on a wide definition of "participating interest," with the clear intention of preventing artificial structures designed to achieve the purposes of off-balance sheet finance schemes.'[40] Thus, 'actual dominant influence' and 'managed on a unified basis' were included as 'potentially a "catch-all" clause designed to capture other relationships,'[41] the substance of commercial relationships rather than their legal form.

37 *Ramsay (WT) Ltd* v *IRC* [1982] AC 300; *Furniss* v *Dawson* [1984] AC 474.

38 Companies Act 1985, ss 226(5), 227(6). According to the Companies Act 1985, individual and group accounts shall give a true and fair view of the state of affairs of the company or group for the year in question (for group accounts only, so far as concerns the members of the parent company (ss 226(2), 227(3)). The accounts shall comply with the provisions of Schedule 4 (annual accounts) or 4A (group accounts) to the Act as to the form and content of the balance sheet, profit and loss account and additional information in the notes (ss 226(3), 227(4)). The Law Society Company Law Committee have expressed the view, which we do not share, that if additional information can be provided to give a true and fair view, there is no call for the true and fair override: ED 55, *Accounting for Investments* (London: Law Society, December 1990) (hereinafter L Soc ED 55).

39 'During the negotiations, it became clear . . . that a real harmonisation could only be effective on the basis of the legal power of control': Van Hulle, *Developments in Financial Accounting and Reporting of the European Community* (Amsterdam: KMG, 1987) p 8. See generally Petite, 'The Conditions for Consolidation under the 7th Company Law Directive' (1984) 21 *Common Market Law Review* 81, 85.

40 Ernst & Young, *op cit* n 11, p 123.

41 Nailor, *Reflecting the Substance of Transactions in Assets and Liabilities* (London: Coopers & Lybrand Deloitte, October 1990) p 35.

A third approach is to avoid tight definitions. The expression 'true and fair' replaced 'true and correct' 'to encourage observance of the spirit as well the letter of the law.'[42] The Act does not define the expression or the 'special circumstances' in which it is to be applied. The Seventh Directive does not define 'dominant influence' which is referred to twice in the Companies Act 1989, as in the Seventh Directive. In introducing the phrase into the Act, the government declared that it wanted 'the ordinary spirit of the language of the legislation to be followed.'[43] It has been defined for the purposes of section 258(2)(c), but not in relation to the more important section 258(4)(a), and that definition 'shall not be read as affecting the construction of the expression "actually exercises a dominant influence" in section 258(4)(a).'[44] The government gave 'very careful consideration to a possible definition of "dominant influence",' but decided that any such definition would result in either a narrowing or widening of the natural meaning:

> Our intention is to curb the use of off balance sheet financing schemes through controlled non-subsidiary undertakings. Any definition of the term will encourage attempts to avoid the provision by artificial constructions with the intention of escaping from the letter of the definition. By leaving the term undefined in the legislation there is scope for guidance as to its meaning for practical purposes to be given in statements of standard accounting practice.[45]

This indicates a fourth aspect of anti-formalism — addressing the legalism and ossification associated with law and courts by relying on professional self-regulation.[46] Statements of Standard Accounting Practice (SSAPs) are 'authoritative statements on accountancy practice,'[47] that is, rules of professional conduct applicable to all financial statements. The exact relationship between self-regulation and all-out legal control has been the subject of much recent discussion.[48] However, the profession has been explicitly delegated the role of fleshing out the details of accounting regulation. The profession has a long-standing statement of principle that SSAPs be enforced according not to their letter but to their spirit,[49] while SSAPs, since the first explicit reference in SSAP 21 in 1984, have increasingly emphasised a substance over form approach to regulation. ED 49 has retained ED 42's 'approach of establishing fundamental principles designed to outwit those who might look for loopholes in detailed rules. It does so by requiring that the *substance* of the enterprise's transactions should be reflected.'[50]

Indeed, the very foundations of financial reporting are now seen in the Accounting Standard Committee's (ASC) ED 49 (as adopted by the Accounting Standards Board (ASB)) as depending on accounting standards 'Reflecting the Substance of Transactions in Assets and Liabilities.' According to paragraph 1, financial statements are intended to assist the user's understanding of an enterprise's affairs by presenting condensed, structured information on the resources, obligations and performance of the reporting enterprise. Such a presentation 'is useful only if the underlying

42 Tolley, *op cit* n 14, p 9.
43 Nailor, *op cit* p 36.
44 Companies Act 1985, Sched 9, para 4(3).
45 Lord Strathclyde, HL Deb vol 503, col 1018.
46 DTI, *Report of the Review Committee under the Chairmanship of Sir Ronald Dearing on the Making of Accounting Standards: a consultative document* (London: DTI, 1989).
47 Ernst & Young, *op cit* p 8.
48 *The Dearing Report*, *op cit* para 10.2. The adoption of some recommendations means that SSAPs now have more legal status; see the contribution by McGee below p 874.
49 ASC, Explanatory Foreword to *Accounting Standards* (London: ASC, 1975).
50 Pimm, 'Off Balance Sheet Finance' in ICAEW, *Financial Reporting 1990–91: A Survey of UK Reporting Practice* (London: ICAEW, 1991) p 137.

classification and analysis are based on the substance of transactions and arrangements.' The intention of ED 49 is to ensure that transactions are accounted for in accordance with their substance, reflecting their commercial effect. It sets out the principles to be followed in determining the substance of transactions and arrangements, analyses the essential characteristics of assets and liabilities for the purposes of financial reporting, and provides application notes to clarify the application of the principles to a range of transactions and arrangements. ED 49 envisages use of the true and fair override to depart from legal detail, to substitute authoritative interpretation and to ignore, modify or even reject legal rules. It also brings in another strand of anti-formalism. Economic substance replaces legal form as the sole or even paramount consideration. This represents a form of anti-closure: the rejection of law as the sole criterion for evaluation and the injection of non-legal criteria.

In both taxation and financial reporting, current approaches to control have been explicitly presented as a campaign against the limits of formalism. The question we address now is whether these anti-formalist approaches can survive.

The Discourse of Resistance

The first obstacle faced by an anti-formalist approach has been political controversy and resistance at a number of levels. If there is a tension between broad and narrow approaches, standards and rules, substance and form endemic in the law, this tension is also a reflection of, arena for, or stimulus to tensions and conflicts of interest in the wider social context which law is seeking to regulate. A move to anti-formalism predictably stimulates 'counterpoised functionalist arguments'[51] in opposition. The debates in legislatures, the press, and general lobbying over the Seventh Directive, the Companies Act 1989, the new SSAP on OBSF and the 'new approach' in tax avoidance have all been characterised by real life counter-arguments which in jurisprudence would be labelled a formalist critique.

The anti-formalist approach has been declared untenable for a range of reasons from the political to the practical. Some or all of these arguments have been expressed by various committees of the Law Society and accounting bodies, by the Big Six accounting firms, members of the legislature at European and national levels, even by the Inland Revenue and the DTI. The discourse is permeated by tensions between formalism and its opposite, or by wistful hopes of some ideal halfway house combining the two, as in the Law Society Revenue Law Committee's (the Revenue Law Committee) request for legislation which would keep up with tax avoidance 'by means of provisions which are sufficiently wide to cover perceived "loopholes" but not so wide as to introduce uncertainty into innocent transactions.'[52] Documents supporting the anti-formalist move in general terms also call for specific changes in terms of a formalist critique. Different sectors of the very organisations and professions calling for anti-formalist control have simultaneously launched formalist critiques.[53] At almost exactly the same time as ED 42 was published by

51 Kelman, *op cit* p 16.

52 L Soc Rev Co, *op cit* p 42.

53 See eg The Law Society Company Law Committee, *Comments on ED 49 Reflecting the Substance of Transactions in Assets and Liabilities* (London: Law Society, September 1990, No 232) (hereinafter L Soc ED 49); Law Society Company Law Committee, *Comments on ED 50 Consolidated Accounts* (London: Law Society, October 1990, No 236) (hereinafter L Soc ED 50); L Soc Rev Co, *op cit*; The Special Committee of Tax Law Consultative Bodies, *Tax Law after Furniss v Dawson* (London: Law Society, 1988) (hereinafter Special Committee); Chartered Association of Certified Accountants, *Accountancy*, September 1988, p 5; Van Hulle, *op cit*; Inland Revenue, letter to the ICA, 20 September

the ASC, March 1988, the various UK accounting bodies were participating in the Special Committee of Tax Law Consultative Bodies (Special Committee) which produced its report in May.[54] ED 42 argued for the predominance of substance over form in an effort to combat OBSF techniques; the Special Committee did exactly the opposite; it launched a powerful concerted attack on the judicial use of substance over form in tax. This report was published just before the start of the *Craven* v *White* case in which the judges began to withdraw from the substance over form approach.[55] The Committee favoured not 'anti-avoidance legislation of a general nature' but 'sharply targeted codes, of the traditional type, aimed at maximum precision and certainty.' The call, albeit in a different setting, was not for substance but for form.

Anti-formalism has been criticised on grounds of legitimacy. Formalism is at its most explicitly political in the invocation of the rule of law: a citizen has the right to know what the law is, what it prohibits, what it allows; law should be prestated, not retrospective; there should be legal limits on state discretion and on arbitrary state action. The idea of the rule of law played a major role in the 'discourse of resistance' to the new approach in tax, with letters in the press on the breakdown of law, democracy and justice.[56] There was a vociferous lobby against judicial policy-making, *post hoc* decisions and the uncertainty of substance over form. The Revenue Law Committee reviewed the new approach and criticised it as unconstitutional.[57] Legal and accounting professions combined in the Special Committee to lobby against the new approach and for clearer rules, and expressed concern over the potential for abuse: 'the applicability of the New Approach can all too easily be alleged by the Revenue, while the majority of taxpayers do not have the resources to resist such claims.'[58] Objections to the new approach were explicitly framed in terms of the unconstitutionality of judicial law-making in *taxation*, but more generally applicable 'rule of law' arguments were pressed too — the unacceptability of retrospectivity, unsettled 'evolving' law, and uncertainty. Uncertainty has also been objected to in relation to financial reporting[59] in terms of the operation of the market: 'I'd rather have no standard at all than one which left the marketplace in disarray' was how a spokesman from the Chartered Association of Certified Accountants put it in relation to ED 42.[60] Broad, vague standards are presented as conflicting with the policy goal of producing comparable accounts.

Issues of legitimacy and formalistic conceptions of law also permeate the Law Society Company Law Committee's (the Company Law Committee) critique of the accounting profession's proposed new standard, in its comment, for example, that TR 603 was 'dangerous and undesirable . . . we consider that what is proposed is contrary to the law.'[61] Several years on, there are still complaints about the lawfulness of sections of ED 49, as we shall see. The Company Law Committee also presents an image of law as a coherent interdependent patchwork of rules in

---

1985; DTI, *op cit*; Nailor, *op cit* pp 10–11; and see the *Dearing Report*, *op cit* p 12, which criticised legalism but came out in favour of 'tighter standards.'

54 *ibid*.

55 *Craven* v *White* [1989] AC 398; McBarnet and Mansfield, 'The Politics of Case Law,' paper presented at Law and Society Association Conference, Chicago, May 1986.

56 McBarnet, *op cit* (1988).

57 L Soc Rev Co, *op cit*.

58 Special Committee, *op cit* p 8.

59 Nailor, *op cit* pp 49, 50, 56.

60 (1988) *Accountancy*, p 5.

61 Law Society Standing Committee on Company Law, *Off-Balance Sheet Finance and Window Dressing* (London: Law Society, 1986).

which it is simply impractical to radically change one part; there are too many ramifications elsewhere; while there is also a clear notion of formalistic 'closure' of the legal system in the objection to the idea of economic substance taking precedence over legal rules. Although, for the ASC 'control' is the key criterion for deciding whether an enterprise is to be treated as a subsidiary[62]; for the Company Law Committee, 'ownership is an essential feature of consolidation . . . Without some degree of ownership . . . the criterion would simply be a matter of economic analysis,'[63] with the clear implication that this is not appropriate.

Broad rules have been criticised as imprecise, over-inclusive, or leading to outrageous results. Concern was expressed that the law would be applicable beyond the intentions of policy and would catch innocent parties. Politicians tend to be quick to dissociate themselves from such inequity.[64] So there were assurances in Parliament that 'straightforward commercial transactions' would not be affected by the 'new approach' in tax.[65] Likewise, the broad scope of the 'dominant influence' provision was criticised at EC level and in the UK as being too over-inclusive. The proposal to consolidate groups under the control of unincorporated businesses was dropped, it being suggested that the 'worldwide commercial interests of the Catholic church would have to be consolidated because they were controlled by the Pope.'[66] The proposal to consolidate subsidiaries controlled by a foreign parent was also dropped on the grounds that the various subsidiaries of Ford would have to be consolidated, even though none of them owned or controlled any of the others.[67] In the UK's original proposal for implementation of the clause on the right to exercise a dominant influence by virtue of a 'control contract' or provisions in the memorandum or articles of association, the phrase 'dominant influence' was not used. Instead, reference was made to the right to direct the operating and financial policies of the subsidiary undertaking. The government expressed concern that 'dominant influence,' the actual words of the directive, might catch a considerable number of undertakings where it was entirely inappropriate for the company to be consolidated by the parent, for example, the suppliers of one of the major retailers in the affairs of whom that company took a close interest — the 'Marks and Spencer' problem.[68]

Anti-formalism has been criticised as unacceptable because it will not result in effective control or because it is impossible to implement. Of ED 42 it was said: 'as presently drafted it contains insufficient specifics to be implementable in practice'[69]; of the new approach in tax, that uncertainty had damaged the 'practical workability of the tax system.'[70] In short, the arguments raised in practice against the anti-formalist approach in taxation and financial reporting sum up much of the

62 ED 50, *op cit* para 8.
63 L Soc ED 50, *op cit* pp 1, 2.
64 See, eg in the context of taxation, HC Standing Committee D, cols 913–14 (21 June 1977), statement by Mr Barnett: 'There is no question of catching innocent parties' (cited by the L Soc Rev Co, *op cit* p 117).
65 The Chief Secretary to the Treasury in the debate over the Finance Bill 1984, cited by L Soc Rev Co, *op cit* p 18.
66 Nobes, 'The United Kingdom and the Seventh Directive' in Gray and Coenenberg (eds), *International Group Accounting: International Harmonisation and the Seventh Directive* (London: Croom Helm, 1988) p 131.
67 See generally Petite, 'The Conditions for Consolidation under the 7th Directive' (1984) 21 *Common Market Law Review* 81.
68 Lord Strathclyde, HL Deb vol 503, col 1018.
69 Technical Partner, Ernst & Whinney (1988) *Accountancy, op cit.*
70 Special Committee, *op cit* p 4.

abstract formalist model of law, assuming a positivist image of how law ought to operate and a procedural rather than a substantive definition of justice. Resistance to broad catch-all substantive anti-avoidance laws and standards in financial reporting and taxation demonstrates very clearly the discourse of formalism at work.

The outcome, in practice, has been compromise. In the Companies Act, the concept of 'dominant influence' has become less a matter of substance over form than of substance *and* form, restricted in application by specific legal criteria. Its scope has been restricted in both the Seventh Directive and the amended Companies Act 1985. Undertaking A shall not be regarded as having the right to exercise a dominant influence over undertaking B, unless there is a written control contract (authorised by the memorandum or articles and permitted by the law under which it is established) which confers a right to give directions with respect to the operating and financial policies of B, and which B's directors are obliged to comply with whether or not they are for the benefit of B.[71] This definition represents a narrowing of the rule. An undertaking will not be regarded as having the right to exercise a dominant influence over another '"unless" it has a right to give directions' and 'the directions are such that the directors are obliged to comply.'[72]

A broader approach was taken in the definition of 'dominant influence' for the purposes of s 258(4)(a). The phrase 'actually exercises a dominant influence' was deliberately left undefined. Yet, it too was linked in closely with more specific criteria. If an undertaking A does not have a 'participating interest' in undertaking B, the issue of dominant influence does not arise.[73] Although the definition in relation to 'participating interest' is very wide,[74] it does dilute the substantive concepts of both 'actual dominant influence' and 'managed on a unified basis' and opens the way once again to rulebound avoidance. In both cases where dominant influence is used, therefore, the substantive concept has been narrowed down by associated rules. In professional regulation, the ASC succumbed to pressure for guidance on how a broad substantive standard should be applied, and produced application notes, to be regarded as standard practice, along with definitions of 'actual exercise of dominant influence' and 'managed on a unified basis.' Indeed, the DTI, while insisting on broad legal rules, had nonetheless assumed more detailed guidance would be added by the profession. The broad open rules were not expected to stand alone.

In tax, too, there has been a narrowing of the new approach. After the *Dawson* decision, the Institute of Chartered Accountants of England and Wales (ICAEW) and the Revenue Law Committee met with the Inland Revenue to seek guidance on how the substantive doctrine would be applied. In a subsequent exchange of letters, the Revenue, while retaining the caveat that 'there may be individual cases where . . . the Revenue would nonetheless feel obliged to follow the *Ramsay* and *Dawson* approach,' agreed particular areas where it would 'not as a rule seek to invoke' the new approach.[75] The House of Lords has also retreated from the new approach in more recent cases, notably *Craven* v *White*.

In short, there has already been a retreat from broad, open, flexible laws and

71 Companies Act 1985, Sched 10A, paras 4(1), 4(2).

72 L Soc ED 50, *op cit* p 6.

73 Companies Act 1985, s 258(4).

74 A participating interest is an interest held by an undertaking in the shares of another undertaking (including interests convertible into an interest in shares and options to acquire shares) which it holds on a long-term basis for the purpose of securing a contribution to its activities by the exercise of control or influence arising from or related to that interest. A holding of 20 per cent or more of shares is presumed to be a participating interest unless the contrary is shown. Companies Act 1985, s 260.

75 Letter from ICA, 8 July 1985; response from Inland Revenue, 20 September 1985.

standards to tighter, narrower rules. Tensions in legal ideology, conflicts within legislative and regulatory approaches, disagreements over how best to achieve efficient control or at what price, vested interests, powerful lobbies against the broad approach, all voiced in the discourse of formalism, have provided the first nail in the coffin of anti-formalist control. A watering down of the anti-formalist approach has occurred before it has even reached the statute or standard books, or broad rules have been preserved in the books only at the expense of accepting that tighter guidance will be operated in practice. Even so, the process is far from complete. In relation to ED 49, to cite but one example, Arthur Anderson & Co, despite agreeing with the draft's main proposition, the need to account for a transaction according to its substance, has still called for 'more specific, detailed, concrete and conclusive guidance with specific examples.'[76] The demand for narrower rules goes on.

The Application of Anti-formalism and the Drift Back to Formalism

Political demands for narrower rules are supplemented at operating level. In practice, a number of mechanisms in the enforcement and organisation of regulation tend to lead to a drift over time to narrow rules. The very activity of operationalising broad rules itself produces a process of 'clarification'; if there is positive demand for such clarification and narrowing, the process can also be helped along.

Guidelines

Even fairly specific laws may spawn further details on how they will be operationalised. The Inland Revenue regularly publish press releases, explanatory notes, extra-statutory concessions, and statements of practice. The ASC and its successor the ASB publish, in addition to standards, interim statements which are intended to give guidance on the interpretation of legislation.[77] As recommended by the Dearing Committee, the ASB, in order to provide an immediate and authoritative response to emerging issues, has established the Urgent Issues Task Force with a capability of publishing authoritative, though non-mandatory, guidance on emerging issues.[78]

It may seem hardly surprising, therefore, that both the Inland Revenue and the ASC have succumbed to pressure to produce guidance on the application of broader regulation. However, guidance is contradictory to the anti-formalist approach to control, and experience suggests that this may create an 'Achilles heel' in its likely effectiveness. SSAP 21 on leasing, despite, controversially, expressing a substance over form approach, gave guidelines for deciding whether 'substantially all the risks and rewards' have passed to the lessee via a 90 per cent test.[79] This 'test,' according to a Big Six accountancy firm,

76 Arthur Anderson & Co, letter to the ASC, 28 September 1990, on file at the ICAEW Library.

77 See, in particular, ASB, *Interim Statement — Consolidated Accounts* (London: ASB, 1991). The main impetus for revising SSAPs 14 'Group Accounts' and 1 'Accounting for Associated Companies' was the 7th Directive, and its implementation in the Companies Act 1989: see ED 50, *op cit* para 1.1.

78 *Dearing Report*, *op cit* pp 27–29.

79 'It should be presumed that such a transfer of risks and rewards occurs if, at the inception of a lease, the present value of the minimum lease payments, including any initial payment, amounts to substantially all (normally 90 per cent or more) of the fair value of the leased asset': SSAP 21, *Accounting for Leases and Hire Purchase Contracts* (London: ASC, 1984) para 15. Its introduction was controversial: 'SSAP 21 was one of the most controversial accounting standards, as it effectively invoked a substance

appears to have been used in practice as a fairly definitive test instead of being just one factor in deciding whether substantially all of the risks and rewards have been transferred to the lessee under a lease. It seems that the 90% test has been widely interpreted as a rigid rule rather than a guide.[80]

The same approach is predicted for the guidelines in the current draft standards. For example, the ICAEW has expressed the view that if the proposal in ED 49 — that application notes 'should be regarded as standard in relation to the transactions fitting the circumstances they describe'[81] — is adopted, 'then it is likely to encourage a strict rulebook approach.'[82] In ED 49, Application Note B on sale and repurchase agreements gives an example of a housebuilder selling land to a 'special vehicle' company and providing it with a subordinated loan equal to 40 per cent of the consideration.[83] According to the ICAEW, if the example is incorporated into a standard, 'people will do it, but with 30%, and avoid by accounting for the transaction as a sale.'

The Courts

Clarification and narrowing of broad rules may also emerge — or be sought — through the courts. Even in the 'new approach' taxation cases themselves, limits were implicit. In the reasoning on why the schemes in those cases failed lay guidelines on how to fashion schemes which would, in those terms, succeed. So, when one of the reasons given for the failure of the *Ramsay* scheme was its lack of a 'business purpose,' it became practice, according to interviews with tax practitioners, to ensure an element of commerciality was included in business schemes. If 'business purpose' schemes were to be excepted they would be likely to become the norm. The Revenue Law Committee pointed out that implicit in the judgement was also the assumption that 'single step transactions' leading to tax avoidance would be excepted from the new approach.[84] Subsequent cases, in particular *Craven* v *White*, have limited the application of the new approach and provided guidelines on how to escape the legal net. The message was: spread the steps of the scheme over time (it had been commented in *Dawson* that the various sales and purchases which comprised the scheme were 'all over by lunch'[85]); leave an element of uncertainty or at least do not tie up all the ends ahead of time; and ideally, add some element of commercial motivation to meet the 'business purpose test.' In short, indications of what will be excluded from the net of legal control have begun to emerge.

over form approach to give an accounting treatment possibly different from the legal ownership position': Ernst & Young, *op cit* p 686. See also Taylor and Turley, 'The Views of Management on Accounting for Leases' (1985) 15 *Accounting and Business Research* 59.

80 Ernst & Young, *op cit* p 714. KPMG Peat Marwick McKlintock, in their letter to the ASC dated 1 October 1990 (on file at the ICA Library) in response to ED 49, also state that the 90 per cent test is used by the profession. According to Ernst & Young, *op cit* p 715, it is the use of the words 'in exceptional circumstances' to determine when the presumption may be rebutted which has resulted in the 90 per cent test being taken as a firm rule. TR 644, *Implementation of SSAP 21* (London: ICA) attempted to influence the practice of treating the 90 per cent test as a firm rule: '[The 90% test] does not provide a strict mathematical definition of a finance lease. Such a narrow interpretation would be contrary to the spirit of SSAP 21 and SSAPs generally' (para 5).

81 ED 49, *op cit* para 65.

82 ICAEW, *Memorandum of Comments from the Institute of Chartered Accountants in England and Wales on ED 49 'Reflecting the Substance of Transactions in Assets and Liabilities'* (London: ICA, 1990).

83 ED 49, *op cit* Application Note B, Example 2.

84 L Soc Rev Co, *op cit* p 31.

85 Mansfield, *op cit* p 7.

Case law on 'sale or charge' cases, while endorsing a substance over form approach, gives guidance on how to manipulate the finding of the court. In *Curtain Dream*,[86] for example, the court identified particular features of the transaction which affected its characterisation.[87] Using a substance over form approach led to these parties failing in their common purpose, but the decision of the court provides others with guidance on how to reconstruct the transaction. In the leading case of *George Inglefield*,[88] Romer LJ analysed the differences between a transaction of sale and a transaction of mortgage or charge.[89] In the United States, 'Long check-lists have been developed by courts to determine the existence of the necessary degree of control'[90] to reveal 'dominating control' and allow them to pierce the corporate veil. In short, as soon as substance is applied to particular cases, rules emerge, either overtly as criteria of acceptability or covertly as exceptions.

In the UK, accounting issues have rarely been resolved in the courts.[91] However, the role of the courts may well increase following the introduction in the Companies Act 1989 of procedures for the voluntary and, after notice by the Secretary of State, court-ordered revision of annual accounts.[92] The new Financial Reporting Council has been authorised by the Secretary of State to make applications to the court, and £1 million of the £1.2 million provided to the FRC is to enable it to secure compliance with the accounting provisions of the Act. Increased powers and sanctions are likely to stimulate increased opposition, if necessary in the courts.

Legal Opinions

Guidance on the application of broad rules — or any rule — need not come from regulatory authorities or the courts. It may also be sought privately, for example, via legal opinions. Barristers are asked to give an opinion on the lawfulness or legal consequences of proposed transactions. This guidance can, in practice, assume the quality of a rule, being treated as an authoritative statement of what is or is not likely to be caught in the net of legal control. Anyone concerned about uncertainty may seek a legal opinion. For example, credit agencies in their assessment of companies' financial status for the market, at a loss over how to treat companies' use of complex financial instruments, have sought legal advice.[93] That legal advice may then be extended to other cases and become a practical operating rule in the credit agency business. The vaguer the regulation, the more uncertain its application,

---

86 *op cit* n 19.

87 Neither party was able to withdraw from the global transaction; there was an 'indissoluble link' between the parties; the destiny of the material was pre-determined; there was an overall agreement to establish a credit line; an interest rate was specified; and 'there was an exact degree of mutuality in both directions with regard to the passing of the title to the property': *per* Knox J, p 937.

88 *op cit* n 18.

89 The vendor in a sale is not entitled to get back the subject-matter of the sale by returning the money, the mortgagor is, until foreclosed; if the mortgagee realises the subject-matter of the mortgage for a sum more than sufficient to repay him, he must account to the mortgagor for the surplus, if a purchaser sells and realises a profit, he has not got to account for the profit; if the mortgagee realises for a sum that is insufficient to repay, the mortgagor is entitled to recover the balance, if the purchaser resells at a price which is insufficient to recoup him the money he had paid to the vendor, he is not entitled to recover the balance: *Re George Inglefield*, *op cit* pp 27–28.

90 Hofstetter, 'Parent Responsibility for Subsidiary Corporations: Evaluating European Trends' (1990) ICLQ 576, 592.

91 For a review, see Radcliffe, 'Accounting Standards and the Judiciary' (1990) *Accounting and Business Research* 329.

92 Companies Act 1985, ss 245, 245A, 245B.

93 *Financial Times*, 9 January 1991.

the more likely interested parties are to go for legal clarification as protection if things go wrong. Likewise, the more important the claim to legal certainty is, whether for legal protection in the normal course of business or for marketing avoidance schemes complete with 'fraud insurance,'[94] the more likely it is that opinions will be sought and acted upon as though they were rulings.

Clearances and Operational Decisions

Simply in the process of operation, decisions are taken which begin to 'clarify' the substantive approach and to narrow the broad rules. This process can occur in a number of ways, formal and informal. Any system of clearances produces an informal cookbook of what can and cannot be got away with. There may be attempts to resist this process. For example, in the USA it is claimed that in broad legislation aimed at deterrence, guidelines are rarely published.[95] However, it may be difficult to resist a process of 'clarification' and dissemination taking place regardless.[96] Clearances may be sought informally even where there is no statutory right to them. Interviews on tax avoidance found that there were frequent requests to the Technical Office of the Inland Revenue for informal advice on 'hypothetical' or 'no-names' transactions. The research also showed that tax inspectors had an ambivalent attitude to giving informal clearances of this kind. On the one hand, they preferred to keep rules vague in order to keep avoiders guessing about the tax consequences of particular schemes. On the other hand, requests for clearances provided inspectors with a valuable source of information on (some of) the latest lateral thinking of creative compliance, which might be hard to come by in other ways. There is a symbiotic interest in an information exchange; but the trade-off is a drift to narrow rules.

Indeed, however abstract regulations may be in statute or standard, and however hard regulators try to keep the rules in the books general, enforcing regulations inevitably involves application to concrete situations, and decisions about whether a practice or instrument is to be treated as caught by the regulation or not. These then spread remarkably quickly through the network of practice and become informal precedents. The trend to bureaucratisation[97] in big accountancy firms, with auditing done by teams, internal rulebooks, computerised databases of the latest decisions and technical departments providing guidance in tax and accounting, can only encourage this process.

Decisions by Default

Even where regulators try to stay above the process of demarcating the acceptable from the unacceptable, it is hard to avoid endorsement, positive or negative. Regulators cannot simply stand back and stay above the game. There is a dynamic process involved in which the regulator is forced to play a part. When regulators announce a broad flexible regulatory approach, business does not stop. It goes on; people try schemes; if they come to the attention of the regulators, they have to

94 McBarnet, 'Whiter than White-Collar Crime: Tax, Fraud Insurance and the Management of Stigma' (1991b) 42 Brit J Sociology 3.

95 L Soc Rev Co, *op cit*.

96 Heller, 'Public Interest Law and Federal Income Taxes' in Weisbrod, Handler and Komesar (eds), *Public Interest Law* (Berkeley: University of California Press) p 446.

97 Whittington, 'Accounting Standards in the UK after Twenty Years: A Critique of the Dearing and Solomons Reports' (1989) 19 *Accounting and Business Research* 195.

be responded to with clearance or rejection; others copy the scheme; guidelines begin to emerge. 'The vagueness couldn't last,' said one Revenue official resignedly after the initial shock of the *Furniss* v *Dawson* decision gave way to more and more testing of the waters. If the regulators do not respond, the lack of reaction is taken as lack of rejection, and therefore of endorsement. Schemes may even be leaked to the press to test the water. Rules emerge by default. They disseminate through the industry and the professions and become accepted practice. If this is considered undesirable by the regulators, more regulation is required to control it. Cases go to court. Guidelines emerge again and the dynamic process goes on with increasing reversion to formalism. The broad flexible approach simply becomes a mechanism for substituting new rules for old, and the drift back to specific rules is under way.

Drifting and Steering

In the process of applying anti-formalist, or any, regulation, it is difficult to avoid producing operational rules or quasi-rules — decisions or agreements without legal authority but treated in practice as rules[98] — which narrow the broad anti-formalist approach. But the process is not entirely neutral. The levers operating the process can also be pushed into action. Those who want a more specific, form-based approach to control — for professional, cynical or protective reasons, in order to facilitate creative compliance, increase control, cut costs or many other different and even contradictory reasons — may not only call for clarification at the rule-making stage but may also take action themselves to push for clarification through the mechanisms of application. Rules are constructed not just by regulators but through the actions of the regulated — trying out schemes, seeking clearances, asking for informal rulings, acquiring legal opinions or initiating judicial limitation via carefully selected court cases. Judges do not always spell out specific rules and guidelines in cases; those with an interest in finding guidelines also dig over judicial reasoning and construct them. The mechanisms, institutions and structures of law are thus *used* to narrow down, tighten and define broad open-textured anti-formalist controls. Law not only *drifts* from substance to form, from broad to narrow, from open to closed, it can also be steered quite deliberately.

The Incorporation of Anti-formalism

Decisions made in relation to particular cases would not constitute quasi-rules were it not for some notion of their general applicability being called into play. Decisions become rules when precedential value is claimed for them. However hard those making decisions try, for their part, to keep them on the basis of one-off specific decisions, if there is pressure and demand for rules, there is also recording and networking of decisions, citation of how other cases have been treated, claims, rooted in formalist legal ideology, for like cases to be treated alike. Even in the context of anti-formalist strategies of control, formalist concepts such as precedent, parity and the rule of law, persistently pressed, may prove difficult arguments to openly resist. Instead of countering formalist thinking, anti-formalism can thus be incorporated, in practice, into a formalist framework of thinking or acting. Anti-formalist approaches may in this way be turned against themselves.

98 See the discussion on 'working certainty' below.

Formalistic Substance

Broad substantive regulations do not necessarily eliminate formalistic avoidance of legal control. Ironically, even broad 'substance over form' regulations have been used legalistically against their own declared purposes. If substance over form can itself be used as a rule, it ceases to be a safety net beyond particular rules. Rather, it becomes a particular rule itself, amenable to use in the creation of loopholes. It is incorporated into a formalistic framework.

Debt defeasance is one example of how (economic) substance-over-(legal) form regulation has been used for creative compliance. 'In-substance' defeasance involves the purchase of virtually riskless government securities which are placed in a trust, the sole purpose of which is to meet the cash payments due on a company's debt. The company is freed from making any further payments on the debt as long as the cash flows on the trust's riskless assets match those promised on the company's debt. In substance, therefore, it is argued that the debt has been eliminated, even though in law the liability remains. The debt is taken off the balance sheet by offsetting the trust investment against the liability. The purchased securities are also removed from the balance sheet.

In the United States, the possibility of defeasing debt has been utilised in ways not envisaged by the regulators.[99] To cite just one example, Wall Street bankers have developed 'instantaneous in-substance' defeasance.[100] Newly issued debt rather than existing debt has been defeased in a form of arbitrage transaction. For example, a US corporation borrows DM 100 million at 8 per cent and uses it to buy DM 100 million German government security yielding 8¼ per cent in trust to cover the debt *and* create an excess. Not only is the debt extinguished, a gain is also recognised. The Federal Accounting Standards Board has stated that this is not what it intended with its regulation and has introduced a subsequent specific rule. The proximity of the borrowing and the acquisition of securities suggest that these are 'borrow-and-invest' activities, rather than the true elimination of debt; they should be reported as borrowing and investment rather than defeasance.[101] In other words, instantaneous in-substance defeasance should be left on the balance sheet. This response, however, is both an acceptance of the use of formalistic substance and a resort to form for control.

The anti-formalist approach to consolidation introduced in the Companies Act 1989 — through broad concepts such as the actual exercise of dominant influence and the regulation of quasi-subsidiaries through SSAPs — can also be treated formalistically in practice, with the criterion of control used to defeat its purpose of ensuring consolidation. On the contrary, the broad anti-formalist criterion is used not only to justify but to require non-consolidation. Our research has revealed a variety of methods, some in place before provisions of the Companies Act 1989 became effective, which have been adopted to achieve this result. One example — use of a joint venture (JV) — might illustrate how creative compliance can be used to nullify the anti-formalist approach.

Several JV escape routes from consolidation are possible. For example, companies A and B control half the voting rights and directors' voting rights of company C, which they created together. Company C is also 'deadlocked,' that is, the ability

99 Financial Accounting Standards Board, SFAS No 76, *Extinguishment of Debt* (Norwalk, Connecticut: FASB, 1983).

100 See Rosenblatt, (1984) *Corporate Finance*.

101 FASB Technical Bulletin No 84-4, *In-Substance Defeasance of Debt* (Norwalk, Connecticut, 1984).

of A or B (or any other 'external' agent) actually to exercise a dominant influence over C is restricted since C cannot depart from specified policies. As a result, since neither A nor B control it, C need not, under the terms of the amended Companies Act 1985, be consolidated in the balance sheets of either A or B. This is so even though the purpose (and commercial effect) of establishing C may have been to remove assets and the loans used to acquire them from those balance sheets, or to produce paper profits and cash for A or B. Nor can C be proportionally consolidated in the balance sheets of A and B since the Act prohibits such treatment of corporate bodies.[102]

This kind of legal structure disguises the economic substance of a relationship *by complying with the substantive approach*: since there is no actual exercise of a dominant influence, there is no consolidation. Deadlocked JV companies have been used as vehicles for property development, and the discovery, after its collapse, of an estimated £700 million of debt in JVs involving Rush & Tompkins clearly reveals how the joint venture can work to hide liabilities. In practice, however, many of these JVs are likely to take a non-corporate legal form: the JV is for a single purpose, and the company form would present an administrative burden; the accounts of a corporate JV must be publicly filed, prejudicing commercial sensitivity; a non-corporate form also gives the JV partners greater flexibility in terms of utilising tax losses.[103] While the statute permits proportional consolidation for a non-incorporated JV, ED 50 mandates it. If pressure to restore the statutory approach is unsuccessful and the ASB retains the obligation, other forms of creative compliance may be adopted. Any undertaking (or bank) offering to consolidate another undertaking by creating a control relationship with it will provide a valuable service to other undertakings which do not wish to consolidate.[104] Creative compliance with the statutory definitions, including the anti-formalist ones, could provide protection not only against the statute-based attacks but professional ones also. After all, according to the ASC, only one enterprise may have control of another in the manner which makes consolidation the appropriate treatment.[105]

In short, even regulation based on capturing economic substance, brought in precisely to thwart creative compliance, may itself be treated as a cookbook for the creation of new avoidance devices. The ideology of precedent is used to claim rigid rule status for the substance approach. By making substance over form a rigid rule, as opposed to an override of rigid rules, it becomes not a control over creative compliance but further material for its construction.

Capturing Economic Substance: Closure and Incorporation

Incorporation of anti-formalist approaches can occur in other ways. Reliance on regulations which go beyond legal forms and even beyond the legal system (by placing the operation of accounting regulation in the hands of the accounting profession, or judging on the basis of economic substance rather than legal form) assumes that claims of 'closure' of the legal system and 'legalism' of lawyers are irrelevant or can be resisted or accommodated. Otherwise, such regulations may also be incorporated into formalism.

102 Companies Act 1985, Sched 4A, para 19(1).
103 Costain Group, comments on ED 50 dated 12/10/90, on file at the ICAEW Library.
104 Indeed, neither may have to consolidate: one has benefits/risks but no control; the other has control but nothing to report (except its fee).
105 ED 50, *op cit* para 14.

The idea of capturing the 'substance' rather than just the 'form' of a transaction may seem a very sensible approach to control. What 'substance' is to mean, however, remains problematic. Under the current discussions of 'substance over form,' and apparent agreement between lawyers and accountants over the need to capture the substance of a transaction, lie quite different approaches to its meaning. For the ASC, 'Accounting for a transaction in accordance with its substance requires that its accounting treatment should fairly reflect its commercial effect.'[106] Thus, 'a decision that a sale and repurchase agreement ought properly to be regarded as a sale by the seller and a purchase by the buyer will follow a failure to establish through analysis that the transaction is in substance a financing one.'[107] The ED 49 application note approaches the analysis by comparing the position of the seller with that of the borrower; and of the buyer with that of the lender. It focuses on the allocation of risks and rewards between the two parties. The true commercial effect of a transaction is a sale if the seller genuinely relinquishes control of the benefits and transfers the exposure to the significant risks associated with the resource to the buyer.

Current case law, however, suggests that without a dramatic change in judicial approach, this is not necessarily an approach that will survive in law. On the face of it, the judicial approach to such an agreement is similar: 'it is the substance of the transaction that has to be looked at and not just the form.'[108] However, 'to point out that it is a transaction of financing throws no light on the question we have to determine.'[109] That question is not whether the transaction was one of financing, but whether the financing was by means of a transaction of mortgage and charge or by means of a transaction of sale.[110] Thus, to lawyers, the initial reaction of accountants to treat a sale and repurchase agreement as a financing rather than a sale, is 'prejudiced'[111] and is a 'fundamental weakness' in the application notes of ED 49.[112]

At one level, the difference in approach appears semantic; in practice, however, it may be significant.[113] Whereas accountants find the substance following an analysis of the commercial effect of a transaction, lawyers find the substance after a consideration of the legal rights and obligations of the parties to be derived from an examination of the true agreement between them. Whereas accountants, in their analysis, concentrate on the *ends* of the transaction, lawyers in theirs place emphasis on the *means*.[114] One produces the economic substance; the other produces the

106 ED 49, *op cit* para 3.
107 *ibid* para B.21.
108 *Re Curtain Dream, op cit per* Knox J. See also *Re George Inglefield, op cit* p 17 *per* Lord Hanworth MR, p 27 *per* Romer LJ.
109 *Re George Inglefield, ibid* p 27 *per* Romer LJ. See also L Soc ED 49, *op cit* p 12: 'The fact that in substance a transaction is one of financing does nothing to assist in its analysis and cannot of itself justify the accounting treatment of a sale as a loan.' Because factoring is a financing transaction and has the same effect as a loan against the security of the debt 'does not mean that it is a loan and not a sale' (p 10).
110 *Re George Inglefield, ibid*.
111 L Soc ED 49, *op cit* p 16.
112 *ibid* p 12.
113 It may be significant for other reasons too. The approach adopted in ED 49 may result in the 'under-inclusion of information. In discussing the appropriate note disclosure for sale and repurchase agreements, a distinction is made between a transaction which is 'in substance a financing arrangement recognised on the balance sheet' from those which are 'legitimately recognised as a sale and is off balance sheet.' This approach fails to recognise that the *combined* legal and commercial effect may be a financing *and* a legitimate sale. Factoring debts, for example, may be a legitimate sale made to raise finance.
114 See generally Tolley, *op cit* pp 225–228.

legal substance. Even in the 'new approach' to tax and in the long-standing tensions over form and substance, the issue has not been whether economic substance should prevail over legal form, but whether *lawyers'* substance should.[115] In short, the idea of economic substance overriding a more legalistic approach may not survive, but may be incorporated into a legal framework.

Self-regulation: Escaping Law or Incorporated Within It?

Whether the lawyers' approach will prevail depends to some extent on the outcome of another strand of anti-formalist strategy. Because of concern that dealing with accounting standards through statute and the courts would lead to legalism and ossification, the DTI expressed a preference for leaving detailed implementation to the accounting profession.[116] This may, however, be easier said than done. In response to the accounting profession's proposed new standard, the legal profession has launched a critique which is detailed and unequivocal. The lawyers' stance is not simply that there is a clash but that in a clash the legal interpretation dominates. The legal interpretation also tends to be a narrower, legal rule-based approach. The Company Law Committee has observed, for example, that the true and fair override, far from freely overriding compliance with specific legal rules in order to achieve the purpose of accounting, can only be operated in legally specified circumstances. Thus, the Committee observe: 'Where the application of ED 49 leads to a recharacterisation of a transaction which conflicts with the legal analysis . . . the accounting treatment is likely to result in the departure from the statutory requirements. This is lawful only if there are special circumstances which would allow the use of the override . . . where the circumstances are not "special" then use of the override is impermissible and the transaction may not be recharacterised.'[117]

In other words, the Committee reject the ASC's view that the override can be applied 'automatically,' for example because of the mere existence of a quasi-subsidiary or the identification of 'special circumstances' in an accounting standard. Instead,

> it is always necessary to consider whether the circumstances are 'special' and, if so, whether it is necessary to depart from the statutory requirements in order to give a true and fair view . . . Such a process must be undergone wherever there is a conflict between the legal and accounting analysis of a transaction.[118]

There are further clashes; for example, the Committee also rejects what it regards as attempts to deviate from the law in ED 50 over the issue of control:

> There is a danger in the discussion on control that control will become the guiding principle in application of the statement, when that principle should rather be whether the statutory requirements for consolidation are satisfied . . . while we accept the need to correlate the conceptual approach with the law, it is the law which has to be applied.[119]

115 See L Soc Rev Co, *op cit* p 3 referring to *IRC* v *Westminster* [1936] AC 1, 19–21. According to Lord Wright, 'the true nature of the legal obligation and nothing else is "the substance"' (p 31); *Ramsay* v *IRC*, *op cit* pp 305–306.

116 DTI, *op cit* (1989).

117 L Soc ED 49, *op cit* p 14. See also L Soc ED 55, *op cit*.

118 *ibid* p 4.

119 L Soc ED 50, *op cit* pp 2, 3. Thus, it could be 'dangerous' to interpret dominant influence as equivalent simply to directing the operating and financial policies. 'That might equate with "control" as ordinarily understood, but that is not in point here' (pp 7–8).

In short, the idea of avoiding legalism and ossification by regulating through the accounting profession rather than the law is meeting strong resistance from lawyers.

Clearly, there may be a simple clash of interests involved. Research has suggested there is considerable competition between lawyers and accountants, and that the accountants are calling the tune.[120] The legal profession could be seen as having an interest not only in resisting the intrusion of accountants into 'their' territory of company law, but in defining more specific accounting regulation as legal terrain. But there are other obstacles. The legal profession has drawn attention to the enormous practical difficulties involved in introducing any major changes to accounting via a new SSAP. Standards set by the profession have implications for other areas of law, for example in relation to tax allowances, borrowing covenants and capital adequacy regulations.[121] If the going concern assumption no longer applies, 'the test of assets and liabilities is likely to be whether or not they reflect legally enforceable rights and obligations.'[122] The need to characterise a transaction in accordance with legal rules arises also in the context of the registration of charges.[123] There are wider legal contexts too. The Institute of Chartered Accountants of Scotland notes with remarkable casualness that its recommendations for changes in financial reporting would require 'review, and if need be, amendment' of UK company law, which would involve 'the European Commission and other countries within the European Community.'[124] This presents a daunting practical and political task.

Indeed, even in UK company law itself, the power delegated to the profession is explicitly limited. The Companies Acts' new catch-all concepts such as 'actual dominant influence' and 'managed on a unified basis,' about which the profession is asked to give guidance, operate only within the confines of specifically defined situations — where there is also a 'participating interest.' If there is no participating interest, they are inoperative. The power of the accounting profession to fill gaps in the statute as outlined in ED 49 does not operate in a legal vacuum. Indeed, for all its emphasis on the need to avoid legalism and ossification, the approach of the DTI to the issue of how the true and fair override should operate is very reminiscent of its approach following the *Argyll* case which fostered a decade of strict rule-following and creative compliance. Essentially, it has taken the line that where the rules are clear they should be adhered to, despite the views of the professional standard-setters.[125]

The impetus for the profession, both at the level of standard setting and at the level of practice, to adhere to legal rules is particularly enhanced by the threat of, increase in, and current concern among accountants about negligence actions against auditors.[126] While the *Caparo* decision[127] gave a breathing space by limiting auditor liability to the body of shareholders as a whole rather than third parties, the *Morgan Crucible*[128] case has already undermined this. Indeed, our research indicated that

120 See the article by Dezalay above, p 792.

121 L Soc ED 49, *op cit* p 4.

122 *ibid.* The Committee would 'prefer ED 49 to take effect as a conceptual framework, and the application notes as guidelines, rather than as standard accounting practice': p 5.

123 *Re George Inglefield, op cit*; *Re Curtain Dream, op cit.*

124 Institute of Chartered Accountants of Scotland, *Making Corporate Reports Valuable* (London: Kogan Page, 1988) p 95.

125 Crichton, 'A New Approach to Consolidated Accounts' (1990) *Accountancy* 32.

126 Whelan and McBarnet, 'The "Crisis" in Professional Liability Insurance' in Whelan (ed), *The Law and Economics of Professional Liability Insurance* (Geneva: The Geneva Association, special issue of *The Geneva Papers*, vols 13 and 14, 1989–90).

127 *Caparo Industries* v *Dickman* [1990] 2 AC 605.

128 *Morgan Crucible Co plc* v *Hill Samuel & Co Ltd* [1991] 2 WLR 655.

powerful third parties like banks had already adapted to the new situation with new legal instruments to make auditors liable *despite Caparo*. Even though most cases are settled out of court, they are settled in shadow of the law. In such a situation, where conflict arises between strict interpretation of legal rules and professional standards or practices, we would hypothesise a tendency to stick by the legal rules as a matter of self-protection against legal retaliation. In the clash between law and accounting, law has power and sanctions on its side.

Accountants themselves may also be ambivalent or even hostile towards a strategy of broad general rules, effective control of legal avoidance and the allocation or assumption of a key role for the profession in implementing it. Accounting is said to be an increasingly competitive market, with auditing not only a market in itself but an entree to more lucrative management consultancy. Accountants may prefer formalistic rules requiring more mechanistic compliance work and cutting auditing costs. Competition, or fear of competition, between lawyers and accountants may exacerbate the situation. One accountant observed in interview: 'Now a client will ask, "how can I capitalise my costs? How can I keep liabilities off the balance sheet?" If I don't tell him he'll go to a solicitor down the road who will.' The Dearing Committee commented: 'It would be idealistic to assume that all auditors at all times are unmindful of the risk of losing business.'[129] If clients want clear rules or indeed avoidable rules, the pressures of the market may mean that the profession's regulatory interest in a substance approach is countered by its commercial — or professional — interest in giving clients what they want.

Conclusion: Formalism, Indeterminacy and Legal Control

Can Anti-formalist Control Survive?

As a strategy of legal control, anti-formalism has been presented as a potential solution to the shortcomings of formalism and as a way of curbing creative compliance. However, there is an irony in introducing anti-formalism to control the creative compliance of sophisticated regulatees backed by resources of finance and expertise. Creative compliance is stimulated by strong motivations for resisting control. These motivations do not disappear with the first threat of a different form of control. On the contrary, they become motivations for resisting and undermining anti-formalism. Sources of resistance can be found within legal structures and ideologies themselves. Creative compliance demonstrates the manipulability of the legal system, and the system can be used not just by playing with the substance of law, as in the construction of specific formalist devices to avoid control, but by using the mechanisms of law to force out narrow rules, and using its ideologies as justification.

Not that all resistance to anti-formalism is based on a wish to boost creative compliance. There are many reasons for people wanting in good faith to know where they stand legally; there are uncertainties about anti-formalism as a strategy of control, both in terms of its likely effectiveness and in terms of its costs; while there are multiple layers of politics, conflicts, tensions and ambivalences within the system and the organisations, professions, legislators, regulators and regulatees involved in and affected by it. All these factors contribute to undermining anti-formalism in the demand for, and production of, clearer rules. If anti-formalist policy is to

129 *Dearing Report*, *op cit* p 11. See, too, Wallace and Cooke, 'The diagnosis and resolution of emerging issues in corporate disclosure practices' (1990) 20 *Accounting and Business Research* 143, 145.

survive in this area as more than mere rhetoric, there are major obstacles to be overcome. This raises the question of whether formalism is inevitable in law.

Is Formalism Inevitable?

This has been a one-sided argument. It has explored the obstacles to anti-formalist control and the factors which are likely to stimulate a return to formalism and cookbook control. There are undoubtedly also pulls and pressures in the opposite direction, as the rise of the anti-formalist approach itself demonstrates. What our analysis does suggest, however, is that where there are powerful motivations to formalism backed by opportunities, resources and political clout, there are available, in the ideologies and structures of the legal system, a range of mechanisms for steering regulation in policy and practice back to formalism, and a repertoire of powerful rhetorical gambits to justify this move — the inequity or impracticality of over-inclusive controls, the need for the rule of law, for controls on arbitrary discretion, for like treatment of like cases, and so on.

There are, of course, competing notions of justice and fairness, but it may be that there is a fundamental formalism inherent in the very idea of legal control in the liberal democratic state which makes formalist arguments difficult to resist or easy to justify. Any policy can be resisted politically. A policy of anti-formalist control is, however, particularly vulnerable to such ideological critique, not just at the political level but in more routine dealings with regulators. To talk of a fundamental formalism legitimising law is not to reify the role of ideology. Ideology of itself determines nothing. But it *can* be brought into play to legitimise resistance and present controllers as overstepping the mark. It is E.P. Thompson's point about the real potential of the ideology of the rule of law.[130] The irony is that if the rule of law may be used as a weapon to limit rulers and further the interests of underdogs, it is much more readily available for use by those who already have the resources, expertise and power to use the rhetoric, and the mechanisms of law, effectively.[131]

This is not, however, to say formalism is inevitable in law. The drift to form we describe here in the context of law and finance is the product of a complex and dynamic interplay of structures, situations, ideologies and motivations. The repertoire of formalist mechanisms and ideologies is available but only brought into play when there is motivation to do so, and when those with such motivations have adequate resources, organisation or political muscle to use the system in this way. Rules are not always 'privileged' in practice. Broad standards may be tolerated, even by sophisticated subjects, in other situations with other motivations in play. There need not always be a perceived interest in clear rules. There may also be countervailing interests in vague open regulation. Creative compliance is just one of several strategies in dealing with law. Negotiation may be preferred by regulatees and may be seen to be enhanced by vague laws. Negotiation may also be preferred by regulators. Parties may settle out of court to *avoid* establishing rules. Law may be perceived as symbolic and ineffective anyway so that there is a preference for simply keeping quiet and letting policies of anti-avoidance and anti-formalism prevail, but only as empty words. In short, demand for formalism is not inevitable. Nevertheless, where formalism *is* wanted and pressed for, it may be hard to resist within the current structures and ideologies of law.

130 Thompson, *Whigs and Hunters* (London: Allen Lane, 1975).
131 McBarnet, *op cit* (1984).

Does Formalism Matter? Limiting Indeterminacy and Constraining Control

Of course, if in reality law is indeterminate and enforcement characterised by discretion and autonomy, regulators are not in practice constrained by legal rules, and whether those rules are broad or narrow is of little practical relevance to the issue of control. If regulators want to control they can. If they do not, the reasons must lie somewhere other than in the constraints of formalism. More generally, indeterminacy implies endemic uncertainty, and the mere uncertainty of outcomes may itself constrain creative compliance by creating too much risk. In short, if law is indeterminate and outcomes uncertain, formalism, and the fate of anti-formalism, may be, in effect, irrelevant. However, active regulatees and their advisers can take steps to confront this endemic uncertainty, manage the risk of control and reduce the practical relevance of indeterminacy.

The anti-formalist strategies described here in a sense espoused uncertainty. Narrow definitions were eschewed in order to keep meanings open and flexible. However, in practice, additional provisions, guidelines and application notes clarified meanings. Common understandings were constructed in negotiation with regulators. Even the uncertainty implicit in judicial references to an 'evolving doctrine' was undermined by agreements on how the controversial judicial decisions would be applied. Such negotiations, along with careful monitoring of cases, can also pre-empt the judicial role by limiting the likelihood of cases reaching the courts; the evolution of doctrine may not be invited. Indeed, the judges' own reasoning, even in turning point cases, provides guidelines for future *successful* creative compliance.

Even negotiated meanings may, of course, be applied in different ways; language is flexible. However, meaning is not necessarily left, in sophisticated circles with vast sums of money at stake, to chance or to *post hoc* decisions by regulators. Specific clearances are sought in relation to specific cases. Legal opinions are taken. Technical advice is sought from regulators. Meaning is negotiated and cleared before transactions take their final form. The *post hoc* autonomy of the regulator is constrained; a working certainty is created. Likewise, resort to regulatory bluff can be called; legal opinions produced; practice monitored; complaints made. Bluff may work on the small trader; it is less likely to control the sophisticated.[132] Covert anti-formalism may simply not be allowed to work without legal or political challenge.

Of course, judges can still come along *post hoc* and overthrow the status quo of negotiation and practice. The losers in a turning point case — the taxpayers in *Ramsay* or *Furniss* v *Dawson*, the disappointed parties in *Curtain Dream* — are effectively controlled, as are those who settle in the wake of such cases. Yet there are political limits to how far or how often the judges can do this. We have seen how overt anti-formalism by judges can be resisted politically with all the repertoire of formalist rhetoric in support. More covert anti-formalism can also be rendered overt, publicised, and resisted, if motivated parties do not agree with it.[133] In practice, there are therefore periods of calm during which narrow rules operate by working consensus.

Certainly, creative compliance frequently works. It may only work for a while — tax scheme promoters talked in interview of having a 'season' for any particular

132 See Bardach and Kagan, *Going by the Book* (Philadelphia: Temple University Press, 1982); Mann, *Defending White-Collar Crime* (New Haven: Yale University Press, 1985); McBarnet, *op cit* (1991b).

133 Although *Argyll* was just a magistrates' court case, it was publicised and not, in this case, resisted, but welcomed and used for creative compliance.

scheme before the rules were changed to stop it — but in practice lawyers, accountants, consultants and bankers operate on the working assumption that regulators can be expected to play by the common understanding of the rules until they are explicitly changed, and call foul if they do not. Regulators, as implied in the call for a change to anti-formalist policy, claim they *are* constrained by formalist rules.[134] This may be delusion or political bluff; it may be that their real powers to control would be revealed if only they read the critical legal theory which says they can do what they like within the law. Or it may be that, despite the theoretical freedom possible within the meaning and operation of law, real practical and political limits can be constructed. In theory, law is at least moderately indeterminate; in practice, a working determinacy can be agreed or imposed.

Beyond Control?

If regulation cannot in practice transcend formalism, the spirit of the law will remain elusive and creative compliance continue to escape effective legal control. Yet our analysis suggests that in the context of finance, anti-formalism is unlikely to survive as more than rhetoric or theory. New situations arise and new rules are produced to deal with them. But new rules cannot control creative compliance. How do you control those playing by the rules? New rules simply mean new games. No rules, rules broad enough to be flexible in application, mean resistance, and the use of legal structures and ideologies to re-establish working rules, which can then be manipulated. There may be limits in turn to this process. Frequent change may result in effective control by making the costs too high. Debate and scandal may impose some sense of moral obligation. This discussion is based only on study of the area of law and finance. Further research in wider contexts is required. Yet where the stakes are high, where there is strong motivation to circumvent legal control, and where there are the resources to achieve this, we would expect law to be avoided and control to be resisted.

This has implications beyond academic debate. We have described elsewhere the limits of formalism in providing effective control. If anti-formalism is doomed to fail, or to revert to the cookbook approach, then creative compliance, and the powerful economic elites usually associated with it, may be beyond legal control.

134 See McBarnet and Whelan, *op cit* (forthcoming); McBarnet, *op cit* (1991a).

[17]

When Compliance is not the Solution but the Problem: From Changes in Law to Changes in Attitude

A cooperative taxpaying culture is the ultimate goal of the Compliance Model of enforcement adopted, among other regulatory agencies (see, for example, Hawkins, 1984), by the Australian Taxation Office (ATO) (Cash Economy Task Force, 1998; Australian Taxation Office, 2000a). This volume, therefore, includes chapters on why people comply – or do not – and on the best way for enforcement agencies to secure compliance. Securing compliance is seen as the key, as the solution to the regulatory problem of making policy effective in practice. This chapter offers a different perspective. It asks: What happens to the Compliance Model when compliance is not the solution but the problem?

The Compliance Model focuses on the strategies adopted by those enforcing the law. They should be cooperative, understanding, focusing on fostering compliance rather than on leaping immediately to punishing non-compliance, with 'big stick' sanctions reserved for those recalcitrants who continue with non-compliance regardless (Ayres and Braithwaite, 1992). But choice of strategies is not the preserve of enforcement agencies. Different strategic responses can be adopted by those on the receiving end of the law too, and these translate into different approaches to compliance. Faced with a tax bill, people may choose to comply willingly. We might think of this as *committed compliance*. They may choose to comply unwillingly, complain but pay up nonetheless. We might think of this as *capitulative compliance*. They may invent false expenses, pack their cash in a suitcase and whisk it out of the country without declaring it, or simply operate in the cash economy, opting for *non-compliance*. Or, if they have the resources, they may set their lawyers to work[1] on the legal form of their activities to package or repackage them in ways they can claim fall beyond the ambit of *dis*advantageous, or within the ambit of advantageous, law. They can engage in *creative compliance*.

It is the essence of creative compliance that it can be defended as *not* non-compliance. Indeed, that is exactly how it is often presented, as 'not illegal', or more positively, in that well-worn phrase, as 'perfectly legal'. Nonetheless, just like non-compliance, the essence of creative compliance is that it escapes the intended impact of law. The creativity inherent in creative compliance involves finding ways to accomplish compliance with the letter of the law while totally undermining the policy behind the words. It is therefore when compliance takes the form of creative compliance that it becomes, for those vested with the task of enforcing policy, a problem not a solution.

Creative compliance devices abound in the area of tax, but are not confined to it. Far from it. Creative compliance will be found in any area of law in which those subject to it have the motivation and the resources (in terms of money and/or know-how) to resist legal control legally.

Recognising this will help those concerned with tax to realise that creative compliance is not a tax issue but a much more general law issue, and a fundamental one at that. Recognising that the issue goes beyond tax avoidance to law avoidance means we can try to learn from experience in other areas of law, in such areas, for example, as that first cousin of tax avoidance, creative accounting. Indeed, creative accounting is pertinent to tax not only as a parallel area of creative compliance, but as potentially integral to tax computation.[2] In the analysis that follows I draw not only on my own research on tax avoidance in the United Kingdom (UK)[3] and in Australia,[4] but on joint research on creative accounting[5] to draw out the challenges posed for effective enforcement by creative compliance.

Creative Compliance

Two factors contribute to the practice of creative compliance. One significant factor is the nature and operation of law itself. The law-making process leads to lobbying and compromise, legislators cannot address every contingency that might arise, drafting is fallible. More fundamentally, it is in the nature of law that it is open to different interpretations, and that its meaning and application are arguable.

Creative compliance, however, does not arise deterministically from the nature of law. It also requires a particular attitude to law, an attitude which, far from seeing law as an authoritative and legitimate policy to be implemented, sees it as a material to be worked on (McBarnet, 1984), to be tailored, regardless of the policy behind it, to one's own or one's client's interests. And it requires active legal work.

Law is open to alternative interpretations. Innovations in practice can leave law behind. But grey areas, alternative interpretations and innovative legal forms do not only arise 'naturally'. Rather, they may be motivated precisely by the desire to outflank the law. Creative compliance involves careful scrutiny of law in order to seek out material for and actively construct alternative and innovative arguments and legal forms. Creative compliance involves seeking out: (a) gaps facilitating the 'where does it say I can't do that?' argument; (b) the ex-files of law, expressing exemptions, exceptions, exclusions, with practices then restructured to fit within them; and (c) rules, the more prescriptive and rigid the definitions and thresholds involved, the better, with legal forms adopted to fit inside or outside their literal ambit (a practice of working to rule).

Regulators often express concern about uncertainties in the law being exploited,[6] but creative compliance operates particularly effectively in the context of a rule-bound regime, where the words of the law can be treated as recipes for avoidance.

How this works in practice can be readily demonstrated from research. When it was proposed in the UK that value added tax (VAT) should be levied on domestic fuel, hitherto exempt, there was extensive protest on the basis that the old and the poor would suffer. In the event, not everyone suffered. Some institutions, including university student residences, found a nice way to avoid the new costs involved in heating and hot water. They would sell their boilers, which of course remained exactly where they were in the institution's basement, to a separate company. The company would buy the fuel to heat the water. The company would have to pay VAT on the fuel but, as a commercial enterprise, could reclaim it. The company then sold the water to the institution. There is as yet no VAT on water so, hey presto, nobody pays any VAT. And the 'where does it say I can't do that?' argument, along with a quick referral to the rules, can be brought into play to justify it.

UK national insurance is currently being avoided in the North Sea oil industry by transferring UK staff to overseas agencies. Transnational tax avoidance by using tax havens or differential rules in different jurisdictions (for example, the 'Delaware Link' device (McBarnet, 1992)) is common practice. But avoidance can also be readily accomplished within a jurisdiction simply by working to, or playing with, the rules. For example, to avoid UK national insurance contributions (national insurance contributions being paid by employer as well as employee), a practice was developed in the financial sector of paying part of the salary in the form of large bonuses in shares. No national insurance contributions were payable on shares, though they had a clear monetary value and could be converted immediately into cash. To deal with this, the law was changed to impose national insurance on any payment in a 'traded commodity on a recognised exchange'. The result was a shift to payments in fine wine, also of clear monetary value, also amenable to immediate conversion to cash, but not traded on a recognised exchange.

Creative compliance is pervasive in corporate practice in many areas of law and has, over time, involved a vast array of techniques (see Griffiths, 1986, 1995). Take an example from my research with Christopher Whelan on creative accounting, one we have frequently cited because it demonstrates so clearly the problems posed by creative compliance. This specific example, the 'orphan subsidiary', was widely used in the 1980s to cosmetically enhance a corporate group's paper profits and assets, with knock-on effects for share prices, performance-related pay and borrowing capacity. A parent company must, under company law, produce accounts, which include the profits/losses and assets/liabilities of its subsidiaries. The idea is that it should provide the full picture for all the companies it controls, and not hide away poor performances or liabilities in a separate entity whose details it does not disclose. But what if parent company A sets up a company B which it controls, but which is nonetheless carefully structured to fall outside the legal definitions of a subsidiary? In this 'orphan subsidiary' it would have the perfect vehicle to use in ventures which involved high risk or high borrowings – such as a highly leveraged acquisition – without the losses or liabilities appearing, detrimentally, in its group accounts.

The statutory definition of a subsidiary under Section 736(1) of the *Companies Act 1985* involved two criteria. Company B was a subsidiary of company A if (a) A owned more than half B's equity capital, or if (b) A controlled the composition of B's board of directors. With a little creativity, both criteria could be readily circumvented. There were many ways of achieving this, one of the simplest being to set up two types of shares, ordinary shares and preference shares, 50 per cent of each. Company A would own the ordinary shares, while its bank would own the preference shares. Company A would not therefore own more than 50 per cent of the equity capital. Company A and its bank would each appoint half the directors. Company A would not therefore control the composition of the board of directors. But the directors representing the ordinary shareholder (Company A) would have two votes to the preference share directors' one. Company A would not control the composition of the board of directors, but it would control the board's votes.

These are typical examples of creative compliance at work, and they demonstrate how the material of law is actively used to circumvent legal control. The constructs that emerge are backed with legal arguments and the opinions of leading counsel and, if challenged, a case can be produced (however 'bullish' – see ahead) to claim compliance with the law. And these are merely examples. Creative compliance is not a practice operating at the statistical margins, or at the margins of society. On the contrary, it is pervasive, and pervasive among leading lights in the social and corporate world. The orphan subsidiary, for example, was just one of a vast range of creative accounting devices, used routinely in the UK by household name companies.

Creative Compliance and Non-compliance

That creative compliance *is* compliance is, of course, only a claim. Whether it is perfectly legal or not is an unanswerable question, until it has won or lost in court. Often it is a claim that succeeds simply because it is not contested. Even if it is successfully challenged, the fact that it is a case based on applying the law rather than ignoring it[7] provides protection from the sanctions and stigma associated with simple non-compliance. A tax planning device may fail in court without being branded a tax fraud.[8] It is an essential element and attraction of creative compliance that it can claim to be 'not illegal', to be quite distinct from non-compliance.

But the line between the two is not always so clear as that suggests (McBarnet, 1992). The Australian Commissioner of Taxation (2000) has recognised that aggressive tax planning can in practice slip over the line into evasion: 'The competition in the market has also stretched the boundaries of arrangements, with some edging to the fraudulent' (p. 5).

What is more, creative compliance and non-compliance can intertwine. There has recently been a furore over Australian barristers going bankrupt with one creditor, the ATO, to whom they owed debts in unpaid taxes to the tune of millions of dollars (Commissioner of Taxation, 2000, pp. 6-7). In this case the actual non-payment of tax would not appear to be a matter of creative compliance, but of simple non-compliance under tax law. But resort to a different branch of the law, bankruptcy, permitted escape from the sanctions of tax law. Of course no one can go into bankruptcy unless they have run out of assets. But the reason for the furore was concern that assets remained in the family, accessible to and enjoyed by the bankrupt, despite the bankruptcy and the protection it offered regarding the enforcement of tax law. In short, there was concern that bankruptcy law had been used creatively. Certainly, bankruptcy can be planned and creatively constructed. The ATO Auditor-General Audit Report (1999) observed (on a broader base than the bankrupt barristers mentioned in the press) that the individuals concerned 'are generally well prepared for bankruptcy' (Auditor-General, 1999, p. 113).

Tackling Creative Compliance: 'Big Powers'

How is creative compliance to be dealt with? In the ATO Compliance Model, if a taxpayer is not won over to compliance via gentle cooperative control, there is a next step – a shift of gear from gentle persuasion to legal force, from cooperation to sanctions. The Compliance Model has two sides. It involves not just cooperation but 'big sticks'. Despite the primary consensual approach, there is a need to remember the power of the punch behind this velvet gloved approach (Clayton Utz, 1997). In the Compliance Model, law and sanctions may be a matter of last resort, but they are there, and they are there to be used.

But what happens when it is the taxpayer who is resorting, as a matter of first resort, to the law, and using it, whatever the enforcement agency's view, to claim compliance? Big sticks are for dealing with non-compliance. How do enforcers bring in legal sanctions to deal with what is claimed to be legal compliance? In this situation the issue is no longer a matter of enforcement style, of the agency choosing whether to bring in the big sticks or not. The enforcement agency cannot bring in the big sticks until it contests the claim to compliance. The issue, in short, is no longer one of enforcement, but one of enforceability. Before big sticks can be brought into play, the claim to compliance must first be contested.

To challenge the foundations of creative compliance, then, one first needs 'big powers'. Big powers mean more than just new specific rules, which can result merely in a cat and mouse game of new creative compliance adapted to the new words of the new rule. Big powers need to be of a qualitatively different kind.

There have been attempts to produce big powers in a number of areas, including tax in the UK and Australia, and financial services and financial reporting regulation in the UK. In many ways the UK's new regime in accounting regulation, driven in particular by the wish to control creative accounting, has been at the cutting edge of the big power approach.

Key big power strategies have included: (a) a shift, in the form of regulations, from rules to principles; (b) a focus on the substance of practice, not just its legal form; (c) taking a conceptual approach to the construction of definitions; and (d) an emphasis on 'super-principles'. Each will be discussed in turn.

Rigid detailed rules have been recognised as providing too fertile a soil for creative compliance. Where regulations involve rigidly defined categories, they can be too readily avoided by repackaging activities into a form that falls outside the clear delineations. The orphan subsidiary or the national insurance examples given above are classic examples. Hence, the approach of the Australian Accounting Standards Board (1994) of trying to write its regulation for dealing with such matters as off-balance sheet financing (in the Accounting Standards Board's financial reporting standard known as FRS5) in terms of a simple general principle: companies should report the substance of their transactions. The Australian Review of Business Taxation (Ralph Report, 1999) has also advocated 'a system based on clearly enunciated principles' as the best way to 'ensure horizontal equity and to reduce tax avoidance and hence to improve the integrity of the system' (p. 15).

FRS5 not only set out its regulation in the style of a principle not a rule, but it clearly stipulated that it was substance, not form, that counted. This notion of substance over form is also at the heart of the UK's 'new approach' to tax avoidance, introduced through judicial doctrine in the 1980s in the cases of *Ramsay (WT) Ltd v IRC [1982] AC300* and *Furniss v Dawson [1984] AC474*. The Australian Review of Business Taxation has also proposed a focus on 'economic substance rather than legal form' (Ralph Report, 1999, p. 15), and recommended that 'transactions with similar economic substance should be taxed in a similar manner' (p. 14).

The orphan subsidiary was based on a very specific definition in the *Companies Act 1985*, as we have seen, including the criterion of 'control of the composition of the board of directors'. The *Companies Act 1989* changed that, by including a much broader definition that went for the essence of control regardless of its specific form. One 'entity' was the parent of another (its subsidiary) if it had a 'participating interest' in it, and 'actually exercised dominant interest' over it. This was seen as a 'catchall' definition that avoided the invitation in more specific rules to slip beyond the parameters they set.[9]

Another strategy is to set up 'super-principles' which cut through or override literal compliance with specific rules. Australia's General Anti-Avoidance Rule can be seen as an example. The idea of substance overriding form can also be seen in this light. In the UK the epitome of the super-principle is the 'overriding' requirement in company law that accounts should give 'a true and fair view'. There is also an express clause requiring directors to depart from, rather than comply with, specific rules, if following them will not result in a true and fair view (see Sections 226(5) and 227(6) of the *Companies Act 1989)*.

What all of these strategies are about is bringing into play big powers that undermine the material for, cut through, or override claims to compliance based on the letter of the law, rather than on what those producing or enforcing the law see as its spirit. But these big powers pose their own problems.

Problems

A number of problems arise where big powers involve basing regulation on principles rather than on specific detailed rules. One problem is how to sustain principles and prevent them from being converted or reduced to rules, which can then be used once again as material for creative compliance.

Sustaining Principles

This kind of reduction can happen in a number of ways. It may occur through demands for guidance on how principles will be applied in specific contexts. FRS5, the Accounting Standards Board's regulation requiring the reporting of the substance of transactions, not just their legal form, took nine years to reach the standards book. Demands for guidance produced detailed examples which some have certainly looked to as new rules and potential material for creative compliance (McBarnet and Whelan, 1999). What happens in effect is that we get rules about how principles can be used.

Lobbying may result in negotiated curtailment behind the scenes of what looks in the books to be big powers. After the 'new approach' in UK tax, for example, the Inland Revenue responded to lobbying and met with legal and accounting professional bodies to negotiate the parameters within which they would apply the new approach in practice.

Something similar can be found in the Australian context in the Ralph Report (1999). Australia's big power is the General Anti-Avoidance Rule (GAAR), but the Ralph Report has sought a clear statement that 'the GAAR will not apply to the mere use in a straightforward and ordinary manner of structural features of the law to best advantage'. A 'statement of policy should confirm the circumstances in which the GAAR could be applied and reduce the perception that valid business practices could unintentionally be subject to the application of the GAAR' (p. 241). It has recommended that there should be a board to review the application of the GAAR, including rulings on whether or not a practice is caught by the rule. It has argued the need for producing clarity without mapping the minefield (Ralph Report, 1999, p. 44). This unfortunately is not a solution but a restatement of the problem – just how to produce the clarity requested without mapping the minefield. There is a real danger that in pursuit of 'clarity', the big power of the GAAR may be limited to narrower parameters and reduced to rules, undermining its capacity to override rule-based avoidance.

This narrowing can also be produced through the courts, not just through the enforcement agency losing but through the process of decisions being made (whoever wins or loses), reasoning being set out, and new material being provided for those bent on exploiting creative compliance. In the context of the new approach to tax avoidance in the UK, new 'rules', and therefore material for creative compliance, were found by scrutinising the arguments used by the judges, even in the *Ramsay* case, which introduced the anti-avoidance principle of looking through form to substance.

The *Ramsay* case comprised a circle of 'self-cancelling' transactions used to create an artificial loss, not unlike the recent Australian 'investment schemes' (Senate Economics References Committee, 2001), though more complex. The transactions required two companies and a subsidiary controlled by the taxpayer, two companies controlled by the scheme promoters (the Rossminster group). It involved two loans, one share issue, the exercise of options on interest levels (the interest rate on one loan was changed from 11 per cent to 22 per cent, on the other from 11 per cent to zero), the sale of the 22 per cent loan to a company controlled by the scheme promoter, which then sold the loan to the subsidiary of taxpayer company B, two liquidations, loan repayments, and exchange of shares for loanstock in another promoter-controlled company. Yet it was, as the judges observed, 'all over by lunch'. What is more, these multiple deals had 'no business purpose'. These observations were seized upon and steps taken in subsequent tax avoidance schemes to factor in a business purpose (with 'careful minuting', as one interviewee put it, to record it) to build in gaps and contingencies, and to change the timescale.

Even without resort to courts, precedents build up. In the context of rulings on the application of the General Anti-Avoidance Rule, it has been observed that 'an important body of case law is building up' (Clayton Utz, 1999). Rulings or clearances may be sought informally whether there is a statutory right to them or not, and interviews with UK tax officials and accountants indicated frequent requests to the Technical Office of the Inland Revenue for informal advice on 'hypothetical' or 'no-names' transactions. Tax officials had an ambivalent attitude to such requests, preferring to avoid rulings on such a basis but finding the requests a valuable source of information on the latest creative thinking. Potential new material for creative compliance is also produced every time there is a decision on the part of the agency on how a principle should apply to a specific situation. Even a simple failure to challenge a practice can be treated as endorsement by default, and built upon.

Application

Big powers are only as big as their application, and application may in practice be curtailed by a range of factors. These can be illustrated by looking at the record of enforcement in the new UK accounting regime.[10] The body responsible for enforcement is the Financial Reporting Review Panel, which came into being in 1991, armed with the extensive new powers listed above; and with a big stick sanction in the background in the judicial power to make directors personally liable for all the costs of revising and reissuing accounts which were successfully challenged by the Panel, along with legal costs. The Panel announced that it would use the true and fair super-principle to stop creative compliance:

> Where we are firmly of the view that accounts are not true and fair, we will not be deterred from taking action by the fact that there is room for forensic argument as to technical compliance with the particular FRS [accounting standard] (Financial Reporting Council, 1992, p. 24).

In other words, the Panel would use the true and fair principle to override what it saw as creative compliance.

But to date this power has never been used for this purpose. Rather, the Panel has monitored those situations where companies have invoked the true and fair principle to override compliance with specific rules. Indeed, it has tended to require companies to adhere to the rules even where there is strong opinion that following the rules does not produce true and fair accounts. In doing so the Panel may indeed be damaging its big powers. It may be setting a precedent that following the rules is more important than following the principle of a potentially clashing true and fair view. The big power of FRS5, requiring companies to report substance not just legal form, has been used only once against a small company. No directors have had to face personal liability costs, because no cases have gone to court.

It could be argued, of course, that all this tells us is that creative compliance has died off in the face of the new regime. But there are still many instances of practices that others see as 'bullish', or 'sailing close to the wind' (Griffiths, 1995; McBarnet and Whelan, 1999), and there is some danger that by not addressing them the Panel is in fact legitimising them.

Why then has the Panel been so circumspect in its use of its big powers? For, although the Panel has big powers in the books, our interpretation of what was happening was that a kind of 'self-regulation' was taking place, in the sense that the enforcers themselves were limiting their invocation of the powers at their disposal. Indeed, reflecting on the position of the Panel, or any agency in the same position (the ATO with its General Anti-Avoidance Rule, for example), the fact is that putting big powers into practice is not as straightforward as it might seem. Indeed, there are risks in using big powers which can foster caution.

There is a risk of 'winning but losing' in court with decisions and reasoning used in unforeseen but very damaging ways. In the accounting context, the *Argyll* case in 1981[11] involved successful prosecution of company directors for including in their group accounts a company they had not yet fully acquired. They argued that they effectively controlled it, it was in substance a subsidiary, and including it would result in true and fair accounts. The Department of Trade followed the case with a statement, underlining the message that specific definitions in the law had to be strictly adhered to. The unintended consequence was the highly damaging device of the orphan subsidiary, with the case and the statement pointed to as a powerful basis for arguing not only that the practice was not illegal, but that directors had no legal alternative but to keep a company that did not meet the specific definitions of a subsidiary out of their group accounts.

More generally, going to court means losing control to the judges who may, whether in ways favourable to the enforcement agency or not, come up with approaches with complex implications for other instances. And of course there is a risk of losing, not only opening the floodgates to copycat cases of the same type, but encouraging avoidance more generally. 'A daft judge can kill a standard', as one of our UK accounting regulators put it (McBarnet and Whelan, 1999, p. 88). The ATO has had experience of this in the past in terms of judicial treatment of the General Anti-Avoidance Rule. After the new approach cases in UK tax, the Inland Revenue required tax inspectors not to invoke the *Ramsay* ruling without getting central clearance to do so. Inland Revenue did not want taxpayers challenging them in court on the reach of the new doctrine in the context of just any case; the new doctrine of 'substance over form' was too important not to keep it carefully controlled.

Small wonder then if the pragmatic approach is to avoid confrontation in court. Indeed, big powers may be stronger for not testing them in court. The (until recently) chairman of the Accounting Standards Board, David Tweedie, observed of the new principle-based regime:

> We're like a cross-eyed javelin thrower competing at the Olympic Games: we may not win but we'll keep the crowd on the edge of its seats.[12]

He was reflecting on the (continuing) uncertainty surrounding how effective the new regime can really be. But the comment also captures the power of uncertainty. Uncertainty over where the regulatory javelin will fall (both because the regime is new and because it is based on principles) may make for greater caution among the regulated in embarking on creative compliance.

From the perspective of the regulators we can use another metaphor, and think of the benefits of the 'Oz factor'. The power of the Wizard of Oz lay in projecting big powers without exposing the mere mortal behind the image. For enforcement agencies, the image of big powers, never used, may be more effective in securing control than actually using them and taking the risk that they may be revealed as less powerful in practice than the image suggests.

This becomes in fact, an argument for the compliance strategy of enforcement, albeit on a very different grounding from that propounded by the ATO. But that has its dangers too, since a big power never used can soon lose its deterrent effect, and the failure to invoke big powers, may be taken as tacit admission that there are doubts on their reach.

There are other restraints on the use of big powers: concerns over the possibility of compensation demands if, for example, the agency loses a case and a regulated company attributes to it damage to reputation and loss of share value. Since, as the ATO explicitly acknowledges, there is always room for 'disagreements or different views on the law and compliance' (Australian Taxation Office, 2000a, p. 6), this is always a possibility – the more so where the application in practice of broad untested principles is concerned.

There can also be a real concern that the powers are just too big. The then chairman of the Financial Reporting Review Panel, which actually enforces the new regime in accounting, described the powers available to the Panel as 'draconian'. If the big powers were little used for cutting through creative compliance, it reflected a concern on the part of the enforcement body itself, that, for example, the 'true and fair' principle is too 'blunt' an instrument, and indeed that it should not be used to counter something 'which Parliament, rightly or wrongly, wrote in' (McBarnet and Whelan, 1999, p. 226). An agency dealing with such powers may see itself as structurally vulnerable to judicial review, or these days in the UK, litigation under the Human Rights Act.

A regime based on big powers is always vulnerable to lobbying on the basis of a rule of law critique. Big power regulation (based on principles, on a capacity to override literal compliance with specific rules by invoking broader purposes, or on a general anti-avoidance rule) can readily be presented as too uncertain, as involving retrospectivity, as giving regulators too much power, or as opening the way to arbitrary decision-making. All of these points were made in the wake of the UK's new approach to tax avoidance, notably in a booklet published by a joint committee of solicitors and accounting professional bodies, the Special Committee of Tax Law Consultancy Bodies (1998).

The Ralph Committee's concern about uncertainty in the reach of the Australian General Anti-Avoidance Rule, has already been noted. The committee's general terms of reference included assessment of how far current arrangements 'meet the aims of', among other things, 'certainty of taxation treatment' and 'clarity of law' (Ralph Report, 1999, p. vi). The ATO has also experienced direct criticism of its recent attack on artificial investment schemes (see Griffiths, 1995; McBarnet and Whelan, 1999) on the basis of retrospectivity (Senate Economics References Committee, 2001). The Accounting Standards Board's FRS5 took nine years and four drafts to reach the standard book precisely because of vociferous criticisms that the principled approach was too vague, too uncertain, and too impractical.[13] The big power response to creative compliance can only too readily be presented as 'creative control' (McBarnet and Whelan, 1999, p. 272).

Small wonder that enforcement bodies are inclined to be circumspect with big powers. It is precisely because they are regulating or 'taxing democracy', as this book's title underlines, with all its inherent tensions between due process and effective control.

Attitude

Finally, big powers, far from destroying creative compliance, may still fall prey to it. Even big powers can be treated as 'material to work on'. We have already seen how the judicial reasoning in the UK's new approach tax cases was mined for 'rules' which could be used to argue that new tax avoidance schemes lay beyond the reach of the new approach.

Regulations, even regulations geared to principles or anti-avoidance doctrines, have to be expressed in words, and even the words expressing the big powers to curb creative compliance can be subjected to the creative and advantageous interpretation on which creative compliance is based. Consider the orphan subsidiary. We saw earlier how it was based on careful scrutiny of and adaptation to very specific definitions in company law. We also saw how the law was changed. Definitions of a subsidiary under new legislation included the 'catchall' requirement to include an 'entity' in group accounts if the parent company had 'a participating interest' in it (a far cry from 'more than half the equity capital') and 'actually exercised control' over it (much wider than 'controlled the composition of the board of directors'). Legislators set out definitions of a broader, more abstract nature, and refused to define them further, precisely (and they were quite explicit about this) in order to stop feeding creative compliance.

Yet creative compliance continued. Even big powers have exemptions and exceptions ('ex-file' clauses) which were sought out and used. But more significantly still, the words in the catchall definition were themselves scrutinised and responded to with the 'deadlocked joint venture'. This involved two companies forming a 50-50 joint venture in which, it was claimed, neither 'actually exercised control', so that it remained off the accounts of both.

The power to override compliance with specific rules in order to require compliance with the overarching principle of producing true and fair accounts, has itself been scrutinised and resisted on the basis that it is complied with if companies give the 'true and fair' version of their accounts in the *notes* but leave the *numbers*, in the same accounts, based on literal compliance with specific rules – even though it is accepted that compliance at this level does not give a true and fair view.[14] The numbers of course, are more important than the notes, not only because the significance of the notes may be lost on the less expert reader, but because the numbers are what are used in calculating market ratios such as leverage or gearing. These ratios, in turn, are what are used by analysts in assessing share value, by banks in lending covenants to stop excessive additional borrowing by management, or which, when they reach a certain level, oblige management to consult shareholders. The numbers are, in other words, the basis of legal controls on a number of fronts.

In short, even big powers designed to counter creative compliance may themselves be vulnerable to it if they meet with the same attitude to the law – an attitude that treats the law as merely a material to work on. It is not only how big powers are applied that determines their impact, but how they are received.

A Change of Attitude

Creative compliance, I suggested earlier, is the product of two factors: the nature of law and the attitude taken to it. The application of law *is* problematic, given to grey areas and alternative interpretations. But the problem posed by creative compliance depends on those on the receiving end of law actively working on and taking advantage of those intrinsic problems. The enhanced uncertainty associated with principles and general anti-avoidance rules is a genuine concern. Yet the resort to such measures is itself a response to active abuse of more specific rules. The drift of principles to rules I have designated a 'problem', but it would not be a problem if those rules were not likely to be actively seized on and used to escape legal control, and if there were not a culture which treated the law as fair game for such activity.

What this suggests is that changes in law, however sweeping, are unlikely, alone, to eliminate creative compliance and the problems it poses for law and enforcement. The second factor, the attitude to law, needs to change too. The ATO, and the Compliance Model of law enforcement itself, recognise the need to foster a cooperative taxpaying culture, and indeed recognise that it is not just law that has to change, but attitude: 'Changing attitudes to our tax system is the remaining element that can give a major impetus to achieving a genuine new tax system in its fullest sense' (Commissioner of Taxation, 1999, p. xiii). The ATO is currently working to counter non-compliance by fostering an image of tax as a positive contribution, not as a negative imposition. It seeks to relate tax payment to the provision of public services: 'Our tax system is important to our community. It is about education, health treatment, support for those in need and roads and other community assets' (Commissioner of Taxation, 2000, p. 8). The ATO, in effect, is appealing for tax compliance as a mark of responsible citizenship (see also Australian Taxation Office, 2000b). The UK's Inland Revenue has announced a similar approach. It will be promoting the payment of tax as a 'badge of good citizenship', 'explicitly linked to public goods'.[15]

But this chapter, and the larger bodies of work on which it draws, indicates that tackling the attitude to non-compliance, appealing for compliance, is not enough. Whether compliance is enough depends on how people are complying. Compliance can itself be a creative construct, and a mark of resistance to tax policy, not cooperation with it. In aiming to construct a culture of compliance, then, the aim must be not just a culture of compliance as opposed to non-compliance, but a culture of compliance with the spirit of the law, rather than creative compliance with its letter.

Creative compliance is not just a tax problem but a law problem. The ATO is working to change the general attitude towards tax. But if a change of attitude is required, it is not just in the attitude to tax, but in the attitude taken to law, policy and compliance. This is true not just for taxpayers, but for their professional advisers – the lawyers and accountants whose creative work lies at the heart of creative compliance. What needs to be fostered is a change of attitude to the law, in which it is seen not as a game of words, a material to be worked on to one's own or one's client's advantage, but as an instrument of legitimate policy to be respected, with the policy, not just the words, looked to as the measure of compliance. That, I know, is itself problematic in many ways. But without some shift in that direction, the concern must be that compliance will remain not a solution but a problem for tax policy and tax enforcement, and, indeed, for legal policy and legal control in general.

Notes

1 Or if they are lawyers, as in the celebrated recent cases of Australia's bankrupt barristers (Auditor-General, 1999), set themselves to work.

2 The more so where taxable profits and financial reporting profits substantially overlap. There is variability between jurisdictions as to how far this is the case. See, for example, Touche Ross (1989).

3 Funded by the Economic and Social Research Council and based on in-depth interviews with lawyers, accountants and regulators (including the Inland Revenue, Accounting Standards Board, Financial Reporting Review Panel, Australian Taxation Office), along with key players from business as relevant.

4 As a Visiting Fellow at the Centre for Tax System Integrity, researching the ATO Compliance Model of enforcement and issues posed for it by legal creativity.

5 With Christopher Whelan. Funded by the Jacob Burns Fund for Socio-Legal Studies and the European Commission. See McBarnet and Whelan (1999), on which this chapter draws.

6 See for example, Australian Commissioner of Taxation's reference to 'tax arrangements which seek to exploit deficiencies or uncertainty in the law' (Commissioner of Taxation, 1999, p. xiii).

7 The Ralph Report (1999) distinguishes tax avoidance as a 'mis-use or abuse of law rather than a disregard for it' (p. 243).

8 I have elsewhere described one of the functions of creative compliance as 'fraud insurance' (McBarnet. 1991).
9 Drawn from European law. See McBarnet and Whelan (1991).
10 This section draws on analysis based on joint research with Christopher Whelan (McBarnet and Whelan. 1999).
11 Unreported magistrates' court case, but very influential. Reported unofficially in Ashton (1986).
12 Hence the 'cross-eyed javelin thrower' of our book.
13 See McBarnet and Whelan (1991) for a deeper analysis of 'the discourse of resistance' in relation to both tax and accounting regulation changes.
14 There was a controversial debate over this in the 1980s between accountants David Tweedie and James Kellas, on the one hand, and Ralph Aldwinckle of the Law Society, on the other. Even after a change of statutory wording, the debate continues. See McBarnet and Whelan (1999, Chapter 15) for a detailed analysis.
15 *Financial Times* weekend 20-21 January, 2001, quoting Nick Montagu, chairman of Inland Revenue, who also argued that a similar approach had 'worked in the Netherlands'.

References

Accounting Standards Board (1994), *FRS5: Reporting the Substance of Transactions*.

Ashton, R.K. (1986), 'The Argyll Foods Case: A Legal Analysis', *Accounting and Business Research*, vol. 17(65), pp. 3-12.

Auditor-General (1999), *Audit Report No. 23 1999-00: The Management of Tax Debt Collection*, Auditor-General's Office, Canberra.

Australian Taxation Office (2000a), *Cooperative Compliance: Working with Large Business in the New Tax System*, Australian Taxation Office, Canberra.

_____ (2000b), *Strategic Statement 2000-03*, Australian Taxation Office, Canberra.

Ayres, I. and Braithwaite, J. (1992), *Responsive Regulation*, Oxford University Press, Oxford.

Cash Economy Task Force (1998), *Improving Tax Compliance in the Cash Economy*, Australian Taxation Office, Canberra.

Clayton Utz (1997), 'When the Commissioner Comes Knocking', *Tax Litigation Issues*, Issue No. 2, Clayton Utz, Sydney.

_____ (1999), 'Challenging Private Rulings', *Tax Litigation Issues*, Issue No. 3, Clayton Utz, Sydney.

Commissioner of Taxation. (1999), *Annual Report 1998-99*, Commonwealth of Australia, Canberra.

_____ (2000), *Annual Report 1999-00*, Commonwealth of Australia, Canberra.

Financial Reporting Council (1992), *Annual Report*, Financial Reporting Council, London.

Griffiths, I. (1986), *Creative Accounting*, Sidgwick and Jackson, London.

_____ (1995), *New Creative Accounting*, Macmillan, London.

Hawkins, K. (1984), *Environment and Enforcement*, Clarendon Press, New York.

McBarnet, D. (1984), 'Law and Capital: The Role of Legal Form and Legal Actors', *International Journal of the Sociology of Law*, vol. 12(3), pp. 231-38.

_____ (1991), 'Whiter than White Collar Crime: Tax, Fraud Insurance and the Management of Stigma', *British Journal of Sociology*, vol. 42(3), pp. 324-44.

McBarnet, D (1992), 'It's Not What You Do But The Way That You Do It: Tax Evasion, Tax Avoidance and the Boundaries of Deviance', in D. Downes (ed), *Unravelling Criminal Justice*, Macmillan, Basingstoke, pp. 247-68.

McBarnet, D. and Whelan, C. (1991), 'The Elusive Spirit of the Law: Formalism and the Struggle for Legal Control', *Modern Law Review*, 54(6), pp. 848-73.

McBarnet, D. and Whelan, C. (1999), *Creative Accounting and the Cross-eyed Javelin Thrower*, John Wiley, Chichester.

Ralph Report (1999), *A Tax System Redesigned: More Certain, Equitable and Durable*. Report of the Review of Business Taxation, Commonwealth of Australia, Canberra.

Senate Economics References Committee (2001), *Inquiry into Mass Marketed Tax Effective Schemes and Investor Protection: Interim Report*, Parliament of the Commonwealth of Australia, Canberra.

Special Committee of Tax Law Consultancy Bodies (1998), 'Tax Law After Furniss vs Dawson', The Law Society, London.

Touche Ross (1989), *Accounting for Europe*, Touche Ross, London.

Appendix

Further publications by Doreen McBarnet

Books

Conviction: Law, the State and the Construction of Justice, Macmillan, 1981; paperback edition, 1983

Creative Accounting and the Cross-Eyed Javelin Thrower, John Wiley, London, 1999 (with C. Whelan)

Edited Volumes

Law, State and Society, Croom Helm, 1981 (edited with A. Hunt, B. Fryer and B. Moorhouse)

Law and Capital, Special Issue of *International Journal of the Sociology of Law*, Academic Press, 1984

Journal Articles

1976

'Pretrial Procedures and the Construction of Conviction' in P. Carlen (ed), *Sociological Review Monograph on the Sociology of Law*, 1976, pp. 172–199

1978

'The Fisher Report on the Confait Case: Four Issues', *Modern Law Review*, July 1978, pp. 455–463

1981

'The Royal Commission and the Judges' Rules', *British Journal of Law and Society*, Spring 1981, pp. 109–117

'Balance and Clarity: Has the Royal Commission Achieved Them?', *Criminal Law Review*, July 1981, pp. 445–453

'Magistrates' Courts and the Ideology of Justice', *British Journal of Law and Society*, Winter 1981, pp. 181–197

1982

'Legal Form and Legal Mystification: An Analytical Postscript to the Scottish Criminal Justice Act, the Royal Commission on Criminal Procedure, and the Politics of Law and Order', *International Journal of the Sociology of Law*, November 1982, pp. 409–417

1983

'Victim in the Witness Box – Confronting the Victimological Sterotype' in *Contemporary Crises*, 1983, pp. 293–303

1984

'Law and Capital: The Role of Legal Form and Legal Actors' in D. McBarnet (ed), *Law and Capital*, 1984, pp. 231–238

1988

'Law, Policy, and Legal Avoidance: Can Law Effectively Implement Egalitarian Policies?', *Journal of Law and Society*, Spring 1988, pp. 113–121

1989

'The "Crisis" in Professional Liability Insurance', *The Geneva Papers on Risk and Insurance*, 14(53), October 1989 (with C. Whelan), pp. 296–307

1991

'Whiter than White Collar Crime: Tax, Fraud Insurance and the Management of Stigma', *British Journal of Sociology*, Sept 1991, pp. 323–344

'The Elusive Spirit of the Law: Formalism and the Struggle for Legal Control', *Modern Law Review*, November 1991, pp. 848–873 (with C. Whelan)

1992

'Legitimate Rackets: Tax Evasion, Tax Avoidance and the Boundaries of Legality', *Journal of Human Justice*, Spring 1992, pp. 56–74

'Lawyers in the Market: Delivering Legal Services in Europe', *Journal of Law and Society*, Spring 1992, pp. 1–20 (with C. Wheelan)

1993

'Adversary Accounting: Strategic Uses of Financial Information by Capital and Labour', *Accounting, Organizations and Society*, 18(1), 1993, pp. 81–100 (with C. Whelan and S. Weston)

2001

'When Compliance is not the Solution but the Problem: From Changes in Law to Changes in Attitude', *Centre for Tax System Integrity Working Paper* no. 18, 2001

Chapters in Books

1978

'The Police and the State: Arrest, Legality and the Law' in G. Littlejohn *et al* (eds), *Power and the State*, Croom Helm, 1978, pp. 196–216

'Arrest: The Legal Context of Policing' in S. Holdaway (ed), *The British Police*, Edward Arnold, 1978, pp. 24–40

'False Dichotomies in Criminal Justice Research' in J. Baldwin and A.K. Bottomley (eds), *Criminal Justice*, Martin Robertson, 1978, pp. 23–34

1981

'Law, State and Society' in *Law, State and Society*, Croom Helm, 1981, pp. 9–20 (with A. Hunt, B. Fryer and B. Moorhouse)

1984

'Victim in the Witness Box – Confronting the Victimological Stereotype' reprinted in W.G. Chambliss (ed), *Criminal Law in Action*, Second Edition, Paperback, Wiley, USA, 1984, pp. 328–335

1990

'Rethinking White Collar Crime: Tax, Fraud Insurance and the Management of Stigma' in C. Kemp (ed), *Current Issues in Criminological Research: Collected Papers from the British Criminology Conference*, Volume 2, 1990, pp. 1–27.

1992

'It's Not What You Do But The Way That You Do It: Tax Evasion, Tax Avoidance and the Boundaries of Deviance' in D. Downes (ed), *Unravelling Criminal Justice*, MacMillan, 1992, pp. 247–268

'The Elusive Spirit of the Law: Formalism and the Struggle for Legal Control' reprinted in J. Freedman and M. Power (eds), *Law and Accountancy*, Paul Chapman, 1992, pp. 80–105 (with C. Whelan)

'Lawyers in the Market: Delivering Legal Services in Europe' reprinted in P. Thomas (ed), *Tomorrow's Lawyers*, Blackwell, 1992, pp. 49–68 (with C. Whelan)

'Lawyers in the Market: Delivering Legal Services in Europe' reprinted in G. Weick (ed), *Current Issues in British and German Law*, University of Giessen Press, Germany, 1992 (with C. Whelan)

'Regulating Accounting: Limits in the Law' in Hopwood *et al*, *Accounting and the Law*, Prentice-Hall, 1992, pp. 99–111 (with C. Whelan)

'The Construction of Compliance and the Challenge for Control: The Limits of Non-Compliance Research' in J. Slemrod (ed), *Why People Pay Taxes*, University of Michigan Press, 1992, pp. 333–345

'International Corporate Finance and the Challenge of Creative Compliance' in J. Fingleton (ed), *The Internationalisation of Capital Markets and the Regulatory Response*, Graham and Trotman, 1992, pp. 129–141 (with C. Whelan)

1993

'Law Policy and Legal Avoidance' reprinted in W. Chambliss and J. Katz, *Crime and Criminal Justice: A Conflict Perspective*, McGraw-Hill, 1993

1994

'Magistrates' Courts and the Ideology of Justice' reprinted in R. Cotterrell (ed), *Law and Society*, Dartmouth, 1994

'Whiter than White Collar Crime: Tax, Fraud Insurance and the Management of Stigma' reprinted in D. Nelken (ed), *White-Collar Crime*, Dartmouth, 1994, pp. 597–618

'International Corporate Finance and the Challenge of Creative Compliance' reprinted in S. Wheeler (ed), *The Law of the Business Enterprise*, Oxford University Press, 1994, pp. 403–416 (with C. Whelan)

'Legal Creativity: Law, Capital and Legal Avoidance' in M. Cain and C. Harrington (eds), *Lawyers in a Postmodern World*, Open University Press, 1994, pp. 73–84

'Law and the Level Playing Field' in T. Kende (ed), *Europai Politika es Jog*, Szazadveg, Budapest, 1994 (with C. Whelan)

'Two Tiers of Justice' in N. Lacey (ed), *Criminal Justice*, Oxford University Press, 1994

1996

'Law, Policy and Legal Avoidance' reprinted in A. Sanders (ed), *Prosecution in Common Law Jurisdictions*, Dartmouth, 1996

'Resisting Discretion', Council of Europe *Administrative Discretion and Problems of Accountability*, 1996, pp. 121–128

1997

'Creative Compliance and the Defeat of Legal Control: The Magic of the Orphan Subsidiary' in K. Hawkins (ed), *The Human Face of Law*, Oxford University Press, 1997, pp. 177–198 (with C. Whelan)

1998

'The Elusive Spirit of the Law: Formalism and the Struggle for Legal Control', extracts reprinted in D. Chalmers (ed), *European Union Law: Texts and Analysis*, Ashgate, 1998

1999

'Challenging the Regulators: Strategies for Resisting Control' in C. McCrudden (ed), *Regulation and Deregulation*, Clarendon Press, Oxford, 1999, pp. 67–77 (with C. Whelan)

2002

'Transnational Transactions: Legal Work, Cross-border Commerce and Global Regulation' in M. Likosky (ed), *Transnational Legal Processes*, Butterworths, 2002, pp. 98–113

2003

'When Compliance is Not the Solution but the Problem: From Changes in Law to Changes in Attitude' in V. Braithwaite (ed), *Taxing Democracy*, Ashgate, 2003, pp. 229–243

'The New Corporate Accountability' in W. Cragg and C. Koggel (eds), *Contemporary Moral Issues*, McGraw Hill Ryerson, Toronto, 2004

Shorter Articles

1993

'Financial Reporting and Financial Risk' in Oxford in North America, *Financial Markets: Regulation, Risk and a Global Economy*, 1993, pp. 1–13

1999

'Creative Accounting and the Cross-Eyed Javelin Thrower', *European Accounting Focus*, June 1999, pp. 12–16 (with C. Whelan)

'Painting by Numbers', *Accounting Technician*, November 1999, pp. 16–18 (with C. Whelan)

'Waving the Red Flag', *The Accountant*, June 1999, pp. 14–15 (with C. Whelan)

'Creative Accounting: Will the Javelin find its Mark?', *Accounting and Business*, October 1999, pp. 39–42 (with C. Whelan)

'The Defective Detectives', *Accountancy*, November 1999, pp. 105 (with C. Whelan)

Name Index